TIMOTH

REVIVALISM

and

SOCIAL REFORM

In Mid-Nineteenth-Century America

Chapters I-XI and XIV Comprise
*The Frank S. and Elizabeth D. Brewer Prize Essay
for 1955*
THE AMERICAN SOCIETY OF CHURCH HISTORY

ABINGDON PRESS

NEW YORK NASHVILLE

REVIVALISM AND SOCIAL REFORM

SET UP, PRINTED, AND BOUND BY THE
PARTHENON PRESS, AT NASHVILLE,
TENNESSEE, UNITED STATES OF AMERICA

To
KAREN

PREFACE

∽

Could Thomas Paine, the free-thinking pamphleteer of the American and French revolutions, have visited Broadway in 1865, he would have been amazed to find that the nation conceived in rational liberty was at last fulfilling its democratic promise in the power of evangelical faith. The emancipating glory of the great awakenings had made Christian liberty, Christian equality and Christian fraternity the passion of the land. The treasured gospel of the elect few passed into the hands of the baptized many. Common grace, not common sense, was the keynote of the age.

The Calvinist idea of foreordination, rejected as far as it concerned individuals, was now transferred to a grander object—the manifest destiny of a Christianized America. Men in all walks of life believed that the sovereign Holy Spirit was endowing the nation with resources sufficient to convert and civilize the globe, to purge human society of all its evils, and to usher in Christ's reign on earth. Religious doctrines which Paine, in his book *The Age of Reason*, had discarded as the tattered vestment of an outworn aristocracy, became the wedding garb of a democratized church, bent on preparing men and institutions for a kind of proletarian marriage supper of the Lamb.

This is not the place, of course, to measure the vast gap between these hopes and their fulfillment. Historians acquainted with the scandalous conduct of good churchmen like Jay Gould and Daniel Drew will be understandably skeptical. Instead of a marriage supper after the Civil War we had what Vernon Louis Parrington called the Great Barbecue. And only men of privilege were invited. Those who lived through the twenty-five years before 1865, however, thought the hopes were grounded in reality.

What has made the preparation of this book exciting has been the dawning discovery that revivalistic religion and the quest of Christian perfection lay at the fountainhead of our nation's heritage of hope. My original purpose was simply to trace the extent and significance after 1850 of what I thought

7

was by then the declining influence of these two spiritual traditions in America. The simplest justification for such a study was that ignorance of these matters hindered understanding of the exact way in which other-worldly faith had nurtured the impulse to social reform. Another was the guess that the persistence of popular religious ideas had been too much overlooked, leaving even theologians no alternative but to attribute the rise of small sects and the recurrent sweep of revivals in the twentieth century to economic and social tensions. The stanchest adherents of modern holiness and evangelistic movements, I knew, were the children and grand-children of shouting Methodists and praying Presbyterians. And most of them took literally the Biblical injunction to be fruitful and multiply and replenish the earth.

As the work progressed, so many unsuspected but obviously interrelated facts came to light that a general revaluation of mid-nineteenth-century Protestantism seemed necessary. The manuscript which was finally pre-sented for a graduate degree set forth a new interpretation of that era. It seems advisable, therefore, to state the major thesis clearly at the begin-ning of this published version, so as to let the reader know where he is going. Relevant facets are repeated at the beginning or toward the close of each chapter.

The gist of it is simply that revival measures and perfectionist aspiration flourished increasingly between 1840 and 1865 in all the major denomina-tions—particularly in the cities. And they drew together a constellation of ideas and customs which ever since have lighted the diverging paths of American Protestantism. Lay leadership, the drive toward interdenomina-tional fellowship, the primacy of ethics over dogma, and the democratiza-tion of Calvinism were more nearly fruits of fervor than of reflection. The quest of personal holiness became in some ways a kind of plain man's transcendentalism, which geared ancient creeds to the drive shaft of social reform. Far from disdaining earthly affairs, the evangelists played a key role in the widespread attack upon slavery, poverty, and greed. They thus helped prepare the way both in theory and in practice for what later became known as the social gospel.

I do not mean to debate whether material and social factors—such as the tremendous expansion of capitalist economy, the advance of science, the growth of cities, and the increasing social and geographic mobility of the people—were less important than religion in shaping American ideals. What is proposed is that insofar as equalitarian, perfectionist optimism

8

is a *spiritual* inheritance in America, John Wesley, George Whitefield, and Samuel Hopkins more than Benjamin Franklin or Jean Jacques Rousseau were its progenitors. And the path of its progress is as clearly seen in the revivals and missionary labors of countless Baptist, Methodist, and New School Calvinist preachers as in the social thought of an Emerson or a William Ellery Channing.

The reader has the right to know about two important points of view which have pervaded the research and the writing for this book. One is that the beliefs and practices of the mass of ordinary men are most important. Preoccupation with the learned and sophisticated minority is as misleading as overattention to the crackpot fringe. Neither course will disclose the part which religion really played in our country's development. Especially must we go beyond the solemn quarterlies published for clergymen and sift the literature which their parishioners read. Vast collections of devotional and biographical tracts, popular histories of revival and reform movements, and files of weekly denominational newspapers remain almost unexplored. Here lie the records of events as contemporaries actually saw them, interpreted in the light of their own doctrines, hopes, and prejudices. The only problem is to avoid spending the flower of one's youth in those dark and dusty areas where university librarians shelve religious books.

The second viewpoint is that during the nineteenth century the vital center of American Protestantism was in the cities rather than the rural West. It is strange that long after historians with other special interests have sharply revised Frederick Jackson Turner's thesis that the frontier was the matrix of American ideals, students of church history are still absorbed with it. A recent example is Charles A. Johnson's fine work on the frontier camp meeting, which explains at length the disappearance of the institution in the very years when it was hitting its stride in the Middle Atlantic and New England states. The day came, as we shall see, when revival measures were as proper in Boston as in Kentucky. Oberlin College, often considered a product of Western enthusiasm, was fully as much an arm of Eastern urbanity. Charles G. Finney repeatedly raised funds for it in England.

Further investigation may demonstrate that the currents of religious fervor which swept back and forth across the Atlantic were more important than anything which happened on the frontier. It is significant that every prominent American evangelist, from Lorenzo Dow to John Wilbur Chapman, gained his reputation in part from reports of his success in overseas cities. Great churchmen of the 1850's—like Robert Baird, founder of the Evangelical Alliance; Edward N. Kirk, pastor of Mt. Vernon Church, Boston; and William Arthur, a leader among British Wesleyans—thought their revival faith not a wilderness byway, but an avenue of ecumenicity down which the gospel army would roll to conquer the world. In our day, Billy Graham seems to have reawakened this belief.

A final note is in order to persons other than professional historians who I hope will read this book. The purpose of historical study is to explore fully and summarize accurately what really happened in the past. Scholars do not pretend to have achieved absolute objectivity, any more than the old-time Methodist preachers who professed sanctification meant to claim sinless perfection. Accuracy and impartiality are, however, the historian's cherished goals. It happens that I hold deep affection for the faith of the revivalists whose labors this book recounts. Had this not been so, the volume would very likely not have been written. But my intent has been to get the facts straight. Unless Christianity is dependent upon propaganda, its case is better served when historians hew to this line as best they can, letting the chips fall where they may.

Without attempting to name all of those to whom I am indebted for aid, I should mention particularly Arthur M. Schlesinger, Sr., now professor emeritus at Harvard, without whose counsel and encouragement I should never have completed the task; my wife, Anne Wright; the staffs of the marvelous group of libraries clustered around Boston; the members of the Brewer Prize Committee of the American Society of Church History; and, finally, my father and mother—holiness preachers and friends of reform —at whose knees I learned to appreciate both Christian faith and social compassion.

Timothy L. Smith

CONTENTS

❧

11

CONTENTS

I
The Inner Structure
of American Protestantism

ᠸᢧᠧ

Evangelical Protestantism reached the summit of its influence in America during the last half of the nineteenth century. If the years after the Civil War witnessed its maturity and initial decline, the twenty-five years before were the era of its painful but portentous adolescence.

During this period revival fervor emerged from the frontier to dominate the urban religious scene. A widespread aspiration for Christian perfection complemented in many ways the social idealism which endeavored to reform the drunkard, free the slaves, elevate womankind, and banish poverty and vice from the country. Exuberant churchmen rededicated themselves to the dream of making America a Christian nation.

But they found that both sectarian division and the readjustments of our society to industrial and urban growth complicated their task. Catholic immigration, the misery of city slums, and a burgeoning worship of wealth made more difficult the work of converting the nation and the world. Meanwhile, the paradox and danger inherent in the mounting crisis over Negro slavery laid cold hands upon evangelical hopes.

The impulse to retreat to the simpler childhood of both the church and the state was, in such circumstances, inevitably widespread. Fletcher Harper, editor of the nation's most flourishing young magazine, expressed this urge clearly in an editorial written in 1854. "There can be no doubt," he wrote, "that the tendency at the present day is to magnify the political, the social, the secular, or what may be called the worldly-humanitarian aspects" of "professedly religious movements." He lamented the fact that at anniversary meetings of religious societies it was becoming "almost as common to hear about the regeneration of the *race* as the salvation of souls." The Christian millennium seemed increasingly expected to be ushered in by political movements "and to be itself a sort of politico-religious golden age." Missionary and Bible societies won greatest praise for their civilizing rather than their spiritual influence.

Harper complained that clergymen and laymen alike rejoiced when they could persuade a politician or "some old hero of a general" to "harangue on such utilities before the annual religious gatherings"—as though the testimonies of public men were necessary to vindicate the gospel. He warned that if these aspects of religion continued to be presented as the chief ground of its support, Christianity would cease to serve the republic. Instead of the church evangelizing the world, the world would secularize the church.[1]

The young editor's statement points up many of the problems which have beset social Christianity ever since. But it also brings into focus the perplexing issues which faced American Protestantism in the twenty years prior to the Civil War. Harper was a "spiritual" Methodist and a loyal democrat whose successful publishing ventures had only recently brought him to wealth and fame. Political conservatism, particularly on the issue of slavery, fitted well the pattern of his life. Men such as he felt most keenly the tensions arising from the renewed efforts of Protestantism to dominate American society. Political caution combined with sectarian loyalties to make them skeptical of the reforming spirit which the Bible, tract, mission, and antislavery societies had spread in the churches. Their yearning for a return to spiritual religion, thus avoiding the pain of dealing with the hard facts of social evil, conflicted with an equally strong and authentically Christian desire to see those evils done away.

Controversies inevitably arose over the means by which churchmen were seeking to make America a godly commonwealth. What was the function of revivalism? How might human efforts to win souls be reconciled with the older Calvinist view of divine election? Whence was the power by which men and societies could be lifted to a higher ethical plane, God's grace, or man's resolution? Was either a pure heart or a perfect society attainable in this world? What were the nature and meaning of the millennial hope? How could Christian liberty become a bridge to democracy for all mankind when year by year the South laid a heavier yoke upon its Negro slaves? If it were granted that slavery was an evil, how and under whose leadership ought it to be destroyed?

Such were the painful issues of revival religion's hectic youth. From the effort to resolve them came many of the conflicts, the achievements, and the tragedies of twentieth-century Protestantism. These were the years of decision which were to shape the character of America's faith.

[1] *Harper's New Monthly Magazine*, IX (1854), pp. 115-16; XII (1856), pp. 841, 843.

Before we venture upon the fascinating story of how the churches met these issues, however, we must first survey their temporal and physical resources and make clear a few of the chief differences between the various denominations.

Numerically, organized Protestantism had attained a strength greater than at any previous point in our history. The census of 1860 reported 38,183 church buildings, one for every 608 persons, valued at $87,000,000. Only one-twentieth of their total seating capacity was in Roman Catholic edifices. While between 1832 and 1854 the population had increased 88 per cent, the number of evangelical clergymen had grown 175 per cent. Numerous part-time ministers, including 8,500 local preachers of Methodist persuasion, supplemented the work of 26,842 professionals. The census did not attempt to enumerate communicants, but a compilation from various of the better sources indicates that in 1855, 4,088,675 persons out of a population of more than 27,000,000 held membership in a Protestant congregation.[2]

[2] See Robert Baird, *State and Prospects of Religion in America. . . .* (London, 1855), pp. 27-31 and the table below, pp. 20-21.

United States, *Statistics of the United States . . . in 1860, compiled from the Original Returns of the . . . Eighth Census* (Washington, 1866), "Miscellaneous Volume," pp. 352-501, will yield the following statistics, gathered by Lewis G. Vander Velde, *The Presbyterian Churches and the Federal Union, 1861-1869* (Harvard Historical Studies, XXXIII, Cambridge, 1932), p. 5.

	Accommodations	In Slave States	Property Value
Methodist	6,259,799	2,788,338	$ 33,093,371
Baptist	4,044,220	2,413,818	21,079,104
Presbyterian	2,565,949	943,746	27,840,525
Roman Catholic	1,404,437	266,313	26,774,119
Congregational	956,351		13,327,511
Protestant Episcopal	847,296	287,546	21,665,698
Lutheran	757,637	143,603	5,385,179
Christian	681,016	273,900	2,518,045
Union	371,899	157,235	1,370,212
German Reformed	273,697	26,975	2,422,670
Friends	269,084		2,544,507
Universalist	235,219		2,856,095
Dutch Reformed	211,068		4,453,850
Unitarian	138,213		4,338,316
Jewish	34,412		1,135,300
Moravian	20,316		227,450
Adventist	17,128		101,170
Swedenborgian	15,128		321,200
Spiritualist	6,275		7,500
Shaker	5,200		41,000
Minor Sects	14,150		895,100
TOTALS	19,128,761		$172,397,922

17

The records of both the census takers and the churches were, of course, subject to considerable error. But a greater distortion would result from thoughtless comparison of these figures with those of either contemporary Europe or modern America.

To sympathetic Old World observers the state-church system to which they were accustomed seemed more efficient in enrolling members but afforded no guarantee of the sort of active religious life they found in America. Philip Schaff noted in 1854 that Berlin's forty churches, serving a population of 450,000 but attracting only about 30,000 weekly worshipers, compared poorly with the 250 which ministered to New York City's 600,000 citizens, all supported by voluntary contributions. "There are in America probably more awakened souls," Schaff declared, "and more individual self-sacrifice for religious purposes, proportionally, than in any other country in the world, Scotland alone, perhaps, excepted." Alexis de Tocqueville had earlier affirmed that there was "no country in the whole world in which the Christian religion retains a greater influence over the souls of men than in America." Even a rather skeptical Tory like Thomas C. Grattan was compelled to agree.[3]

Certainly by modern standards, church membership was a strenuous affair. All evangelical sects required of communicants a personal experience of conversion and a consistent life. Two worship services and Sunday school on the Sabbath were customary, along with a midweek gathering for prayer. The Methodists invariably kept new converts on "probation" for many months.[4] Wesley's followers also attended a weekly class meeting and more than the usual number of revivals and camp meetings throughout the year. Laymen of most denominations were responsible for a large amount of missionary and benevolent work in the towns and cities. All these activities were pursued with a seriousness absent today.[5]

Contemporary observers frequently praised the homogeneity of American Protestantism. Though there were numerous sects, Christianity abroad, taken as a whole, was no less divided. Twenty-six of the forty-odd groups in the United States had migrated across the Atlantic. Most others were

[3] Philip Schaff, America. A Sketch of the Political, Social, and Religious Character of the United States . . . (New York, 1855), pp. 94, 118; Alexis de Tocqueville, Democracy in America (tr. Henry Reeve; New York, 1900), I, 308; Thomas C. Grattan, Civilized America (London, 1859), II, 337, 340.

[4] Isabella (Bird) Bishop, The Aspects of Religion in the United States of America (London, 1859), pp. 168-69; cf. Schaff, op. cit., pp. xii, 117.

[5] See J. H. Grand Pièrre, A Parisian Pastor's Glance at America (Boston, 1854), pp. 69-100.

simply new combinations of Old World ethnic and religious divisions. Methodistic sects accounted for a fourth of the 300,000 members enrolled in the twenty-seven smaller denominations which claimed less than 50,000 members. Two stanchly conservative ones, the Dutch Reformed and Associate Reformed Presbyterian, owned another fourth. Neither Shakers, Mormons, nor Adventists were really typical of these small groups. All made such little impact, particularly in the cities, that their influence was generally disparaged.[6]

Several travelers agreed that, in the absence of a state church, "the distinction between church and sect properly disappears."[7] A Parisian pastor who had supposed that the multiplicity of denominations must of necessity "present an obstacle to the progress of the spirit of brotherly love" was astonished at the genuineness of their "harmony and good feeling." "I have understood better, since my visit to the United States," he wrote, "why our American brethren have shown so little forwardness to unite with us in the Evangelical Alliance. It is because they have its reality at home." Isabella Bishop noted with pleasure the numerous exchanges of pulpits, union prayer meetings, and joint efforts in Bible Society, Sunday school, and mission work. She decided that the sectarian spirit of Europe's churches arose not so much from "conscientious scruples and differences of opinion on government or doctrine" as from the fact that some had endowments and some did not.[8]

Further generalization about Protestants as a whole, however, would be misleading without an elementary differentiation of the various denominations. The religious life of the average American was centered around one of these. He followed its guidance and discipline and earnestly defended its customs. Though differences in doctrine and church polity may have arisen from variations in environment or social status, the members took them seriously. Until these are understood, the danger of quoting Old School Presbyterians or Universalists for "typical" Protestant views is always near.

[6] See especially Georges Fisch, *Nine Months in the United States During the Crisis* (London, 1863), pp. 32-33; Robert Baird, *The Progress and Prospects of Christianity in the United States of America* (London, 1851), pp. 268-69; Schaff, *op. cit.*, p. 125. Cf. the table below, pp. 20-21.

[7] Schaff, *op. cit.*, pp. xiv, 115, 117, 120-21; Fisch, *op. cit.*, pp. 23, 64; James Dixon, *Personal Narrative of a Tour through a Part of the United States and Canada* . . . (New York, 1849), pp. 188-89.

[8] Grand Pièrre, *op. cit.*, pp. 63, 66; Bishop, *op. cit.*, pp. 166-67. Cf. Agénor Étienne de Gasparin, *The Uprising of a Great People. The United States in 1861* (tr. Mary L. Booth; New York, 1861), pp. 60-68.

The statistical table below lists the ten organizations numbering over 100,000 members with which we have primarily to deal. They were separated from the twenty-seven small groups by seven which claimed between 50,000 and 100,000 communicants. Five of these latter—the Methodist Protestant, United Brethren in Christ, Antimission Baptist, Freewill Baptist and Cumberland Presbyterian—were largely rural and sectional, and the German Reformed was confined to a single ethnic stock. The seventh, the Society of Friends, suffered from the Hicksite division and was, in any case, so predominantly rural as to sustain in 1861 only four of the four hundred churches in Philadelphia. However, the Quaker interest in social problems raises them, together with the even less numerous Unitarians, to a place of significance alongside the ten larger denominations.[9]

CHURCH MEMBERSHIP STATISTICS

Church	In 1855	In 1865	Increase	Per Cent
M. E. (North) .	. 783,358	929,259	145,901	19
M. E. (South)	579,525	708,949	129,424	22
Meth. Protestant .	.. 70,015	105,120	35,105	50
United Brethren	67,000*	102,983	35,983	53
Wesleyan Meth.	23,000*	25,620	2,620	10
Evang. Assoc.	21,076	51,185	30,109	140
A. M. E. (Bethel) .	21,237	84,270	56,830	208
A. M. E. (Zion)	6,203	(Reported in 1865 with A.M.E. Bethel)		
Calvinistic Meth.	4,500	4,500*	......	..
Primitive Meth.	1,100	1,805	705	65
TOTAL METHODISTS	1,577,014	2,013,691	436,677	22
Reg. Bapt. (North)	311,321	400,197	88,876	28
Reg. Bapt. (South)	497,433	640,806	143,373	28
Disciples	170,000*	200,000*	30,000	18
Antimission Bapt.	66,507	50,000*	−16,507	−25
Freewill Bapt.	51,775	56,738	4,963	9
Seventh-Day Bapt.	6,321	6,796	475	6
General Bapt.	2,189	3,000*	811	37
TOTAL BAPTISTS	1,105,546	1,357,537	251,991	22

* Fisch, *op. cit.*, p. 33.

Presb. (O. School)	219,263	287,360	68,097	29
Presb. (N. School)	140,452	138,074	–2,378	–1
Cumberland Presb.	90,000*	103,062	13,062	14
Assoc. Reformed	27,000*	2,561		
Assoc. Presb.	19,000*	1,000*		
United Presb.	. ....	67,900	42,121	91
Reformed Presb.	......	16,660		
TOTAL PRESBYTERIANS .	495,715	616,617	120,902	24
Evang. Lutheran	200,000*	269,985	69,985	28
German Reformed	75,000*	91,200	16,200	22
Dutch Reformed	36,297	54,268	17,971	49
Mennonites	10,000*	....	.....	..
Ch. of the Brethren ..	8,000*	......	.... .	..
Moravians	5,000*	5,859	......	..
Tenn. Synod, Lutheran ..	5,049	......	. . . . .	..
Reformed Mennonites ...	5,000*	......	......	..
Amish	5,000*	....	. ....	..
Schwenkfelders	1,000*	....	.... .	..
TOTAL GERMAN & REF'D	350,346	......	.....	..
Congregationalists	207,608	268,015	60,407	34
Prot. Episcopal	105,350	154,118	48,768	46
Universalist	100,000*	140,000*	40,000*	40
Unitarian	13,550	31,670	18,120	138
Christ. Connection . .	32,046	36,000*	3,594*	11
Friends	64,500*	94,672	......	..
Hicksite Friends	10,000*	......	......	..
Winebrennarians . . .	12,000*	23,800	11,800	99
Swedenborgians	9,000*	......	......	..
Shakers	6,000*	......	......	..
TOTAL ALL OTHERS ...	560,054	.....	. ...	..
TOTAL PROTESTANTS	4,088,675[10]	.. ...	. ...	.-.

[10] The figures for 1855 are compiled from Baird, *State and Prospects*, p. 31, and Joseph Belcher, *The Religious Denominations in the United States: Their History, Doctrine, Government and Statistics* (Philadelphia, 1857), pp. 242-938, *passim*. Those for 1865 appear in Charles C. Goss, *Statistical History of the First Century of American Methodism* ... (New York, 1866), pp. 110-13. Starred figures seem to be estimates.

The outstanding fact is that by 1855 the Methodists and Baptists had come to a dominant position, accounting for 2,712,560, or nearly 70 per cent of the total number of Protestant communicants. Wesley's followers alone numbered 38 per cent of the whole. Although Regular Baptists—including those in both North and South—formed the most numerous single group, the Northern and Southern branches of the Methodist Episcopal Church, claiming 783,000 and 579,000 members respectively, were together far more numerous and each more than twice the size of any of the others. The New and Old School wings of Presbyterianism when combined, for example, numbered scarcely half as many members as the Methodist Church, North.

The major difference between the two sects is that, whereas the Baptists were predominantly rural and Southern, mid-century Methodism had made great advances in the cities and in the Eastern states. By 1865 New York, Pennsylvania, Maryland, and New Jersey were among the seven states most heavily populated with John Wesley's followers. The Philadelphia, Pittsburgh, East Baltimore, New York, and New York East conferences—the latter centered around New York City—outnumbered in that order the largest Western conferences of the church. The denominational publishing business was located in the national metropolis, as were the tract and missionary societies. The bishops who did not reside there were thus frequent visitors to Manhattan's forty congregations. Cincinnati filled a similar place for Methodists beyond the Alleghenies.[11] The ten most populous Baptist states in 1854 were, by contrast, all to be found in slave territory except New York, second to Virginia with 87,538 communicants, and Massachusetts, ninth, with 32,107. In the six years preceding, the Baptist population in most Eastern states was at a standstill or actually declining, while rapid growth continued in the West and South.[12]

[11] Goss, op. cit., p. 109; William Warren Sweet, The Methodist Episcopal Church and the Civil War (Cincinnati, 1912), p. 111. Grand Pièrre, op. cit., p. 59, lists the churches in New York City in 1853 as follows: Presbyterian, 54; Protestant Episcopal, 46; Methodist, 42; Baptist, 33; Dutch Reformed, 17; Congregational, 9; Unitarian, 2; and Roman Catholic, 22. Schaff, op. cit., p. 94, gives a somewhat different set of figures, but without change in the proportions, except that he notes five Lutheran congregations.
[12] Tabulations taken from the denominational almanacs for the years 1848 and 1854 appear in John Winebrenner, ed., History of All the Religious Denominations in The United States ... (Harrisburg, 1848), p. 71, and Belcher, op. cit., p. 242. They show the relative change as follows:

	1848	1854		1848	1854
New York	87,573	87,538	Virginia	79,563	89,929
Massachusetts	29,926	32,107	Kentucky	60,991	69,098
Pennsylvania	28,125	30,053	Georgia	48,357	65,639

Thus when the moral earnestness characteristic of both denominations provoked the divisions over slavery, the result was to increase greatly the relative strength of Methodism in the North. The Southern Baptist Convention, organized in May, 1845, to sponsor home and foreign missions in which slaveholders might be admitted to service, represented by 1854 over 60 per cent of the Regular Baptists. The 311,000 adhering to the Northern church compared poorly with their Methodist fellows, who numbered two and one-half times as many.[13]

The Southern branches were, of course, in both cases more rural and provincial, more bound by the association with slavery to a conservative outlook. Tennessee contained more members of the Methodist Church, South, than any other state. Approximately a fourth of the whole membership—in South Carolina as much as 60 per cent—was listed under the heading "colored and infants."[14] The Baptists, it should be noted, considered that their denomination was not divided, but simply organized separately for the better prosecution of missionary work. Rancor between the two divisions was considerably less than in the case of the Methodists, whose communion, being more closely knit, required more force to sunder.[15]

Undoubtedly the organizational structure of Methodism contributed to its greater success in the cities. Government of the denomination was in the hands of the clergymen, who seemed as self-sacrificing a band as any Wesley's stern discipline might have asked. The bishops, elected by the quadrennial General Conference—chief governing body of the church —had complete power to transfer the ministers to any place where their services might promote the corporate aim "to reform the nation and to spread scriptural holiness over these lands." Lest any become attached to green pastures, all were moved every two or three years. It was thus comparatively easy to send the best men to the cities. There they usually

---

Maine	21,223	19,775	Ohio	24,612	24,693
Connecticut	16,061	16,355	Illinois	12,594	19,259
New Jersey	11,637	13,362	Missouri	16,769	24,006

Belcher, a Baptist pastor in Philadelphia, evidently did not think any of the buildings housing the thirty-three congregations of his persuasion in New York City equal to those in Southern cities whose pictures he printed, pp. 189, 215-23.

[13] See again the statistical table above, pp. 20-21.

[14] Belcher, op. cit., p. 604.

[15] Cf. Albert Henry Newman, A History of the Baptist Churches in the United States (Philip Schaff and others, eds., The American Church History Series, II, New York, 1894), pp. 447-51, with Charles Baumer Swaney, Episcopal Methodism and Slavery; with Sidelights on Ecclesiastical Politics (Boston, 1926), pp. 117-88.

maintained "free churches" in the face of the growing custom of charging pew rents, a prop for social pretension.[16]

Lifelong membership in such an organized, mobile fellowship of ministers provided a training in preaching and pastoral skills denied to the long-term shepherd of a congregationally governed flock. Facing a new challenge every two years was a fair substitute for the formal education which Methodist preachers, no less than Baptist, usually lacked. The former profited, too, from frequent exposure to the sermons and platform versatility of the bishops, who preached often and well at conferences and camp meetings.

Whether in rural or urban areas, however, both churches appealed to the plain men of the period. Only occasionally did they win converts from the upper ranks of society. The Negroes free to make a choice joined one or the other. A French visitor found in 1860 that the colored population of Louisville was divided into two coteries—the "aristocracy" being Baptist. Among whites, wherever only a simple class structure had developed, members of the two sects might completely dominate society. Eleven of the thirteen congressmen representing Indiana in 1852 were Methodists, as well as the governor and one of her senators.[17]

Intense denominational zeal, frequent revivals stressing individual conversion, and displays of great fervor in hymns and "heart-touching" sermons were the chief means by which both won the loyalty of the common people. The rite of baptism by immersion, whose emotional symbolism was doubtless more impressive to the average man than the long sermons demonstrating it to be the scriptural "mode," was no stronger advantage to the one than the camp meeting and class meeting were to the other. Laymen were encouraged to share active leadership in the services of both, thousands of Methodist "local ministers" filling with better supervision the place which farmer-preachers supplied in the other communion. Women were as welcome as men to participate in revivals and in testimony, prayer and class meetings, as often as not becoming spiritual leaders.[18]

The doctrines of salvation which each proclaimed heightened these

[16] Wade Crawford Barclay, *Early American Methodism, 1769-1844*, vol. II, *To Reform the Nation* (*History of Methodist Missions*, Part I, New York, 1950), pp. 287-301; Goss, *op. cit.*, pp. 171-73.

[17] Fisch, *op. cit.*, pp. 29-30; Goss, *op. cit.*, pp. 165-80.

[18] See criticisms in Schaff, *op. cit.*, pp. 173-75, 207-12, and Alexander Blaikie, *The Philosophy of Sectarianism; or, a Classified View of the Christian Sects in the United States* (Boston, 1855), pp. 324-28, 330-40.

anti-aristocratic tendencies. Neither was stanchly Calvinistic. The Baptist endeavor to maintain the form of orthodoxy amidst revival efforts resulted in a practical nullification of the idea of unconditional election but not of final perseverance. The consequent stress which they eventually laid upon the "eternal security" of baptized believers appealed powerfully to weak and sinning men. In contrast, Methodists had proclaimed free will and free grace from the beginning. Wesley modified the Calvinist notion of man's total depravity, to which the doctrine of predestination was related. He taught instead that God had mitigated our sin by giving every man the ability to respond to the call of the gospel. Free, but morally responsible to yield to God, every sinner might hope to find at the Methodist mourner's bench a positive inner assurance of personal salvation. He then might seek with confidence the "second blessing," called entire sanctification, which would cleanse away the moral depravity of his soul.

Thus to the hopeful concepts of free will and a universal atonement, Methodism added the promise of man's immediate perfectibility, not by reason or education, but through the operation of the spirit of God. Both doctrines hastened the church's growth. So the Rev. Alexander Blaikie, pastor of the Associate Reformed Presbyterian Church in Boston, complained in 1854: "Every man . . . is born an Arminian, and while he must be born again to be a true Calvinist, in the mean time all that is requisite to make him a Methodist is the adoption of the chosen opinions, order and usages of the Rev. John Wesley." The one which pandered most, he felt, to human pride was the aspiration for "personal and sinless perfection.[19]

The general popularity of Arminian views in America is indicated by the fact that, although both the Methodist and Baptist denominations suffered from several secessions, only those from the latter involved chiefly doctrinal issues. The withdrawal of the Methodist Protestants in 1830 was due to a dispute over lay participation in the church government, and that of the Wesleyan Methodist Connection in 1843, over slavery. The Antimission Baptists, on the other hand, numbering 66,500 members by 1854, represented an arch-Calvinistic reaction against the "creaturely activity" of missionaries sent to the West. Their leaders were frontier preachers who felt themselves overshadowed by better educated Easterners.

[19] Goss, op. cit., pp. 183-86; Blaikie, op. cit., pp. 324, 325. On the subject of sanctification generally, see Barclay, op. cit., pp. 314-19; John L. Peters, Christian Perfection and American Methodism (New York and Nashville, 1956), pp. 39-46, 90-133; and ch. VIII of this book.

The Freewill Baptists were at the opposite extreme, sectionally and theologically. Nearly 60 per cent of their members resided in rural New England. The church dated its history from 1780, when the Regular Baptist Church in New Hampshire ejected Elder Benjamin Randall "on account of his belief in free will and in a free and full salvation." It had grown by means of revivals and opposition to the closed communion, but at mid-century its increase proceeded at the slow pace characteristic of all Eastern Baptists. The Antimission group was steadily declining; after six years in America, Philip Schaff knew of it only by hearsay.[20]

Despite their fewer numbers Presbyterians exerted a greater social influence than either Methodists or Baptists, particularly when they were able to act in co-operation with New England's Congregationalists. Their church was, in the words of one observer, "the religious form preferred by the industrial and commercial classes, by men of enterprise and initiative." Although both Baptists and Methodists far outnumbered the 500,000 Presbyterians in the nation, New York City contained more of their congregations than of either of the more popular sects.[21]

But the principal denomination of the group was seriously divided. In 1837 the conservative Scotch element in the Presbyterian Church, U.S.A., found itself in control of the General Assembly. They voted to exclude several "Puritan" synods which had in previous years blocked action against the revival methods and alleged Arminian heresies which Albert Barnes, N. S. S. Beman, Lyman Beecher, and George Duffield had championed. The ousted brethren formed the "Constitutional Assembly," commonly called the New School, after an abortive attempt to force re-entry into the parent group at its session the next year. Thereafter, synods and presbyteries throughout the church, including those in the Southern states of Virginia, Tennessee, and South Carolina, split into factions adhering to one or the other of the two bodies.

That slavery was not the chief divisive issue is plain from the fact that the Huguenot element dominant in the Charleston, South Carolina, Union Presbytery was able to force out the Scotch minority and carry most of the churches there into the New School Assembly. The Southern members

---

[20] On the Wesleyan Methodists, contrast Peters, op. cit., pp. 124-27, with Whitney R. Cross, The Burned-Over District . . . (Ithaca, N. Y., 1950), pp. 263, 267. See also Belcher, op. cit., pp. 242, 319; anon., The American Christian Record: Containing the History, Confession of Faith, and Statistics of Each Religious Denomination in the United States and Europe (New York, 1860), pp. 32-34; Schaff, op. cit., p. 206.

[21] Fisch, op cit., p. 28; see earlier, p. 22.

in the New School were sufficiently numerous to block effective action against slavery until the eve of the Civil War, though they were unable to silence the long and feverish debates on the question. In the Old School the proportionately larger membership from slaveholding states and the conservatism of the Scotch on social issues combined to muzzle entirely discussion of the institution.

A more important line of demarcation than slavery was the conflicting attitude which the two assemblies took toward co-operation in nonsectarian missionary ventures. The New School favored interdenominational organizations. It supported the American Home Missionary Society, the American Education Society, and the American Board of Commissioners for Foreign Missions. Its leaders were, therefore, deeply embarrassed when the rising tide of sectarian sentiment among Congregationalists caused them in 1852 to scuttle the historic Plan of Union between the two denominations and to develop parallel organizations of their own for Western work.[22]

The Old School grew rapidly in the South and Southwest, untroubled by competition from other strictly Calvinist groups. The New School made slower progress, hardly gaining enough in twenty years to offset the loss in 1857 of its proslavery presbyteries. Prolonged indecision over the slavery issue made its synods prey to the Congregationalists in sections like northern Ohio and New York where abolitionism was rife. The Scotch following was scattered widely through rural America, however, while over one half of the New School membership was concentrated in New York and New Jersey. Nevertheless, the Old School exercised powerful influence in the urban East through Princeton University, *The New York Observer*—an important religious weekly—and a dozen great metropolitan pulpits. The noise of Presbyterian strife thus rose not along sectional boundaries but in the halls between college classrooms and across busy New York and Philadelphia street corners.[23]

The division illustrates how revivalism and Arminianism went hand in hand. The Cumberland Presbyterians, organized in 1810 out of the great awakening in Tennessee and reporting 90,000 members by 1855, had

---

[22] E. H. Gillett, *History of the Presbyterian Church in The United States of America* (Philadelphia, 1864), II, 553-55, 558-63 and *passim*.
[23] *Ibid.*, II, 555-58; anon., *American Christian Record*, p. 192. For figures by states see Belcher, *op. cit.*, p. 690.

Belcher's account of the nature of the division, pp. 683-84, resembles that in Winebrenner, *op. cit.*, pp. 497-98; Vander Velde, *op. cit.*, pp. 13-15 and *passim*, stresses the Scotch-Puritan conflict. See later, pp. 185-87.

long since declared for free will and a universal election of grace. Although the New School Assembly preserved the old Confession of Faith, no one could forget that the schism had originated during the argument about the trials of Duffield, Barnes, and Beecher for their Arminian views. As successive revivals swept the cities of the North, free grace became the Assembly's most prominent doctrine.

To be sure, few thoughtful New School clergymen accepted Finney's extreme view that all men possessed a "natural ability" to choose the right. They did, however, replace the notion that original sin was imputed guilt with the view that it was a diseased condition of the moral nature. This was very near to the Wesleyan position. It was only one step to the conception that salvation was also subjectively real, that divine grace might heal the sinfulness of the soul. William E. Boardman and many others took this path to perfectionism. By the late 1850's, as we shall see, Methodist, New School, and Oberlin perfectionists found little practical difference in their doctrines.[24]

But whether they were New or Old School Presbyterians, Dutch or German Reformed, Congregationalists or Cumberland Presbyterians, the followers of Calvin in America were contenders, as Philip Schaff put it, for the absolute supremacy of the Holy Scriptures, "thorough and moral reform, individual, personal Christianity, freedom and independence of congregational life, and strict church discipline."[25] The salvation in which they believed may have begun as a transaction in the inscrutable mind of the Eternal, but it ended in the radical moral transformation of human character. For the elect, at least, this was as optimistic a hope for man's perfection as some others in vogue in the nineteenth century. And the preaching of a Finney or an Albert Barnes readily suggested that a larger proportion than earlier supposed of those "called" might indeed be "chosen."

Aside from the Congregationalists, whose gradual departure from the old theology under the leadership of Nathaniel W. Taylor and Horace Bushnell are well known,[26] and the Episcopalians, described on every hand as "the fashionable church of America,"[27] no other group exerted an influence remotely approaching that of the Methodists, Baptists, and

[24] See anon., *American Christian Record*, pp. 170-71; George Duffield, "The Doctrines of the New School Presbyterian Church," *Bibliotheca Sacra*, XX (1863), pp. 608-15; Schaff, *op. cit.*, p. 145; Winebrenner, *op. cit.*, pp. 493-94. See ch. VII.

[25] Schaff, *op. cit.*, pp. 111-12.

[26] The issues were intertwined with the question of revivalism, to be discussed later.

[27] Fisch, *op. cit.*, p. 28; Bishop, *op. cit.*, p. 33; Schaff, *op. cit.*, pp. 154-55.

Presbyterians. The Disciples of Christ, who claimed over 100,000 members by 1855, were growing rapidly in the West, led by their founder, Alexander Campbell. But they were not yet in a position greatly to influence American society and suffered in any case from the common cause made against them by the three dominant sects. Although the Universalists in New England were still expanding, they were no longer the church of the common people. Methodists and Baptists on the one hand and erratic movements like Millerism and Spiritualism on the other were increasingly filling this place.

Both the Evangelical Lutheran and the Protestant Episcopal Churches deserve a separate word, however, in view of their unique problems and future rapid growth.

The middle twenty years of the nineteenth century witnessed a sharp controversy among the heirs of the Anglican tradition in America, made possibly more bitter from the fact that their church remained an organic unity. Differences between evangelicals and High-churchmen had existed for nearly a century. In 1840 the leaders of the former party were Stephen H. Tyng, popular pastor in Philadelphia, Alonzo Potter, later Bishop of Pennsylvania, Bishop Philander Chase of Ohio, and Dr. William Sparrow, head of the Virginia Theological Seminary. Chief defenders of the High Church position were Bishops G. W. Doane of New Jersey, Horatio Potter of New York, the powerful corporation of Trinity Church, New York City, and the faculty of the General Theological Seminary located there.

The publication of the Oxford Tracts, especially the seemingly pro-Roman "Tract 90," brought this division into the open, in America no less than in England. When in 1843 the Bishop of New York consented to the ordination of Arthur Carey, a recent graduate of the General Theological Seminary who avowed his adherence to the views expressed in "Tract 90," Low-churchmen were thoroughly aroused. Feeling reached its climax when certain evangelical bishops brought three of their brethren to trial—Bishops Henry U. Onderdonk of Pennsylvania, for intemperance, B. T. Onderdonk of New York, for unchastity, and G. W. Doane of New Jersey, for the unethical conduct of financial affairs. In 1847 the Low Church party organized the Society for the Promotion of Evangelical Knowledge and, in 1860, the American Church Missionary Society—both aimed at infiltrating the church with their principles. The evangelicals reached the pinnacle of their influence in the late 1850's, by which time

Stephen H. Tyng, Sr. and one of his sons had built large congregations in New York City, and Bishops Manton Eastburn of Massachusetts and Charles P. McIlvaine of Ohio had joined their ranks.[28]

Differences between the two groups lay not so much in their observance of liturgy and sacraments or their respect for episcopal powers as in the way in which they regarded these matters. As the church's historian put it sixty years ago, evangelicals emphasized the individual reception of grace; High-churchmen, the institutional administration of grace. "The watchword of the one was experience; that of the other, authority." To the former group, then, sacraments and ritual liturgy were simply means to inspire the believer to live in vital, spiritual relation to his Lord. To the other, they were significant for their own sake, objective channels of grace. The Low Church emphasis upon experience led them to approve affiliation with other Christians in evangelistic endeavors, as well as to introduce prayer meetings, extemporaneous exhortation, and, in some cases, seasons of revival into their program of worship. Laymen inevitably found a larger place of usefulness under their banner. Conversely, admirers of the Oxford Movement feared religious enthusiasm, opposed all measures of gospel work other than those which the liturgy allowed, and considered their church a divine institution rather than a voluntary association. They were, by definition, sectarian and conservative.

That throughout these years the one Episcopal party "accounted itself as having all the piety, and the other all the loyalty and good manners in the church" did not, strangely, inhibit the growth of the whole. The denomination's membership increased 46 per cent in the decade following 1855. The evangelicals provided the mass appeal and their sedate opponents the pomp and circumstance which together fit the church for an important role in urban America.[29]

As for the Lutherans, Philip Schaff explained to a Berlin convocation in 1854 that Methodism, which held the same spiritual relation to the English church as pietism did to Lutheranism, had greatly influenced German immigrants to the United States—especially those from pietistic Würtemburg. Not only had German-speaking Wesleyan sects like the

---

[28] Charles C. Tiffany, *A History of the Protestant Episcopal Church in The United States of America* (Philip Schaff and others, eds., *The American Church History Series*, VII, New York, 1895), pp. 459-61, 467-68, 472-81.

[29] *Ibid.*, pp. 461-69, 489. Tiffany's chapter is far more sympathetic to the evangelicals than William W. Manross, *A History of the American Episcopal Church* (New York, 1935), pp. 277-85.

United Brethren in Christ, the Evangelical Association, and the German Methodists emerged, but all the German churches in America, he said, had adopted the system of revivals and the emphasis upon "subjective, experimental religion."

Schaff complained that the powerful "New Lutheran" party, which controlled the schools at Gettysburg, Pennsylvania, Springfield, Ohio, and ·Springfield, Illinois, had "entirely given up all the points which distinguish the Lutheran theology from the Reformed, substituting for the Calvinistic doctrine of predestination, however, the still un-Lutheran, Arminian theory of free will." Revivalism had increased steadily in favor among them after 1830, with the mourner's bench being used "not rarely with the wildest hyper-Methodistic excess." The Old Lutheran group, inclined to liturgical worship, had, he said, recently gained strength from the growing study of German theology and a gradual return in at least some of the Eastern branches to the more traditional forms of service. But the strife over re-vival measures had been so great that Schaff declared that one might "make a book on the anxious bench controversy in the German churches of America." [30]

The Society of Friends and the Unitarians, though often portrayed in terms of the liberalism of Elias Hicks and Theodore Parker, more generally revealed a similar attachment to personal and evangelical faith. Under the leadership of the Englishman John Joseph Gurney and Elisha Bates of the Ohio Yearly Meeting, the Friends experienced a decided revival of faith in the atonement as the means of sanctification, in contrast to the Hicksite predication of the innate capacity of man for a perfection of attainment. For a large majority of Quakers the Cross thus became more important than the "Inner Light," precisely because it was the source of grace by which the light might shine within. [31]

Similarly, from the day that Ralph Waldo Emerson resigned his pulpit in 1832, a widening breach had split the ranks of Unitarianism. Amidst the sharp controversy of the 1850's, the note dominant in Unitarian preaching seems to have been devotional and spiritual. One sizable group, led by Frederic Dan Huntington, Harvard Professor and preacher at the Appleton Chapel, consistently assailed liberals of Parker's variety and taught a religion

[30] Schaff, op. cit., pp. 168-69, 175-76, 183, 186, 188-89, 193, 204. See later, pp. 55-59.
[31] Elbert Russell, The History of Quakerism (New York, 1942), pp. 331-32 may be compared with John Joseph Gurney, Essays on the Evidences, Doctrines, and Practical Operations of Christianity (Philadelphia, 1856), pp. 529-30, and Elisha Bates, The Doctrines of Friends . . . (Philadelphia, 1868), pp. 119-31.

of personal communion with God through prayer and faith in the atonement.[32]

This is not to suggest that the peculiar social impact of Unitarianism arose from anything other than its tolerance of skeptical and independent intellectuals, but rather to illustrate the fact that with the masses of the people liberal Christianity was making little headway. The "Christian Connection" in the West, which opposed all creeds but practiced baptism by immersion, seems to have claimed more members in 1854 than did the Unitarians, with whom the group frequently co-operated. The total number in both, however, did not exceed 65,000, and the portion of these whose tendencies were radically liberal must have been quite small.[33]

The most important conclusion to be drawn from the foregoing analysis is that there was neither a typical Protestant point of view on religious and social matters nor even, in most cases, one which was common to the great body of believers within any major denomination. Every sermon, newspaper article, and essay must be studied in the light of its author's relation to the contending groups in his sect.

Nor can mid-nineteenth-century American clergymen be divided simply into the two categories of "orthodox" and "liberal." Four significant strains of thought and feeling flowed freely across denominational lines. *Traditionalism* is the term which best describes the mood common to High Church Episcopal and Old Lutheran leaders. *Orthodox Calvinism*, the bogeyman of social historians, was a dying dogma. Old School Presbyterians, Antimission Baptists, a small party of the most conservative Congregationalists, and two or three minor Presbyterian sects were its sole champions. What we will call in this book *Revivalistic Calvinism* was, paradoxically enough, almost Arminian on the matters of election and free will and leaned as well toward "new measures" and interfaith fellowship. This point of view characterized New School Presbyterians, most Congregationalists, Low Church Episcopalians, Regular Baptists, Disciples of Christ, and those

[32] The account in Joseph Henry Allen and Richard Eddy, *A History of the Unitarians and the Universalists in The United States* (Philip Schaff and others, eds., *The American Church History Series*, X, New York, 1894), pp. 205-20, is factually sparse, though written from distant memory of the events. The files of *The Monthly Religious Magazine* for the 1850's are revealing, especially the articles as follows: "Editor's Collecteana," XIV (1855), pp. 51-58; Rufus Ellis, "Our Gross Injustice to the Great Body of Unitarian Believers," XXV (1861), pp. 255-59; and E. H. Sears, "Theodore Parker and His Theology," XXIV (1860), pp. 73-78. See Chap. VI.

[33] See Schaff, *op. cit.*, p. 206; Grand Pièrre, *op. cit.*, pp. 46-47; and Marianne Finch, *An Englishwoman's Experience in America* (London, 1853), pp. 269-70, for general comments.

of the New Lutherans who were not thoroughgoing Arminians. *Evangelical Arminianism* claimed the allegiance of a vast army of Methodists of all sorts, the German Wesleyan sects, the Friends, many New Lutherans, the Cumberland Presbyterians, and the Freewill Baptists.

Low Church Episcopalians and New Lutherans were thus in thought and feeling closer to New School Presbyterians and Regular Baptists than to High-churchmen. All four revealed more openness to John Wesley's doctrines than to the old orthodoxy. The line dividing Evangelical Arminians from Evangelistic Calvinists seems, in retrospect, to have been more a matter of custom than of creed. The doctrine of Christian perfection became a leading concern in both camps.

American religion was organized outwardly into denominations, the knowledge of whose structure and inner relationships is fundamental to an understanding of the whole. But the easiest fallacy is to treat each one of these as a homogeneous unit. The next easiest, if scholarly works on the subject are any evidence, is to label everyone who believed in man's sinfulness a "Calvinist."

II

The Social Influence
of the Churches

ে৵৩

The irreligious had prophesied ever since 1785 that
sectarian conflict would gradually strangle Christianity in the new nation.
True, the multiplicity of denominations had required the early divorce of
the national government from religion. The rapid growth of dissenting
groups eventually compelled the states in turn to abolish whatever vestiges
of an established church they had retained. But legal status, in religion as
in other matters, may often indicate an empty tradition rather than a social
fact; its absence may be equally deceiving. What was the real influence of
Protestant Christianity on American life on the eve of the Civil War?

Denominational rivalry had certainly not lessened the zeal to win converts.[1] Revival enthusiasm and personal consecration had fashioned a rod
stronger than legal sanctions to herd the lost sheep in. Moreover, the government adopted measures which belied its professed neutrality in religious
affairs. Stephen Colwell, Philadelphia Presbyterian and reformer, declared
that statutes requiring observance of the Sabbath, proclamations calling the
nation to prayer, state laws against blasphemy, court rulings in church
cases, oathswearing on the Bible and the maintenance of chaplains in
legislative halls and the armed services all proved that evangelical Protestantism was indeed "legally recognized as the popular religion of the
country."[2]

But, Colwell asserted, the power of Christianity is in any case "moral,
not physical"; its security in the hearts of the people was "higher than the
Constitution itself," for it was "the very atmosphere in which our institu-

---

[1] See Robert Baird, *The Progress and Prospects of Christianity in the United States of
America* (London, 1851), pp. 26-27, 44; Philip Schaff, *America . . .* (New York, 1855),
pp. 117, 120-21; and Stephen Colwell, *The Position of Christianity in the United States
. . .* (Philadelphia, 1854), pp. 78-81.

[2] Colwell, *op. cit.*, p. 53; cf. pp. 1-89, *passim*. See also Baird, *Progress and Prospects*,
pp. 27-28, and the same author's *State and Prospects of Religion in America . . .* (London,
1855), pp. 116-29.

tions exist, . . . the basis of our morality, and the mould in which our civilization has been cast." Philip Schaff likewise held that the nation was "still Christian" though it refused "to be governed in this deepest concern of the mind and heart by the temporal power." Because American Christianity was "the free expression of personal conviction and of national character," he believed it had "even greater power over the mind, than when enjoined by civil laws." The revolutions of 1848, he noted, had shown the European system to rest principally on "grand illusions." [3]

What had happened was that the American Christians had created a new pattern of church-state relations, unknown since the first century. It was called the "voluntary system," to distinguish it from the state-church tradition in Europe. Thoughtful visitors from the Old World expressed amazement at its success. Alexis de Tocqueville pointed out in 1833 that the efforts American clergymen made to avoid political strife actually increased their hold upon society. Religion, he said, regulated the community through its power over manners and morals. It was, therefore, "the foremost of the political institutions of the country." Tocqueville noted that citizens of all classes and shades of political opinion held Christianity to be indispensable to the maintenance of republican government. Wherever the church attempts to share the temporal power of the state, he concluded, it cannot avoid being "the object of a portion of that animosity which the latter excites." [4]

Gilbert Haven, a Boston abolitionist who became a Methodist bishop after the war, explained the social responsibilities of clergymen under the American system in a fast-day sermon for 1863 called, "The State a Christian Brotherhood, the Mission of America." Haven believed that the nation's destiny was to prove that "the utmost liberty of worship and the utmost liberty of no worship" can "co-exist with a ruling Christianity," and that "the utmost liberty and equality of all men can co-exist with a stable and prosperous government." Democracy would fail, he said, if "this attempt to trust the human race with the offers of salvation, without

[3] Colwell, op. cit., p. 68; Schaff, op. cit., pp. xiii, 91. Cf. William Henry Milburn, The Rifle, Axe, and Saddle-Bags, and Other Lectures (New York, 1857), pp. 56-57, 77-78.
[4] Alexis de Tocqueville, Democracy in America (tr. Henry Reeve; New York, 1900), I, 310, 315-17; see generally the whole passage, 313-20. Cf. Winthrop S. Hudson, The Great Tradition of the American Churches (New York, 1953), pp. 63-79, 98-99, and passim.

endeavouring, in the least degree, to compel their acquiescence" did not succeed in bringing about a Christian society.[5]

Haven warned, however, that grave dangers arose from the tendency to discourage ministers from speaking out on political and social issues.

The Gospel . . . is not confined to a repentance and faith that have no connection with social or civil duties. The Evangel of Christ is an all-embracing theme. It is the vital force in earth and in heaven. . . . The Cross is the centre of the spiritual, and therefore of the material universe,

the divine touchstone before which "literature, science, politics, business, the status of society, all charities, all reforms" must be brought to test. It is thus alone, he cried, that "the kingdom of Christ can be universally established." [6]

Regardless of the validity of these theoretical explanations, there is abundant factual witness to the immense power of the clergy. Higher education, developed from the first under the supervision of Presbyterian and Congregationalist ministers, centered increasingly around religion, now that the popular sects undertook a larger role. By 1860 Northern Methodists operated 26 colleges and 116 institutes and academies. Regular Baptists, North and South, maintained 33 colleges and 161 secondary schools.[7] Ministers edited scores of denominational newspapers and magazines whose total circulation had grown to phenomenal proportions by 1860. Strongly religious journals like *Harper's Monthly, Harper's Weekly,* and *The Ladies Repository,* to mention only three under the influence of Methodism, filled a place held later by more secular publications.[8]

Clergymen inspired the dominant social movement of the period, the crusade for humanitarian reform, at every stage. They were the principal arbiters of manners and morals and the most venerated citizens of every community. A young Methodist circuit rider, returning in 1845 from the

[5] Gilbert Haven, *National Sermons. Sermons, Speeches and Letters on Slavery and Its War* . . . (Boston, 1869), pp. 342-44.

[6] *Ibid.,* pp. 337-38. See later, pp. 220-22, 235.

[7] Anon., *The American Christian Record* . . . (New York, 1860), pp. 273-75, 278, 295, 359. Cf. Donald G. Tewksbury, *The Founding of American Colleges and Universities Before the Civil War; with Particular Reference to the Religious Influences Bearing Upon the College Movement* (Teacher's College, Columbia University, *Contributions to Education,* New York, 1932), pp. 66-91, 108-11, 113 and *passim;* excellent tables appear on pp. 93-95, 104-05, 115-16. See also Lewis G. Vander Velde, "The Diary of George Duffield," *The Mississippi Valley Historical Review,* XXIV (1937-38), pp. 23, 25.

[8] Frank Luther Mott, *A History of American Magazines, 1850-1865* (Cambridge, 1938), pp. 301-5, 383-91.

West in broken health, actually won election as chaplain to the national legislature through the efforts of three congressmen whose respect he had won by publicly castigating their drunkenness and gambling aboard an Ohio River steamboat. According to Robert Baird, New Orleans was the only American city which in 1851 permitted omnibuses to operate on Sunday. New York got along with one horse-drawn street railway in service. A reviewer of a volume of Henry Ward Beecher's sermons wrote in *The Atlantic Monthly*: "No class has such opportunities for influence, such means of power" as the American preachers. Even now, he declared, the press ranks second to the pulpit. "Sunday morning all the land is still. Broadway is a quiet stream, looking sober, even dull. Even in this great Babel of Commerce one day in seven is given up to the minister." [9]

A sampling of the opinions of Europeans who traveled in the United States between 1850 and 1865 will readily verify this judgment. Dissenters might naturally rejoice to find the voluntary system of support working well, but proponents of an established church also admitted its success, as did several who professed disinterest in religion.[10] Evangelicals were especially heartened to discover that the elimination of legal privilege seemed to lessen sectarian rivalry.[11]

The latter group agreed unanimously that the ideals of evangelical Protestantism seemed to dominate the national culture. They pointed to the rigorous observance of the Sabbath, even in cities filled with German immigrants—like Milwaukee and Chicago—and the evident enthusiasm of large segments of the population for temperance reform, as proof that a national religion was more effective than merely a state church. They thought the Bible House, built in New York City in 1853 at a cost of $280,000, a fitting monument to the book which in politics as in religion served as final authority.[12] Several argued that the previous generation of

[9] Baird, *Progress and Prospects*, p. 28; *The Atlantic Monthly*, I (1858), pp. 862-63; William Henry Milburn, *Ten Years of Preacher-Life: Chapters from an Autobiography* (New York, 1859), pp. 113-14.

[10] See dissenters' statements in A. É. de Gasparin, *The Uprising of a Great People* . . . (tr. Mary L. Booth; New York, 1861), pp. 63-65; Georges Fisch, *Nine Months in the United States* . . . (London, 1863), p. 23; and anon., *America As I Found It* (London, 1852), p. 100. Cf. Schaff, *op. cit.*, pp. 90-95; J. H. Grand Pierre, *A Parisian Pastor's Glance at America* (Boston, 1854), pp. 57, 66; T. C. Grattan, *Civilized America* (London, 1859), II, pp. 338-40; Henry A. Murray, *Lands of the Slave and the Free: or, Cuba, The United States, and Canada* (London, 1857), p. 423; and William Hancock, *An Emigrant's Five Years in the Free States of America* (London, 1860), pp. 109-10.

[11] See earlier, p. 19.

[12] Isabella (Bird) Bishop, *The Aspects of Religion in the United States* . . . (London,

visitors, prejudiced in favor of state churches and representing principally, as one put it, "the *beau monde* of London and Parisian society," had amused their readers with caricatures of revivals and strange sects which wholly misinterpreted the nature and influence of American religion.[13]

Europeans were particularly astonished at the vast sums given for church buildings, religious benevolence and charity. It seemed incredible that clerical salaries in New York and Boston ranged between $4,000 and $5,000 a year, or that the Rev. William Adams expected to raise $150,000 from his New York City congregation for a new church building within a few weeks.[14] They frequently attributed this to the fact that American ministers, appointed as they were for their zeal and abilities and usually responsible only to the people, preached better sermons than those in Europe and exercised much greater personal power over their congregations. Nothing was so rare in America, Georges Fisch observed, as "a worldly or immoral clergyman," for under the voluntary system the people would not allow it. Here, he believed, was the most distinguished body of pastors in the world, "not only at the head of their churches, but at the head of the nation as well." An English woman commented that "an aristocracy of moral worth and consistent piety" existed in the country, for a minister's influence as chairman of a meeting carried more weight than that of a "real live lord" in Britain.[15]

Thus by 1860 the clergy had recovered whatever influence over public affairs they had lost in the generations of Thomas Jefferson and Andrew

1859), pp. 26, 66, 126, 128, 138, 140-42, 165; James Dixon, *Personal Narrative of a Tour Through a Part of the United States* . . . (New York, 1849), p. 178; anon., *America As I Found It*, p. 110; Grand Pièrre, *op. cit.*, pp. 59, 66, 75-76, 86; Gasparin, *op. cit.*, pp. 56-71, 84-85.

See also the comments on temperance, some of them amusing complaints of the alcoholic aridity of the new nation: Hancock, *op. cit.*, p. 108; David W. Mitchell, *Ten Years in the United States* (London, 1862), pp. 86-87; Charles Mackay, *Life and Liberty in America; or Sketches of a Tour in the United States and Canada in 1857-58* (London, 1859), I, 60, 217; and Johann Georg Kohl, *Travels in Canada, and Through the States of New York and Pennsylvania* (tr. Mrs. Percy Sinnett; London, 1861), pp. 223-24.

[13] Dixon, *op. cit.*, pp. 167-68; Bishop, *op. cit.*, pp. 5-23, *passim*; Fisch, *op. cit.*, p. 94.

Max Berger, *The British Traveler in America, 1836-1860* (New York, 1943), pp. 129-36, relies principally on secular-minded visitors in describing foreign views of American religion.

[14] Grand Pièrre, *op. cit.*, pp. 58-61. Cf. Gasparin, *op. cit.*, pp. 68-71; Bishop, *op. cit.*, pp. 28-29; Schaff, *op. cit.*, pp. x-xi, 94. Joseph Belcher, *op. cit.*, pp. 982-86, noted, conversely, the great disparity between the salaries of rural and city pastors; he estimated the national average to be little better than $400 annually.

[15] Marianne Finch, *An Englishwoman's Experience in America* (London, 1853), p. 75. Cf. Fisch, *op. cit.*, p. 43; anon., *America As I Found It*, p. 110; Grand Pièrre, *op. cit.*, pp. 69-70; and Bishop, *op. cit.*, pp. 28-29, 140-63.

Jackson, and enjoyed it without let or hindrance from legal sanctions. Significantly enough, Abraham Lincoln was the last of the long line of American presidents who were reluctant to identify themselves publicly with a church organization. In fact, the religious conviction which permeated Lincoln's statements and addresses set the tone for a new generation of public figures, ready—at times all too ready—to affirm their Christian faith. The form of godliness, however odious when displayed by men like Daniel Drew or Jim Fiske, became a prerequisite for eminence. By the end of the Civil War, as secular a journal as *The Nation* was found thoughtfully urging increased salaries for rural ministers and support for the expanding program of the Y.M.C.A., lest "the religious culture of this generation" should "leave very few traces on the next." [16]

Such general approbation was in part a reward for the social responsibility which the churches had assumed for the evangelization of the West and the religious and moral instruction of the nation's unchurched youth. By 1850 nine separate societies were employing 2,675 home missionaries to establish churches and Sunday schools in "destitute" communities at a total annual expenditure of $500,000. Most of these organizations were denominational offshoots of the nonsectarian American Home Missionary Society, which supported 40 per cent of the workers. A vast river of Bibles, books, magazines and pamphlets flowed from the presses of the American Bible and Tract societies and scores of denominational concerns to water the gospel seed.[17] Recent immigrants, come in great poverty from what many Americans regarded as "lands of darkness," received much attention. By 1860, for example, 229 of the 289 domestic missionaries of the Methodist Episcopal Church worked among the German population, and thirty others among Scandinavians. O. G. Hedstrom inspired and often guided the latter group, from the contacts he made with Swedish newcomers aboard the "Bethel Ship," "The John Wesley," in New York Harbor.[18]

[16] *The Nation*, March 15, 1866, pp. 326-27. Cf. Hudson, *op. cit.*, pp. 103-7; Carl Russell Fish, *The Rise of the Common Man, 1830-50* (Arthur M. Schlesinger and Dixon Ryan Fox, eds., *A History of American Life*, VI, New York, 1927), p. 179.

[17] See statistics for 1850 in Baird, *Progress and Prospects*, pp. 24-25. Although Tewksbury, *op. cit.*, pp. 72, 76-78, 80-81, 83-85 stresses the sectarian nature of the college movement in the West, much of the evidence he cites illustrates that its impetus was a general concern for the maintenance of a religious culture.

[18] *Zion's Herald*, Dec. 1, 1852; anon., *American Christian Record*, pp. 290, 306; J. M. Reid, *Missions and Missionary Society of The Methodist Episcopal Church* (New York, 1879), I, p. 434. Cf. Paul F. Douglass, *The Story of German Methodism. Biography of an Immigrant Soul* (New York, 1939), pp. 1-90.

Most of the details of this home missionary crusade are well known, of course. The significant point here is that its leaders considered themselves as much civilizing and Americanizing agents as soul winners. "If you converse with these missionaries of Christian civilization," remarked Alexis de Tocqueville in 1832, "you will be surprised to find . . . that you meet with a politician where you expected to find a priest." [19]

The same is even more true of the Sunday-school movement. Prominent laymen representing several communions had organized the American Sunday School Union in 1830 for the purpose of supplying both rural and urban children with the religious education forbidden in the public schools. Though by 1850 a parallel Methodist organization led the way by far in the number of schools and scholars, the co-operative group still received the most financial assistance. It had originally helped organize many of the units which later passed into denominational hands. [20] The Union began about that year also to employ ministerial students as temporary missionaries during their summer vacations. In 1853, 214 men from twenty-six colleges organized 695 schools and induced over four thousand persons to serve as teachers. They were very active in city slums, where they served as unofficial truant officers, rounding up many children for the public schools. [21]

A long debate raged on the question whether Sunday schools were an adequate substitute for a religiously oriented state-educational system, as was possible in Europe. Old School Presbyterians, like the Lutherans and Catholics, were planning parochial schools in the 1840's. Ministers of some other communions seem to have held back only because of the expenditure required. [22] Stephen Colwell published an important book in 1854 which called the American system a failure. He recommended that all Protestants

[19] Op. cit., I, 311-12. Cf. Edward Norris Kirk, The Church Essential to the Republic. A Sermon in Behalf of the American Home Missionary Society . . . (New York, 1848), passim; Milburn, op. cit.; the same author's Pioneers, Preachers, and People of the Mississippi Valley (New York, 1860); James L. Batchelder, The United States, The West, and the State of Ohio, as Missionary Fields (Cincinnati, 1848), pp. 1-7. See also Tewksbury, op. cit., pp. 22-23, 72-75; for interesting quotations.
[20] See Baird, Progress and Prospects, pp. 24-25; Belcher, op. cit., pp. 594, 603.
[21] The Watchman and Reflector, Jan. 19, 1854; Mary M. Boardman (Mrs. Wm. E.), Life and Labours of the Rev. W. E. Boardman (New York, 1887), pp. 96-101. See later p. 167.
[22] Anson Phelps Stokes, Church and State in The United States . . . (New York, 1950), II, pp. 676 and 645-79, passim; Hugh Seymour Tremenheere, Notes on Public Subjects Made During a Tour in The United States and Canada (London, 1852), pp. 42-43.

agree immediately on a common creed, so as to make possible a committedly Christian program of state education. The chief difficulty was not so much the reluctance of the clergy to act in political matters, Colwell said, as their sectarian strife.[23]

The American Sunday School Union had tried twenty years earlier to persuade Horace Mann to adopt its "select library" for religious instruction in Massachusetts. When Mann countered with the proposition that the Bible alone be employed, in a manner consistent with Unitarian prejudices, he displayed equal rejection of the idea of an entirely secular system. Meanwhile, even Methodist preachers served as superintendents of public schools, one of them as a New Hampshire state commissioner.[24]

Unsolicited advice from European critics helped confuse Protestant thinking on the subject, as did the publicity given Roman Catholic views when Archbishop John Hughes conducted an unsuccessful campaign to secure state funds for parochial institutions in New York.[25] The figures which one English investigator gathered in 1851 to discredit the Sunday-school movement actually gave much evidence of its success. Hugh Seymour Tremenheere found that in New York the average weekly attendance of 30,000 equalled three-fourths of that in "public, ward and corporate schools." Elsewhere, his polls revealed that 67 per cent of the public-school children in Cleveland, 40 per cent in Pittsburgh, 80 per cent in Philadelphia and 80 per cent in Boston attended church schools on the Sabbath. The low figures for Pittsburgh, however, were borne out in other industrial or mining communities, like Jamestown, Rhode Island, and Pottsville, Pennsylvania. In many places, moreover, the public-school attendance was far below the potential which the census of the population indicated.[26]

Tremenheere noted approvingly that the Christian-education movement was lessening sectarian tensions, particularly in areas where only one school could be supported. The Sunday School Union had contributed effectively, so the secretary of the Massachusetts State Board of Education

[23] Colwell, op. cit., pp. 80, 84-85, 98, 118 and 89-130, passim.

[24] Stokes, op. cit., II, pp. 55-56; Zion's Herald, Jan. 7, 1852; George Prentice, The Life of Gilbert Haven . . . (New York, 1883), p. 110; Abel Stevens, Life and Times of Nathan Bangs (New York, 1863), p. 361.

[25] W. O. Bourne, History of the Public School Society of the City of New York (New York, 1873), Chs. X-XV; Tremenheere, op. cit., pp. 26-27, 48-49; anon., America As I Found It, pp. 49-57. But contrast favorable views in Fisch, op. cit., pp. 73-74, 80-82, and Bishop, op. cit., pp. 172-75.

[26] Tremenheere, op. cit., pp. 14, 16, 19, 24-27.

told him, to the growing conviction that peculiarities of doctrine were subordinate to the great truths which the churches held in common. A writer in *The Sunday School Journal* for 1854 declared that, despite the opposition of ecclesiastical leaders, if all the Christians could be heard, a great majority would speak for relaxing denominational bonds and strengthening "those which unite them as followers of Christ. *The sentiment of the church, at this moment, is for union.*" [27]

The mutual understanding which thus blossomed from the sowing of home-mission and Sunday-school workers further strengthened the reviving social prestige of religion. It bore many fruits, none more significant than the ill-fated efforts to form a world Evangelical Alliance. Robert Baird, temperance agitator and European representative for several organizations seeking to convert Roman Catholics, seems to have joined with other American clergymen in suggesting such an ecumenical organization to the British and Continental churches. A distinguished American delegation, including Edward Norris Kirk, Samuel S. Schmucker, Stephen Olin, Abel Stevens, Emerson Andrews, and Lyman Beecher, attended the first conference at London in 1846. The British, however, seized the initiative and wrecked hopes for active American participation by insisting upon a clause barring slaveholders from membership. [28]

The United States representatives returned home to organize a national alliance of the same name, as did those from the Continent. Baird founded and edited for three years a monthly organ, *The Christian Union and Religious Memorial*, and attended numerous meetings of the English and Continental sections. But his hopes of securing removal of the antislavery clause and, thereby, a revival of ecumenicity, were never fulfilled. Meanwhile, opposition from both the left and right enfeebled the American alliance, as did bickering over slavery and the ill feeling created between Presbyterians and Congregationalists at the disruption of their co-operative association, the Plan of Union, in 1852. [29] George B. Cheever, famous pastor of New York's Church of the Pilgrims, and many others who could

---

[27] *Ibid.*, pp. 40-41; *The Sunday School Journal*, March 1, 1854, quoted in Colwell, *op. cit.*, pp. 82-83. Cf. anon., *America As I Found It*, pp. 114-19.

[28] Henry Martyn Baird, *Life of the Rev. Robert Baird, D.D.* (New York, 1866), pp. 227-35.

[29] *Ibid. The Independent*, March 29, 1855, bitterly attacked Isaac V. Brown, *Vindication of the Abrogation of the Plan of Union by the Presbyterian Church in The United States of America* (Philadelphia, 1855), and Old School Presbyterianism in general. Cf. E. H. Gillett, *History of the Presbyterian Church . . .* (Philadelphia, 1864), II, 558-63.

not be accused of proslavery sympathies supported the project, however, both as a counterweight to Catholicism and a means to the fulfillment of the scriptural promise of the world's conversion through Christian union in evangelism.[30] Others in the liberal wing of Congregationalists in New York City opposed it, as did Horace Bushnell, on the grounds that its creed was so narrow as to make it a "new eclectic sect" from which many sincere Christians were excluded.[31]

Typical of the residual bigotry was Alexander Blaikie's volume, *The Philosophy of Sectarianism*, published in 1854. Its arguments proved, at least to the author's satisfaction, that the burst of brotherly activity in charity, evangelism, and religious education was spurious, since it rested on other than Calvinistic doctrine and called for "unscriptural" organizations. Clearly the world's conversion awaited the adoption by the churches of the principles of the Associate Reformed Presbyterian Church.[32]

The next year the New School *New York Evangelist* and *The Independent*, organ of liberal Congregationalists, heatedly debated the question whether what the former called "a legitimate denominationalism" was equivalent to sectarianism. The editors of the latter paper insisted that the whole spirit of denominational loyalty must be overcome "before a true Christian unity can be manifested to the world; before the millennial glory can be ushered in." It is doubtful, however, that their references a month later to the "minor ingenuities of perversion" and the "sub-acid smartness" of *The Evangelist* hastened the dawning day.[33]

Succeeding chapters will endeavor to show how revivalism helped to melt these ancient prejudices as well as to popularize socially constructive versions of perfectionist and millenarian doctrines. In fact, the awakening of 1858-59 set the stage for a tremendous advance in interdenominational social and religious work, quickening the pace by which the churches Christianized the land. Old benevolent societies took on new functions, new ones like the Y.M.C.A. and the Christian Labor Union appeared,

[30] *The Independent*, May 17, 1949; *Zion's Herald*, Feb. 18, 1852.
[31] *The Independent*, Jan. 11 and 25, 1849. The issue of May 17, 1849, nonetheless carried a long and favorable report of its annual meeting.
[32] Alexander Blaikie, *The Philosophy of Sectarianism* . . . (Boston, 1855), pp. 4-6, 240-41.
[33] *The Independent*, July 19 and August 16, 1855. See also the same, May 3 and 10, 1855, for the report of the second annual meeting of the Congregational Union; the issue of July 5, 1855, p. 212; and the utterly silly controversy over a review of Henry Ward Beecher's *Plymouth Collection of Hymns* in those for November 22 and December 13, 1855. Cf. Colwell, *New Themes for the Protestant Clergy* . . . (Philadelphia, 1851), p. 176.

and for a brief period the churches themselves joined hands and hearts to usher in the kingdom of Christ.

The opinions of both European and American observers, therefore, seem verified in solid fact: the churches were making a far greater impact upon American society than their numbers or separation from the state would imply. Nor was sectarianism as strong as is commonly supposed. The interdenominational Bible, tract, missionary, and temperance associations did not seem to contemporaries the projects of men who had divorced themselves from active church life. They were rather the symbols of a growing spirit of union which the greatest ecclesiastical leaders heartily endorsed. From the very beginning, moreover, and increasingly as years passed, these organizations sought to reform earthly institutions as well as to prepare the souls of men for heaven. Most churchmen were keenly aware of their role in shaping America's destiny—even Methodists like Gilbert Haven. Otherworldly convictions imparted a sacred potency to their crusade to sanctify the national culture and convert the world to Christian principles.

III

The Resurgence of Revivalism
1840-1857

ᥱᵔᵓ

The cutting edge of American Christianity after 1850 was the revival, adopted and promoted in one form or another by major segments of all denominations. One writer declared on the eve of the Civil War that the most characteristic feature of the religious history of the century was "the increasing recognition, cultivation, and expectation of revivals." The previous twenty-five years especially had witnessed "such a succession and general distribution" of them as to encourage his hopes for the day of their permanent and continuous enjoyment.[1] No less a figure than Robert Baird stoutly defended them before European audiences and adorned the magazine he edited for the American branch of the Evangelical Alliance with reports of their progress. Two of his articles in 1849 urged that a state of continuous awakening was the normal condition of the church and sectarian strife the greatest hindrance to attainment of this goal.[2]

Though historians have in the past two decades become increasingly aware of the contributions of revivalism to nineteenth-century culture, interest has been focused principally upon the events which transpired before 1842 and particularly upon the careers of individuals like Charles G. Finney and Lyman Beecher. Relatively little attention has been paid to the later extension of their kind of crusade in the churches, except to unusual outbursts like that of 1858. What, then, can be found in the inner life of the larger denominations which will indicate the wider setting in which such extraordinary awakenings took place?

The answer to this question is particularly important if it be true that evangelists and evangelistic pastors led the way in liberalizing Calvinistic

[1] William C. Conant, *Narratives of Remarkable Conversions and Revival Incidents* . . . (New York, 1858), p. 359.
[2] Robert Baird, *Religion in America* . . . (New York, 1844), pp. 203-15 ff.; *The Christian Union and Religious Memorial*, II (1849), pp. 77-78, 146. See revival reports in the same, I (1848), pp. 59, 121-23; and II (1849), pp. 252-54.

theology and inspiring humanitarian effort. During the revival of 1858, for example, James Freeman Clarke wrote in the Unitarian *Monthly Religious Magazine* that the churches were rising "out of dogmas into the life of the Spirit," where new manifestations of "liberality of opinion and practical goodness" would add strength to their common bonds. In such epochs, he declared, "the essential features of Calvinism disappear; for the doctrine of total inability must be put aside, if not openly rejected. . . . The necessary subjects are those connected with sin and salvation, and must be treated, not in a speculative, but in a practical manner." [3]

The fact that since 1890 mass evangelism has often been associated with theologically obscurantist and socially negative religion makes such a statement seem incredible. Modern students find it difficult to understand the constructive contributions of a tradition chiefly remembered for the barbarities evidenced at frontier camp meetings. If, however, by revivalism we mean the use of special efforts to secure conversions amidst excited group emotions, its enlightened and disciplined flowering among urban Christians at mid-century is far more significant than anything which happened before. [4]

No argument is required to establish the popularity of religious awakenings among Methodists before the Civil War. Long promotion of camp meetings had stamped Wesleyanism with a fervor which city churches expressed in yearly seasons of special religious interest called "protracted meetings." Here sinners were bidden each night to the "anxious seat," or mourner's bench, devised about 1808 in a crowded New York City chapel to enable saints to deal with seekers more conveniently. [5] The fact that only four noteworthy full-time evangelists appeared in the church before 1857 —John Newland Maffitt, James Caughey, and Dr. and Mrs. Walter Palmer, who were laymen—only emphasizes the point that every bishop, college president, presiding elder, and circuit rider was expected to be a constant winner of souls. Revivals of "perfect love" were the catalyst which

---

[3] James Freeman Clarke, "The Revival," *The Monthly Religious Magazine,* XIX (1858), p. 351.

[4] Richard C. Wolf, "The Middle Period, 1800-1870. The Matrix of Modern American Christianity," *Religion in Life, a Christian Quarterly of Opinion and Discussion,* XXII (1952-53), pp. 72-84, suggests this idea, as do several other recent writers: Robert T. Handy, "The Protestant Quest for a Christian America, 1830-1930," *Church History,* XXI (1953-54), pp. 11-13; Charles Howard Hopkins, *History of the Y.M.C.A. in North America* (New York, 1951), pp. 6-8, 16-39, *passim;* and Charles C. Cole, Jr., *The Social Ideas of the Northern Evangelists, 1826-1860* (New York, 1954), pp. 71-95.

[5] Frank Grenville Beardsley, *A History of American Revivals* (2nd ed., New York, 1912), pp. 194-95, 202-3.

enabled an authoritarian church government to control effectively the followers of an intensely democratic faith.[6] They also helped to congeal the intense concern for social reform which sprang up among Northern Methodists around 1840. Every abolitionist periodical published in the denomination unceasingly promoted them.[7]

The story of Baptist revivalism is more involved. The spread of the Antimission schism after 1820, and of its prejudices within Western associations not formally separated from Regular Baptist fellowship, demonstrated the force of ultra-Calvinistic rejection of special measures for the conversion of the lost. Ohio, Georgia, Alabama, and Tennessee were greatly affected, Tennessee associations almost unanimously spurning evangelizing efforts in the two decades after 1830.[8]

Though the opposite tendency prevailed in the East, progress was slow before 1850. One deterrent was the unwillingness to countenance measures championed for so long in rural New England by the Freewill Baptists, whose devotion to Arminianism and evangelism was displayed anew in the protracted meetings which gave birth to their first organizations in New York and Boston in 1849 and 1850.[9] Another was the controversy over Elder Jacob Knapp, first professional evangelist in the denomination.

Knapp's ministry in the 1830's was principally to rural and small-town communities in New York, where he became known as a chief supporter of Madison University at Hamilton. His first urban successes, in union campaigns sponsored by the Baptist churches in Rochester, Baltimore, and Boston, were cut short in 1842 when antirevival clergymen charged that he wore old clothes in the pulpit in order to secure a more sympathetic response in the offerings. His supporters hotly contested the accusation, and he was officially cleared. But the institution at Hamilton suffered

[6] James Caughey, *Glimpses of Life in Soul-Saving* . . . (New York, 1868), pp. i-viii; George Hughes, *The Beloved Physician, Walter C. Palmer, M.D., and His Sun-Lit Journey to the Celestial City* (New York, 1884), pp. 164-68. On the last point, see Richard Wheatley, *The Life and Letters of Mrs. Phoebe Palmer* (New York, 1876), pp. 311-12. See Chap. VIII.

[7] See "Revivals—Why Are They Not Permanent," *Zion's Herald*, Nov. 17, 1852, and subsequent editorials in the issues of Dec. 1 and 15. On the abolitionists of western New York, see later pp. 129-33, 205-7, 212-13.

[8] Albert Henry Newman, *A History of the Baptist Churches in The United States* (Philip Schaff and others, eds., *The American Church History Series*, II, New York, 1894), pp. 437-41.

[9] William Hurlin, "The Free Will Baptists, Their History and Doctrines," *The Christian Review*, XXVII (1862), pp. 565-69, 571-72; Helen Dunn Gates, *A Consecrated Life. A Sketch of the Life and Labors of Rev. Ransom Dunn, D.D., 1818-1900* (Boston, 1901), pp. 89, 92, 136.

secessions which eventually provided nuclei for Lewisburg University (now Bucknell) and the University of Rochester. Knapp spent the next fifteen years in small churches, some of them farther West.[10]

Jabez S. Swan and Emerson Andrews, two other revivalists active during the period, seem also to have labored principally in small towns in New England and the Middle Atlantic states. This may be due to the fact that most Baptist congregations were located in such communities. Although their success was occasionally phenomenal, the extent of revival activity in the denomination cannot be measured by the careers of such professionals, all of whom suffered from the prejudices against Jacob Knapp.[11]

For in time, promoters of colleges, missionary projects, and Bible, Sunday-school, and temperance societies discovered, in the words of R. Jeffry—a pastor prominent in Philadelphia during the Civil War—that it was "never so easy to induce a church to make large contributions for a benevolent object . . . as when it is in the full tide of a religious revival." Baptists generally regarded such enterprises as "unwarrantable innovations on the methods of grace," Jeffry said, until "new measures" won general acceptance. And the strongest and latest opposition came from rural and frontier areas.[12] In the East college presidents like Francis Wayland of Brown University and Martin Brewer Anderson of the University of Rochester set out to inspire and train a new generation of evangelistic preachers.[13]

The editors of Boston's *Watchman and Reflector* believed in 1854 that with "living Christians in our evangelical churches" there was no longer any question as to "the vast utility, and . . . indispensableness of revivals of religion." Evidence for the statement might well have come from the bulging revival column of this Baptist newspaper.[14] After New Year's

[10] Jacob Knapp, *Autobiography of Elder Jacob Knapp* (New York, 1868), pp. xv, xix-xxvi, contains a dispassionate summary by R. Jeffry. Cf. *The National Cyclopaedia of American Biography* . . . (New York, 1917), XII, pp. 243-44.

[11] P. C. Headley, *Evangelists in the Church. Philip, A. D. 35, to Moody and Sankey, A. D. 1875* (Boston, 1875), pp. 252-58, summarizes Swan's long career, stretching from 1823-70; Emerson Andrews, *Living Life; or, Autobiography of Rev. Emerson Andrews, Evangelist* (Boston, 1875), pp. 120-82, *passim*, and especially pp. 158, 164.

[12] Knapp, *op. cit.*, pp. x-xi; *The Watchman and Reflector*, March 12, 1857 and March 4, 1858.

[13] James O. Murray, *Francis Wayland* (Boston, 1891), pp. 124-34, 246-49; Charles G. Finney, *Memoirs* . . . (New York, 1876), pp. 438-40; sketch of Anderson in *National Cyclopaedia of Biography*, XII, 243-44. Theodore Collier's summary of Wayland's career in *The Dictionary of American Biography* ignores his soul-winning interests.

[14] "How Shall We Promote Revivals," *The Watchman and Reflector*, March 2, 1854; cf. revival reports in the issues for Jan. 12 and 19, Feb. 9 and 16 and March 2, 9, and

Day, 1857, its entire editorial policy focused on a campaign to promote awakenings "throughout New England." The paper gave extensive coverage to Elder Knapp's long union meetings in Baltimore and Cincinnati. His return to popular favor helped to erase doubts about his methods in the Northeast. The *Watchman's* news columns from January to April reported hundreds of special efforts to precipitate revivals—including notable ones in Charlestown, Massachusetts, Providence, Rhode Island, Brooklyn, and a half-dozen New York City churches. Weeks of nightly meetings at Pittsfield, Massachusetts, catapulted that Baptist congregation up among the largest in the state. Fifty Methodists, a cheering omen, were among Emerson Andrews' converts at North Adams. Scores of New England towns were deeply stirred. On April 2 the editors announced that "the year 1857 promises, beyond any for the last ten, at least, to be one of increase to Zion. . . . We believe that the people of God may now believingly address themselves to the work of promoting revivals everywhere." [15]

Primitive Piety Revived, a much-discussed volume which Henry Clay Fish published in 1857, became a keynote of Baptist revival propaganda. Fish was a Union Theological Seminary graduate who had just completed the first seven years of a highly successful quarter century as pastor in Newark, New Jersey. George B. Ide, pastor at West Medway, Massachusetts, and formerly at the First Baptist Church, Philadelphia, and Heman Humphrey, Congregational evangelist and former president of Amherst College, chose Fish's manuscript from those submitted in a prize competition. Its ringing plea for a return to the soul-winning enthusiasm of the early Christians helped pave the way for the awakening of 1858 and won its author an honorary doctorate from the University of Rochester. "What can save our large cities but a powerful revival of religion," he cried. "What one thing does this whole country so loudly call for, as the descent of the Holy Ghost upon the churches?" [16]

---

16. The Baptist *Christian Review*, like most theological quarterlies, was more conservative; but see "Christian Experience and Its Relation to Ministerial Success," XXI (1856), pp. 584-86, and G. W. Hervey, "Congregational Music," XXIII (1858), pp. 249-51.

[15] *The Watchman and Reflector*, Apr. 2, 1857. See also editorials in the issues of Jan. 15 and 29, 1857; the revival columns from January to April, especially those for March 19 and 26; and the report of the further awakening at Pittsfield, March 4, 1858. Cf. Andrews, *op. cit.*, p. 220.

[16] Henry Clay Fish, *Primitive Piety Revived, or the Aggressive Power of the Christian Church. A Premium Essay* (Boston, 1857), pp. iii, 242; see also pp. 231 ff. A sketch of Fish's life appears in *National Cyclopaedia of Biography*, III, p. 523. Cf. George B. Ide, *The Ministry Demanded by the Present Crisis* (Philadelphia, 1845), p. 88 and *passim*.

That the Congregational publishing house in Boston should print and widely advertise Fish's book is evidence that by the 1850's measures to promote awakenings were coming to characterize that denomination as well.[17] Educational leaders were here even more obviously responsible. That generation of clergymen had grown to maturity who had heard Ebenezer Porter declare before the student evangelistic associations at Andover in 1832 that he deemed it "all important that ministers, and those who are preparing to become ministers, should be revival men." [18] At Amherst, Heman Humphrey, president from 1823 to 1845 and a spiritual product of the Yale College awakening of the first decade of the century, made seasons of revival a central feature of college life and a chief goal of ministerial training. From the time of his retirement there until his death in 1861, Humphrey was employed as a "new measures" evangelist among the New England churches.[19] Mark Hopkins's presidency at Williams College was likewise contemporaneous with a thoroughly revivalistic program. His own son, Henry, was an active soul winner and a close friend of the future evangelist, Edward Payson Hammond, during their student days in the 1850's.[20]

Leonard Bacon carried on at Yale the traditions of the generation of Nathaniel W. Taylor and Asahel Nettelton. Bacon was pastor of The First Church, New Haven, from 1825 to 1866, and was a chief figure in the development of a stronger denominational consciousness. Before Taylor's death in 1858, he and Bacon joined forces many times in protracted meetings in New Haven. They often employed the revivalist Edward Norris Kirk—the last time in 1850, after Kirk had become minister of Mt. Vernon Church, Boston. In later years Bacon expressed the conviction that Taylor's long and rich experience in revivals was the inspiration of his progressive theology. "The passion of his life was so to preach—and to instruct and train his pupils so to preach—that conversions

---

[17] As conservative contemporaries often noted: Philip Schaff, *America . . .* (New York, 1855), pp. 183, 173 ff.; Alexander Blaikie, *Philosophy of Sectarianism . . .* (Boston, 1855), pp. 166-68.

[18] Ebenezer Porter, *Letters on the Religious Revivals which Prevailed about the Beginning of the Present Century* (2nd. ed., Boston, 1858), pp. 2-3.

[19] Heman Humphrey, *Revival Sketches and Manual* (New York, 1859), pp. 329-38; *The Puritan Recorder*, Feb. 16, 1854. Frederic L. Thompson sketched Humphrey's life for the *D.A.B.*

[20] P. C. Headley, *The Harvest Work of the Holy Spirit, Illustrated in the Evangelistic Labors of Rev. Edward Payson Hammond* (6th ed., Boston, 1862), pp. 41-61.

should follow, not at some future day, but immediately." [21] The revivals at Yale in 1857 and 1858 were thus in accord with the liberal, evangelistic spirit which had permeated the religious life of the college for the previous half-century.[22]

Kirk's great success at Mt. Vernon was an instruction to his fellow pastors. He had first come to prominence in the 1830's while at the Fourth Presbyterian Church, Albany, New York. Five years of travel and evangelism followed before he accepted in 1842 the pastorate of the Boston congregation, organized as a result of the revivals he conducted there that year. Mt. Vernon soon became the major soul-winning institution in the city, responsible for the work with young men which produced in 1851 the first Y.M.C.A. and, a few months later, the conversion of Dwight L. Moody. Throughout his ministerial career, Kirk was a principal sponsor of some educational institution and an inveterate promoter of college revivals. His *Premium Essay on Prayer for Colleges,* published in 1855 by the Western College Association, appeared later in many forms.[23]

Congregational newspapers mirrored the influence of such men at mid-century in numerous editorials and regular columns of revival news. In Boston *The Puritan Recorder,* representing the traditions of Orthodox Calvinism, agreed with the liberal *Congregationalist* in urging efforts for more and greater awakenings. Accounts of them in both papers differed from similar Methodist reports only in that here sinners were "hopefully converted" instead of confident of "the witness of the Spirit." [24] In 1854, for example, the churches in industrial Nashua, New Hampshire, and Lawrence, Massachusetts, reported scores of conversions in nightly union meetings lasting several weeks. Campton, New Hampshire, had enjoyed throughout the previous year a powerful awakening, concerning which a witness wrote, "We could no longer hesitate to say, 'The Pentecost has fully come.'" [25]

[21] Quoted in David O. Mears, *Life of Edward Norris Kirk, D.D.* (Boston, 1877), p. 334; cf. pp. 332-35.

[22] For revival accounts, see *The Puritan Recorder,* Jan. 15, 1857, and Conant, *op. cit.,* p. 378. Sidney Earl Mead, *Nathaniel William Taylor, 1786-1858; a Connecticut Liberal* (Chicago, 1942), pp. 147-57 and *passim,* explains the close relationship between Taylor and Lyman Beecher and describes the place of revivalism in their program before 1832.

[23] Harris Elwood Starr wrote the sketch for the *D.A.B.;* cf. Hopkins, *op. cit.,* p. 17, and Mears. *op. cit.,* p. 336 and *passim.* See later pp. 53-4, 73.

[24] "We Need A Revival of Religion," *The Puritan Recorder,* Feb. 2, 1854. Cf. the issue of March 23, 1854, and the extensive notes on college revivals, Apr. 6, 1954.

[25] *The Puritan Recorder,* Feb. 16, 1854. See generally the "revival columns" each succeeding winter and spring both in this newspaper and *The Congregationalist.*

The Independent, a weekly newspaper founded in New York City in 1848 to propagate the views of liberal Congregationalists outside New England, was no less friendly to revivalism. From the very first the paper carried full accounts of unusual awakenings among Baptists, Presbyterians, and Methodists, as well as in its own churches.[26] In the winter of 1849-50 a series of letters appeared offering the thesis that the revival method "conforms to the natural laws of the mind" since man's emotions and intellect are awakened most effectively when he acts with a group. "A thorough religious conviction," the writer argued, "together with the sympathies, associations and friendships of such an era, form the beginnings of a heartily religious life, such as may be looked for elsewhere in vain. ..."[27] Editorial and news items supporting this view appeared frequently in succeeding years. In 1855 the successful Iowa intinerary of pastor-evangelist George Clark, formerly of Connecticut, received a glowing notice; and Henry Ward Beecher wrote from Boston that there was "great hope and promise of revivals of religion once more in the old Puritan city."[28]

Here, at least, were men not identifiable with antiquated orthodoxy upon whom Horace Bushnell's criticism of new measures evangelism had had little effect. It may be significant that one of Bushnell's young parishioners, Richard Morse, who was for much of his adult life national secretary of the Y.M.C.A., remembered his boyhood pastor of the 1850's most for the seasons of "special religious interest" which Bushnell sponsored each year and the young people's prayer meetings held every week.[29] In any case, when the Boston pastors invited Charles G. Finney to conduct a six-week union campaign at Park Street Church in 1857, none could doubt that the revivalism Finney championed had at last won the approval of Eastern Congregationalists.[30]

Perhaps one reason for this was that Oberlin College had become a chief

[26] *The Independent,* Dec. 28, 1848, Jan. 4 and 11, and May 3, 1849.

[27] *The Independent,* Jan. 10, 1950. Cf. the articles, "What Directions Shall We Give to Inquirers?" and John Dudley, "Means of a Revival," in the issue of March 14, 1850; and "Times of Refreshing," Sept. 20, 1855.

[28] *The Independent,* Jan. 11 and March 29, 1855. See also, "How to Have a Revival" and "Preaching to the Heart," Jan. 12, 1854, and, in the same issue, "Direct Labors for Souls," reprinted from *The Oberlin Evangelist.* Cf. revival news in the issues of Jan. 4, Jan. 18, March 15, March 29, and May 3, 1855.

[29] Richard C. Morse, *My Life With Young Men; Fifty Years in The Young Men's Christian Association* (New York, 1918), pp. 24, 26. Cole, *op. cit.,* p. 45, calls Bushnell "an evangelist in spite of himself."

[30] Finney, *op. cit.,* pp. 441-42. Cf. *The Watchman and Reflector,* Jan. 22, 1857, quoting

agent in crystallizing denominational sentiment in the growing Western wing of the church. Lyman Beecher's difficulties at Lane Theological Seminary, Cincinnati, like those his son Edward experienced while president of Illinois College, amply demonstrated the prejudices which many Presbyterians in the West held against new measures. When it became apparent in 1835 that Oberlin men were to be excluded from the Plan of Union presbyteries, President Asa Mahan and Professor Henry Cowles spearheaded the withdrawal of "The General Association of the Western Reserve." The college church, which was its center, remained for decades the largest Congregational body beyond the Alleghenies. Though Finney himself refused confinement to either sect or section, churches of the denomination were the chief beneficiaries of his many "union" campaigns in Eastern and Western cities. In the long run they dared not bind the hands that served them.[31]

Nor could the New School Presbyterians, whose leaders in the East, at least, closely followed the progressive Congregationalists in the use of the new soul-winning techniques. Albert Barnes, for forty years pastor of the First Presbyterian Church, Philadelphia, and a chief promoter of Union Theological Seminary in New York, was foremost among the distinguished group of revival men who dominated the New School synods. Others were George Duffield, Lyman Beecher, Nathaniel S. S. Beman, and George Barrell Cheever, editor in the 1850's of Finney's old paper, *The New York Evangelist,* by then the most influential weekly in the denomination.[32] Barnes published in 1841 a significant series of articles calling for united efforts to promote revivals in urban centers. He insisted that there was nothing in the nature of city populations to prevent their occurrence there; rather, they ought to flourish where social ties of communication and interdependence were strongest.[33] The next year, New School and Congregational pastors planned Edward N. Kirk's union campaigns in Phila-

an article, "Direct Preaching," from the Old School Presbyterian *New York Observer* praising Finney's manner of preaching; and *The Watchman,* March 19, 1857.

[31] See Henry Cowles, "Ohio Congregationalism," *The Congregational Quarterly,* V (1863-64), pp. 140-41; Robert S. Fletcher, *A History of Oberlin College, from Its Foundation Through the Civil War* (Oberlin, Ohio, 1943), I, pp. 220-21; and Finney, *op. cit.,* pp. 435-40. Lewis G. Vander Velde, ed., "The Diary of George Duffield," *The Mississippi Valley Historical Review,* XXIV (1937-38), p. 33, records Finney's influence over Detroit Congregationalists and Presbyterians in 1847.

[32] Frederick T. Persons wrote the sketch of Cheever for the *D.A.B.;* Charles Noble, the excellent one on Barnes.

[33] Albert Barnes, "Revivals of Religion in Cities and Large Towns," *The American National Preacher,* XV (1841), pp. 3, 7-8.

delphia, New York, New Haven, and Boston in order to test this theory.[34] The sharp resistance which greeted their efforts faded as passing years made Barnes and Kirk respected names in American church life.[35]

Nathaniel Beman, pastor for forty years of the First Presbyterian Church, Troy, New York, and president from 1845-65 of the institution which later became Rensselaer Polytechnic Institute, exerted a comparable influence. Rebuked by his associates for undertaking a series of revivals in 1826, Beman later won such esteem that he became moderator of the General Assembly in 1831 and nominal leader of the New School secession in 1838. Promotion of awakenings and of educational institutions remained his twin passions, as illustrated by the "Troy and Albany Theological School," where he and Kirk joined in the 1830's in turning out revival preachers. By mid-century, virtually all New School colleges shared their aims. The results were recorded in the religious press, where news of Presbyterian awakenings apppeared almost as frequently as that from Methodists.[36]

That the new evangelism also made noticeable inroads in Old School Presbyterian circles further supports the thesis that a basic shift in attitudes was taking place. The success of a professional soul winner like Daniel Baker, who traveled in the South and Southwest and supported the college founded in 1849 at his suggestion at Austin, Texas, is significant, but less so than the accommodation of urban congregations to the same methods. It was necessary, of course, not to seem to approve New School practices. Thus a writer in *The Ohio Observer* belabored the "high pressure" system of modern revivals, while expressing thanksgiving that they were increasing both in number and power in all churches. He urged a return to the "old system" in which the whole congregation bore responsibility instead of delegating it to the pastor or evangelist.[37]

As early as 1858, Lewis Cheeseman, Old School pastor at Rochester,

[34] Mears, *op. cit.*, pp. 222-23.

[35] See, for attacks on this crusade, Martin Moore, *Boston Revival, 1842; a Brief History of the Evangelical Churches of Boston* . . . (Boston, 1842); and Arthur Cleveland Coxe, *Revivalism and the Church. A Letter to a Reviewer in Reply to Several Articles in The New Englander* . . . (Hartford, 1843), pp. 34-45, an episcopalian view. Cf. Robert Woodward Cushman, *A Calm Review of the Measures Employed in the Religious Awakening in Boston, 1842* . . . (Boston, 1846).

[36] Ray Palmer Baker's sketch of Beman in the *D.A.B.* is complete on these points. See also *The Christian Union and Religious Memorial*, I (1848), pp. 121-23; and II (1849), pp. 252-54; *The Puritan Recorder*, Apr. 6, 1854; and the revival columns cited from various newspapers in the foregoing pages.

[37] Quoted in *The Puritan Recorder*, March 23, 1854. Headley, *Evangelists in the Church*, pp. 195-208, 288-96, reviews from contemporary sources the careers of Baker and O. Parker.

denied that efforts to promote revivals distinguished his group from New School Presbyterians. Protracted meetings which resulted in awakenings of marked extent were common, he asserted, at their "sacramental seasons." Old School men heartily approved of the anxious bench, the inquiry room, and emotionally powerful preaching, so long as they were not accompanied by the doctrinal heresies current among their more liberal brethren.

When we see the Spirit undervalued and set aside, except in name, and the Son dishonored in His reconciliation, and depravity denied, and human ability, and men and measures exalted; the work of reformation, however widespread and imposing, is not of God, but is a fearful apostasy from a primitive Christianity, and will end in popery, or infidelity, or in some other form of ultimate evil, to which it tends.[38]

The argument was no longer over revivals or measures, but only the theological framework within which their success was to be interpreted.

Revivalism was the core of the issues which racked the Lutheran synods after 1830. Samuel Simon Schmucker was the leader of the Americanized, or "New Lutheran" party, which, according to Philip Schaff, was probably the most numerous and certainly "the most active, practical and progressive" branch of the communion. Schmucker was the dominant figure in the General Synod's struggles to unite the church until 1856, and from 1826 to that date the most important professor at its seminary in Gettysburg, Pennsylvania. He was a Princeton graduate, stanch Arminian, active supporter of the American Tract and Bible Societies and one of the first advocates of the Evangelical Alliance.[39]

Benjamin Kurtz, editor from 1833-58 of *The Lutheran Observer*—the denomination's most influential English newspaper—likewise supported revivals and opposed with equal fervor liturgical worship and the concept of a confessional church. Another important figure was Samuel Sprecher, president of Wittenberg College and Seminary, Springfield, Ohio. Sprecher was mentor of the synods which had withdrawn from the conservative Joint Synod of Ohio in 1840. He succeeded to the leadership of the evan-

[38] Lewis Cheeseman, *Differences Between Old and New School Presbyterians* . . . (Rochester, 1848), p. 170; cf. pp. 150, 174, 182-85.

[39] Schaff, *op. cit.*, p. 183; Samuel Simon Schmucker, *The American Lutheran Church, Historically, Doctrinally, and Practically Delineated,* . . . (5th ed., Philadelphia, 1852), pp. 247-73, *passim.* Two of the essays in the latter volume, pp. 11-40 and 90-119, are valuable historical accounts of American Lutheranism before 1840. Cf. Robert Fortenbaugh, "American Lutheran Synods and Slavery, 1830-1860," *The Journal of Religion,* XIII (1933), pp. 72-73.

gelistic party after Schmucker's retirement. The seminary at Springfield, Illinois, and the one sponsored by the Hartwick Synod in New York also adhered to the New Lutheran position. The Hartwick Synod, organized in 1831 expressly to promote new measures and Americanization, was still too conservative for those of its members who withdrew in 1837 to found the radically revivalistic and antislavery Franckean Synod.[40]

Such men rejected both Calvinism and a rigid adherence to the Augsburg Confession. They insisted that Lutheranism was a "reformation in progress." They supported new measures heartily, including the hotly contested mourner's bench, and divided their synods into "conferences," containing ordinarily from five to ten ministers, for the purpose of holding several protracted meetings each year within their boundaries. "This feature," wrote Schmucker, "mainly resembles the quarterly meetings of our Methodist brethren, and presents to pious and zealous ministers who are thirsting for the salvation of souls, the most direct opportunity they can desire, to glorify God, and advance his spiritual kingdom."[41]

The German-speaking confessional party, however, reigned supreme in the ministerium of Pennsylvania and its offspring, the Joint Synod of Ohio. Missionaries from Pennsylvania, shocked by the extensive use of evangelistic methods in the North Carolina Synod, instituted in the 1820's the antirevival Tennessee Synod. It soon spread widely over Virginia and the Carolinas, as well as in its home state.

Both clergy and laity in the Old Lutheran sections of the church were poorly educated, and the congregations were located chiefly in rural areas— facts which explain the conservatism which they otherwise displayed by clinging to the German tongue. They were never able properly to support their few educational institutions. The Pennsylvania ministerium finally threw its strength to the Gettsyburg school, in an arrangement guaranteeing them one crucial faculty appointment. The town and college became thenceforward a sort of theological no man's land, but revivals showed no signs of disappearing.[42]

[40] Henry Eyster Jacobs, *A History of the Evangelical Lutheran Church in The United States* (Philip Schaff and others, eds., *The American Church History Series*, IV, New York, 1893), pp. 365-69, 385-86, 487. Jacobs's account of the controversy, pp. 353-460, is complete, though confusingly organized. Cf., on the Franckean Synod, Fortenbaugh, *loc. cit.*, pp. 73, 74, 91.

[41] Schmucker, *op. cit.*, pp. 66-67, 200, 243-44; Francis Springer, "Lutheranism in The United States," *The Evangelical Quarterly Review*, XI (1859-60), pp. 98-99; Schaff, *op. cit.*, pp. 168-72, 204.

[42] Jacobs, *op. cit.*, pp. 391, 393-94. *The Puritan Recorder*, March 12, 1854 reported a powerful revival at Gettysburg and various other Lutheran congregations.

After 1840 the new immigration combined with a dawning desire for symbols of denominational identity and the influence of German theology to support a resurgence of conservative Lutheran strength. The Buffalo Synod, dating from 1845, and the far more important Missouri Synod took a determined stand for a full and literal acceptance of the Augsburg Creed as the basis for a confessional communion. The Missouri Synod was organized at Chicago in April, 1847, under the leadership of C. F. W. Walther, one of the first German immigrants to St. Louis, and F. C. D. Wynekin, of Fort Wayne, Indiana, a graduate of Göttingen and Halle Universities. Close ties with Germany enabled it to rally a large portion of the incoming settlers to its standard. Less rigid, but equally unresponsive to Americanizing tendencies, were the new Iowa and Michigan synods.[43]

Scandinavian immigrants, it should be noted, seem to have gravitated more readily to the New Lutheran position. Elling Eilsen, a Norwegian revival preacher, founded a small Midwestern synod for his countrymen in 1846. The pioneer Swedish home missionary in America, Lars Paul Esbjörn, had also been a revivalist in his homeland. The American Board of Home Missions, a Congregational organization, supported Esbjörn after 1849. He first shepherded his people into the Americanized synod of Northern Illinois, associated with the Springfield seminary. Two of the eight pastors who founded it had come from the Franckean synod. In 1860 Esbjörn led the Scandinavians into the independent Augustana Synod.[44]

The new strength of the liturgical party was dramatized in 1853 when the Pennsylvania ministerium led a group of its members back into the General Synod as the first move in a campaign to regain leadership of the church. Continual trumpeting for denominational distinctiveness was their chief tactical weapon. A writer in *The Evangelical Quarterly Review*, for example, denounced the anxious bench as an "un-Lutheran" method of dealing with the awakened. One synodical pastoral address blamed the slow rate of the church's growth on the "extreme latitudinarianism" of New Lutheran ministers. They had, it charged, so effectively established the similarity of the Lutheran to other evangelical denominations that their own members were transferring in large numbers. "We have an historical

---

[43] Jacobs, *op. cit.*, pp. 397-410; Schaff, *op. cit.*, pp. 188-89.

[44] Florence E. Janson, *The Background of Swedish Immigration, 1840-1930* (Chicago, 1931), pp. 187-92, 196-99, 203, 206, is very complete at this point. Cf. Jacobs, *op. cit.*, pp. 411-15, and Oscar N. Olson, *The Augustana Lutheran Church in America: Pioneer Period, 1846-1860* (Rock Island, Ill., 1950), pp. 242-61. Olson, in these pages and on pp. 239-41 and *passim*, disowns the revivalistic background of early Augustana Lutheranism.

prestige and a confession of faith," the address ran. "Why, then, do we not avail ourselves of the armor furnished to our hands and get to ourselves a name and a position which shall be to the glory of Protestantism?"[45]

On the other hand, however, reunion required traditionalists to accept the contention which Schmucker had elaborated at great length that the revivalists were indeed true Lutherans. The Gettysburg professor himself delivered the synodical sermon at the union meeting in 1853. Though moderate in tone, Schmucker's address rejected any return to sectarianism, liturgical forms, or confessional dogmatism. Its climax was a strong appeal to promote "genuine piety" through revivals and active support of "the great Christian enterprises of the day," the tract, temperance, Bible and home mission societies. He cried:

Without holiness no one shall see God. As all men are by nature and practice sinners; unless a man be born again, be converted from sin to holiness, he cannot see the kingdom of heaven. The grand object of ministers and congregations should be, to admit none but sincere professors into the church, men who have experienced a change of heart. . . . The various means of grace and privileges of the church, are designed to promote this spiritual renovation and sanctification. . . . Let us, therefore, my brethren, unitedly set our faces against dead formality in religion . . . . Let us employ every means to call sinners to repentance. . . . Yea, we should labor and pray for the effusion of the Holy Spirit, that every congregation may be visited by a pentecostal season of revival. . . .[46]

For many years the evangelicals were able successfully to defend their position in the Lutheran Church. Though Schmucker failed to achieve general acceptance of his revision of the Augsburg Confession, some conservative synods came "fully up to the Spirit of the times," as one of their defenders wrote, in supporting Bible and tract societies and measures of active evangelization.[47] Benjamin Kurtz organized in 1857 the Melancthon

[45] Quoted in Jacobs, op. cit., pp. 453-54. See also A. M. Ziegler, "Treatment of the Awakened," The Evangelical Quarterly Review, IX (1857-58), pp. 237-38 and passim.

[46] S. S. Schmucker, The Peace of Zion: a Discourse Preached before the General Synod of the Evangelical Lutheran Church . . . (Gettysburg, Pa., 1853), pp. 36-37; cf. pp. 19, 29-30, 32-33, and Schmucker, American Lutheran Church, p. 213.

[47] "The Present Position of the Lutheran Church," The Evangelical Quarterly Review, XI (1859-60), pp. 31, 35-37, by a moderate conservative, is to be compared with Francis Springer, "Lutheranism in The United States," the same, pp. 97, 101-2. "Dr. Schmucker's Lutheran Symbols," the same, VIII (1856-57), pp. 453-85 is a doctrinal and historical examination of the controversy which had raged around the professor's proposal and, in part, an answer to his American Lutheranism Vindicated; or Examination of the Lutheran Symbols, on Certain Disputed Topics . . . (Baltimore, 1856).

Synod in Maryland, the liberal creed of which was a slightly revised version of the one drawn up for the Evangelical Alliance. He established the next year a training institute for revival preachers at Selinsgrove, Pennsylvania. Many younger men joined Kurtz and Sprecher in the fight for a liberal, progressive church, one which would stay in the main channel of American Protestantism. Though the compromise finally reached involved surrender of the Methodist mourner's bench, it also required Old Lutherans to accept an historical rather than a literal interpretation of the creeds.[48]

A detailed chronicle of the incidence of revival measures among Cumberland Presbyterians, Disciples of Christ, and Friends is unnecessary for the purpose of this chapter. Albert Henry Newman suggested over fifty years ago that discontent with the antirevival movement among Baptists made possible the success of Disciples evangelism in the West. Though the Friends were weakened by the divisions over the liberalism of Elias Hicks, John Joseph Gurney's visit in 1837 directed the more orthodox yearly meetings along the path of evangelism toward the Puritan and quietly Methodistic customs which they were following by 1880.[49]

There can be no doubt that the popularity of revival men and methods surged forward in the major segments of American religion between 1840 and 1860. Particularly striking is the fact that rural and frontier areas seemed by the decade of the slavery crisis to have been supporting laggardly the measures which had nurtured their religious life fifty years before. Now Eastern and urban evangelism played the dominant role. What are the reasons for these changes?

The system of voluntary church membership and support, peculiar to this country, was probably the chief factor. Since the decision to become an active member was made in adulthood, the ancient Baptist concept of a "believer's church" inevitably flourished, even among Lutherans and

---

[48] Jacobs, op. cit., pp. 424, 432; "The Present Position of the Lutheran Church," loc. cit., pp. 40-43; R. Weiser, "A Want in the Lutheran Church Met by the Founding of the Missionary Institute," The Evangelical Quarterly Review, X (1858-59), pp. 332-47. Cf., generally, Jacobs, op. cit., pp. 421-70, and Philip Schaff's wishful prediction of the decline of Lutheran revivalism in America, p. 176.

[49] Newman, op. cit., pp. 440-41; Benjamin B. Tyler, A. C. Thomas, and others, A History of the Disciples of Christ, The Society of Friends, The United Brethren in Christ, and The Evangelical Association (Philip Schaff and others, eds., The American Church History Series, XII, New York, 1894), pp. 267-71, 302-4; Robert V. Foster, "A Sketch of the History of The Cumberland Presbyterian Church," in the same volume, p. 291 and passim.

Episcopalians. And sinners became believers most readily when emotional tides ran high.[50]

On the other hand, the decline of uncouth expressions of emotion made protracted meetings more palatable to educated clergymen and city dwellers conscious of the social graces. Charles G. Finney opposed loud praying and pounding on benches with the observation that "inquirers needed more opportunity to think than they had when there was so much noise." Robert Baird insisted that in thirty years of revivals he had "never, but in one instance, and that a very slight one and for a moment, witnessed any audible expression of emotion" in an evangelistic service. Though his statement was not applicable to the Methodists, critical witnesses were more than once surprised when "a stillness and a solemnity, almost oppressive" pervaded their places of worship. Even at camp meetings they placed great emphasis upon the "blessed quietness" of the Spirit's presence and expected leaders to restrain the fervor of the flock.[51]

The role of educational leaders was all important. Nearly every prominent evangelist gave time and raised money for a college which he hoped would train young ministers to follow in his steps. In this respect Oberlin was only in degree more significant than Amherst, Rensselaer, Rochester, Wittenberg, Connecticut Wesleyan, Ohio Wesleyan, Gettysburg, and Western Reserve colleges and Lane, Yale, Andover, and Union theological seminaries. Here men of piety and scholarship purged American revivals of their fanaticism, grounded them on liberalized Calvinist or Arminian doctrines, and set their course in a socially responsible direction.

It is difficult but necessary for modern students to realize, moreover, that in the nineteenth century revival measures, being new, usually went hand in hand with progressive theology and humanitarian concern. Only thus could they have won the support of so many, both in and outside the churches, who wished Christianity to become a dynamic force for the reformation of human society. Albert Barnes and Emerson Andrews were in this respect not a step behind Charles G. Finney, who insisted as late as 1868 that "the loss of interest in benevolent enterprises" was usually evidence of a "backslidden heart." Among these, Finney specified good

[50] Thomas Fenner Curtis, *The Progress of Baptist Principles in the Last Hundred Years* (Boston, 1857), pp. 60-72, presents an amusing interpretation.

[51] Finney, *op. cit.*, pp. 462-63; Baird, *Religion in America*, p. 205; *The Watchman and Reflector*, Jan. 19, 1854. Charles A. Johnson, "The Frontier Camp Meeting: Contemporary and Historical Appraisals, 1805-1840," *The Mississippi Valley Historical Review*, XXXVII (1950-51), pp. 91-110.

government, Christian education, temperance reform, the abolition of slavery, and relief for the poor.[52]

Societies devoted to these ends—education, Bible, home mission, tract, Sunday-school and temperance organizations—generally cut across denominational lines. By mid-century they had become to thoughtful Protestants the symbols of a common national faith. The prominent part which liberal revivalists played in them could not but win favorable attention from a generation which was earnestly seeking a basis for Christian union. The antirevival Orthodox Calvinists, on the other hand, usually isolated themselves from such "creaturely activities." Inevitably, their doctrinal excuses seemed to the average man mere sectarian cant.

Another factor in their success was the way in which the revivalists popularized an enlarged concept of the work of the Holy Spirit. They thus carried one step further the long process of accommodating Calvinism to free grace and, by implication, to the ideals of an equalitarian society. Men like Knapp and Kirk and Schmucker clothed measures once regarded as human devices with the garb of divine sanctity. Their very efficiency seemed a mark of God's favor. The greater the uniqueness and emotional power of an awakening, the more easily was such supernatural agency affirmed.[53]

Finally, on the practical level revivals meant many things to many people. Those blessed with a wide social vision thought of them as a chief means of converting human institutions to Christian principles. Individual converts, in many cases, sought only fulfillment of the aspiration for forgiveness and personal union with the Saviour. Pastors saw church problems melt away and financial surpluses appear. Treasurers of benevolent associations happily tallied increasing returns from recently awakened communities. Denominational leaders were as gratified by the growth in members as editors and publishers were pleased with new subscriptions to religious journals. The rise of tremendous individual congregations under liberal, revival clergymen was a pointed lesson to all. The substantial fruits of fervor thus became an authoritative object lesson to pragmatic Americans. The author of *Primitive Piety Revived* was soon offering expert advice

---

[52] See the 1868 preface to Finney's *Lectures on Revivals of Religion* (New York, 1898), pp. v and 415-16; and Barnes's introduction to Samuel Davies, *Sermons on Important Subjects* . . . (2nd. ed., Edinburgh, 1867), p. 6.

[53] See the editorial, "The Holy Spirit," *The Independent*, Nov. 22, 1855.

on "power in the pulpit." And Boston had at last believed in Finney for the very works' sake.[54]

In summary, the revival fervor which had earlier seemed typical of the rural West became in the years between 1840 and 1857 a dominant mood in urban religious life. Under the sponsorship of city pastors, the "new measures" which had from their beginnings characterized Methodist and New School Presbyterian churches managed at last to conquer Calvinistic scruples against them in Baptist, Congregational, and Reformed communions, and to make deep inroads in Old School Presbyterian circles as well. Lutheranism's strongest party, though not by any means entirely urban, was as thoroughly evangelistic in work and worship as many of the German Methodist sects. The most provincial rural sections of the Lutheran, Baptist, and Presbyterian churches were now the strongholds of antirevival feeling, though the Cumberland Presbyterians, Disciples of Christ, and Freewill Baptists kept the fire burning on several frontiers. The common notion that, except for occasional sporadic outbursts led by Finney, Moody, and the Y.M.C.A., revivalism declined steadily after the great Western awakening burned out around 1840, seems in direct contradiction to the facts.

The awakening of 1858, as we shall see in a moment, was both the climax of these long trends and the result of united efforts by urban churchmen of many denominations. In the two years immediately preceding it, hundreds of them had labored to precipitate a national Pentecost which they hoped would baptize America in the Holy Spirit and in some mystic manner destroy the evils of slavery, poverty, and greed. Thereafter, and during the Civil War especially, "union" city-wide campaigns and protracted meetings in churches of every description, metropolitan and rural, became the order of the day.

[54] Henry C. Fish, "Power in the Pulpit," *The Christian Review*, XXVII (1862), pp. 118-42, exhorted clergymen to sound Christian experience and revival methods.

IV
Annus Mirabilis—1858

～

What attracted the attention of secular newspaper reporters to the awakening of 1858 was the frenzied growth after February 1 that year of daily, noontime interdenominational prayer meetings. Although weekly laymen's gatherings had dotted New York City the previous fall, Jeremiah C. Lanphier, a neighborhood missionary employed by the Old Dutch Church on Fulton Street, had organized on September 23 the first one to come to prominence in connection with the revival. Increasing interest converted it into a daily gathering on October 7, just a few days before the stock-market crash brought unrest and unemployment to clerks and businessmen in the financial district nearby. By midwinter the crowds had overflowed into the John Street Methodist Church, around the corner.[1]

Late in February James Gordon Bennett, one of America's pioneers in sensational newspaper editing, began to exploit revival news in his *New York Herald*. Horace Greeley, editor of the *New York Tribune*, responded to the challenge with a stream of editorials and news stories. These came to a climax in April with a special revival issue of the *Tribune's* weekly edition. Simultaneously, religious and secular newspapers all over the country began giving prominent notice to noonday prayer meetings.[2] Groups of clergymen and local units of the Y.M.C.A. found it easy to begin such gatherings. Some which had been struggling for survival suddenly attracted huge crowds.[3] By April twenty were in progress in New

[1] The three most important contemporary accounts of the revival are Talbot W. Chambers, *Noon Prayer Meeting of the North Dutch Church* . . . (New York, 1858), pp. 39-90; Samuel Irenaeus Prime, *The Power of Prayer, Illustrated in the Wonderful Displays of Divine Grace at the Fulton Street and Other Meetings* . . . (New York, 1859), pp. 20-43, by a Methodist minister who had access to Lanphier's diary; and William C. Conant, *Narratives of Remarkable Conversions and Revival Incidents* . . . (New York, 1858), pp. 354-444, which summarized newspaper material available at the height of the excitement around May 1.

[2] Russell E. Francis, Pentecost: 1858. A Study in Religious Revivals (unpublished Ph.D. dissertation, The University of Penn., 1948), is a somewhat dramatic treatment of what may be known from Y.M.C.A. literature and the files of secular newspapers; it analyzes Greeley's role, pp. 68-74.

[3] See, for example, first reports of large crowds at the meetings in Boston, Providence, and Portland in *The Watchman and Reflector*, March 25, 1858.

York alone, including two famous ones at Burton's Theater and the Music Hall. Dozens of churches there had begun nightly meetings. The Metropolitan Theater in Chicago was crowded with two thousand daily attendants. In Philadelphia mammoth prayer services in Jaynes Hall, Handel and Haydn Hall, and the American Mechanics Auditorium finally gave way in the summer to those held for four months under a great tent. The most spectacular of many revivals in public high schools was in Cleveland, where all but two boys professed conversion.[4]

The mode of worship was the same in all the meetings. There was no ritual or prepared plan. Any person present might pray, exhort, lead in song, or give testimony as he felt "led," only keeping within the five-minute time limit and avoiding controversial subjects like water baptism or slavery. Distinctions between the sects and between ministers and laymen were ignored. The joyous liberty of the camp meeting "love feast" was thus transferred to an urban setting. The sound of the leader's bell provided a businesslike touch appropriate to the new environment.[5]

The revival is often attributed to mass hysteria resulting from both the long strain of the slavery crisis and the shock of the panic of 1857. Certainly the latter was an important factor. James Waddell Alexander, pastor of the largest Old School Presbyterian Church in New York, for example, joined many contemporaries in thinking the financial crisis proof that God had been pleased "by the ploughshare of his judgments to furrow the ground for the precious seed of salvation."[6] Two new means of mass communication, the "penny" press and the national telegraph system, helped to snowball enthusiasm. They were, as one observer remarked, "taken possession of

---

[4] Frank Grenville Beardsley, A History of American Revivals (2nd. ed.; New York, 1912), pp. 222-26, summarizes these reports; cf. Prime, op. cit., p. 171, and The Watchman and Reflector, March 4 and and 18, 1858, for church revivals and prayer meetings.

[5] Chambers, op. cit., pp. 47-54.

[6] James Waddell Alexander, The Revival and Its Lessons . . . (New York, 1858), p. 6. Cf. Humphrey, Revival Sketches and Manual (New York, 1859), pp. 269-79; Harper's Monthly, XVI (1858), pp. 840-41; The Watchman and Reflector, Dec. 17, 1857, and Jan. 14, 1858; and A. P. Marvin, "Three Eras of Revivals in The United States," Bibliotheca Sacra, XVI (1859), pp. 296-97.

Two European visitors in close touch with American evangelical leaders emphasized the economic factor: Gasparin, Uprising, p. 67; and Fisch, Nine Months, p. 151. It is treated cautiously in Beardsley, op. cit., pp. 216-17, but with some abandon by Russell E. Francis, loc. cit., pp. 77-93, and Carl Lloyd Spicer, "The Great Awakening of 1857 and 1858," Ohio State University, Abstracts of Dissertations Presented by Candidates for the Degree of Doctor of Philosophy, Summer Quarter, 1935 (Columbus, 1935), pp. 149-57. Similar but less completely documented interpretations appeared earlier in Henry Steele Commager, Theodore Parker (Boston, 1936), pp. 269-71, and Grover Cleveland Loud, Evangelized America (New York, 1928), pp. 216-32.

by the Spirit, willing or unwilling, to proclaim his wonders." Lanphier, sensing the value of publicity, had early in January solicited the New York dailies to report his meetings.[7] Heman Humphrey felt that the newspaper coverage was so complete as to distort comparisons with previous revivals. He remembered that in the awakenings of 1832 it had been impossible to get "even a short paragraph of religious intelligence into a secular city paper." Now that revivals had become interdenominational, he noted, these papers could report them fully without offense to any sect. This fact explains why even in 1858 the secular press gave much greater attention to the activities of the nonsectarian Y.M.C.A. than to the churches, in strong contrast to the reports in denominational weeklies.[8]

The latter, in fact, reveal a movement reaching deep into the life of the churches and related more directly than is generally believed to their recent efforts to quicken the spiritual and moral currents in American society. A healthy alarm over the standstill of proportionate membership in evangelical communions in Boston, New York, and Pittsburgh had been evident for some time, despite the knowledge that most of the population increase was from Roman Catholic immigration and that many Protestant families were moving to suburban communities.[9] Those conservatives whose real concern was the waning prestige of Mr. Calvin's five points, to be sure, offered only dark forebodings as to the "low state of religion." Their later disposition to ascribe to the Divine Spirit alone all credit for the wonders of 1858 further dimmed public memories of the hopeful efforts others put forth to precipitate the awakening.[10]

Especially important was a carefully organized program to evangelize New York City's impoverished masses. In September, 1856, the New York Sunday School Union allocated to each church responsibility to visit homes and organize mission Sunday schools in a destitute area. The plan caught the imagination of laymen in such great churches as those where George B. Cheever, J. W. Alexander, and William Adams were serving as

[7] Conant, *op. cit.*, pp. 395-96; Prime, *op. cit.*, p. 36.
[8] Humphrey, *op. cit.*, pp. 281-82. Charles H. Hopkins, *History of the Y.M.C.A. in North America* (New York, 1951), pp. 81-84, even more than Francis, *loc. cit.*, pp. 64-66 and *passim*, emphasizes the singular function of the Y.M.C.A.
[9] Henry C. Fish, *Primitive Piety Revived* . . . (Boston, 1857), pp. 23-25; Alexander Blaikie, *Philosophy of Sectarianism* . . . (Boston, 1855), pp. 327-28; *The Watchman and Reflector*, Feb. 5, 1857.
[10] "Where Are We Drifting," *The Puritan Recorder*, Feb. 5, 1857; Humphrey, *op. cit.*, pp. 276-79; Chambers, *op. cit.*, p. 267. *The Christian Register* (Boston's Unitarian weekly), Oct, 17, 1857, lampooned *The Recorder's* pessimistic conservatism.

pastors. The following spring two thousand visitors, working in teams of two for each block, blanketed the city from the lowliest to the most fashionable streets. They visited the unchurched every month and ministered to whatever spiritual or material needs they found. In July, 1857, the Old Dutch Church employed Jeremiah Lanphier to superintend such work among the poor who had crowded into the Fulton Street neighborhood, as an alternative to following other Protestant congregations uptown. The famous prayer meeting which Lanphier instituted that fall for his band of lay visitation assistants was, in fact, no different from those in progress in a score of churches. The events which in succeeding months gave him lasting prominence served to obscure the memory of the others.[11]

By January, 1858, when an agent of the Sunday-school union described the New York plan to a large interchurch group at Dr. Edward N. Kirk's meetinghouse in Boston, it was operating with similar success in Brooklyn, Hartford, Detroit, and Buffalo. That revivals followed immediately should be no surprise. A working laity rapidly developed the necessary attitudes of concern and expectancy. And they brought new grist to the mill.[12]

In other ways as well church leaders were striving for a national awakening. New School Presbyterian "Revival Conventions," held at Pittsburgh and Cincinnati in the fall of 1857, set aside the first Sunday of the new year for sermons on the necessity of a general awakening and the Thursday following for fasting and prayer in its behalf. Late in December New York Baptist pastors were conducting each week an all-day union meeting of intercession for the Spirit's outpouring. Old School Presbyterians soon followed suit.[13] Congregational pastors in Rochester and Boston, Methodists in Philadelphia, and Baptists in Baltimore and Cincinnati united about the same time in massive evangelistic campaigns in which Finney, Caughey, and Knapp prepared the way of the Lord. Finney's return to Boston for the second long meeting in twelve months drew larger crowds and, according to Beecher's Independent, suffered even less from prejudice than the preceding year.[14]

[11] Conant, op. cit., pp. 358, 360, 413; Alexander, op. cit., pp. 171-74; Prime, op. cit., pp. 21-22; Chambers, op. cit., pp. 27-38.
[12] The Watchman and Reflector, Feb. 4 and March 4, 1858. Many accounts stressed the fruits of the revival among the poor: Prime, op. cit., pp. 220 ff., 258-63; James W. Alexander, Forty Years Familiar Letters of James W. Alexander . . . (John Hall, ed., New York, 1860), II, pp. 276-77.
[13] Conant, op. cit., p. 358; The Watchman and Reflector, Dec. 17, 1857.
[14] Beardsley, op. cit., p. 224; Alexander, Letters, II, p. 227; The Independent, Jan. 7, 1858. Cf. Jesse T. Peck, "Can We Have a Revival," The Guide to Holiness, XXXI (January-June, 1857), pp. 12-14.

That many New England congregations meanwhile were spontaneously instituting days of fasting and prayer for the "descent of the Spirit" seemed to the editors of *The Watchman and Reflector* to foreshadow a deluge of divine grace. They praised the increasingly simple, direct preaching characteristic of so many pulpits and called all Christians to "self-examination, humility, and prayer." Though at New Year's "God's Chariot" seemed yet "stayed in its coming," the editors urged faith and work for a Pentecostal outpouring which would "repress those scandalous vices which are making our great cities resemble Sodom and Gomorrah" and arm Christians for the early conversion of the world.[15] God's chariot arrived in time for the next week's mail. Revival reports poured in from the length and breadth of the land. A New York Baptist paper tabulated twelve thousand converts for a part of January alone, weeks before Greeley and Bennett helped to make the noonday meeting a national craze.[16]

In the record of the climactic five months from February to June, two facts stand out. Small towns and rural communities were as powerfully affected as the great cities; and support and participation came from major portions of every Protestant sect.

The union prayer meeting was never an exclusively metropolitan institution. As early as December, 1857, the daily one at Worcester, Massachusetts, and the weekly gathering which the Presbyterian, Dutch Reformed, Methodist, and Baptist churches sponsored at Utica, New York, had moved to larger quarters. Dozens of such places as Peekskill, New York, and Bethel, Connecticut, eventually organized them. The one held in the latter place at 4:00 P.M. each day, attended by "farmers, mechanics and storekeepers," reported 200 conversions.[17]

Nor were protracted meetings in rural and small-town churches unimportant. William C. Conant's compilation reveals that 88 towns in Maine, 40 in New Hampshire, 39 in Vermont and 147 in Massachusetts experienced unusual awakenings. Some of these, to be sure, may have been quite ordinary meetings which persons caught up in the universal excitement glowingly reported. But other evidence abounds. Methodists Walter and Phoebe Palmer wrote of conversions by the hundreds and crowds of 5,000-6,000 at obscure camp meetings in Ontario and Quebec in 1857. That fall an afternoon prayer meeting in Hamilton, Ontario, stretched into

[15] *The Watchman and Reflector*, Nov. 26, 1857 and Jan. 7, 1858.
[16] *The Watchman and Reflector*, Jan. 14, 1858 and succeeding issues; *The Puritan Recorder*, Feb. 18, 1858.
[17] *The Independent*, Jan. 7, 1858; Conant, *op. cit.*, pp. 367-79.

a ten days' revival in which 400 were converted and scores sanctified. Lay testimonies rather than sermons, particularly in the afternoon meetings for holiness, were, Mrs. Palmer believed, chiefly responsible for these results.[18]

The winter's excitement found the Palmers successively in Owego, Binghamton, and Union, New York, for campaigns which Presbyterian, Congregationalist, and Baptist pastors united to support. They reported from the Maritime Provinces in August, 1858, that 400 had been converted and 200 sanctified in twenty-three days at St. John, and 170 converted at Halifax. In October a tide of glory swept Prince Edward Island; more than 700 were at the mourner's bench, and all the ministers on the district experienced the "second blessing."[19]

A very great number of Baptist awakenings likewise broke out in small towns before the excitement in the cities reached its peak. In New England Boston seems to have been the least and last affected.[20] Typical examples were Sheldonville, Massachusetts, where five successive Mondays of fasting and prayer won twelve heads of families to the church, and Pawtucket, Rhode Island, blessed with seventy conversions from six weeks spent in nightly gatherings for testimony and exhortation. In mid-March unusual revivals were in progress at Waterford, Mystic River, Southington, Banksville, North Lyme, and Norwich, as well as Hartford and New Haven, Connecticut. Reports from Nantucket, West Royalton, Fairhaven, and Dartmouth, Massachusetts, appeared alongside the news of 500 converts in Newburyport and 600 in New Bedford.[21]

[18] Conant, op. cit., pp. 426-30; Richard Wheatley, The Life and Letters of Mrs. Phoebe Palmer (New York, 1876), pp. 316-31, passim.
[19] Ibid., pp. 312, 334-35, 337-44. Cf. Homer S. Thrall, A Brief History of Methodism in Texas (Nashville, 1894), pp. 131-33.
[20] The Independent, Jan. 7, 1858; The Watchman and Reflector, Oct. 14, 1858. Following is a list of places where revivals were reported in The Watchman and Reflector between Dec. 24, 1857, and Feb. 4, 1858; the figure in parentheses represents the number of converts when it was given: Connecticut: Hampton (30), Brooklyn, Winstead (200) and Meriden (50); Rhode Island: Charlestown, Dorrville, South Ferry, Kingston, Usquequag, East Greenwich, Wickford, and Central Falls; New York: Wetskill (25), Weston (70), Ft. Edward (46), and Saratoga County; Massachusetts: Rock (80 in eleven weeks), Long Plain (15), North Tewksbury (30), North Uxbridge (30), Southwick, Scituate, North Cambridge, Andover, and Wales; Vermont: Whitingham (25), Lunenberg, Saxonville, North Easton, Bridgwater, West Barre, St. Albans, Swanton, Fairfax, and Westford; New Hampshire: Manchester and Nashua (extensive community-wide awakenings); Maine: Thomaston. The distribution between town and city churches remained constant throughout the year.
[21] The Watchman and Reflector, Feb. 18 and March 25, 1858. Emerson Andrews, Living Life; or, Autobiography of Rev. Emerson Andrews, Evangelist (Boston, 1875), pp. 173-82 does not, however, record anything remarkable about 1858.

If the awakening dramatized the nearly complete acceptance of revivalism among Baptists, it evoked surprising support from Old School Presbyterians, Episcopalians, and even Unitarians and Universalists. James W. Alexander's correspondence provides an intimate glimpse of a very conservative Old School Calvinist being pulled along by the popular tide. On New Year's Day, 1858, Alexander had written sarcastically of the New York City churches which were "using terrible blast bellows to get up artificial heat." On March 1 he admitted rather grudging pleasure at having received fifteen members, but expressed fear that the Fulton Street meetings would succumb to a "go-ahead, joyous, auction-like, unreverent elation" unless the ministers assumed control as they had uptown.

By April, however, "ten leading gentlemen" of his congregation had instituted a nightly prayer meeting at their mission chapel for the poor, and this Old School pastor was compelled to acknowledge that his efforts "to keep down and regulate excitement" had failed. He wrote to a friend at Princeton:

Study I cannot, being run down by persons, many of whom I never knew, in search of counsel. . . . The openness of thousands to doctrine, reproof, etc., is undeniable. Our lecture is crowded unendurably, many going away. The publisher of Spurgeon's sermons says he has sold a hundred thousand. . . . You may rest assured there is a great awakening among us, of which not one word gets into the papers; and that there are meetings of great size, as free from irreverence as any you ever saw.[22]

Alexander remained adamant against "the license given A, B, or C, to teach or pray" in the union meetings. But he remarked that, nonetheless, a "still, solemn, and tender" atmosphere usually prevailed in them, "more like a communion than a prayer meeting." [23]

Low-Church Episcopalians, whose best-known leaders were Charles Pettit McIlvaine, bishop of Ohio, and Stephen Higginson Tyng and his sons, pastors of immense congregations in Philadelphia and New York, welcomed the awakening with more abandon. Dudley A. Tyng was a prominent leader of the Jayns Hall meetings in Philadelphia. One observer believed that those "slain of the Lord" through one of his appeals outnumbered the results of "any sermon in modern times." When the young preacher died suddenly in April, his fame spread along with the

---

[22] Alexander, *Letters*, II, 275-77. Cf. Fletcher Harper's similar judgment, *Harper's Monthly*, XVI (1858), p. 840.
[23] Alexander, *Letters*, II, 277-79.

hymn, "Stand up for Jesus," which he had recently written—an exhortation aimed, perhaps, at churchly timidity in testimony meetings.[24]

In Ohio, Bishop McIlvaine devoted his annual diocesan report of June 3, 1858, almost exclusively to the revival. He declared that its simplicity and "freedom from unwholesome excitement," the display of "brotherly love and union among Christians of different evangelical denominations," the reliance upon the regular ministry and ordinances of grace and the wide extent of the work all confirmed him in "the decided conviction that it is 'the Lord's doing.'" He reported:

Our own churches in this diocese, and in others have largely participated in this blessing. . . . Our own diocesan college [Kenyon] is thus favored. Pray for it, brethren. . . . Pray for our whole church, that no part of it may be unvisited in these "times of refreshing from the presence of the Lord." [25]

Meanwhile, the editors of *The Church Journal*, organ of the High Church party, felt called upon to print a series of articles claiming that the "church system" could give "full range for the proper working of the revival element, and at the same time furnish all requisite safeguards against the mischiefs of excess." Their chief recommendation was that ministers in all larger parishes conduct continuous evening services during the Advent and Lenten seasons featuring free seats and "popular singing and preaching." [26]

Even more remarkable is the fact that Unitarian churches in New York and Boston united that spring in "densely crowded" weekly meetings for testimony and prayer. "The speaking," ran one report, "interspersed with one verse from hymns and tunes that have been sung from childhood, seemed to be taken home to every heart present." At Harvard, Frederic Dan Huntington, Plummer professor of Christian morals and preacher at the Appleton Chapel, conducted such a service on Wednesday evenings.[27]

After mid-March the editors of the denominational newspaper, *The Christian Register*, kept its readers abreast of events in the revival, always

[24] See William Wilson Manross, *A History of the American Episcopal Church* (2nd. ed., New York, 1950), pp. 251-52, 275-78, and *passim;* the sketches of the elder and younger Stephen H. Tyng in *National Cyclopaedia of Biography*, II, 187-88; Prime, *op. cit.*, pp. 46, 287-91; Chambers, *op. cit.*, pp. 277, 279; and *Stand Up For Jesus; a Christian Ballad* . . . (Philadelphia, 1858). The better-known hymn with the same title, by a New School Presbyterian pastor in New Jersey, also appeared in 1858.

[25] Charles Pettit McIlvaine, *Bishop McIlvaine on the Revival of Religion* . . . (Philadelphia, 1858), pp. 4, 11, 22.

[26] *The Revival System and the Paraclete. A Series of Articles from The Church Journal* (New York, 1858), pp. 11-15; see also pp. 18, 20, 31-40, 44-45.

[27] *The Christian Register*, March 20 and April 17, 1858; Conant, *op. cit.*, p. 377. Frederic Dan Huntington, *Permanent Realities of Religion, and the Present Religious*

approving the absence of sectarianism and emotional excitement. They agreed to "greet it and forward it, as far as it aims to promote pure religion in its practical, and therefore universally acknowledged truths." The editorial for April 3 praised the tearful testimony which a recent convert had given at a Unitarian-Universalist religious conference in Brookfield, devoted to the theme, "What must I do to be saved?" And it criticized Portsmouth, New Hampshire, clergymen for giving "the Rev. Mr. Patterson, of the Universalist Church, a hint that his participation in the prayer meetings was not desired." [28]

The Monthly Religious Magazine, dominated by Huntington and the evangelical wing of the church, published three serious articles in defense of the awakening. Theodore Tebbetts declared that Unitarians had too much disregarded "the mysterious and spontaneous power of the union of hearts for the accomplishment of spiritual purposes." He believed the recent events had produced a "quickening of the general conscience" and "an advance in political and social morality" which would enable Christians to "carry their consecration into their daily lives in business and politics." A little later a Methodist journal reported with amazement that a London Unitarian quarterly meeting had professed itself virtually unanimous in the belief that revivals were the result of "direct and immediate agency of the Holy Spirit." [29]

When a year had passed, the leaders of the Fulton Street meeting conducted an anniversary service at which numerous clergymen testified to the fact that unity in evangelism had routed sectarian controversy. The venerable Methodist Nathan Bangs joined many others in declaring that he had "laid aside the polemic armour." He had determined to preach "principally upon experimental and practical religion" and to join in fellowship with every man who would share that theme. The great question was, Bangs declared:

Interest (Boston, 1858), a hearty approbation, received a friendly review in *The Watchman and Reflector*, Apr. 29, 1858.
[28] *The Christian Register*, Apr. 3, 1858.
[29] *The Methodist Quarterly Review*, XLII (1860), p. 312. Cf. Theodore Tebbetts, "Revivals, Past and Present," *The Monthly Religious Magazine*, XIX (1858), pp. 333, 335-36, with similar ideas in Richard Pike, "Times of Refreshing," in the same volume, pp. 273-78; James Freeman Clarke, "The Revival," the same, pp. 343-51; and those in a sermon by Henry W. Bellows, Universalist pastor in New York, reviewed in *The Christian Register*, March 27, 1858, p. 2.
    Less enthusiastic were Solon W. Bush, *The Revival. A Sermon Preached at The First Congregational Church, Medfield* . . . (Dedham, 1858), pp. 7-8, 13; William Henry Ryder, *Religion and the Present Revival. A Sermon* (Boston, 1858), pp. 8, 10.

Shall this revival continue? I think it may continue and it ought to continue. It depends upon the fidelity of the people of God whether it will or not. If the professors of religion . . . fix their minds upon the mark . . . of holiness of heart, of life, and of conversation, . . . [the Lord Jesus] certainly will not forsake His church, but will continue to pour out His spirit more and more abundantly.[80]

Perhaps his generation was disappointed. But to a modern observer these hopes seem to have been amply fulfilled.

Very little reaction against revival methods appeared as the excitement of the "year of wonders" passed away. Union city-wide campaigns became a familiar part of American church life. Unusual ones occurred during the war at Boston and Fall River, Massachusetts; Portland, Maine; Utica, Troy, and Brooklyn, New York; Evansville, Indiana; and Montreal, Canada.[31] The columns of the religious press remained as filled as ever with news of revivals, and responsible churchmen turned out a score of guidebooks to instruct pastors and laymen in winning souls.[32] Reports of extensive awakenings in Europe during 1859 seemed to American evangelicals an extension and in some sense a validation of the Spirit's work begun here.[33]

Chief reapers in the whitened harvest fields were the evangelists, whose special usefulness now secured more general recognition. Jacob Knapp, deeply humbled by the honor, returned to Boston in 1860 for meetings

[80] Chambers, *op. cit.*, pp. 247-48 and *passim*.
[31] Samuel Irenaeus Prime, *Five Years of Prayer, with the Answers* (New York, 1864), pp. 29-45, *passim*; *The Watchman and Reflector*, March 26 and Apr. 9, 1863; P. C. Headley, ed., *The Harvest Work of the Holy Spirit, Illustrated in the Evangelistic Labors of Rev. Edward Payson Hammond* (Boston, 1862), pp. 226-30.
[32] The American Tract Society published Horatius Bonar, *Words to the Winners of Souls* (Boston, ca. 1859), for pastors, and Humphrey, *op. cit.* The Congregational Board of Publication reprinted Ebenezer Porter's *Letters on the Religious Revivals Which Prevailed About the Beginning of the Present Century* (Boston, 1858). Harvey Newcomb, *The Harvest and the Reapers; Home Work for All, and How to Do It* (Boston, 1858), received favorable comment in the Baptist *Christian Review*, XXIV (1859), p. 153, as did Horatius Bonar, *God's Way to Peace: a Book for the Anxious* (New York, 1862), the same, XXVII (1862), p. 347.
Somewhat later appeared Henry C. Fish, *Handbook of Revivals: for the Use of Winners of Souls* (Boston, 1874); Francis Wayland, *Salvation By Christ* (Boston, 1859); Edward N. Kirk's lectures on revivals given at Andover in 1866 and 1867, as well as numbers of his evangelistic sermons, such as *The Waiting Saviour* (Boston, 1865); and Albert Barnes, *The Way of Salvation* (Philadelphia, 1863), one of many variations of his famous sermon of 1829. Thomas Guthrie, *Speaking to the Heart; or Sermons for the People* (New York, 1863), exemplifies the contribution of several English preachers to this kind of literature.
[33] William Gibson, *The Year of Grace; a History of the Revival in Ireland, A.D. 1859* (Boston, 1860), "Introduction" by Baron Stow, *passim*; Prime, *Five Years of Prayer*, chs. xvii-xx.

which were held first at the Baldwin Street Baptist Church, then for ten weeks nightly at the Union Church, Merrimac Street, and, finally, five weeks at Tremont Temple. In the years immediately following, Knapp appeared at the Wabash Avenue Church, Chicago; Second Baptist Church, Wilmington; Fourth Baptist Church, Philadelphia; and various ones in Newark and Trenton. At his meeting in New York City in 1866 every Baptist pastor professed to have been converted in a revival.[34] Edward Norris Kirk continued to spend part of each year conducting evangelistic campaigns, notably at Mt. Holyoke College, where he headed the Board of Trustees from 1858 until the time of his death in 1874. Professor William S. Tyler later recalled several remarkable awakenings under Kirk's ministry there. In the winter of 1863-64, for example, a four-day flood tide of emotion swept eighty-five students into salvation.[35] Charles G. Finney and Dr. and Mrs. Walter Palmer, who conducted evangelistic meetings in Europe in the years immediately following 1858, were swamped when they returned with more calls than they could accept. Emerson Andrews, James Caughey, and Heman Humphrey likewise shared the increased prestige of the older group of soul winners.[36]

Meanwhile, public attention was shifting to a new generation. Edward Payson Hammond, a graduate of Williams College who had served as a student volunteer worker in New York during the revival of 1858, returned in 1861 from two years' study at Free Church College, Glasgow. The news of his successful revivals in Scotland had preceded him to New England. There his success was immediate, first at Salem Street Congregational Church, Boston, where one hundred professed conversion, and then at the Second Parish Church, Portland, where a month of his preaching ignited a series of major religious conflagrations in Maine. The Rev. Paul A. Chadbourne—a professor of natural history at Bowdoin College who was later to be president in turn of the University of Wisconsin, Williams College, and the Massachusetts Agricultural College—assisted Hammond in the several weeks' meeting at Bath. He counted as many as six hundred in the inquiry room there at one time. News of the Maine awakenings gave

[34] Jacob Knapp, *Autobiography* . . . (New York, 1868), pp. 175-79. See pp. 164, 181-82, 184, 186.

[35] David O. Mears, *Life of Edward Norris Kirk, D.D.* (Boston, 1877), pp. 340-41; cf. pp. 338, 347-48, 352-53. See also anon., *The Power of Christian Benevolence Illustrated in the Life and Labors of Mary Lyon* (New York, 1858), pp. 244, 249, 255-56.

[36] Charles G. Finney, *Memoirs* . . . (New York, 1876), pp. 473-75; Andrews, *op. cit.*, pp. 101, 104; George Hughes, *The Beloved Physician, Walter C. Palmer, Jr.* . . . (New York, 1884), p. 221; P. C. Headley, *Evangelists in the Church* . . . (Boston, 1875), p. 294.

Hammond a national reputation and brought him invitations to conduct union campaigns in Montreal, New York, and other Eastern cities.[37]

Among Baptists the new figure was A. B. Earle of Boston, chief leader in the general awakening at Fall River in 1863. Earle, who avoided both sectarianism and sensationalism, spent most of his time after 1860 in interdenominational campaigns in which he stressed the Finney-Methodist doctrine of sanctification.[38] Alfred Cookman and John S. Inskip were chief among a score of young Methodist evangelists devoted to the same theme. The group included the colorful William Taylor, fresh from seven years' pioneer street preaching in California. Taylor launched his career in the East with numerous Methodist meetings conducted during the excitement of 1858.[39] Such men made America revival conscious, preparing the way for the evangelistic giants of a later day, Dwight L. Moody, Reuben A. Torrey, and J. Wilbur Chapman.

Meanwhile, religious assemblies and publications defended revivals much more strongly than in the previous decade. In 1863, for example, when the Rev. Robert Aikman addressed the Presbyterian Synod of New York and New Jersey on the "Relations of the Ministry to Revivals of Religion," he recognized no differences of opinion about them save on the question of whether professional evangelists were preferable to neighboring pastors. It was the "high and sacred duty" of every preacher, he declared, to learn how best to plan and promote them.[40] Even the conservative *American Theological Review* praised Heman Humphrey in 1859. *The Evangelical Quarterly Review*, long silent on the issue so divisive in Lutheran circles, printed in 1856 a Hartwick Seminary professor's strong defense and exposition of measures to secure mass conversions. A prominent Baptist minister reported at the end of the Civil War that the traditional antipathy to revivals in his denomination had completely disappeared, the

[37] Headley, *Hammond*, pp. 41-61, 76-216, *passim*, 218-19, 226-30, 246-47, 250-89. *The Independent*, Jan. 1 and 8, 1863; *The Watchman and Reflector*, Jan. 8, 1863. The sketch of Chadbourne's career in *The Dictionary of American Biography* is by Frederick Tuckerman.

[38] Absalom B. Earle, *Bringing In Sheaves* (Boston, 1869), pp. 38-62, 89-107, 269-80. Cf. *The Watchman and Reflector*, March 26, 1863.

[39] William Taylor, *Seven Years' Street Preaching in San Francisco* . . . (New York, 1857).

[40] Robert Aikman, *The Relations of the Ministry to Revivals of Religion* . . . (New York, 1863), pp. 13, 15 and *passim*.

On professionalism see *The Independent*, Dec. 23, 1858, and the issue of Jan. 8, 1863, responding to criticism of E. P. Hammond from *The Presbyterian Banner*.

acceptability of pastors to large city congregations now resting frequently on their ability to conduct them.[41]

It is not surprising, perhaps, that holy pandemonium still broke out occasionally at Methodist camp meetings. But it is intriguing to find the editor of a Unitarian magazine writing, upon his return from one of them, "how much more efficient is the Word when free from the restraints of primness and formality, in breaking up the fountains of the heart and convincing and converting souls." In commenting on the absence of fervent prayer at a large Disciples of Christ camp meeting in the Western Reserve, Henry Ward Beecher's paper, *The Independent*, praised its leaders for realizing that in doing away with the mourner's bench entirely, they had carried their reaction against emotionalism to "a dangerous extreme"![42]

The greatest leaders in New England Congregationalism swung their support to revivals with similar enthusiasm. In 1861 the learned Henry Martyn Dexter, editor of the *Congregational Quarterly*, rejoiced that his denomination's loose organization, freedom from liturgy, and emphasis upon lay initiative uniquely fitted it to promote them. The previous year a prominent pastor cast the mantle of historic sanctity about them with an article on the revival spirit of the Pilgrims.[43] The National Congregational Council which met in Boston during June, 1865, issued a call for "revivals of religion in our churches and colleges . . . deep and powerful in their effects." Without them, it declared, the church could never produce a ministry "steeped in devout affection, and consecrated by the baptism and rich indwelling of the Holy Spirit of God."[44] The Puritan City's answer was to engage A. B. Earle, then concluding a highly successful campaign in nearby Chelsea, for a city-wide effort the next spring.[45]

Among the twelve sermons which the Boston Council recommended for

[41] *The American Theological Review*, I (1859), pp. 698-708; Levi Sternberg, "Revivals," *The Evangelical Quarterly Review*, XV (1864), pp. 278-79, 281-84. Cf. R. Jeffry's statement in Jacob Knapp, *op. cit.*, p. ix, with *The Watchman and Reflector*, Apr. 9, 1863.

[42] *The Monthly Religious Magazine*, XXIV (1860), p. 297; *The Independent*, Jan. 13, 1859, p. 2. The account of a Tennessee Methodist camp meeting in *The Watchman and Reflector*, Feb. 5, 1863, pp. 1-2, may be overdrawn, but cf. *Zion's Herald*, Nov. 17, 1852.

[43] Henry M. Dexter, "Congregationalism Specially Adapted to Promote Revivals of Religion," *The Congregational Quarterly*, III (1861), pp. 52-58; Joseph S. Clark, "A Lesson from the Past: The Revival Spirit of the Pilgrims," the same, II (1860), pp. 404-08. See also Erdix Tenney, "A True Revival of Religion," the same (1862), pp. 241-46.

[44] "Official Record of the National Council at Boston, June, A.D., 1865," *The Congregational Quarterly*, VII (1865), pp. 323, 325; cf. pp. 343-45.

[45] For a sharply critical account, see Charles K. Whipple, "The Boston Revival, and Its Leader," *The Radical: A Monthly Magazine Devoted to Religion*, I (1865-66), pp. 429-38.

lay reading that winter was one by the Rev. John E. Todd answering the question, "Are Revivals Desirable?" He began thus:

It is too late to discuss this question. As well might we discuss the desirableness of summer showers. It is evident that they are a part, and a blessed part of the Divine administration. . . . Whatever of life and earnestness there is in any of our churches has originated in and been fed by revivals. Most of those who have been redeemed . . . were converted in revivals; almost every faithful minister of the Gospel and missionary has traced his conversion to a revival.[46]

The evangelistic methods of the 1850's were institutionalized in two national organizations, the Y.M.C.A. and its wartime offspring, the United States Christian Commission. Charles Howard Hopkins's recent illumination of the fervently religious orientation of the mid-century Y.M.C.A. leaves insufficiently stressed only one point—its intimate bond with the churches. Leading ministers participated in "Y" affairs at all levels. Contemporaries seem never to have regarded the organization's union prayer meetings, visitation evangelism directed toward unchurched young men, or the annual tent-meeting revival efforts which it sponsored in Boston, Philadelphia, and many other cities as anything other than a united expression of the soul-winning fervor of evangelical Protestantism.[47]

This held particularly true of the Christian Commission. Although George H. Stuart, an active Y.M.C.A. leader, served as its president, he would have been surprised at any who thought him not a stanch churchman. Edmund Storer Janes, senior bishop of the Methodist Episcopal Church, was an original and effective member of the small executive board. William E. Boardman, a New School Presbyterian minister and author of the recent perfectionist volume, *The Higher Christian Life*, became executive secretary early in the war and organized the Commission's work. Many of the 1,375 clergymen who served as volunteer "delegates" to the army camps were Methodists. Among the important leaders were earnest revivalists like Alfred Cookman, C. C. McCabe, Edward N. Kirk, and Dwight L. Moody.[48]

[46] John E. Todd, *Revivals of Religion* (*Addresses to Church Members by the Congregational Pastors of Boston, Recommended by the Boston Congregational Council*, No. 6, Boston, 1866), pp. 3, 4.

[47] Hopkins, *op. cit.*, pp. 18, 26-27, 45-47. Cf. Y.M.C.A., Baltimore, *Proceedings of the All-Day Prayer Meeting . . . September 27, 1859* (Baltimore, 1859), pp. 3-4; and Boston Y.M.C.A., *Annual Report . . . May, 1866*, pp. 15-16.

[48] Lemuel Moss, *Annals of The United States Christian Commission* (Philadelphia,

The blending of concern for the physical and the spiritual needs of the soldiers in the Commission's activities was similar to that directed toward the urban poor after 1856. The primary goal was, of course, the conversion of souls. Personal witnessing, tract distribution, preaching services, and camp revivals were simply more obvious means to this end than providing books and magazines for camp libraries, giving medical care to the wounded, or writing letters home for the hospitalized and supplying food for men in prison. Agents reported the latter activities principally in terms of their power to win converts from among those previously skeptical of Christianity's practical social compassion.[49] The extent of the Commission's success is difficult to measure, but in any event, by 1865 the revival in the armed forces was a major interest of the times.[50]

Churchmen in the North remained oblivious to the awakening going on at the same time in the Southern armies. Missionaries and book agents of the Evangelical Tract Society and the Bible Society of the Confederate States joined with scores representing various denominational organizations and hundreds of pastors serving on their own to fan the flames of religious anxiety which broke out in the Army of Northern Virginia early in the war. Interest soon spread through all the Confederate forces. Dr. Moses D. Hodge of Richmond helped to bring in past the Union blockade thousands of copies of the Bible and Gospel portions—all gifts of the British and Foreign Bible Society. Christian officers like Stonewall Jackson heartily co-operated.[51]

Particularly during the period between the battles at Fredericksburg

---

1868), pp. 67, 76, 106, 116-17, 130-31. Cf. Mary M. Boardman (Mrs. Wm. E.), *Life and Labours of the Rev. W. E. Boardman* (New York, 1887), pp. 119-20; Hopkins, *op. cit.*, pp. 89-94; Mears, *op. cit.*, pp. 300-305; and William Warren Sweet, *The Methodist Episcopal Church and the Civil War*, pp. 149, 162-65.

[49] See especially Boardman's chapters in *Christ in the Army: a Selection of Sketches of the Work of the U. S. Christian Commission* (Philadelphia, 1865), pp. 1-16, 23-46, and testimonies and accounts of revivals, pp. 59, 62-63, 82-83, 97, 107-12. Cf. Boston Y.M.C.A., *Annual Report . . . 1864*, pp. 39-40; Hopkins, *op. cit.*, p. 94; Mary M. Boardman, *op. cit.*, pp. 123-25; and Moss, *op. cit.*, pp. 91-93.

M. Hamlin Cannon, "The United States Christian Commission," *The Mississippi Valley Historical Review*, XXXVIII (1951-52), pp. 61-80, omits any mention of Boardman and, p. 67, deprecates revivalistic fervor.

[50] "The United States Christian Commission," *The Evangelical Quarterly Review*, XVI (1865), pp. 266-71; "The United States Christian Commission," *The Baptist Quarterly*, II (1868), pp. 194-227.

[51] W. W. Bennett, *A Narrative of the Great Revival which Prevailed in the Southern Armies . . .* (Philadelphia, 1877), pp. 46-48, 51-52, 68-70, 74-77, 251-362, 368, and *passim*; John William Jones, *Christ in the Camp; or, Religion in Lee's Army* (Richmond, 1887), pp. 50-51, 89, 148-51.

and Chancellorsville Confederate prayer meetings and open-air revivals multiplied. The Rev. Enoch Marvin, later a bishop in the Methodist Episcopal Church, South, initiated in an Arkansas force the first regimental "Army Church," in which membership was open to men of all evangelical persuasions. Since both war and spiritual fervor made sectarian lines seem less important, the idea spread through the whole army. Enthusiasts estimated 150,000 converts in all.[52]

The revivalistic, missionary Christianity predominant in the South since 1875 owes much to this wartime awakening. Certainly that section had not experienced the flood tide which earlier engulfed the Northern churches. Rather, in the decades immediately preceding the war, Old School Presbyterian, Old Lutheran and Antimission Baptist sentiments had claimed a wide allegiance from men who favored slavery or wished to dodge the issues which it raised.[53]

Thus did the symphony of salvation fill the atmosphere of American Christianity from the days when its first thundering notes awakened the nation to the wonders of 1858. To the irreligious, still a large minority of the population, the rendition must have seemed a painful farce. Few contemporaries, however, could ignore the spell which revivalism had cast upon the minds of the masses. Nor could any clergyman overlook the revolution in thought and practice which, as we shall see, the new fervor had wrought in Protestant religion. Far from rejecting material and social progress in a romantic retreat to the past—a mood exemplified by such varied figures as Brigham Young, Herman Melville, and Bronson Alcott—the most avid proponents of revival measures regarded themselves as civilization's most indispensable agents. They were progressive in their theology, catholic in their sentiments, and thoroughly in tune with the current belief that American society must become the garden of the Lord.

Church historians of a later day, anxious to make plain the origins of modern religious outlooks, wrote the history of the great popular sects in such a way as to becloud the memory of evangelism's power. They have made familiar the deeds of pioneers of liberal Christianity like Horace Bushnell, Mark Hopkins, and Washington Gladden. But we know very little of the lives of Albert Barnes, George B. Cheever, Samuel S.

[52] Bennett, op. cit., pp. 54-55, 252-54, 365-66; Jones, op. cit., pp. 223-24, 312-53, 390-91, and passim; John Shepard, Jr., "Religion in the Army of Northern Virginia," The North Carolina Historical Review, XXV (1948), pp. 367, 369.
[53] Contrast Shepard, ibid., pp. 350, 356, 365-66.

Schmucker, Robert Baird, Stephen H. Tyng, Edward· N. Kirk, and William E. Boardman—men who seemed to their contemporaries the most distinguished spiritual leaders of the age. Methodists Matthew Simpson and Phoebe Palmer have recently escaped anonymity; but after one hundred years, Charles G. Finney awaits a biographer, and Frederic Dan Huntington remains Unitarianism's forgotten man.[54] Little wonder that today's thoughtful clergyman considers the evangelistic and perfectionist traditions which all these in some manner represented to be perennial obstructions to human progress.

Secular historians, meanwhile, have paid more attention to bizarre groups like the Shakers, Mormons, and Millerites than to the Methodists and Baptists.[55] Even Alice Felt Tyler's book, *Freedom's Ferment,* which elaborately illustrates how pious enthusiasm nurtured the spirit of reform, devotes only one chapter to evangelical religion while assigning seven to "cults and utopias." Charles C. Cole's fine treatment of *The Social Ideas of the Northern Evangelists* chops the narrative off at the point where its most significant developments begin.[56] The myth persists that revivalism is but a half-breed child of the Protestant faith, born on the crude frontier, where Christianity was taken captive by the wilderness. The triumphs of Billy Graham, in prim Boston and ancient Oxford no less than in adolescent Los Angeles, point to another interpretation.

---

[54] Earle Morse Wilbur, *A History of Unitarianism in Transylvania, England, and America* (Cambridge, 1952), does not mention Huntington. Wade Crawford Barclay, *Early American Methodism, 1769-1844* . . . (New York, 1949), ignores Mrs. Palmer; but cf. John L. Peters, *Christian Perfection and American Methodism* (New York, 1956), pp. 109-13, and Robert D. Clark, *Life of Matthew Simpson* (New York, 1956).

[55] See, for example, Merle Curti, *The Growth of American Thought* (2nd. ed., New York, 1951), pp. 306-13; and Whitney R. Cross, *The Burned-Over District; the Social and Intellectual History of Enthusiastic Religion in Western New York, 1800-1850* (Ithaca, N. Y., 1950).

[56] Alice F. Tyler, *Freedom's Ferment: Phases of American Social History to 1860* (Minneapolis, 1944); and Cole, *op. cit.,* pp. 221-27, 238.

V

The Fruits of Fervor

❧

The mid-century revivals brought to a climax four fundamental changes in the inner life of American Protestantism. The traditional predominance of the clergy in the spiritual and organizational work
of the churches now gave place rapidly to the enthusiastic expansion of
lay participation and control. The spirit of interdenominational brotherhood, which had struggled for survival ever since its beginning in the
crusade to Christianize the West after 1800, came swiftly to maturity
and caught the imagination of the greatest churchmen in the land. Ethical
concerns replaced dogmatic zeal in evangelical preaching and writing. And,
equally important, Arminian views crowded out Calvinism in much of
the dogma which remained.

The increased wealth and education of lay persons was, to be sure, an
important factor in their rise to religious leadership. Time and money
for study and cultural refinement brought many men whose fathers sat
in awe of the learned clergy to a feeling of social and intellectual equality.
Many successful businessmen invested their new resources in such useful
ways that they inevitably gained a larger voice in church counsels. They paid
the bills for the fine new church buildings which adorned the better neighborhoods. In the large cities, therefore, the congregational system of church
government began to fulfill its democratic promise, and Methodist laymen
staked out new claims on territory which the preachers had long occupied
alone.[1]

A more important bulwark of the minister's sovereignty, however, had
been his supposed spiritual eminence. In the free atmosphere of the
great revivals, where the Holy Spirit bestowed his gifts without respect
of persons, this mystic monopoly, too, was done away. Prayer-meeting

[1] See Abel Stevens, "Letter to Bishop Simpson," *The National Magazine*, VII (1855),
pp. 75-85; and *The Methodist Quarterly Review*, XXXIII (1853), pp. 323-28. For later
debate see Abel Stevens, "Methodism: Suggestions Appropriate to Its Present Condition,"
the same, XLII (1860), pp. 129-32, and Francis Hodgson, "Lay Representation," the same,
pp. 228-44.

testimonies now ranked with sermons in converting souls, often above them. Many pastors shared Francis Wayland's discovery at Providence in 1858 that a permanent system of apportioning to laymen responsibility for the spiritual care of families in a parish would yield excellent results. Only the Methodists, through their class leaders and local preachers, had theretofore exploited this possibility. Even conservative clergymen plunged into Sunday-school visitation crusades, Y.M.C.A. tent revivals, and Christian Commission rallies where the unordained helped to usher in the dispensation of the Spirit. The old-time evangelist, who had invaded single-handedly the precincts of Satan, now gave way to a team of influential clergymen and practical businessmen, who advertised and engaged the preacher for the moment made propitious by their months of careful effort.[2]

Ever since Charles G. Finney had generated among the people the support which ministers had denied him for Oberlin College and other benevolent ventures, revival men had encouraged this trend. Samuel S. Schmucker rejoiced that talented and spiritual laymen had conducted a large share of the business at the General Synod of Lutherans which united their church in 1853. Benjamin Kurtz at his institute in Selinsgrove, Pennsylvania, seems to have aimed at training Lutheran men for roles analogous to those of Methodism's local preachers.[3]

When the good Baptist, Henry Clay Fish, caught the vision of a nation-wide awakening, he did not hesitate to point to the Methodists, as well as to the New Testament church, as exemplars of the power of a soul-winning laity. Mrs. Phoebe Palmer was the author of a widely read tract entitled "A Laity for the Times," first published in 1857 in the New York *Christian Advocate and Journal*. It urged church members to take the lead in the crusade of personal evangelism.[4] Two years after the awakening of 1858 had demonstrated the soundness of this program, a conservative Lutheran editor hailed the "modern era of revivals, missions,

[2] James O. Murray, *Francis Wayland*, (Boston, 1891), pp. 132-34; "What Can I Do for Christ," *The Independent*, Jan. 20, 1859.
[3] Charles G. Finney, *Memoirs* . . . (New York, 1876), pp. 336-37, 344-45; Samuel S. Schmucker, *The Peace of Zion: a Discourse Preached before the General Synod of the Evangelical Lutheran Church* . . . (Gettysburg, 1853), p. 4; R. Weiser, "A Want in the Lutheran Church Met by the Founding of the Missionary Institute," *The Evangelical Quarterly Review*, X (1858-59), p. 345.
[4] Henry C. Fish, *Primitive Piety Revived* . . . (Boston, 1857), pp. 209-30, *passim*; Richard Wheatley, *Life and Letters of Mrs. Phoebe Palmer* (New York, 1876), pp. 554-57; *The Guide to Holiness*, XXXII (1857-58), pp. 174-75.

and benevolent institutions" for bringing consecrated laymen to their rightful position in the church.[5]

The usefulness of women to an emotionally awakened Christianity, a fact obvious to every evangelist after Finney, illustrates another aspect of the growth of lay activity. The co-educational experiment at Oberlin was too far in advance of the times to set a pattern as yet, but it did demonstrate a new attitude. Even here, however, girls were discouraged from preparing for the ministry, despite the fact that revivalistic churches like the Freewill Baptists and later the Wesleyan Methodists sometimes ordained them.[6] More influential was the example which Mrs. Palmer and the second Mrs. Finney set in the immensely successful testimony and prayer meetings which each held in connection with her husband's campaigns. Both encouraged women to participate in gospel work, undercutting the usual antifeminist objections by quoting the apostle Peter's words at Pentecost: "And it shall come to pass in the last days, saith God, I will pour out of my Spirit upon all flesh: and your sons and your daughters shall prophesy" (Acts 2:17).

This, at any rate, was the biblical basis for the solid book Phoebe Palmer published in 1858, *Promise of the Father; or a Neglected Specialty of the Last Days*, which established woman's religious rights on the authority of the Holy Spirit. She had discussed the manuscript at some length with Harriet Beecher Stowe and Francis Wayland and dedicated the book to the Philadelphia Episcopalian pastor, Dudley A. Tyng![7] That same year when the businessmen's noonday prayer meetings were thrown open to the ladies, social acceptance of their new role, though by no means complete, was in the long run assured. A glance at the reports of the dozens of religious-humanitarian enterprises operating in New York by

[5] "The Prayer Meeting," *The Evangelical Quarterly Review*, XII (1860-61), p. 106. Cf. A. P. Marvin, "Three Eras of Revivals in The United States," *Bibliotheca Sacra*, XVI (1859), p. 292.

[6] See William Hurlin, "The Free Will Baptists; Their History and Doctrines," *The Christian Review*, XXVII (1862), p. 566; Robert S. Fletcher, *A History of Oberlin College; from Its Foundation through the Civil War* (Oberlin, 1943), I, pp. 291-93; and, for the United Brethren, A. W. Drury, *History of the Church of the United Brethren in Christ* (Dayton, Ohio, 1924), pp. 424-26.

Wesleyan Academy, Wilbraham Connecticut, was co-educational from its founding in 1825; see George Prentice, *Wilbur Fisk* (Boston, 1890), pp. 64-65, 72.

[7] Phoebe Palmer, *Promise of the Father* . . . (Boston, 1859); Wheatley, *op. cit.*, pp. 336, 606-07, 611, 613 ff.; Finney, *op. cit.*, pp. 285, 412-13, 438, 443, 456.

the end of the Civil War removes all doubt that a women's corps had at last been organized to "stand up for Jesus" in the army of the Lord.[8]

A soul-winning laity understandably cared less than ministers about dogmatic distinctions between the sects. New York City and Brooklyn laymen who protested the disruption of the New School-Congregationalist Plan of Union argued that the two churches were "essentially united" on "a sound common orthodoxy, evangelical sentiments, and revivals, and missions, in the hands of the Holy Spirit, for the conversion of the world."[9] Revivalists were likewise foremost among those clergymen who abandoned feuding among themselves in favor of a united front against the devil. All of the principal advocates of the Evangelical Alliance were evangelists. Edward Norris Kirk, Samuel S. Schmucker, Robert Baird, Emerson Andrews, Lyman Beecher, and Methodists Stephen Olin, George Peck, and Abel Stevens attended the fruitless London conference in 1846. They joined laymen of a similar outlook in promoting the Bible, tract, and home mission societies. Inevitably, like Finney, such men emphasized the saving simplicities of the gospel, stressed compassion over creeds, and regretted more and more the weakness which internal dissension brought to Christianity.[10]

In 1850 a Methodist pastor wrote in his denominational quarterly that "the present division of Christians for opinion's sake" was a sin. He declared it his belief that all the bishops were "deeply interested" in the growing movement for church union. The catholicity of both Wesley's work and doctrine was, he asserted, the example all Methodists

[8] Henry Cammann and H. N. Camp, The Charities of New York, Brooklyn and Staten Island (New York, 1868), passim; New York City Tract Society, Thirty-Sixth Annual Report. . . . 1862, pp. 63-68. Cf. W. W. Bennett, A Narrative of the Great Revival which Prevailed in the Southern Armies . . . (Philadelphia, 1877), pp. 55-60; Joseph Belcher, The Religious Denominations in The United States . . . (Philadelphia, 1857), p. 539; and, for a typical objection, "Ought Women to Keep Silence in Religious Meetings," The Watchman and Reflector, Oct. 28, 1858, and its response in the issues for Nov. 18 and 25.

[9] An Earnest Plea of Laymen of the New School Presbyterian and Congregational Churches of New York and Brooklyn . . . (New York, 1856), p. 5; cf. pp. 6, 8, 9.

[10] Cf. Emerson Andrews, Living Life; or Autobiography . . . (Boston, 1875), pp. 72-76; Julia M. Olin, The Life and Letters of Stephen Olin, D.D., L.L.D. (New York, 1853), II, pp. 275-320, passim; Stephen Olin, Works (New York, 1860), II, pp. 466-75; Samuel S. Schmucker, Fraternal Appeal to the American Churches, with a Plan for Catholic Union, on Apostolic Principles (New York, 1839), passim; P. C. Headley, Evangelists in the Church. Philip, A.D. 35, to Moody and Sankey, A.D. 1875 (Boston, 1875), p. 257; Robert Baird, The Progress and Prospects of Christianity . . . (London, 1851), pp. 26-27, 44; Charles Adams, Evangelism in the Middle of the Nineteenth Century . . . (Boston, 1851), p. 21; George O. Peck, Our Country: Its Trial and Its Triumph . . . (New York, 1865), p. 34.

should follow.[11] Soon after, the bishops of the Episcopal Church as well as the Old School newspaper, *The New York Observer,* issued calls for the immediate union of all denominations—one, of course, from the traditionalist, but the other from the evangelical point of view. In 1854 Philip Schaff reported that "the noblest and most pious minds in America" deeply disapproved of the "sect spirit."[12] The Rev. Dexter A. Clapp observed at a Unitarian ordination service in 1856 that "the days of theological difference and separation" seemed to be drawing to a close. Controversial zeal and practical godliness were no longer spiritual synonyms. "Love of the heart" outranked intellectual belief. A "new and vital faith" which emphasized simply "the divine incarnation and human regeneration" was, he believed, "spreading in our Christian community, and beyond us in the wide world."[13]

It is perhaps ironic that the revivals which he and other Unitarians once detested were to bring to flower in 1858 the spirit of tolerance they loved. The union visitation crusades and noonday prayer meetings bathed America's churches in a transfiguring illumination of brotherly love. Hundreds of clergymen whose vision for the salvation of souls had been confined to the borders of their own denomination discovered new horizons on the mount of blessings.

Many considered that the absence of sectarian bigotry was the chief characteristic distinguishing this from previous revivals, though one thoughtful observer remarked, "this spirit of union has been growing for years, and has only gained a fresh development at the present time."[14] At the height of the awakening George Peck, recent editor of *The Christian Advocate and Journal* and *The Methodist Quarterly Review,* summoned prominent New York ministers and laymen to a meeting to study "means to perpetuate the present union of Christian effort" in bring-

[11] Charles Adams, "Wesley the Catholic," *The Methodist Quarterly Review,* XXXII (1850), pp. 177-78, 191; cf. the same author's *Essay on Christian Union* (New York, 1850), *passim.*

[12] Philip Schaff, *America . . .* (New York, 1855), p. 119; "Overtures for Christian Union," *The Puritan Recorder,* Jan. 1, 8, 15, and 22, 1857; Benjamin B. Tyler, A. C. Thomas and others, *A History of the Disciples of Christ, the Society of Friends, the United Brethren in Christ and the Evangelical Association* (Philip Schaff and others, eds., *The American Church History Series,* XII, New York, 1894), p. 801.

[13] *The Monthly Religious Magazine,* XV (1856), pp. 50-51.

[14] A. P. Marvin, "Three Eras of Revivals in The United States," *loc. cit.,* p. 292. See earlier pp. 70-72. Cf. James W. Alexander, *The Revival and Its Lessons . . .* (New York, 1858), p. 11; A. É de Gasparin, *The Uprising of a Great People . . .* (New York, 1861), p. 67.

ing religious services within reach of the poor. Baron Stow, a Baptist pastor in Boston, thought the year suitable for publishing his antisectarian book, *Christian Brotherhood*, a manuscript he had withheld since 1842.[15] In the following decade, Y.M.C.A.'s and Christian Commission units, union prayer meetings, and city-wide revivals joined in proclaiming the triumph of interchurch accord. J. M. Sturtevant, president of Illinois College, wrote in *The New Englander* in 1860 that in the work of Christian collegiate education

the very spirit and principle of denominationalism must be abjured. . . . We must found them upon a broad and comprehensive platform of Evangelical Faith. We must cooperate in sustaining them as Christians, and not as Sectarians. . . . We must esteem them as precious, not as instruments of aggrandizing our Denomination, but as blessings to our country, to mankind, and to the distant future.[16]

The notion that revivalism coincided with bigotry in nineteenth-century Christianity must yield to the contrary facts. In denominations where participation in co-operative religious work became an issue, it was the opponents of revivals who held out stubbornly for the narrower path— Old School Presbyterians, High Church Episcopalians, and Confessional Lutherans.[17] Historians must look elsewhere for the sources of the rampant sectarianism of the 1890's—to such factors and conditions as the statistical competition incited when business methods were applied to church affairs, the quest of the insecure for identity with a group ego, or the search for dogmatic antidotes to the new learning. The last was a bitter potion which had at first been sweetened by mixture with a diluted form of the common evangelical creed. It is true that at the end of the century liberal theology and social Christianity replenished the dying stream of interdenominational harmony. But its headwaters were the springs of brotherly zeal which broke forth in the generation of Robert Baird and A. B. Earle.

Interfaith fellowship gained strength in many quarters from the new stress upon common ethical principles about which no ancient controversies

[15] William C. Conant, *Narratives of Remarkable Conversions and Revival Incidents* . . . (New York, 1858), pp. 411-12; John C. Stockbridge, *A Memoir of the Life and Correspondence of Rev. Baron Stow, D.D.* (Boston, 1871), p. 264. Cf. Georges Fisch, *Nine Months in The United States* . . . (London, 1863), pp. 23, 37-57, *passim*.

[16] J. M. Sturtevant, "Denominational Colleges," *The New Englander*, XVIII (1860), p. 87.

[17] For moderate criticism see J. Few Smith, "Denominationalism, Not Sectarian," *The American Theological Review*, II (1860-61), p. 319.

had raged. From a social point of view this is the most important result of the mid-century awakenings. Ever since 1755, when Jonathan Mayhew had preached in the West Church, Boston, that "those who are really the subjects of Christian piety, or evangelical holiness, are the same men *within*, that they are *without*," liberal Christians had assailed the orthodox for neglecting moral themes.[18] Historians have overlooked the fact, however, that revivalists voiced identical complaints throughout the nineteenth century, usually to larger and more responsive audiences.

By the 1860's, similar ethical outlooks prevailed in both camps. Compare, for example, the argument of a Unitarian pastor during the excitement of 1858 that religion was not a thing to be got but a "holy life to be lived," whose power must be seen in "an improved daily life," a "charity that rises above the prejudice of caste and color," and in a "life full of holy usefulness," with a contemporary description of the "modern piety" which a Baptist pastor thought revivals had established in the churches. "It is now more thoroughly understood," the latter wrote, "that the love of Christ in the heart will constrain the life, not merely to acts of sobriety, temperance and godliness, but to a self-sacrificing zeal in good works."[19]

Though Charles G. Finney and George B. Cheever led the way in applying evangelical insights to social evil, they were not alone. Henry Clay Fish vigorously attacked the divorce of religion and economic principle and urged clergymen to use the communal sharing in the early church at Jerusalem as an instruction to modern businessmen on how "secular tasks may be made sacred." The commercial classes hallowed certain times and places, he observed, but "not the whole of life." They consecrated their pews but not their counting rooms to Christ. Industry was "simply another and more respectable name for worldliness."[20] It was possibly unfair to the Methodists but nevertheless significant that other evangelicals often criticized them for stressing the emotional over the ethical fruits of religious experience.[21]

Revivalists brushed aside Theodore Parker's savage attacks on the out-

[18] Jonathan Mayhew, *Sermons* (Boston, 1855), p. 336.
[19] Solon W. Bush, *The Revival. A Sermon* (Dedham, 1858), p. 11; Jacob Knapp, *Autobiography . . .* (New York, 1868), p. ix. Cf. "Moral Enthusiasm," quoted from *The Christian Inquirer* in *The Watchman and Reflector*, Feb. 19, 1857.
[20] Fish, *Primitive Piety*, pp. 47-48, 61, 70, 75. Cf. Charles G. Finney, *Lectures on Revivals of Religion* (New York, 1898), p. 415; and George I. Rockwood, *Cheever, Lincoln and the Causes of the Civil War* (Worcester, Mass., 1936), pp. 52-53, and *passim*.
[21] Knapp, *op. cit.*, p. ix; *The Christian Advocate and Journal*, Jan. 18, 1855, p. 9. See Chaps. X-XII.

burst of 1858, but they paid sincere attention when Horace Greeley's *New York Tribune*, seconded by Harriet Beecher Stowe, inquired whether it would produce any greater concern for business honesty and the lot of the slave.[22] A thoughtful interpreter of the awakening wrote in Andover's *Bibliotheca Sacra* that its distinguishing mark was a rebuke to the love of riches which had stolen across America's churches and a revitalization of the Christian view of property. Among its supporters, even as with Unitarians, both criticism and praise turned, in fact, on the question of its effect upon practical consecration and on the elevation of both personal and social ethics.[23]

The new and enlarged emphasis upon the idea of Christian love, a theme neatly tailored to the romantic bent of the age, was an integral part of this reorientation of ethical values. Its sources were devious. The advocates of Christian union had long made "brotherly love" the supreme virtue.[24] It was certainly the dominant emotional spark of all successful awakenings, particularly the interdenominational prayer meetings and city-wide revivals popular after 1858. Even Jonathan Edwards became a prophet of love to this sentimental century. The Rev. Tryon Edwards, who had charge of the manuscripts of his distinguished ancestor, chose to publish first in 1852 a series of sermons expounding I Cor. 13.[25]

A Baptist editor wrote in 1857 that there had been three types of Christianity in America: transcendentalism, which he called the "religion of dreams"; dogmatism, which ignored "active love, working faith, and

[22] See the editorials in *The Watchman and Reflector* from March 4 to April 15, 1858, *passim;* cf. *The Christian Register,* April 24, 1858.

[23] A. P. Marvin, "Three Eras of Revivals in The United States," *loc. cit.,* pp. 293, 296-97. Cf., again, earlier, pp. 70-72, with Samuel Irenaeus Prime, *The Power of Prayer* . . . (New York, 1859), pp. 184-86; Erdix Tenney, "A True Revival of Religion," *The Congregational Quarterly,* IV (1862), pp. 241-46; and Gasparin, *op. cit.,* pp. 100-101.

[24] See in Robert Baird's *Christian Union and Religious Memorial,* "The Loving Kindness of God," II (1849), pp. 471-73, a reprint from *The New York Evangelist,* and other articles as follows: "New Testament Teaching on the Mutual Love of Christians," I (1848), pp. 25-28; "Heaven the Region of Love," the same, p. 6; "Christian Love Our Bond of Union," the same, p. 593; "Brotherly Love," I, No. 11 (November, 1848), pp. 15-16; "The Unity of the Heavenly Church," the same, pp. 17-20; "The Prominent Position Brotherly Love Holds in the Bible," II (1849), pp. 137-39.

Cf., for Methodist views, Charles Adams, "Wesley the Catholic," *loc. cit.,* p. 191; W. Scott, "Remarks on I Corinthians, xiii, 9-13," *The Methodist Quarterly Review,* XXXII (1850), pp. 377, 380-82, 384; and the sermon by James V. Watson, "Love to God and Man—Christian Union," in Davis W. Clark, ed., *Methodist Episcopal Pulpit: a Collection of Original Sermons from Living Ministers of the Methodist Episcopal Church* (New York, 1850), pp. 274-75.

[25] Jonathan Edwards, *Charity and Its Fruits; or, Christian Love as Manifested in the Heart and Life* (New York, 1852).

operative benevolence"; and the one which was "of faith and works in the true Gospel of Jesus." That religion which "shuns the poor and blushes when in contact with the lowly," he declared, had failed to heed the Bible denunciation of those who cry "Lord, Lord" and neglect charity; "to reach perfection and heaven, men must walk in active love." [26] To those who argued that agitating the slavery issue was shattering brotherly ties as well as dishonoring the central evangelical theme, "Christ and Him crucified," George Barrell Cheever, in whose church Finney preached during the revival of 1858, penned a classic reply:

But what is it to truly preach Christ and him crucified, except to pour the light of a Saviour's sufferings and death upon men's sins, that in that light they may see and feel "the exceeding sinfulness of sin," their own sins, and the sins of the community, and be led, out of love to Christ, and for his sake, to renounce them? . . . Many are very willing to hear about Christ being crucified *for them*, who will not listen for a moment to the proposed crucifixion of their sins *for him*, especially those sins which they call organic, those that have the sanction and protection of human law. . . . But for what purpose was the gospel given, but to turn men from their iniquities, disclosing and condemning them in the light of the cross? [27]

Three decades of such evangelical moralizing lay back of the summary of Christian ethics which Mark Hopkins published in 1869 under the title *The Law of Love, and Love as Law*. His book symbolized the emotional and intellectual redirection of American Christianity which prepared the way for a social gospel.[28]

Theologically, the new evangelical synthesis required frank abandonment of the Old Calvinism. Methodists and, to a lesser degree, Lutherans, Freewill Baptists, Episcopalians, Cumberland Presbyterians, Disciples of Christ, United Brethren, Moravians, and Winebrennerians had long evidenced the appeal in a Christian democratic society of the Arminian doctrines of free will, free grace, and unlimited hope for the conversion

[26] *The Watchman and Reflector*, Dec. 17, 1857. Cf. Fish, *op. cit.*, p. 130; L. P. Brockett, "The Relations of Christianity to Humanitarian Effort," *The Methodist Quarterly Review*, XL (1858), pp. 455-57, 470; and William S. Plumer, *Vital Godliness: a Treatise on Experimental and Practical Piety* (New York, 1864), pp. 375-93.

[27] George Barrell Cheever, *God Against Slavery: and the Freedom and Duty of the Pulpit to Rebuke It, as a Sin against God* (New York, 1857), p. 54. Rockwood, *Cheever, Lincoln*, pp. 40-55, contains a sketch of Cheever's life.

[28] See Mark Hopkins, *The Law of Love, and Love as Law* . . . (New York, 1869); Complaints about Nehemiah Adams's revival sermon, "God is Love," in *The Christian Review*, XXIV (1859), p. 494; and later, pp. 158-61.

of all men.[29] The view of natural ability which Nathaniel W. Taylor
accepted in the 1820's and Charles G. Finney adopted ten years later was, in
fact, more extreme than that which Methodists held. Both Taylor and
Finney arrived at it through their experience in revivals. By the 1840's the
drift of Calvinists toward Arminianism and of the Orthodox toward the
"Taylorism" they once had scorned was noticeable everywhere. The idea
of personal predestination could hardly survive amidst the evangelists'
earnest entreaties to "come to Jesus."[30]

Robert Baird, for example, heatedly denied on one occasion Alexis de
Tocqueville's verdict that American religion was less a doctrine than a
commonly admitted opinion. Yet elsewhere Baird noted happily that the
weight of theological conviction here was tending toward "the simplest and
most scriptural Christianity" whose gospel was "glad tidings to all men."[31]
In New England, Arminianism progressed so rapidly among Baptists as
nearly to destroy the *raison d'être* of the Freewill group. Early in 1858
the editors of Boston's *Congregationalist* answereed one of The Puritan
Recorder's many editorial assaults on their orthodoxy by declaring it doubtful "if any creed or church outside of Hard-Shell Baptists avow and defend
all the principles of original Calvinism." Pointing to The Recorder's own
compromises with modern thought, they asked "how far persons may adopt
actual Arminianism" in preaching "a modified doctrine of original sin;
a partial free will; a universal atonement; man's activity in regeneration,
etc., etc.," and still claim to be original and thorough Calvinists. The Unitarian newspaper reported the incident with ill-concealed glee.[32]

The great revival provided those who halted between the two opinions

[29] D. D. Whedon, "Doctrines of Methodism," *Bibliotheca Sacra*, XIX (1862), pp. 243-
45; Adams, *Evangelism*, pp. 40, 46; Belcher, *Religious Denominations*, pp. 696-97; John
J. Butler, *Natural and Revealed Theology* . . . (Dover, N. H., 1861), pp. 162-69 and
passim (for the Freewill Baptists); Tyler and others, *op. cit.*, pp. 121 and *passim*; Stephen
H. Tyng, *Lectures on the Law and the Gospel* (New York, 1848), pp. 234, 238, 243.
[30] George Duffield, "The Doctrines of the New School Presbyterian Church," *Bibliotheca
Sacra*, XX (1863), pp. 608, 614; Sidney Earl Mead, *Nathaniel William Taylor, 1786-
1858, a Connecticut Liberal* (Chicago, 1942), pp. 125, 223-24. Cf. Taylor's *Man a Free
Agent Without the Aid of Divine Grace* ("Doctrinal Tracts," No. 2, New Haven, 1818),
disputing the Methodist position, with the review of T. F. R. Mercein, *Natural Goodness*
(New York, 1854), in *The Methodist Quarterly Review*, XXXVIII (1855), p. 144.
[31] Robert Baird, *Religion in America* (New York, 1844), p. 291; cf. pp. 32, 299-302.
[32] See *Church History*, XXXIV (1955), 175-76, a review of Norman A. Baxter,
History of the Freewill Baptists; A Study in New England Separatism (Unpublished
Ph.D. dissertation, Harvard University, 1954); "The Freedom of the Will Not Destroyed
in Regeneration," *The Watchman and Reflector*, Nov. 23, 1854; and "The Recorder vs.
The Congregationalist," *The Christian Register*, March 13, 1858.

with thundering assurance that the Divine will was ready to dispense grace in enlarged measure. The sermons, tracts, and books which "Calvinist" ministers prepared for the edification of seeking souls showed a fine disregard for Mr. Calvin's five points.[33] Most startling of all was James W. Alexander's declaration that every man can be saved if he "yields to the moving of the gracious Spirit, takes God at His word, and makes the universal offer his own particular salvation." *The Independent*, needless to say, lost no time in praising the good doctor's volume. When *The Presbyterian* responded with obvious embarrassment that Alexander's position was no different from that which his Old School brethren held, Beecher fired back: "This is the theology of Edwards, Dwight, and Taylor, the theology of New England, but it is not the theology of Princeton."[34]

Now thoroughly alarmed, orthodox forces rallied to launch two quarterly journals designed to halt the heresy among the clergy. *The Boston Review*, promoted by the conservative newspaper, *The Puritan Recorder*, dusted off the old accusation that Arminianism had spawned Unitarianism and compared the doctrine of free will to the temptations of Bunyan's Pilgrim. The first words in *The American Theological Review*, which began publication in New York in 1859, were a stinging rebuke of

this breaking away from old usages and conventional restraints; this re-investigation of moral principles, and reconstruction of ethical codes; this transcendental soaring of perverted minds for the absolute, the perfect; this putting forth of new schemes of reform, and new modes of explicating theological truths. . . . Sound theological views were never more important than at the present juncture of partial waking to Christian responsibilities.[35]

[33] *The New York Pulpit in the Revival of 1858—a Memorial Volume of Sermons* (New York, 1858), *passim*; see especially "Coming to Christ," pp. 187-96, by M. S. Hutton, minister of the Washington Square Dutch Reformed Church, and "What Shall I Do to Be Saved," p. 203, by William Ives Buddington, pastor of the Clinton Avenue Congregational Church. See also the address of the Rev. H. Dunning, pastor of the First Presbyterian Church, Baltimore, in Y.M.C.A., Baltimore, *Proceedings of the All-Day Prayer Meeting . . . September 27, 1859* (Baltimore, 1859), pp. 11-12; and the emphasis upon "only believing" in J. W. Alexander, *op. cit.*, pp. 13, 88, 111, 113. Cf. Edward N. Kirk, *The Waiting Saviour* (Boston, 1865), *passim*; Albert Barnes, *The Way of Salvation* (Philadelphia, 1863), *passim*; and *The Christian Review*, XXIV (1860), pp. 316-17, for comments on Francis Wayland, *Salvation by Christ* (Boston, 1859).

[34] *The Independent*, Dec. 30, 1858 and Jan. 6, 1859.

[35] *The American Theological Review*, I (1859), pp 1-2 ff. Cf. "Spurious Revivals," the same, pp. 82, 83 and the attack on "spurious conversions" in "The Theology of Edwards, as Shown in His Treatise Concerning the Religious Affections," the same, pp. 199-200. See also "Theology, Old and New," *The Boston Review*, I (1861), 97-113, *passim*; "About Beginnings," the same, p. 5 complaining of the theological ignorance of

But the triumphant march of revivalism and free grace was not to be halted by the apparition of the Rev. Cotton Mather's ghost. Arminians had been defending themselves from such attacks for three centuries. Of course God was sovereign, declared revival advocate Levi Sternberg to a Hartwick Lutheran Seminary audience, and no human means would move him if he had not in his sovereignty chosen to work together with man to give the Holy Spirit to those who ask him. A "divine and human co-operation" seemed to such men the Bible plan to save the world.[36]

Methodist educator Wilbur Fisk had long since defined the Wesleyan answer to the charge that his sect preached salvation by works: men were saved by grace alone, but not without exercising the moral power of choice which grace had granted them. Thus Wesley's followers rejected both what John McClintock, editor of *The Methodist Quarterly Review,* called the Oberlin theology's "flippant denial" of man's depravity and the old orthodoxy's extreme insistence upon it. McClintock protested the fashion among liberals to "identify Christianity with Calvinism" and thus to "load Scriptural Christianity with the sins of a superannuated theology." [37] When in 1860 a former student of Nathaniel Taylor ventured to assert in *The New Englander* that his teacher was responsible for establishing the doctrine of free will in America, Daniel Whedon, by then editor of the Methodist quarterly, took him sharply to task.

Principles of divine government which he, with the mass of Dr. Taylor's pupils, imagined to be original with their master, and for which they proclaim him "A Newton in Theology," have for a century been embodied in Wesleyan theology; have in past times been patent in the horn-book of every Methodist circuit-rider, and have constituted much of our strength in demolishing Calvinism, antinomianism, and sin.

"Whether this reviewer happens to be aware of it or not," Whedon added,

---

the younger clergy; and attacks on Nathaniel W. Taylor's theology and Henry Ward Beecher's lack of it, the same, pp. 129-54, and II (1862), pp. 1-24.

[36] Charles Adams, *Evangelism,* p. 19; L. Sternberg, "Revivals," *The Evangelical Quarterly Review,* XV (1864), p. 278. Cf. the immensely complicated reasoning of *The Watchman and Reflector,* Aug. 20 and Dec. 3, 1857, endeavoring to maintain the form of orthodoxy.

[37] George Prentice, *Wilbur Fisk,* pp. 90, 111-38, analyzes Fisk's book, *Calvinistic Controversy. Embracing a Sermon on Predestination and Election* (New York, 1837). Cf. John McClintock, "The Conflict of the Ages," *The Methodist Quarterly Review,* XXXVI (1854), pp. 176, 189-90; and "The Princeton Review on Arminianism and Grace," the same, XXXVIII (1856), pp. 257-59, 261, 263, 265.

"the reality of human freedom is the great point of division between Arminianism and Calvinism." [88]

The strength of the new Samson was its unshorn orthodoxy. Evangelical Arminians, unlike radical liberals, would join as humbly as any in the solemn confession, "All we like sheep have gone astray, we have turned every one to his own way; and the Lord hath laid on Him the iniquity of us all." But their Christ was the good Shepherd who sought out even the last, lost sheep; their God, the loving Father who welcomed every returning prodigal to a life of holiness and love. Precisely because theirs was a new, emotionally dynamic combination of old tenets, rather than a radical departure, they were able to accomplish what Emerson and Parker could not.

To be sure, Arminian orthodoxy can be just as dry as Jonathan Edwards' bones and just as sterile of saving compassion. But in the nineteenth century it was nurtured in the warm tides of revival fervor and conditioned by a controversy which made it as conscious as it was cautious of its liberalism.

Whether as a religious doctrine it really affected the social outlook of the churches is a problem heavily if inconclusively documented by scores of writers who have found Unitarianism's denial of human depravity the fountain of its enlightened social views. Unless their work is utterly pointless, it must be of some significance that America's largest sect laid most stress on man's freedom and God's readiness to "cleanse us from all unrighteousness," and that by the time of the Civil War all but the Scotch Presbyterian, Antimission Baptist, and German Reformed denominations in the Calvinist fold had moved decidedly toward free will. Wherever the belief that the saving power of God was at work in the world was applied to social relationships, it was bound to sustain a more liberal social ethic. The problem, as we shall see, was how it might be applied.

An important by-product of revivalism's triumph over Calvinism was that American theology stood increasingly upon the practical, empirical foundation of Christian experience. Finney remarked after his first visit to England, "I found that their theology was to a very great extent dogmatic, in the sense that it rested on authority. . . . When I began to preach, they were surprised that I reasoned with people." [39] Ten years later a Baptist editor and promoter of revivals warned that utilitarianism was pulling men's minds from the hope of heaven. But he did not realize the pragmatism implicit in his own complaint that theology had remained "meagre and dry," lacking an "internal, vigorous life," because its principles had not yet been reconstructed to express "the realities of the spiritual life in which they are founded." [40] Many Methodists thought that their greatest contribution to Christianity was "heart earnestness," or the belief that sanctified affections, not the intellect, were the chief aggresive instrument of the gospel. "The truth," said revivalist Levi Sternberg in 1865, "meets a response in Christian experience." [41]

In the same romantic-pragmatic mood Mark Hopkins arranged the wedding of Puritan virtue and the pursuit of happiness; man's end was neither holiness nor happiness alone, but a holy happiness, a happy holiness. As a Methodist preacher put it, "Godliness is the sum of our duty and the summit of our bliss." The offspring of Zeno and Epicurus had at last joined hands in Christian love. [42]

A prophet might have foreseen that such sentimentalism would undermine the intellectual bulwarks which had withstood the earliest onslaughts of liberal theology. A new generation would trust the Holy Spirit to be "the conservator of orthodoxy." The joyous adulation of "experience" strengthened, too, the credulous strain in the American character. A people grown romantically attached to the phenomenal in religion would at length find a place for Mary Baker Eddy, P. T. Barnum, Billy Sunday, and William James, professor of philosophy at Harvard University and author of *The Varieties of Religious Experience*.

Thus did the national faith of the nineteenth century approach a measure of integration. Lay-centered, tolerant of minor sectarian differ-

[39] *Memoirs*, p. 451; cf. Finney, *Lectures on Revivals of Religion* (New York, 1868), pp. 375-92. Richard C. Wolf, "The Middle Period, 1800-1870, the Matrix of Modern American Christianity," *Religion in Life, a Christian Quarterly of Opinion and Discussion*, XXII (1952-53), p. 83, contains comments on this theme.

[40] *The Watchman and Reflector*, Nov. 30, 1854. Cf. *Harper's Monthly*, XXI (1860), pp. 122-23.

[41] J. McClintock, "Stephen Olin," *The Methodist Quarterly Review*, XXXVI (1854), p. 24, contains a similar statement; see Levi Sternberg, "Pilate's Question," *The Evangelical Quarterly Review*, XVI (1865), pp. 587-88; and W. T. Willey, "The Spirit and Mission of Methodism," *The Methodist Quarterly Review*, XXXVI (1854), pp. 57-76, *passim*.

[42] See the review of Hopkins's *Lectures on Moral Science* (New York, 1862) in *The Christian Review*, XXVIII (1863), pp. 328-29; and Clark, *M. E. Pulpit*, p. 332.

ences, ethically vital and democratically Arminian, it was a creed of practical piety, and of compassion which went beyond fine intentions. Though still centered in the historic Christian views of man and God and of salvation through Christ, it was actively devoted to making the world a place where men might more readily choose the good path.

VI

Evangelical Unitarianism

෬~෨

The growing rapprochement between evangelicals and the conservative group dominant in the American Unitarian Association illustrates most dramatically the wide significance of the new patterns of Protestant work and thought. By 1854 the Baptist newspaper in Boston was confident that the "right wing" Unitarians were "steadily advancing towards a pure, evangelical faith." [1] During the next three years the religious press pulsed with a hopeful discussion of this theme, set in motion by two Unitarian ministers, George E. Ellis and Frederic Dan Huntington. That every periodical serving theirs and the Universalist denomination participated suggests how strong was the reaction against Theodore Parker's radicalism.

Huntington, youthful pastor at the South Church, Boston, and editor of *The Monthly Religious Magazine*, explained that the chief Unitarian blind spot was to think that the orthodox actually regarded the Father as vengeful, when they in fact identified him with the Saviour's love and thought the Atonement the crowning work of his compassion. Huntington questioned whether men were truly liberals who were "tolerant of skepticism and persecutors of orthodoxy." In 1855 he declared that a large group of Unitarians believed the essence of Christianity to be a "special, supernatural redemption from sin, in Christ Jesus" the "eternally begotten Son of God," the "ever-living present Head of the Church and personal intercessor for his disciples." The next year when a Miss Plummer, of Salem, endowed at Harvard a "professorship of the heart, not the head," whose incumbent she wished to serve as minister and friend to the students, the university corporation elected Huntington to the post and proceeded to build the Appleton Chapel for his use.[2]

---

[1] *The Watchman and Reflector*, March 23, 1854. Cf. *The Independent*, Jan. 2, 1851, summarizing a recent amicable discussion with *The Christian Register*.

[2] *The Monthly Religious Magazine*, XIV (1855), pp. 53, 56-57; XV (1856), pp. 110-11; Cf. the same, p. 104 and XVI (1856), pp. 44-45. Robert Baird quoted the 1855 article in his *State and Prospects of Religion in America* . . . (London, 1855), pp. 88-91. See also,

Ellis, meanwhile, published in *The Christian Examiner* a long series of articles seeking to conciliate the Congregationalists. Both sides ought now to recognize, he urged, that neither humanism nor Calvinism any longer exerted a powerful religious influence. The only question still dividing them was whether Christ possessed "the underived honors of the Godhead" so as to be "an object of worship and prayer and of our ultimate religious dependence." The Harvard Corporation made Ellis professor of systematic theology the next year. In his inaugural address he proclaimed that the spirit and power of the "old orthodoxy" which was dead among Congregationalists ruled again at Harvard. That the current of Unitarian preaching was moving away from the "excesses of rationalism" toward a "more fervent and heart-satisfying Christology" and a "religion which springs up from experience" seemed to one of their prominent pastors a fact "too obvious to be more than stated." [3]

The retreat from radicalism could not have taken this direction had not orthodoxy been so recently and powerfully liberalized by the common evangelistic faith. The new drive toward Christian union, for example, matched the long Unitarian antipathy to sectarianism and also magnified experience over creeds. The age had discovered, as one put it, an earnest belief in Christ which was antisectarian in nature and displayed as well "a wider range of inquiry and toleration than the most indifferent skepticism." Huntington praised the more earnest catholicity of evangelical Unitarians and professed the hope that soon the gospel of inward love and self-forgetful devotion to Christ would "take the place of all sectarian strifes . . . and absorb the entire church in an undivided and joyful amity.[4] His associates soon discovered, as had he, that the quest of personal religious

Arria S. Huntington, *Memoir and Letters of Frederic Dan Huntington* . . . (Boston, 1906), pp. 103, 168.

[3] See *The Watchman and Reflector,* Aug. 13, 1857, and Solon W. Bush, "The Autumnal Convention," *The Monthly Religious Magazine,* XVI (1856), p. 256. Cf. "Stumbling-Blocks of Liberalism," the same, pp. 300, 303-04.

Ellis's articles were reproduced in George E. Ellis, *Half-Century of Unitarian Controversy* (Boston, 1857), from which, p. 105, the quotation is taken; cf. pp. viii, xxiv, 5, 7, and the essay, "The New Theology," pp. 343-405, *passim.* *The Christian Register,* Jan. 19, and 26, 1856, reviewed the first article as well as an editorial on "Fellowship with Unitarians" which had appeared in *The New York Evangelist;* succeeding issues carried more of the series. See also "What Does It Mean?" *The Puritan Recorder,* Jan. 29, 1857; and *The Methodist Quarterly Review,* XLI (1859), pp. 386-401.

[4] *The Monthly Religious Magazine,* XV (1856), p. 53; Dexter A. Clapp, "Sects, the Broken Body of the Church," the same, XVII (1857), p. 151. See also, the same, XIV (1855), p. 53; XV (1856), pp. 264-65, 267; XVII (1857), p. 3; and *The Watchman and Reflector,* March 23, 1854. Cf. Ellis, *Unitarian Controversy,* pp. xiii-xiv.

experience led them to a new appreciation of the doctrines of the Trinity and the Atonement. For the foundations of a "living faith," one of them wrote, was not any system of dogmatic truths, but "Christ, the Saviour who died . . . [and] is made unto us wisdom and righteousness and sanctification and redemption."[5]

Revivalism's rejection of predestination and emphasis upon the continuous availability of the Holy Spirit proved equally helpful. Unitarian affirmations of the latter doctrine in 1858 compare identically with one made by an Episcopalian, seeking to show that revivals were unnecessary, and others by a Methodist and an Old School Presbyterian declaring them to be indispensable! The new stress upon the reality of the Divine presence in Christian prayer was a variant of the same theme.[6] Thus the Rev. Edward E. Hale, Huntington's successor at the South Church, welcomed Finney's preaching at Park Street in 1858 as an illustration of how "orthodoxy melts in the fire."

The churches of the sad confession, at an epoch like this, come up to our position. . . . He believes, as we believe, that the tide of the Spirit is always at high water. And so, in his own side of the church, they criticize him, and his, as much as they dare, as "Perfectionists." . . . Nor does he reject the criticism. . . . The doctrine beneath [his] language is the doctrine from which the Old Calvinism is to meet its inevitable doom. It is the Quaker doctrine, the Methodist doctrine, the Ultra-Unitarian doctrine, the Transcendental doctrine —that God is, every moment, with every child, in a union so close that nothing can be compared with it.[7]

[5] J. I. T. Coolidge, "The Foundations of a Living Faith," *The Monthly Religious Magazine,* XVI (1856), p. 292. Cf. L. S. S., "What Is the True Doctrine of 'the Cross,' Viewed as the Central Doctrine of the Gospel?" the same, XIV (1855), pp. 74-75; Horace Bushnell, "The Christian Trinity a Practical Truth," the same, XIII (1855), pp. 113, 115; S. W. Dutton, "The Relation of the Atonement to Holiness," the same, XV (1856), p. 20; and "The Essence of Christianity," the same, XVIII (1857), p. 28. See also, for an interesting interpretation, James Freeman Clarke, *The Hour Which Cometh, and Now Is: Sermons Preached in Indiana-Place Chapel, Boston* (Boston, 1877), pp. 19-20.

[6] Cf. the statements in *The Christian Register,* Feb. 9, 1856 and Apr. 10, 1858, with anon., *The Revival System and the Paraclete. A Series of Articles from the Church Journal* (New York, 1858), p. 32; Samuel Irenaeus Prime, *Five Years of Prayer, with the Answers* (New York, 1864), p. 8; and James Waddell Alexander, *The Revival and Its Lessons . . .* (New York, 1858), p. 13.
See also Frederic Dan Huntington, "Public Prayers in Colleges," *The Monthly Religious Magazine,* XVIII (1857), pp. 270, 271; and L. J. H., "A Sinner," the same, XVI (1856), pp. 205, 206.

[7] *The Watchman and Reflector,* Apr. 15, 1858, quoted this sermon at length; the issue for Apr. 29 reviewed favorably Huntington's sermon, *Permanent Realities of Religion, and the Present Religious Interest* (Boston, 1858), which made the same point. Cf., again,

The idea of the Holy Spirit's nearness seemed to such men an evangelical version of the transcendentalist conception of immanent divinity.[8]

In a reminiscence published in 1860, Rufus Ellis, now editor of Huntington's old magazine, reasoned that an Emerson was bound to appear in New England once Unitarianism had replaced orthodoxy with "a merely historical Christianity,—a reproduction, with miraculous attestations, of the Religion of Nature, . . . a Gospel without a Holy Ghost." Ellis recalled that during the 1840's the shock of radicalism had divided the student body at Harvard Divinity School into "skeptics, mystics, and dyspeptics." Antipathy toward the extravagances of revivalists had thereafter strengthened their tendency to overlook the agency of the Holy Spirit, by which, as he put it, "the miracles of conversion are continually repeated in Christendom and the conclusive evidence of the truth of the Gospel afforded to the individual soul." [9] His advice that the doctrine of a "Divine influx" replace that of self-development in Unitarian preaching illustrates how liberals and evangelicals were finding common ground in Evangelical Arminianism. One camp rejected radical humanism while the other dismembered Orthodox Calvinism. Both would join man's will to God's grace to set the sinner free.[10]

Preaching which called for a morally transforming regeneration and a life of practical service likewise made evangelical faith palatable to liberal Christians. Horace Bushnell's sermon emphasizing this theme was echoed among them in many quarters.[11] Several Unitarian clergymen agreed that they had erred in ignoring the need of a personal spiritual relationship with Christ, of the piety they now saw to be the foundation of good works. The

The Christian Register, Feb. 9, 1856, and James Freeman Clarke, Revivals, Natural and Artificial (Boston, 1860), passim.

[8] Sidney E. Mead, Nathaniel W. Taylor, 1786-1858, A Connecticut Liberal (Chicago, 1942), pp. 125-27, shows the same parallel for an earlier period.

[9] Rufus Ellis, "Our Gross Injustice to the Great Body of Unitarian Believers," The Monthly Religious Magazine, XXV (1861), pp. 256, 257-59.

[10] A. P. Marvin, "Three Eras of Revivals in The United States," Bibliotheca Sacra, XVI (1859), pp. 285-90. Cf. George E. Ellis, "The New Theology," The Christian Examiner, LXII (1857), pp. 321-22, 328, 337, 341-42, and especially 353-54, with the same author's affirmations of human ability fifteen years before in Regeneration and Sanctification. Two Sermons Preached . . . Sunday, March 6, 1842 (Charlestown, 1842), pp. 11, 19.

[11] Horace Bushnell, "The True Problem of Christian Experience," The Monthly Religious Magazine, XX (1858), p. 119; James Walker, "The Gospel a Remedy for Sin," the same, XVIII (1857), pp. 218, 220, 222-23; F. D. Huntington, "Three Dispensations in History and in the Soul," the same, XX (1858), p. 167; H. M., "Inward Renewal, the Work of the Spirit," the same, pp. 289-97, and passim.

kingdom of Christ could not be ushered in by benevolent enterprises and charitable societies, said one, unless these were supported by "personal consecration, the enthusiasm of holy hearts," and "the union of spirits with Christ." What Unitarians needed, he cried, was the Pentecostal baptism of the Holy Ghost![12]

Another declared that their churches were at a "dull, lifeless standstill" because in opposing the vicarious theory of the atonement, they had ignored the supernatural power of God in regeneration—something which the orthodox, despite their error in symbolizing this power solely by the cross, never had done. He urged both groups to recognize Christ himself, the living Saviour, "as the indwelling eternal life—the Comforter and Sanctifier." They ought, he said, to abandon their preoccupation with a purely objective atonement on the one side, and with an equally objective moral example on the other to seek "the SUBJECTIVE POWER that floweth out of the presence, invisible but real, of the mediatorial Christ."[13]

Similar but more orthodox views in a sermon which S. W. S. Dutton delivered to the Congregational General Association of Connecticut and published in Huntington's magazine in 1856 excited wide comment.[14] Even those who criticized it displayed an utter seriousness about personal holiness, personal consecration. James I. T. Coolidge, pastor of the Purchase Street Unitarian Church, Boston, and Huntington's intimate friend, prayed that Christians everywhere might be taught to surrender their whole souls "to the very Lamb of God, who taketh away the sins of the world." Thus might they live "a life guided, ruled, sanctified in every detail and every relation, by faith in the Son of God, who loved us, and gave himself for us."[15] Little wonder that, while preparing a sermon for Pentecost Sunday, 1858—the year of the great revival—this pastor should find himself writing the words "Trinity in unity and unity in Trinity." Coolidge

[12] "Christian Earnestness," the same, XVII (1857), pp. 154, 155, 158-59. Cf. George W. Briggs, "Civilization Not Regeneration," the same, pp. 299, 300; "The Inefficiency of the Church of Christ," the same, XV (1856), pp. 39, 41; and H. S. E., "A Glance at Ourselves," the same, XVI (1856), pp. 169, 170.

The masthead of *The Christian Register* bore during these years the slogan, "Liberty, Holiness, Love"!

[13] L. S. C., "What Is the True Doctrine of the Cross," *loc. cit.*, pp. 65, 68-69, 72, 75.

[14] S. W. S. Dutton, "The Relation of the Atonement to Holiness," *The Monthly Religious Magazine* XV (1856), pp. 32-33; see also, in the same volume, pp. 106-12, 194-206, *passim*, 235-57, *passim*, 320-23, 359-61. Cf. Arria S. Huntington, *op. cit.*, pp. 154-55.

[15] J. I. T. Coolidge, "The Foundations of a Living Faith," *loc. cit.*, p. 294; cf. "The Essence of Christianity," *The Monthly Religious Magazine*, XVIII (1857), p. 28, and those who criticized Dutton, the same, XV (1856), pp. 108, 236, 255-56.

realized at once that this was his vital faith, and at the close of the sermon offered his resignation. The doctrine of the Holy Spirit, he testified, whose awakening power in the soul had guided him to the Father by way of the Son, had set him firmly on the right road.[16]

Frederic Dan Huntington's pilgrimage into the Episcopal ministry added a dramatic note to this story. The controversy over Dutton's sermon led the Plummer Professor of Morals and preacher at the Appleton Chapel to announce that the magazine he edited must henceforth be regarded as "throughly unsectarian." It would be devoted to the "great doctrines of the New Testament, repentance, regeneration, faith, holiness, the redemption by Christ, humble dependence on God, the supernatural gifts of the Holy Spirit, the personal presence of Christ to the disciple and the Church" and "the unity of Christ's body."

Huntington later testified to the intense agony which the conflict between his increasingly evangelical views and the strong ties of sentiment and belief which bound him to the Unitarian people brought on during his years at Harvard. He had at first aimed "to find a way of so urging the truths of Christ's divine nature and mediatorship, the necessity of a personal relationship to Him, both subjective and sacramental, and the inspiring power of His cross upon character, charities, and missions" as to secure a response to them without needless opposition.[17] By 1858, the decisive year, he doubted if this course were possible, though he could not yet share his friend Coolidge's statement of Trinitarianism. Some time during the next twelve months "the light entered his soul," and he wrote the sermon, "Life, Salvation and Comfort for Man in the Divine Trinity," published in December, 1859. Meanwhile, across Harvard Yard, George E. Ellis leaned as far as he could toward Trinitarianism, as though to woo his friend to stay within the fold.[18]

The event made a profound impact upon New England. Huntington's personal future became a chief topic of discussion. Influential representa-

[16] Arria S. Huntington, *op. cit.*, p. 163; *The Watchman and Reflector*, Aug. 5, 1858. The significance of the perfectionist note struck in many of the foregoing references will be dealt with later.

[17] *The Monthly Religious Magazine*, XVIII (1857), pp. 1-4; Arria S. Huntington, *op. cit.*, pp. 154, 161.

[18] Arria Huntington, *op. cit.*, pp. 163-65; Frederic D. Huntington, *Christian Believing and Living* (New York, 1859), pp. 355-418, *passim*; George E. Ellis, *The Christian Trinity: the Doctrine of God, the Father; Jesus Christ; and the Holy Spirit. A Discourse Preached in Harvard Church, Charlestown, February 3, 1860* (Charlestown, 1860), pp. 4-6, and *passim*.

tives of every denomination extended him a welcoming hand. A large and distinguished group, including the president-elect of Harvard, C. C. Felton, and Manton Eastburn, Low Church Episcopalian Bishop of Massachusetts, wished him to remain where he was, arguing that his drift toward evangelicalism was well known at the time of his election to the Harvard post. Huntington's conscience was far too sensitive to permit this course. He had twice earlier submitted his resignation and left it to President James Walker's discrimination, fearing that to remain would be unfair both to the parents of students who deemed his views erroneous and to those who might readily accept them save for uncertainty as to what they really were. He presented his formal resignation to the Harvard Corporation January 19, 1860, and on the eve of Ash Wednesday made application to be considered a candidate for Episcopal orders. He believed that he had chosen that one among the evangelical communions which best exemplified the authority of Scripture and visible church and which, by the beauty and dignity of its worship, best symbolized the spiritual realities of the Christian religion. That ministers in other sects appreciated the sincerity and liberality of his choice is evident from the "charity" lectures with which they kept him busy during the months following, while he was subject to the canon forbidding the unordained to preach.[19]

Admitted to the Order of Deacons in September, Huntington immediately became pastor of a new congregation, gathered from recent converts out of the Unitarian and other faiths, who wished to locate in the newly developed section beyond the Boston Public Garden, now known as the Back Bay. His original idea was to build there a great "People's Church," in which pew rents would be abandoned in favor of an evangelistic program made sophisticated by Episcopal forms of worship. The expense of constructing the church building combined with the wealthy nature of the new community to make the plan unworkable. But its spirit lived on in the earnest, personal service for which the congregation was carefully organized, in the Sunday school and mission chapel in the slums where Huntington loved to preach, and in the heart and life of the pastor who exhibited the "people's religion" of the nineteenth century at its best.[20]

[19] Arria S. Huntington, op. cit., pp. 167, 168-69, 174-75, 181-95, passim, 197, 198, 209-10. Cf. Frederic D. Huntington, Lectures on Human Society (New York, 1860).

[20] Arria S. Huntington, op. cit., pp. 214, 216, 218-19, 240-43. For the defensive reaction of certain Unitarian clergymen see Thomas Starr King, Trinitarianism Not the Doctrine of the New Testament (Boston, 1860); Thomas Starr King and Orville Dewey, The New Discussion of the Trinity; Containing Notices of Professor Huntington's Recent Defense of That Doctrine (Boston, 1860).

The changes which the new evangelism wrought affected in some similar fashion every significant religious movement of the last half of the century. What makes particularly interesting their impact upon Unitarians is the way in which the spiritual heirs of William Ellery Channing discovered the similarity of the moral and social aims of the evangelicals to their own. By 1840 both Calvinism and humanism had been weighed in the balances and found wanting. The yearnings of Finney on the one hand and Emerson on the other for a vitally transforming faith made this fact plain. But transcendentalism was not to be the answer. Erratic, sophisticated, and at odds with popular religious prejudices, its champions were as much inclined to withdraw from the world as they were to reform it. Their doctrine could serve only as a symbol, not a solace, for the nation's spiritual hunger. In fact, it widened the breach which Channing had opened between the enlightened and the Orthodox.

The Holy Ghost's outpouring on the churches, a transcendent experience of another sort, was the arc which closed the gap. It was not the logic of liberal seminary professors, but the roaring revivals of the 1850's which broke the grip of Calvinism on nineteenth-century Protestantism. The evangelists substituted an existential for the dogmatic concept of original sin, picturing it as a diseased condition of the soul rather than a legal burden of guilt for Adam's fall. More important, as we shall see in the following three chapters, they spread the faith that divine grace was available here and now to cleanse it all away. Sin was real, but God's love in Christ could conquer it—and so regenerate the nation and save the world.

VII

The Holiness Revival
at Oberlin

⟨∞⟩

Christian perfectionism has lately been in such low esteem that church historians have sadly neglected one of the nineteenth century's most persistent and socially significant religious themes. They have depicted it as an illustration of frontier religious radicalism, or, at best, an outgrowth of Methodist earnestness which responsible church leaders neither wanted nor accepted. Actually the hunger for holiness lay near the heart of every movement concerned with developing a more meaningful Christianity.

The revivals of the Jacksonian era produced in Charles G. Finney a perfectionism quite as radical as any that John Wesley's followers ever taught. Since the Oberlin doctrine did not look back to an eighteenth-century prophet, but rather grew out of the religious climate of the age, its history serves well to introduce the current which swept across American Protestantism between 1835 and the end of the Civil War.

Soon after Finney settled in the pastorate of the Chatham Street Chapel, New York City, he tells us that he gave himself to earnest study of the Bible until his mind "was satisfied that an altogether higher and more stable form of Christian life was attainable, and was the privilege of all Christians." John Wesley's *Plain Account of Christian Perfection* and the biography of James Brainerd Taylor fell into his hands during 1836, about the time he began a group of twenty-five "lectures to professing Christians," first published serially in *The New York Evangelist.* He devoted the last nine of these to the doctrine of entire sanctification, an experience which he did not yet profess but believed all Christians could attain. When critics proceeded to identify these views with the antinomianism rife among the Vermont and New York groups who were eventually to congregate around

John Humphrey Noyes and the Oneida Community, Finney was moved to caution.[1]

His terms of duty at Oberlin after 1837, however, inevitably quickened the immense spiritual energies which were concentrated there on the higher development of the Christian graces. A revival season in 1839 especially featured the duty of believers to resist temptation and live a holy life. During one of the daily "religious discussions" a student rose to ask the inevitable question: "Might a Christian expect to attain sanctification in the present life?" President Asa Mahan, deeply affected, at once responded, "yes," and he and the other preachers gave themselves forthwith to seeking this exalted state.[2]

They believed that they found it, and an era of spiritual quickening followed in the wake of their joyful preaching which President James H. Fairchild—an opponent of the "second blessing" idea—believed to be the source of scores of transformed lives. The faculty immediately began publishing their new faith in *The Oberlin Evangelist, The Oberlin Quarterly,* and numerous other books.[3] In general, they said little about "sinlessness." "Perfection" meant perfect trust and consecration, the experience of "the fullness of the love of Christ," not freedom from troublesome physical and mental appetites or from error and prejudice. The preachers early discouraged a student "holiness band," believing that it drew too sharp a distinction between the sanctified and the "merely" justified. They varied, however, in their terminology. Finney preferred the phrase, "entire sanctification"; Henry Cowles, "holiness"; Asa Mahan, "Christian perfection"; and John Morgan, "the baptism of the Holy Ghost."[4]

Modern interpretations have neglected the kinship of this perfectionist

[1] See Charles G. Finney, *Memoirs* . . . (New York, 1876), p. 340, and his *Lectures to Professing Christians* (New York, 1878), pp. 352-53, 358-59.

[2] Finney, *Memoirs*, pp. 349-51; James H. Fairchild, "The Doctrine of Sanctification at Oberlin," *The Congregational Quarterly*, XVIII (1876), pp. 238-40.

[3] Finney, *Memoirs*, pp. 347-50; Fairchild, loc. cit., p. 243. See also Charles G. Finney, *Views of Sanctification* (Oberlin, 1840), and his *Lectures on Systematic Theology* (Oberlin, 1846), pp. 3, 500; Henry Cowles, *The Holiness of Christians in the Present Life* (Oberlin, 1840), first published serially in *The Oberlin Evangelist;* Asa Mahan, *Scripture Doctrine of Christian Perfection* . . . (Oberlin, 1839), and *The True Believer; His Character, Duty and Privileges* . . . (New York, 1847); John Morgan, "The Gift of the Holy Ghost," *The Oberlin Quarterly Review*, I (1845), pp. 90-116, and his volume, *The Holiness Acceptable to God* (Oberlin, 1846).

[4] Fairchild, loc. cit., pp. 240, 241, 243. Recent accounts are Robert S. Fletcher, *A History of Oberlin College, from Its Foundation Through the Civil War* (Oberlin, 1943), I, pp. 223-29; Whitney Rogers Cross, *The Burned-Over District* . . . (Ithaca, N. Y., 1950), pp. 228-51.

outburst to wider strivings of the transcendental age. Edward Beecher, for example, had called in 1835 for "the immediate production of an elevated standard of personal holiness throughout the universal church—such a standard . . . as God requires, and the present exigencies of the world demand." On its success, he believed, depended all hopes for the early inauguration of the kingdom of God on earth.[5] In the same year Mrs. Sarah A. Lankford, of New York City, combined the ladies' prayer meetings of two Methodist congregations to form the "Tuesday Meeting for the Promotion of Holiness." Her sister Phoebe, wife of Dr. Walter C. Palmer, a young physician, experienced sanctification soon afterward and became the acknowledged leader. By 1840 several prominent clergymen were helping these women organize a revival of the Wesleyan experience of perfect love in the metropolitan center of Methodism. At about the same time the radical Franckean Lutheran Synod, organized in upstate New York in 1837, adopted an emphatically perfectionist creed.[6] As Catherine Beecher wrote Finney on receipt of the news from Oberlin, Protestants everywhere were discovering "a practical difficulty arising from past views of Christian imperfection that needs to be met *somehow* . . . tho' the right way" was "not yet *clearly* seen." [7]

Thomas Coggeshall Upham, professor at Bowdoin College and one of the country's most promising young philosophers, became absorbed in this problem in 1839. On a September afternoon while having tea with his wife's new friends, Phoebe Palmer and Sarah Lankford, he found the answer. Upham immediately laid aside his uncompleted series of philosophical treatises to write a dozen books expounding a mystical, experimental version of Wesleyan perfectionism.[8]

[5] Edward Beecher, "The Nature, Importance, and Means of Eminent Holiness Throughout the Church," *The American National Preacher*, X (1835), pp. 193-94, 197, 203. See later, pp. 160, 225.
[6] George Hughes, *Fragrant Memories of the Tuesday Meeting and Guide to Holiness* . . . (New York, 1886), pp. 4-5, 10-35; Henry Eyster Jacobs, *A History of the Evangelical Lutheran Church in The United States* (Philip Schaff and others, eds., *The American Church History Series*, IV, New York, 1893), pp. 457-58.
[7] Catherine Beecher to Charles G. Finney, Nov. 4, 1839, quoted in Fletcher, *Oberlin*, I, p. 225; see Richard Wheatley, *The Life and Letters of Mrs. Phoebe Palmer* (New York, 1876), pp. 606-07 for evidence of Miss Beecher's continued interest.
[8] Benjamin Breckinridge Warfield, *Perfectionism* (New York, 1931), II, pp. 371-459, is a thoroughly antagonistic account. The sketch of Upham by Kenneth M. Sills in the D.A.B. ignores the whole subject. Cf. the strongly perfectionist note in Episcopalian Stephen H. Tyng's *Lectures on the Law and the Gospel* (New York, 1843), pp. 236, 239, 242, 287-90.
George Peck, "Dr. Upham's Works," *The Methodist Quarterly Review*, XXVIII

Horace Bushnell likewise sought a deeper Christian experience, moved in part by the death of his infant son in 1842. "I believed from reading, especially the New Testament, and from other testimony," he wrote later, "that there is a higher, fuller life that can be lived, and set myself to attain it." He read Upham's newest books, including *The Interior Life* and the biographies of Madame Guyon and Fénélon. Though at last rejecting the Methodist view of sanctification, he did not cease seeking. Mrs. Bushnell awakened one morning to find her husband on his knees, staring blissfully toward the sunrise. To her question, "What have you seen," he answered, "I have seen the gospel." [9] Thenceforward his books and sermons expressed in more cultivated fashion the doctrines of personal righteousness, the communication of God's love to men, and the living presence of the Holy Spirit which Finney and Wesley's followers were preaching to the masses. Some Methodists realized this similarity and regretted only Bushnell's exclusion of the idea of substitution from his theory of the Atonement.[10]

William Edwin Boardman, a young Presbyterian grocer living in the tiny lead-mining town of Potosi, Illinois, also began seeking sanctification in 1842 after reading James Brainerd Taylor's biography. He resisted a Methodist circuit rider's instruction until the latter gave him a book containing testimonies by Finney and Asa Mahan. He and his wife then obtained "the blessing" and were soon at Lane Theological Seminary, Cincinnati, making their home a center of holiness testimony to other students. Mrs. Boardman set out to write a book explaining the experience in simple terms. While correcting her crude manuscript, Boardman conceived the idea of his own volume called *The Higher Christian Life,* published at the height of the revival of 1858. He chose this title in the belief that the growing aspiration for perfection in many denominations could best be channeled toward his own views by a term not previously associated with Oberlin or the Methodists. The book was a huge success. We may perhaps dis-

---

(1846), 248-65, analyzes the following of Upham's books: *Principles of the Interior or Hidden Life* . . . (New York, 1843); *The Life of Faith* . . . (New York, 1845); *Life of Madame Catherine Adorna* . . . *with* . . . *Remarks Tending to Illustrate the Doctrine of Holiness* (New York, 1845); and *Life and Religious Opinions and Experience of Madame de la Mothe Guyon* . . . (New York, 1846). See also, *A Treatise on Divine Union* . . . (Boston, 1852); and, among his later works, *Absolute Religion* (New York, 1873).

[9] Mary E. (Bushnell) Cheney, *Life and Letters of Horace Bushnell* (New York, 1880), pp. 190-93; Warren Seymour Archibald, *Horace Bushnell* (Hartford, 1930), p. 67.

[10] See Charles H. Fowler, "Bushnell's Vicarious Sacrifice," *The Methodist Quarterly Review,* XLVIII (1861), pp. 350, 370. Cf. Horace Bushnell, *Sermons for the New Life* (7th ed., New York, 1869), pp. 106-26, 263-81, *passim.*

count Mrs. Boardman's statement that people lined up outside book-sellers' doors to purchase it. But numerous editions did appear in America and England (one publisher reportedly sold sixty-thousand copies by 1875), and Boardman almost overnight became a well-known figure on both sides of the Atlantic.[11]

Frederic Dan Huntington's spiritual journey included a season on the highway of holiness, too, as Phoebe Palmer's correspondence makes plain. He may have been present at a private discussion in March, 1850, which an Episcopalian lawyer arranged for his friends while Mrs. Palmer was engaged in a revival at the Bromfield Street Methodist Church, Boston. Six months later she answered Huntington's request for more information with her usual assertion that we are sanctified by faith, a faith placed in the atonement of Christ and the promises of the Holy Scripture. Since the hour of her sanctification, she testified:

I have not seen the moment but that I have been so far saved from self, as to feel that I would rather die than knowingly sin against God. I have enjoyed the consciousness that He is the supreme object of my affections. This is loving God with all the heart, and "love is the fulfilling of the law" . . . .[12]

Causation in intellectual history is, of course, complex. The perfectionist yearnings which, as we have seen, most evangelical Unitarian preaching displayed in this period no doubt rested principally on the denomination's historic aspiration for a moral religion.[31] It is nonetheless interesting that Huntington's volume, *Christian Believing and Living*, which heralded his break with Unitarianism in 1859, declared his belief in all the doctrines Phoebe Palmer had expounded: scriptural revelation, the atonement of the Incarnate Son, and entire sanctification by faith. He denied that there were spiritual attainments "unfolded in the gospel really and finally beyond the reach of sincere and consecrated persons." By confidence in the

---

[11] Mary M. Boardman (Mrs. W. E.), *Life and Labours of the Rev. W. E. Boardman* (New York, 1887), pp. 43, 48, 64-65, 70, 79, 81, 91, 100, 103-05; William Edwin Boardman, *The Higher Christian Life*, (Boston, 1858), pp. 1-10; Jacob J. Abbot, "Boardman's Higher Christian Life," *Bibliotheca Sacra*, XVII (1860), pp. 508-34; *The Christian*, I (1863), pp. 30-31.

[12] Wheatley, *op. cit.*, pp. 575-76; see also pp. 282-83. Cf. pp. 288-89 and *passim* for notices of other significant union meetings and discussions she held.

[13] See earlier, pp. 97-100. The publication date of George E. Ellis, *Regeneration and Sanctification* . . . (Charlestown, 1842), is significant. Cf. William Ellery Channing, *The Perfect Life, in Twelve Discourses, Edited from His Manuscripts by His Nephew* . . . (Boston, 1873).

Saviour's promises, Huntington said, "Christians do not extol themselves, but honor him." [14]

It is thus small wonder that Finney's perfectionism flourished widely despite considerable criticism.[15] Like other aspects of the Oberlin platform—revivalism and humanitarian reform—it was fitted to the temper of the times. A synthesis of the Quaker, Pietist, Methodist, and Puritan traditions of personal holiness was at work in American religion. Many who at first shared only Finney's belief in the revival path to reform agreed long before the Pentecost of 1858 that the sanctification of believers through the gift of the Holy Ghost was indispensable to the nation-wide awakening which they sought.[16]

The usual theological explanation of the "Oberlin Heresy"—that it was simply a radical extension of the New School doctrine of natural ability—underrates its original association with Wesleyanism. Of course, the moral optimism of Finney's version of free will was obvious then as now.[17] But the antipathy of modern students to the Calvinist view of depravity has made them too willing to accept this interpretation alone. Old School men, in fact, originated it in order to discredit free will. By arguing that preaching human ability led on logically to perfectionism, Princeton theologians hoped to implicate in radicalism all those Presbyterians who had taken the side of Barnes, Beecher, and Duffield in the secession of 1837.[18] The warnings against fanaticism with which they filled the air after 1840 forced New School leaders on the defensive about their most characteristic

[14] Frederic Dan Huntington, *Christian Believing and Living* (Boston, 1859), p. 424; see also pp. 427-28, 430-33.

[15] Much of the incidental criticism is evidence of his influence. See *The Christian Register*, March 20, 1858; *The Watchman and Reflector*, Oct. 21, 1858; Wheatley, *op. cit.*, pp. 571-75, 578-79. Cf. James Challen, *Baptism in Spirit and in Fire* (Philadelphia, 1859), pp. 34-35, and similar criticisms (by a prominent Baptist pastor) in John Winebrenner *History of All the Religious Denominations in the United States* . . . (Harrisburg, Pa., 1848), p. 48.

[16] Merrill Elmer Gaddis, *Christian Perfectionism in America* (unpublished Ph.D. dissertation, The University of Chicago, 1929), pp. 522-25 summarizes, with serious limitations in scope, the American perfectionist traditions. See "The Day of Pentecost," *The Christian Union and Religious Memorial*, II (1849), pp. 457-58.

[17] Fairchild, *loc. cit.*, pp. 237, 247; Fletcher, *Oberlin*, I, pp. 223-24; Charles C. Cole, Jr., *The Social Ideas of the Northern Evangelists, 1826-1860* (New York, 1954), pp. 66-68.

[18] J. C. Lord, "Finney's Sermons on Sanctification, and Mahan on Christian Perfection," *The Princeton Review*, XIII (1841), pp. 231-32, 234-35; S. G. Winchester, "Perfect Sanctification," the same, XIV, (1842), pp. 426-27, 429, a review of W. D. Snodgrass, *The Scriptural Doctrine of Sanctification Stated and Defended Against the Error of Perfectionism* (Philadelphia, 1841). Warfield, *Perfectionism*, I, *passim*, is a later summary of the same arguments.

doctrine, isolated them from the Oberlin evangelists and Oberlin from the Christian community, and supported during the next decade a powerful assault on free will, revivalism, and reform. At this point, for example, George Duffield turned away from both abolitionist and perfectionist radicalism and sought for the next twenty-five years to reconcile the Old and New School positions.[19]

That the preachers at the Ohio college reacted with an even stronger insistence on the doctrine of natural ability, hoping perhaps to identify their perfectionist gospel with the New School tradition, only complicated matters. They had at first taught, as did the Methodists, that entire sanctification was a gift of free grace, not a work of free will. In this way they reintroduced on a bold new level the Calvinist doctrine of dependance upon divine agency, which they had minimized in their explanation of conversion. The result was approximately the same synthesis between an ethic of grace and an ethic of holiness which Wesley set forth a hundred years before. "How many are seeking sanctification by their own resolutions and works, their fastings and prayers, their endeavors and activity," complained Finney in 1836. "It is all work, work, work, when it should be by faith. . . . It is faith that must sanctify, it is faith that purifies the heart." The Old School attack, however, confronted the Oberlin faculty with the alternative of acknowledging their conversion to Methodism or marrying sanctification to the doctrine of natural ability. That they leaned toward the latter course is small surprise.[20]

As early as 1841 the notion of a second experience suffered contradiction because of this inclination. The youthful Professor William Cochran

[19] Fletcher, Oberlin, I, p. 227; Fairchild, loc. cit., p. 244; Finney, Memoirs, pp. 343, 347-48; S. B. Canfield, An Exposition of the Peculiarities, Difficulties and Tendencies of Oberlin Perfectionism (Cleveland, 1841); Enoch Pond, "Christian Perfection," American Biblical Repository, I (1839), 44-58; Nathaniel S. Folsom, "Review of Mahan on Christian Perfection," the same, II (1839), pp. 143-66; Leonard D. Woods, "Examination of the Doctrine of Perfection as held by Asa Mahan . . . ," the same, V (1841), 166-89; Lewis G. Vander Velde, ed., "Notes on the Diary of George Duffield," The Mississippi Valley Historical Review, XXIV (1937-38), p. 57; George Duffield, "The Doctrines of the New School Presbyterian Church," Bibliotheca Sacra, XX (1863), p. 615.

Significantly, some Old School men abandoned even the older view of sanctification through growth in grace; see J. C. Lord, loc. cit., pp. 236-37, and "Legal Holiness, and Not Gracious, That which God has Determined to Establish Throughout His Universe," The American Presbyterian Review, I (1852), pp. 275-89.

[20] Contrast Finney's Lectures to Professing Christians, pp. 362-63, and pp. 352-53, 364, 376, 391, with his Views of Sanctification (1840), pp. 15-16, 61, 68 ff., 167-68, 171 ff. See the review of Calvinist protagonists of Oberlin by George Peck in The Methodist Quarterly Review, XXIII (1841), 307-19, passim.

expounded at a meeting of the alumni association that year his doctrine of "the simplicity of moral action," which declared every moral act perfect by definition. There could be no partial love, incomplete consecration, or imperfect obedience. The biblical exhortation that Christians must, as Cochran's brother, Samuel, delightfully misquoted it, "purify their hearts by faith," referred to perfect obedience. This he called "faith of the Will," as distinguished from "faith of the Intellect." [21] The community responded favorably to this idea and each of the preachers, so President Fairchild tells us, readjusted somewhat his concept of sanctification to conform to it. Henry Cowles re-emphasized his earlier appeal that entire consecration to God is the condition of discipleship. John Morgan and Finney explained that the baptism of the Spirit gave *permanence* to the experience of believers. Mahan and Finney stressed the illumination of the intellect it brought, the new light in which every true Christian would love to walk because his heart was perfect toward the Lord.[22]

Interestingly enough, the very first issues of *The Independent* contained a remarkable discussion of the questions Cochran had raised, provoked when Samuel Cochran received a call to the Sullivan Street Congregational Church, New York. Ten distinguished ministers, including Henry Ward Beecher and George B. Cheever, withdrew from the ordination council after the youthful candidate had declared that "no man has any evidence that he is a Christian who is not in a state of perfect obedience." A majority, however, representing the churches in the pro-Oberlin Evangelical Congregational Association of New York, "fully agreed with Mr. Cochran upon the subject of Christian perfection," so the newspaper regretfully explained, and proceeded to ordain him minister.[23]

Afterward, two long editorials in *The Independent* argued that the Scriptures declare that regenerate persons enjoy only a relative and imputed perfection, whereas the new pastor at Sullivan Street preached an actually sinless life. "If perfect obedience to the moral law is the condition of salvation," the editors pointed out, "the great body of Christians must give up their hope." They did not distinguish, as Cochran had in an answering

[21] Samuel D. Cochran, "Chalmers on the Romans,—Views of Sanctification," *The Oberlin Quarterly Review*, I (1845), p. 461. The Scripture reference is to Acts 15:9, where the Holy Spirit's purifying work is the theme.

[22] This was Fairchild's interpretation in 1873, *loc. cit.*, pp. 247, 252-55, and it may be somewhat forced; see pp. 249, 248-52, *passim*, and George Frederick Wright, *Charles Grandison Finney* (Boston, 1891), pp. 319-22. Cf. John Morgan, "The Gift of the Holy Ghost," *The Oberlin Quarterly Review*, I (1845), pp. 100-02.

[23] *The Independent*, Dec. 28, 1848.

letter, between the perfect law of God and one's immediate comprehension of it, nor between being saved and having evidence of it. The whole discussion was, however, courteous and charitable. Far from rejecting the current aspirations for holiness, the editors encouraged them in these significant words:

There is such a thing as Christian perfection—perfection in the most absolute unqualified sense. This perfection is attainable, and should ever be our aim. We would urge our fellow Christians to it by all the motives of the word of God. . . . But while one may be a sincere Christian though he comes short of perfect obedience to the law of God, let it be remembered that no man can be a Christian who does not keep the commandments of Christ, who has not consecrated himself entirely to the service of the Lord, and who does not *live* in obedience to his commands.[24]

It is significant that President Mahan and Professor John Morgan applied Cochran's concept of perfect obedience to the regenerate state and remained stanch pleaders for a second blessing. Mahan preferred to think that the higher experience subjugated rather than destroyed the propensities for sin; but these were in his eyes emotional and physical, rather than a root principle of depravity, as with Wesley. He agreed with the Methodists, however, in distinguishing carefully between the perfection of the heart, attained through the baptism of the Spirit, and the perfection of character which comes only through growth in grace. And well he might; some members of the Oberlin faculty thought Mahan proud, censorious, and a poor advertisement for the doctrine he taught.[25]

Finney, moreover, drifted steadily back toward the Wesleyan position as years passed, though his primarily empirical description of the second experience was rarely clear or consistent. The Oberlin community, Finney later explained, had first begun discussing sanctification as a "Bible question, . . . an experimental truth, which we did not attempt to reduce to a theological formula . . . until years afterwards." By 1857 he was denounc-

[24] "The Scriptural View of Perfection," *The Independent*, Jan. 11, 1849. Cf. Cochran's letter and its answer, published in the same issue, and the editorial of the previous week.

For later examples of *The Independent's* interest in the subject see "The Theology of the Christian Register," Jan. 2, 1851; Henry Ward Beecher's very friendly review of Upham, *Divine Union*, Jan. 30, 1851; and "A First Visit to Oberlin," Sept. 25, 1851.

[25] Asa Mahan, "The Idea of Perfection," *The Oberlin Quarterly Review*, I (1845), pp. 468, 476, 479-80; Morgan, "The Gift of the Holy Ghost," the same, pp. 96, 111; Fletcher, *Oberlin*, I, pp. 472-88. Cf. Mahan, *Out of Darkness Into Light* . . . (Boston, 1876), pp. 263-80 and *passim*.

ing those who "having begun in the Spirit . . . try to become perfect in the flesh." They rely more on human resolutions than on divine grace. "Men are sanctified by receiving Christ into the heart by faith," he said. "While you affirm your moral obligation, you are more and more oppressed with your moral weakness. But this weakness is what Christ counterbalances with his strength." [26]

The keynote of Finney's later crusades was the plea that Christians should consecrate themselves fully to the Lord. Everywhere he found them living in partial consecration and half-hearted love. A brave evangelist indeed would have been required to announce in the Park Street Church in 1857 that such persons had never really been converted before. The only practical alternative was to urge them to seek a higher work of grace.[27] On the other hand, the two of Finney's *Lectures on Revivals* which were rewritten for the edition of 1868, while making the doctrine of sanctification more prominent, stressed growth more than a crisis of experience.[28]

In any event, those who rejected the second blessing did not abandon the perfectionist ideal. Cochran's teaching simply propagated an exalted view of the first experience of grace. According to President Fairchild, the distinguishing doctrine of what came to be called by 1870 the "Oberlin Theology" was that "every believer is sanctified, in the sense that he has utterly renounced sin in this acceptance of Christ, and given Him his whole heart." [29]

Oberlin-trained advocates of both interpretations whetted the hunger for holiness which was for the next thirty years a dominant strain in American Protestantism. Finney and Mahan ranged the cities of two continents preaching the power of the union of man's will and God's grace to consecrate and to sanctify every believing soul. Finney's appearance at long

---

[26] Finney, *Memoirs*, p. 351; *The Guide to Holiness*, XXXII (July-December, 1857), pp. 132-34. Cf. the same, XXIX (January-June, 1856), pp. 67-68, and XXX (July-December, 1856), pp. 48-50; Wright, *Finney*, pp. 321-22, and Fairchild, *loc. cit.*, pp. 255-58.

[27] See accounts in *The Guide to Holiness*, XXXIII (January-June, 1858), p. 93; *The Christian Register*, March 20, 1858; and Finney, *Memoirs*, pp. 442, 473. Contrast Fletcher, *op. cit.*, I, pp. 480-88.

[28] Cf. Charles G. Finney, *Lectures on Revivals of Religion* (New York, 1868), pp. v, 396, 401, 410, 416, 429-33 with the edition of the same work published in New York in 1835, pp. 398, 400-38, and *passim*.

[29] Fairchild, *loc. cit.*, p. 249.

Merrill E. Gaddis's dissertation, cited above, excluded Oberlinism as "quasi-perfectionist," and ignored all who did not teach a second experience; Cross, *Burned-Over District*, pp. 249-50, does the same, but more defensibly, since his work was limited to the radical fringe.

union meetings in Boston and New York in 1857 and 1858 signaled the collapse of antiperfectionist prejudices against Oberlin men, as well as a new appreciation of their stand against slavery. Meanwhile, a growing army of Revivalistic Calvinists who could not accept the second blessing adopted the view that true conversion made one entirely free from sin. In the awakenings which followed 1858 multitudes of them became convinced that their justification in God's sight must be confirmed by their sanctification in their own and the eyes of the world. The goals were similar, only the method proposed for reaching them varied. Both concepts contributed much to the new ethical seriousness which swept across American Protestantism on the eve of the Civil War.

In retrospect, the quest for Christian holiness seems to have been a popular expression of strivings which on a more sophisticated level produced the transcendentalist revolt of Emerson and Thoreau. That such diverse individuals as Horace Bushnell, Phoebe Palmer, Catherine and Edward Beecher, William E. Boardman, Asa Mahan, Frederic Dan Huntington, and John Humphrey Noyes sought a higher life in the years between 1835 and 1845 indicates a wide surge of thought and feeling of which the events at Oberlin were but a dramatic example. In earlier years the faculty at the Ohio college moved away from the Wesleyan fountain of their perfectionist faith in a vain attempt to marry the doctrine of holiness to the New School concept of natural ability. Generally, however, the evangelical emphasis upon sanctification by grace prevailed. The remarkable fact is that after 1845, as we shall see more clearly in the next two chapters, Christian perfectionism, far from being confined to a colony of frontier fanatics, gained ground steadily among thoughtful leaders of urban Protestantism. The best-loved hymn of the century reveals both the fervor and the faith which the movement caught up:

> Rock of Ages, cleft for me,
> Let me hide myself in Thee;
> Let the water and the blood,
> From Thy wounded side which flowed,
> Be of sin the *double cure*,
> Save from wrath and *make me pure*.

VIII

Sanctification in American Methodism

Methodist perfectionism suffered less from variations in the doctrine of the will than did that at Oberlin. John Wesley and his early preachers understood moral ability to be the gift of God's "prevenient grace." Divine love had saved men from the extreme of depravity which otherwise would have been a consequence of the Fall; Christ had endowed every one with the capacity to respond to the gospel and be saved. Not natural ability but *faith in the atonement* unleashed the regenerating power of the Holy Spirit and raised penitents from the death of sinning to the new life of obedience to God's will.

The progress of this new life was hindered, however, by the remains of the carnal nature within, the "seed" of sin, a bent toward evil perhaps most clearly described as a diseased condition of the soul. Wesley thus considered original sin to be not so much guilt for Adam's transgression as a sinful condition stemming from it. He was less concerned with theological diagnosis of the malady than with declaring God's readiness to heal it—initially in regeneration, entirely in the second crisis of Christian experience called "perfect love." [1]

[1] European students have led the way in recent explorations of Wesley's teaching. The best study is Harold Lindstrom, *Wesley and Sanctification, a Study in the Doctrine of Salvation* (Stockholm, 1946). Cf. R. Newton Flew, *The Idea of Perfection in Christian Theology: an Historical Study of the Christian Ideal for the Present Life* (London, 1934), pp. 313-42; William Edwin Sangster, *The Path to Perfection; an Examination and Restatement of John Wesley's Doctrine of Christian Perfection* (New York, 1943); social implications of the doctrine in Wellman Joel Warner, *The Wesleyan Movement in the Industrial Revolution* (London, 1930), pp. 61-72; and a recent Harvard dissertation, George Allen Turner, *The More Excellent Way: the Scriptural Basis of the Wesleyan Message* (Winona Lake, Ind., 1952).

Aside from George Croft Cell's discussion in *The Rediscovery of John Wesley* (New York, 1935), pp. 337-62, Americans, and particularly Methodists, have until recently neglected the theme. Cf., for example, Wade Crawford Barclay, *Early American Methodism, 1769-1844*, Vol. II, *To Reform the Nation* (*History of American Methodism*, Part I, New York, 1949), pp. 314-19, with William Warren Sweet, *Methodism in American History* (New York, 1933), pp. 341-45.

Wesley chose this term because it exalted divine grace while at the same time emphasizing human responsibility to keep the highest ethical law, the Sermon on the Mount. Christ's love in Calvary, he believed, is not a substitute but a foundation for our holiness. The end of the atonement is both to justify and sanctify men. He believed that gratitude for God's grace in conversion would impel earnest believers toward complete dedication to Christ and at the same time induce discontent with their remaining inner bent to sin. Then, in response to their agonized soul-searching and consecration climaxed in a venture of complete trust which was itself half "works" and half a gift of grace, the "love of God," as the New Testament promised, would be shed abroad in their hearts by the Holy Spirit, "purifying their hearts by faith." Imperfect judgment, the passions and frailties common to men, temptation, and the possibility of falling into sin would remain real. But the bent of the soul would now be toward God's will, not away from it.[2]

Interestingly, Wesley never left a completely clear witness of his own enjoyment of perfect love, although he recorded, studied, and used as examples the testimonies of hundreds of others. Moreover, he so faithfully emphasized the process of self-examination and consecration which preceded the experience and the godly discipline which must follow as to pose the question whether he really understood it to be achieved through spiritual growth rather than, as he often said, by a "second blessing, properly so-called." Recent studies have demonstrated conclusively that Wesley did teach sanctification to be "instantaneous," receivable "now, and by simple faith," though he did not rule out completely the possibility of its attainment through growth.[3]

Considerable evidence suggests that this doctrine did not occupy a chief place in early Methodist preaching in the New World, despite Bishop Francis Asbury's efforts to impress it upon his followers. The moral needs of rural and Western America directed attention to the more elemental work of saving sinners.[4] If the volume of literature devoted to the subject

[2] See Rom. 5:5 and Acts 15:9.
[3] Lindstrom, *Wesley and Sanctification*; Peters, *Christian Perfection and American Methodism* (New York, 1955), pp. 27-66, 201-14; Turner, *More Excellent Way*, pp. 168-72.
[4] Peters, *op. cit.*, pp. 92-101, corrects Merrill E. Gaddis, Christian Perfectionism in America (unpublished Ph.D. dissertation, The University of Chicago, 1929), pp. 223-309, on this point. Cf. A. Kent, "The Work of Holiness in New York Some Years Ago," *The Guide to Holiness*, XXXIII (January-June, 1858), pp. 20-21, 71-72, on the events of 1819-20.

is any index, however, the interest in it which remained alive in urban communities increased rapidly after 1825. In that year Timothy Merritt, a prominent minister in the New York City district, published his *Treatise on Christian Perfection, with Directions for Obtaining That State,* a little handbook which was to appear in thirty-three editions by 1871. Many similar works followed. Adam Clarke's *Commentary* and Richard Watson's *Theological Institutes,* both of which stressed the second blessing, appeared in America in the 1820's and became immensely popular "standard authors" with the Methodist clergy.[5] The bishops called for a revival of holiness at the General Conference of 1832. The pastoral address of the one held eight years later insisted that the usefulness and influence of the church depended upon it. "Let us not suppose it is enough to have this doctrine in our standards," wrote the church fathers; "let us labor to have the experience and power of it in our hearts."[6]

In 1835 the Tuesday Meeting in New York City, mentioned earlier, thrust Phoebe Palmer into a leading role. The weekly gathering was held in her home and confined to women until 1839, when Professor Thomas C. Upham's adherence made it seem providentially intended for men as well. Also that year Timothy Merritt resigned his positions as assistant editor of *The Christian Advocate and Journal* and denominational publishing agent to launch in Boston a monthly magazine, *The Guide to Holiness,* chiefly given over to reports of the testimonies heard at the meeting. Dr. Palmer twice moved to larger houses in order to accommodate the crowds who came from far and near.[7]

The news from Oberlin undoubtedly encouraged the growth of this interest, as did the secession in 1841 of Luther Myrick and the earliest band of Wesleyan Methodists in Western New York. The latter objected to both compromises on slavery and neglect of Christian perfection in the

[5] Timothy Merritt, *The Christian's Manual* . . . (33rd ed., New York, 1871); Adam Clarke, *The New Testament . . . with a Commentary and Critical Notes . . .* (rev. ed., New York, n.d.), II, 105-07, 464, 555; and Richard Watson, *Theological Institutes . . .* (New York, 1840), II, 450-67. See also John Wesley, A. Watmough, and others, *Entire Sanctification, or Christian Perfection, Stated and Defended* (Baltimore, 1838); and Richard Treffry, *A Treatise on Christian Perfection* (London, 1838), both reviewed favorably in *The Methodist Quarterly Review,* XXIII (1841), 123-55; and Aaron Lummus, *Essays on Holiness* (New York, 1826), which first appeared serially in *Zion's Herald.*

[6] *Journals of the General Conference of the Methodist Episcopal Church, 1840 and 1844* (New York, 1844), II, 161; *The Methodist Quarterly Review,* XIV (1832), 346.

[7] George Hughes, *Fragrant Memories of the Tuesday Meeting and Guide to Holiness . . .* (New York, 1886), pp. 161-76; see earlier, p. 105.

parent body. For a brief period around 1842, Oberlin and Methodist forces united in holiness conventions at New York City, Newark, Newburg, Buffalo, Rochester, and points farther west.[8]

Mrs. Palmer's many books spearheaded the popular propaganda of the perfectionist revival. *The Way to Holiness*, a narrative of her own experience, sold 24,000 copies by 1851 and appeared in thirty-six editions before the Civil War. In 1859 her publishers were advertising a twenty-fourth edition of *Faith and Its Effects*—a collection of her correspondence on the subject—a twentieth edition of *Entire Devotion*—first published serially a decade before in *The Christian Advocate and Journal*—and a ninth of *Incidental Illustrations of the Economy of Salvation*. In all her writings, as in the columns of the *Guide*, she combined constant personal testimony to the joys and privileges of entire sanctification with exhortations to believers to lay hold upon the promised blessing by simple faith.[9]

Meanwhile, another monthly magazine, *The Beauty of Holiness*, began publication in Xenia, Ohio, and conference weeklies in many sections showed great interest in the theme. *The Christian Guardian*, organ of Canadian Methodism, printed serially the whole of Mrs. Palmer's *Faith and Its Effects*.[10] In Boston Daniel Wise launched his four-year term as editor of *Zion's Herald* in 1852 with a strong emphasis upon sanctification. Not merely truth acting upon Christian wills, he wrote, but the supernatural agency of the Holy Spirit is the source of purity and power; every

[8] *Ibid.*, pp. 24-35; Robert S. Fletcher, *A History of Oberlin College, from Its Foundation through the Civil War* (Oberlin, Ohio, 1943), I, 227-28; Richard Wheatley, *The Life and Letters of Mrs. Phoebe Palmer* (New York, 1876), pp. 571-72; George Hughes, *The Beloved Physician, Walter C. Palmer, M.D. . . .* (New York, 1884), pp. 241-44. John Peters, *op. cit.*, pp. 109-20, outlines these developments correctly, though without help from most of the pertinent devotional and biographical sources.

[9] Hughes, *Tuesday Meeting*, p. 183, contains a complete bibliography of her works and a record of editions up to 1865. Cf. Wheatley, *Phoebe Palmer*, p. 532; and Phoebe Palmer, *Promise of the Father; or a Neglected Specialty of the Last Days . . .* (Boston, 1859), advertisements on the back flyleaves.

I have seen editions of her works as follows: *Faith and Its Effects; or Fragments from My Portfolio* (45th ed., New York, 1867); *The Way of Holiness, with Notes by the Way; Being a Narrative of Religious Experience Resulting from Determination to Be a Bible Christian* (New York, 1851); *Present to My Christian Friend: or, Entire Devotion* (20th ed., Boston, 1859); and *Incidental Illustrations of the Economy of Salvation, Its Doctrines and Duties* (Boston, 1855).

[10] *The Guide to Holiness*, XXXIII (January-June, 1858), pp. 57-58. The review of the first issue of *The Beauty of Holiness and Sabbath Miscellany* in *Zion's Herald*, Dec. 1, 1853, praised *The Guide* highly but welcomed the second journal. See also notices of the holiness emphasis in *The Northwestern Christian Advocate*, reorganized from *The Michigan Christian Advocate* that year, and *The Nashville Advocate*, in *Zion's Herald*, Sept. 22 and Nov. 3, 1852.

believer should exercise faith for its immediate reception.[11] The newspaper promoted this view freely in the years following, almost without any recognition of the possibility that Methodists ever held another. It printed numerous testimonies of early Wesleyan preachers and praised camp meetings and revivals which featured holiness.[12] From the Plattsburgh, New York, district camp meeting, where several ministers received the blessing in 1854, one of them wrote:

I united with the M. E. Church February 24th, 1819, and thought once or twice I tasted the perfect love of God. But I desire now to say it, to the praise of God: on Wednesday night, 12 P.M., God sanctified my soul in the Rusville tent. The blood of Jesus Christ has cleansed my heart from all sin.

A September editorial which asked, "How Can the Benefits of the Camp Meeting Be Retained at Home," urged those who had "entered into the land of BEULAH, having their hearts 'purified by faith,'" to testify to the experience, but to remain cautious, "humble, melted, subdued in spirit." [13]

The few professional evangelists in the denomination soon joined the crusade, swelling this stream of popular literature. John Newland Maffitt had shown little interest in holiness until his revival at the Bromfield Street Church, Boston, caught the crest of a spiritual wave which had originated in the summer of 1842 at Eastham Camp Meeting on Cape Cod.[14] Two or three years later James Caughey began a strikingly successful career in England and America which was fully recorded by the holiness press. His revivals in Toronto and Hamilton, Ontario, in 1852 seem to have awakened the enthusiasm for holiness among Canadian Methodists to which the Palmers later contributed much inspiration and guidance. Caughey's many books provided plain people everywhere with dramatic calls to seek the blessing.[15] The same is true of William Taylor, who went

[11] Cf. "How Souls Are Purified" and "Faith an Element of Power," *Zion's Herald*, Aug. 25 and Sept. 8, 1852, with "Holiness—Its Effects," the same, Apr. 21, 1852.

[12] See "Conversion of Believers—Sanctification of Believers," and "Holiness—Why Men Are Not Holy," the same, Aug. 16 and 30, 1854; and testimonies of Samuel Hicks, Henry Longden, and John Wesley, Sept. 2, 1852, Aug. 23, and Oct. 11, 1854. Cf. the issues of Aug. 23 and Sept. 6, 1854, for reports of the "German camp meeting" on the New York district, where fifteen were sanctified, of Martha's Vineyard camp, where Phoebe Palmer conducted services, and of the East Brookfield, Mass. encampment.

[13] The same, Sept. 1, 1852, and Sept. 27, 1854.

[14] Martin Moore, *Boston Revival, 1842* . . . (Boston, 1842), pp. 109-12, 117-18, 124. Cf. John N. Maffitt, *Pulpit Sketches* (Louisville, 1839), and Abel Stevens, *A Compendious History of American Methodism* (New York, 1868), pp. 560-61.

[15] W. J. Blackstock, "The Work of Holiness in Canada," *The Guide to Holiness*, XXXIII (January-June, 1858), 57-59. See especially among Caughey's many volumes,

with the forty-niners to become a free-lance prospector for God in the California mining towns. Taylor renewed an earlier association with the Palmers on his return in 1856. During the following three years he made annual tours of important camp meetings in the East and conducted revivals during the winter months in some of the finest Methodist churches in New York, Brooklyn, Philadelphia, and Baltimore. In 1859 and 1860 he blanketed the Midwest with hundreds of one-night stands, featuring evangelism and "news from California."[16]

Securing the support of professional soul winners, always few in number and hampered by the denomination's tight organization, was much less important, however, than enlisting pastors and ecclesiastical officials in the cause. The bishops expected every Methodist pastor to be an evangelist. All were, in fact, "traveling preachers," to use the official phrase, appointed to a wide circuit for terms which rarely lasted more than two years. The bishops themselves were aggressively evangelistic. Elected periodically from the rank and file of the clergy, they wielded power and spiritual influence of immense proportions. They worked closely with the "presiding elders," who directly supervised the pastors and controlled such gatherings as the district or conference camp meetings. The revival of holiness could not get far without substantial encouragement from the top.

That encouragement began early and increased steadily.[17] Bishops Thomas A. Morris and Elijah Hedding were long remembered for their advocacy of the experience in the early 1840's.[18] Bishops Edmund S. Janes and Leonidas Hamline, elected in 1844, were with their wives close friends

Methodism in Earnest: the History of a Revival in Great Britain, in which Twenty Thousand Souls Professed Faith in Christ, and Ten Thousand Professed Sanctification (2nd. ed., Nashville, 1857); *Helps to a Life of Holiness and Usefulness* . . . (5th ed., Boston, 1852), pp. 165-97, and *passim*; and *Showers of Blessing from Clouds of Mercy* . . . (New York, 1868), pp. 339-58. Dr. Walter Palmer's firm in New York published the last of these, along with others as follows: *Light in the Dark, through the Dominions of Unbelief* . . . (1860); *Arrows from My Quiver* . . . (1867); *Earnest Christianity Illustrated* . . . (1868); and *Glimpses of a Life in Soul-Saving* (1868). Cf. *Zion's Herald*, Feb. 25 and July 7 and 21, 1852, for glowing accounts of Caughey's work.

[16] William Taylor, *Story of My Life* . . . (New York, 1896), pp. 73-75, 218, 219-28, 230-32, 244, 251; Hughes, *Tuesday Meeting*, pp. 155-57.

[17] Barclay, *To Reform the Nation*, pp. 339-40, W. M. Gewehr's review of Barclay's work in *The American Historical Review*, LVI (1951), p. 910, and Sweet, *Methodism in American History*, p. 341, suggest the opposite, as did earlier Merrill E. Gaddis, *op. cit.*, p. 393 and *passim*.

[18] Thomas A. Morris, *Sermons on Various Subjects* (Cincinnati, 1841), pp. 41-44, 302-04, 322-24, 378 ff. and *passim*; S.L.C. Coward, *Entire Sanctification from 1739 to 1900* (Chicago, 1900), pp. 211-12; Matthew Simpson, *Cyclopedia of Methodism* . . . (Philadelphia, 1878), pp. 440-41, 630-31.

of Dr. and Mrs. Palmer. Typical of Hamline's role was a letter written in 1845 to a recently sanctified pastor, urging him to "minister on this subject day and night without remission" despite "reproach, contempt, persecution, and every embarrassment that malice, and mischief can devise against us." Janes, who was for twenty-five years the most conservative and influential member of the board of bishops, prepared enthusiastic introductions to two famous volumes explaining instantaneous sanctification.[19] Osmon C. Baker and Matthew Simpson joined this group in 1852. Both were fervent heralds of higher piety, Simpson especially so after the Civil War, when he enjoyed the reputation of being America's greatest preacher.[20]

Nathan Bangs, however, came closer than any of these to being the outstanding Methodist of the first half of the century. Bangs repeatedly declined election as bishop, but served in turn as publishing agent, editor, and presiding elder in New York City until his death in 1852. He attended and presided over the Tuesday Meeting frequently, wrote continually for *The Guide to Holiness*, published an important volume of his own on the doctrine in 1851, and as presiding elder personally led its revival among the pastors in the national metropolis.[21]

Prominent intellectual leaders were meanwhile lending additional respectability to the movement. George O. Peck, editor of *The Methodist Quarterly Review* from 1840–48 and of the New York *Christian Advocate and Journal* for four years thereafter, kept the subject of Christian perfection constantly before the readers of these periodicals. His lectures de-

---

[19] L. L. Hamline, Cincinnati, Dec. 13, 1845, to Rev. C. W. Lean, in "Bishops Autographs and Portraits, 1789-1897," a bound ms. volume in the library of Garrett Seminary. See Janes's introduction in Randolph Sinks Foster, *Christian Purity* (2nd. ed., New York, 1854); and "Life and Works of Hamline," *The Methodist Quarterly Review*, LXIII (1881), pp. 15, 16, 25. Walter Palmer edited the *Life and Letters of Leonidas L. Hamline, D.D.* (New York, 1880) as a token of their friendship. See also Leonidas L. Hamline, *The Works of Rev. Leonidas L. Hamline* (F. G. Hibbard, ed., New York, 1871), pp. 135, 147, 166, 180, 204, and 347-493, *passim*; and Hughes, *Beloved Physician*, p. 242.

[20] John A. Wood, *Perfect Love* (Louisville, 1880), p. 121; George Hughes, *Days of Power in the Forest Temple* . . . (Boston, 1874), p. 65; and A. McLean and Joel W. Eaton, eds., *Penuel, or Face to Face with God* (New York, 1869), pp. 381-85, 468.

[21] Nathan Bangs, *The Necessity, Nature, and Fruits of Sanctification* (New York, 1851) and his *The Present State, Prospects and Responsibilities of the Methodist Episcopal Church* (New York, 1850) won favorable comment for their holiness teachings in *The Methodist Quarterly Review*, XXXIII (1851), 164-65, 333; see p. 59 in the latter work. Cf. Nathan Bangs, "Christian Perfection," *The Guide to Holiness*, XIX (January-June, 1851), pp. 37, 49, 74, 121, and XX (July-December, 1851), pp. 25, 49, 73, 86, 109, 121; and Abel Stevens, *Life and Times of Nathan Bangs*, pp. 52-59, 117-18, 345-47, 350-53, 359.

livered in several New York City churches on the occasion of the Oberlin excitement were published in 1841 and passed through ten editions before the Civil War.[22] Abel Stevens' first historical work, which appeared in 1850, bore his conclusion that the success of early American Methodism was due to the entire consecration of its preachers to Christ. His later writings repeated the same message, especially the famous biography of his close personal friend, Nathan Bangs.[23] Wilbur Fisk, the first president of Wesleyan University, Middletown, Connecticut, and Stephen Olin, who succeeded him in 1842, actively promoted the experience both among their students and at Methodist camp meetings. Fisk had been sanctified at Wellfleet camp meeting, Cape Cod, in 1819, after a sermon by Timothy Merritt, and lay five hours "under the power of the Holy Ghost."[24]

Randolph Sinks Foster, author of a famous holiness apology first printed in 1851, *Christian Purity, Its Nature and Blessedness*, thereafter divided his time until his election as a bishop in 1872 between New York City pastorates, the presidency of Garrett Biblical Institute, Evanston, Illinois, and a professorship and finally the presidency at the new seminary which Daniel Drew endowed at Madison, New Jersey.[25] Jesse T. Peck, a younger brother of the editor, published an equally popular volume in 1856, which maintained that the doctrine of entire sanctification was central not only to Methodism but to the whole tenor of Christian theology. He, too, was elected a bishop in 1872.[26]

[22] George O. Peck, *The Scripture Doctrine of Christian Perfection Stated and Defended* . . . (New York, 1842), pp. 4-6. Among the important articles, some of them no doubt his own, see in *The Methodist Quarterly Review*, "Christian Perfection," XXIII (1841), pp. 123-55, 307-19; "Wesleyan Perfectionism," XXV (1843), pp. 447-61; and "Dr. Upham's Works," XXVIII (1846), pp. 248-65. Cf. George O. Peck, *The Life and Times of George O. Peck, D.D.* (New York, 1874), pp. 207-11.

[23] See Stevens, *Nathan Bangs*, pp. 117-18, 345-47; the same author's *Memorials of the Early Progress of Methodism in the Eastern States* (Boston, 1852), pp. 104, 126-29, 429, 491-92; and his *Compendious History*, pp. 458-61, 566.

[24] Joseph Holdrich, *The Life of Wilbur Fisk, D.D., First President of Wesleyan University* (New York, 1842), p. 72; "The Death of President Olin," *The Methodist Quarterly Review*, XXXIII (1851), p. 654; John McClintock, "Stephen Olin," the same, XXXVI (1854), pp. 17-18; Abel Stevens, *Compendious History*, pp. 458-61; and Abel Stevens, *History of the Methodist Episcopal Church in The United States of America* (New York, 1864-67), IV, 294. Cf. Hughes, *Beloved Physician*, p. 242.

[25] Randolph S. Foster, *Nature and Blessedness of Christian Purity* (New York, 1851), was revised in *Christian Purity; or, the Heritage of Faith* . . . (New York, 1869). Cf. Simpson, *Cyclopedia of Methodism*, pp. 371-72.

[26] Jesse T. Peck, "Holiness," *The Methodist Quarterly Review*, XXXIII (1851), 505-29 is a commendatory review of Foster, *Christian Purity*, containing, pp. 507-18, the germ idea of Peck, *The Central Idea of Christianity* (Boston, 1856). The latter volume

Such books multiplied rapidly. Possibly the most famous of all came from the pen of a scholarly, fervent Englishman, William Arthur, who first won friends in America through a tour to raise funds for Irish Wesleyanism. His *Tongue of Fire,* which urged that the baptism of the Spirit was the source of power for both personal holiness and social service, had sold several editions in England before its simultaneous publication in 1856 for northern and southern branches of the American church.[27]

The rising level of ministerial education seems, in fact, to have aided the widespread rediscovery of the experience of early Methodist saints. Frontier circuit riders had been compelled, despite Asbury's injunction to the contrary, to practice an unfortunate literalization of Wesley's advice that they be "men of one book." Settled pastorates provided them with the opportunity to cultivate more carefully the piety of their members and with a chance to read more books. It is not surprising that they began with the journals and other writings of Fletcher and Wesley and the lives of their early preachers. The same was true of students at the first Methodist theological seminaries at Concord, New Hampshire, Connecticut Wesleyan, Drew, and Garrett. All these institutions were centers of perfectionist fervor during their earliest years.

The remarkable fact is how closely Walter and Phoebe Palmer were associated with the church leaders who encouraged the holiness awakening. Years later John P. Newman, soon to be a bishop, declared to an assembly of dignitaries celebrating the fiftieth anniversary of the Tuesday Meeting that Mrs. Palmer was "the Priscilla who taught many an Apollos 'the way of God more perfectly.'" No other Christian woman of the century, he believed, had exerted a comparable influence. Educators like Stephen Olin and John Dempster—the latter, founder of Concord and Garrett

---

received favorable treatment in turn from Wesley Kenney, of the Philadelphia Conference, in *The Methodist Quarterly Review,* XXXIX (1857), 84-104.

[27] William Arthur, *The Tongue of Fire; or the True Power of Christianity* (New York, 1880), pp. 52-57, 128-32. See also the same author's *Addresses Delivered in New York, with a Biographical Sketch of the Author* (P. Strickland, ed., New York, 1856), pp. 153-88. Among the popular handbooks were William McDonald, *The New Testament Standard of Piety* (Boston, 1861); Thomas Ralston, *Elements of Divinity* (Louisville, 1847), chapters 29-30; and S. D. Akin, *Christian Perfection . . . an Essay Containing the Substance of Mr. Fletcher's Last Check to Antinomianism* (Louisville, 1860).

See also the emphasis upon sanctification in Davis W. Clark, ed., *Methodist Episcopal Pulpit: a Collection of Original Sermons from Living Ministers of the M. E. Church* (New York, 1850), sermons by Noah Levings, financial secretary of the American Bible Society, pp. 137, 141-46, 151-53, Ferderick Merrick, a professor at Ohio Wesleyan University, 136, Nathan Bangs, 343, 348, 350, 353, and others by less prominent figures, 404, 412-13 and *passim.*

seminaries—as well as Bishops Janes, Hamline, and Peck, Newman said, were members of the great company which had "thronged her parlors" and "followed her teachings into 'perfect rest.'"[28] Hamline and Stephen Olin were certainly sanctified under her guidance in the early 1840's, and possibly Janes as well. Nathan Bangs had been her class leader in her youth and remained throughout his life an admirer and close personal friend.[29] Randolph S. Foster sought her advice on the experience while still a member of the Cincinnati Conference and wrote *Christian Purity* to celebrate his attainment of it after he came to be pastor of a New York City congregation.[30]

Undoubtedly Dr. Palmer's generosity toward benevolent enterprises extended their influence. He was for many years a member of the board of managers of the Methodist Missionary Society. Together the physician and his wife seem to have conceived and made the first substantial contributions for the China and Palestinian missions. Their hospitality, too, was a byword among Methodist ministers. The evening meal which followed the Tuesday Meeting invariably included guests from out of town—often as not conference and educational leaders stopping in New York on official business.[31]

Beginning about 1850, the Palmers spent half of each year at Methodist camp meetings and revivals in the Eastern United States and Canada. Since they did not usually accept remuneration, the doctor returned to his medical practice during the winter and spring months and his wife to the leadership of the weekly gathering in their home. Wherever they went, their great prestige with the bishops and church officials enabled these two laymen to win the confidence of the Methodist ministry. Presiding elders usually welcomed them; hundreds of ministers professed sanctification in their camp meetings and returned home to set their circuits aflame with

[28] Quoted from *The Northern Christian Advocate* in Hughes, *Tuesday Meeting*, p. 149. Cf. Stevens, *Nathan Bangs*, 352.

[29] Wheatley, *Phoebe Palmer*, pp. 549, 551; Hughes, *Beloved Physician*, pp. 67-70, 176-80; Stevens, *Nathan Bangs*, pp. 350-53, 368, 370, 383, 390, 395; *The Guide to Holiness*, XXX (July-December, 1856), p. 112. See especially Stephen Olin to Dr. and Mrs. Walter Palmer, Nov. 29, 1841, and July 17, 1844, quoted in Julia M. Olin, ed., *Life and Letters of Stephen Olin* (New York, 1853), II, pp. 43, 45, 197-98; and also II, pp. 32-34, 191-92.

[30] Simpson, *Cyclopedia of Methodism*, pp. 372-73; *The Guide to Holiness*, XVII (1850), pp. 82 ff.; Hughes *Tuesday Meeting*, p. 10. Harris Elwood Starr wrote the sketch of Foster for the *D.A.B.*

[31] Hughes, *Beloved Physician*, pp. 58, 84-88.

holy zeal.[82] While they were awaiting passage in 1858 at Halifax, Nova Scotia, for a four years' crusade in England, a holiness revival broke out which spread to all the major cities of the Maritime Provinces, delaying their departure many weeks.[83] On their return, Dr. Palmer purchased and combined *The Guide* and *The Beauty of Holiness,* making his wife editor in chief. Circulation soon rose from thirteen thousand to thirty thousand monthly. The magazine which so long had sung Phoebe Palmer's praises now carried her optimism and faith to the ends of the earth.[84]

Though Mrs. Palmer so eschewed feminist causes as to leave her name off the title page of most of her books, she inevitably inspired many women to Christian activity. Mrs. Thomas C. Upham was the first to organize in her home at Brunswick, Maine, a counterpart of the Tuesday Meeting. Others followed. In the revival of 1858 important ones were reported in full swing in Baltimore, Wilmington, Philadelphia, and Trenton, along with five in New York and two in Boston. Overseas reports of Mrs. Palmer's meeting in *The Guide* inspired a London lady "peculiarly adopted, by social position, great personal worth, and deep spirituality" to take the lead in establishing a weekday gathering there. Numbers soon sprang up all over the United Kingdom. In 1865 Mrs. Hamline initiated at Evanston, Illinois, the most influential of such meetings in the West. She had moved there following her husband's death. By 1886 238 were in operation, including 15 in Philadelphia, 14 in Boston, 12 in Baltimore, 7 in Toronto, and others in every major city in the United States and a half-dozen foreign countries. These intimate little gatherings brought together the most earnest Christians of all evangelical sects under the leadership of women, an ideal situation for the propagation of perfectionist religion.[85]

The gospel of Christian holiness thus became a chief strain in the

[82] Wheatley, *Phoebe Palmer,* pp. 325-26. Cf. *The Guide to Holiness,* XXX (July-December, 1856), pp. 112, 132; XXXI (January-June, 1857), pp. 1-3; and XXXIV (July-December, 1858), p. 178.

[83] Hughes, *Beloved Physician,* pp. 164-224, describes these years in great detail. See also Wheatley, *Phoebe Palmer,* pp. 337-45, and Phoebe Palmer, *Four Years in the Old World* ... (New York, ca. 1865).

[84] Hughes, *Tuesday Meeting,* pp. 175-76. The account of Palmer's publishing business other than the *Guide* is in the same author's *Beloved Physician,* p. 243.

[85] See *The Guide to Holiness,* XXXII (July-December, 1857), 159; and XXXIV (July-December, 1858), 94-95; Hughes, *Tuesday Meeting,* pp. 97, 142-43; Henry B. Ridgaway, *The Life of the Rev. Alfred Cookman* ... (New York, 1874), pp. 258-59, 292, 346; W. H. Daniels, *The Illustrated History of Methodism* ... (New York, 1880), pp. 683-84.

melody of mid-century Methodism. But precise orchestration of the theme produced occasional discords. The controversy over testimony and terminology, which first came to a head in 1852 and again in 1856, and the Free Methodist schism of 1859 illustrate its divisive properties.

Professing sanctification is a delicate task wherever men are sensitive to the Christian virtue of humility, especially if its witnesses acknowledge in themselves faults which onlookers might call sins. In the popular semifictional novel, *The Methodist*, an old minister advised the hero that although perfect love was a noble and scriptural quest, he must be careful of those who make a specialty of it. No one is "required to profess it in order to continue in the blessing," he said, and many "who do not dream of possessing it" display its evidences more than some who do.[36]

Practically, however, such profession was indispensable to the spread of the holiness revival, a fact evident in every piece of its literature. When Bishops Hamline, Janes, and Hedding neglected in the 1840's to urge public testimony to it, they suffered sharp rebuke from their friend Mrs. Palmer. They were in this respect following John Wesley's example, though not his advice to others. But she knew that few Methodists in America had actually attained perfect love until a militant, joyous group began to bear witness to it. By 1867 when Bishop Janes wrote the introduction for Phoebe Palmer's famous collection of personal experiences, one of a long and influential cycle, her views had won out.[37]

Belief in the immediate availability of sanctification through faith in Christ underlay these testimonies and formed their chief evangelistic content. In order to illustrate and simplify this notion, Mrs. Palmer developed about 1847 the "altar phraseology," as it came to be known, using Paul's figure of placing oneself as a "living sacrifice" on the altar of God to represent complete consecration. The altar, she reasoned, is Christ, the Sanctifier himself. The altar sanctifies the gift. Whoever was conscious, therefore,

[36] Miriam Fletcher, *The Methodist; or Incidents and Characters from Life in the Baltimore Conference* (New York, 1859), I, 171-72. Cf. Daniel Curry, *Life-Story of Davis Wasgatt Clark, D.D., Bishop of the Methodist Episcopal Church* (New York, 1874), pp. 160-61.

[37] Curry, *op. cit.*; Wheatley, *Phoebe Palmer*, pp. 550-54; Phoebe Palmer, ed., *Pioneer Experiences, or the Gift of Power Received by Faith* . . . (New York, 1867), pp. i-v. Hamline had long since changed his mind.

D. S. King, who succeeded Timothy Merritt as editor of *The Guide to Holiness*, edited the first such volume of testimonies, *The Riches of Grace* . . . (Boston, 1848), a book matched in England by John Eyre, ed., *Full Sanctification Realized* . . . (London, 1849).

that he was fully committed to Christ, "all on the altar," might at that moment believe he was sanctified by faith.

The distinction between the "witness of the Spirit" and the exercise of faith for the experience was blurred by this teaching. But it nonetheless released immense optimism by doing away with the chief emotional barrier keeping conscientious seekers from the blessing. When Bishop Hamline expressed misgivings, Mrs. Palmer wrote him that upon her discovery of this truth, she felt that if she were "possessed of a million souls, stained with the most dire pollutions," she could "as confidently bring them to the Christian altar" as she could bring one.[38]

Others beside the good bishop were perturbed. In an otherwise warm defense of the general tenor of her work, written in 1848, Nathan Bangs expressed unwillingness to subscribe to the correctness of all of Mrs. Palmer's terminology.[39] In 1854 when a writer who signed himself "Ida" declared in *Zion's Herald* that earnest seekers for the blessing sinned by not believing that they received it, regardless of the state of their inner consciousness, Hiram Mattison, recent editor of the *Genesee Conference Weekly* and an opponent of all holiness testimony, replied in two long articles which brought the controversy into the open. The whole idea of "only believing," he declared, was a dangerous perversion of what he claimed was Wesley's view that the witness of the Spirit was essential to entire sanctification and would only follow a long period, perhaps years, of striving. The editor, Daniel Wise, refuted Mattison sharply, affirming that faith placed in God's ability to fulfill his promise of holiness and in his willingness to perform it now was neither un-Wesleyan nor unscriptural.[40]

The next year Tobias Spicer, of the Troy Conference, who could not be accused of disbelief in the experience, renewed the discussion in *The Christian Advocate and Journal*, the New York Methodist weekly. Spicer attacked the "religious sentimentality" of urging seekers to "believe that ye have it and ye have it." Mrs. Palmer and others replied with some justice

---

[38] Wheatley, *Phoebe Palmer*, pp. 532-36. Cf. Rom. 12:1-2.

[39] Stevens, *Nathan Bangs*, p. 351. For other echoes of disapproval see the review of Eyre, *Sanctification Realized* in *The Methodist Quarterly Review*, XXXII (1850), 154; and the same, XXXIV (1852), 484. Cf. Wheatley, *Phoebe Palmer*, pp. 587-88, and generally pp. 405-6, 516-17, 583-85.

[40] See "Why Are You Not Wholly Sanctified?" *Zion's Herald*, Sept. 20, 1854; Hiram Mattison's answer, the same, Oct. 25 and Nov. 1, 1854; "Prof. Mattison *vs.* Ida," the same, Nov. 15, 1854. Cf. the editorial, "Saving Faith," Aug. 16, 1854, insisting that sanctification follows faith but is not identical with it, and J. H. Wallace, *Entire Holiness* (Auburn, N. Y., 1853), pp. 3-6, 73-74.

that they did not teach this. A Christian must be conscious of utterly complete consecration, of being "all on the altar," before he may exercise such trust. Moreover, the faith was placed not in his own experience but in "Christ the altar" and the word of God.[41]

The issue was a thorny one, however, and would not die. As late as March 10, 1857, after a long period of praying for guidance a warm friend of Mrs. Palmer's, Nathan Bangs, appeared at the Tuesday Meeting for the specific purpose of refuting the notion that Christians may believe they have the experience before they have the Spirit's witness to it. Wesley, he said, had considered the faith by which we are sanctified to be "inseparably connected with a divine evidence and conviction that the work is done." Hence the "altar phraseology" was unsound, unscriptural, anti-Wesleyan and no doubt in many cases had caused deception. The importance which Bangs attached to the event is indicated in the written charge he left with his diary that if any of it were ever published, the passage reporting the incident must be included *verbatim*.[42]

Meanwhile, Merritt Caldwell, a layman and educator in Maine, proposed a novel terminology of another sort. He believed man was sinful less from the fact that he was depraved than deprived, "constitutionally destitute of the love of God, as a controlling principle of his nature." Depravity results from the fact that the natural appetites and passions find unrestrained indulgence in our early lives and thus warp the personality with habits of sin. The converted believer was still subject to these twisted tendencies until he received the second blessing. Caldwell thus conceived entire sanctification to be a harmonizing rather than a cleansing grace in contrast with, for example, Nathan Bangs's emphasis upon the eradication of the "roots of bitterness."[43]

The pastoral address of the General Conference of 1852 attempted to

---

[41] See the article signed "T. S." on "Self-Deception," *The Christian Advocate and Journal*, Aug. 2, 1855, and the rejoinder in the issue of Sept. 20, 1855. Cf. "Believing and Knowing," *The Guide to Holiness*, XXXI (January-June, 1857), 11; the same, XXXII (July-December, 1857), 59-61; Phoebe Palmer, "The Act of Faith by which the Blessing Is Obtained and Retained," in J. Boynton, *Sanctification Practical* . . . (New York, 1867), pp. 115-29; and Tobias Spicer, *The Way from Sin to Sanctification, Holiness and Heaven* (4th ed., New York, 1857), which otherwise seriously urged Christians to seek and obtain the blessing.

[42] Stevens, *Nathan Bangs*, pp. 396-402, quotes Bangs's journal for March 15, 1857.

[43] Merritt Caldwell, *The Philosophy of Christian Perfection* . . . (Philadelphia, 1848); *The Methodist Quarterly Review*, XXXIV (1852), pp. 589-91; the same, XXX (1848), pp. 148-56, 293-323; and Nathan Bangs's sermon in Clark, ed., *Methodist Episcopal Pulpit*, p. 353. Cf. Peters, *Christian Perfection*, pp. 58-59, 112-14, 121-24, on these controversies.

check innovations in both directions. "The crowning work of the Spirit of holiness," wrote the fathers of the church,

is to sanctify believers wholly—their whole spirit, soul, and body—and to preserve them blameless until death. We would therefore exhort you, dear brethren, that the doctrine of *entire sanctification* or *entire holiness* be not confined to our standards: but that it may be a matter of experience in our hearts, and may be constantly practised in our lives. We advise you, in speaking or writing of holiness, to follow the well-sustained views, and even the phraseology employed in the writings of Wesley and Fletcher, which are not superseded by the more recent writers on this subject. Avoid both new theories, new expressions, and new measures on this subject, and adhere closely to the ancient landmarks.[44]

An ecclesiastical pronouncement, however, could neither make some humble men testify to holiness nor relieve the embarrassment of those who could not if they would. For the latter, that version of the Oberlin doctrine which declared regenerate persons already sanctified offered obvious attractions. Besides, they reasoned, had not Wesley clearly preached that sanctification began at conversion?

In 1854 Davis W. Clark, editor of *The Ladies Repository*, a popular family magazine which the denomination sponsored, began stressing this aspect of the founder's teaching. The event might have passed unnoticed had he not in a biography of Bishop Hedding, published the next year, emphasized the latter's refusal to testify to perfect love so strongly as to question whether Hedding really thought he experienced it. Nathan Bangs responded sharply in *The Christian Advocate and Journal*. The editor of *The Beauty of Holiness*, then published at Delaware, Ohio, printed a collection of quotations from Clark's writings purporting to show that he had entirely rejected the Wesleyan doctrine. What Daniel Curry, Clark's biographer and until much later an avowed opponent of the second blessing, called "a most unedifying controversy" erupted in the church newspapers and spilled over into numerous pamphlets and books. Perhaps Curry felt so because Clark finally defended himself with a statement of his belief in Christian perfection so clear and strong that but for the con-

[44] *Journals of the General Conference of the Methodist Episcopal Church, 1848-1856* (New York, 1856), p. 160.

troversy, Curry thought, "he would have been canonized among its con-
fessors." [45]

Meanwhile in the Genesee Conference of western New York the long
and bitter conflict over holiness which resulted in the organization of the
Free Methodist Church was approaching a crisis. As early as 1848 complaints appeared that the "less spiritual" clergymen of Buffalo and other
cities were joining the Odd Fellows and other secret orders and neglecting
the quest of Christian perfection. These charges grew in the following
years to include worldliness and love of money, compromises on slavery,
political domination of the conference through secret societies and influence over the bishops, and, finally, theological liberalism. The radicalism, anti-Masonry, and abolitionism indigenous to the "burned-over
region" thus burst forth anew—and continuous revivals in rural portions
of the conference combined with holiness camp meetings of immense size
to fan the flames. Perfect love never seemed so unworthy of its name to
the cultivated pastors of weathly city congregations who now moved to
throttle the movement. [46]

The editor of *The Northern Christian Advocate*, Seth Mattison, led
the attack until 1852, when the General Conference replaced him with
William Hosmer, an abolitionist and champion of holiness. However, in
1856 F. G. Hibbard, a more neutral person, gained the post, and Hosmer's
friends united to form *The Northern Independent* and place him in
charge. [47] Every annual conference after 1854 evoked a trial of strength
between the "Nazarites," as the radicals were called, and the "Buffalo
Regency." Whether the latter group engineered the removal of presiding
elders from the affected districts is not clear. Several did go; but those

[45] Curry, *Davis W. Clark*, p. 167; see generally pp. 157-61, 164-66. Cf. Wesley Kenney,
loc. cit., pp. 92-97.

[46] F. W. Conable, *History of the Genesee Annual Conference of the Methodist Episcopal
Church . . . to the Year 1872 . . .* (New York, 1876), pp. 618, 620-21, 635-36, agrees
at these points, despite other wide differences, with the official apology for Free Methodism,
Wilson T. Hogue, *History of the Free Methodist Church of North America* (Chicago,
1915), I, pp. 19-24, 33, 125-26, 129, 130 ff., 149-50. In numerous excerpts from contemporary documents Hogue, I, pp. 19, 24, 30-32, 33-35, 106-8, 110-11, 118, 161-62
demonstrates that the founders of his church felt that secret society membership, slavery
compromise, and worldliness in dress and behavior were the chief evidences of the unconsecrated condition of their opponents. See also, "Dress: a Word to Ministers," *The
Guide to Holiness*, XXXII (July-December, 1857), 143-44, signed by "J. D.," Binghamton,
N. Y.

[47] Hogue, *Free Methodist Church*, I, p. 29; Wheatley, *Phoebe Palmer*, pp. 551-54;
Stevens, *Nathan Bangs*, pp. 321-22. Cf. William Hosmer, *Slavery and the Church*
(Auburn, N. Y., 1853), p. iii.

appointed in the hope that they would "stamp out fanaticism" often became themselves seekers of the blessing.[48]

Early in 1857 Benjamin T. Roberts, one of the more aggressive young men and a convert of Phoebe Palmer, published in *The Northern Independent* an article denouncing the dominant group for their worldliness and doctrinal laxity. He was tried and convicted by the conference for unchristian conduct, sentenced to be reproved by the bishop, and appointed to a miserable rural circuit. At the next annual conference his alleged help in distributing a libelous pamphlet printed in his defense produced a new charge, disobedience to discipline. Roberts was expelled from the ministry and from membership in the church, along with J. M. McCreery, Jr. Both appealed to the General Conference, scheduled to meet at Buffalo in May, 1860.[49]

Meanwhile, they accepted the comforting support of a sizeable movement of laymen who, with the encouragement of several ministers still in the conference, were organizing for the protection of "the sacred doctrines of Methodism." Tensions had reached an explosive stage when Bishop Simpson, as much a believer in discipline as in holiness, arrived to preside over the Genesee Annual Conference in 1859. A large delegation of visiting ministers was present. Some of these who were sympathetic to the perfectionist men boldly organized a camp meeting at the outskirts of the town. The episcopal power, however, was sufficient to subdue the challengers. Four other clergymen were dismissed, several withdrew, and many of the visitors united in a statement approving the action. Characteristically, however, Simpson closed the conference with an exhortation which rebuked coldness and formality in worship. "Hearty prayers and responses," he said, and "praising God aloud" were "the privilege of his children" and fully in harmony with the spirit of Methodism.

The next spring the General Conference denied the appeals of Roberts and McCreery, after a debate which only skirted the issue of sanctification. Several thousand laymen and more than a score of ministers thereafter

[48] Hogue, *op. cit.*, I, pp. 34-35, contains B. T. Roberts's account; see also pp. 74, 76-79. Cf. Conable, *op. cit.*, pp. 616-17. A. A. Phelps, "Memoir of William C. Kendall, A. M.," *The Guide to Holiness*, XXXIV (1858), pp. 80-81, 97-99, 132-34, 161-63 commemorates one of the discharged presiding elders; cf. Hogue, I, pp. 80-82, and Conable, *op. cit.*, pp. 626-27.

[49] Conable, *Genesee*, pp. 643-47, 657; Hogue, the same, I, pp. 69-72, 146-51, 162-80, *passim*. Hogue prints the offending article, "New School Methodism," pp. 96-103. Cf. Hughes, *Tuesday Meeting*, p. 147.

found their way into the Free Methodist Church, and the membership of the Genesee Conference declined nearly one third in the next six years.[50]

There is little to substantiate the "official" Methodist version of the controversy. It alleged that the holiness leaders were fanatics who organized a secret society of their own for the purpose of destroying the reputations of other ministers, and who conducted camp meetings amid scenes of unrestrained emotionalism. Roberts' later writings on the doctrine of sanctification were certainly far from fanatical. They emphasized the ideal of perfect character, toward which he believed perfect love and all other authentic religious experiences tend. He seems also to have denied the eradication of the carnal mind, though this may have arisen from his confused terminology. "A man has but one mind, one intellect, one soul," he wrote; when sanctified wholly, "his mind, his will is so changed that earthly things lose their attractions" but "'the carnal mind' is never so destroyed as to do away with the freedom of the will." [51]

The Free Methodist contention that their exclusion was proof that Wesley's followers had abandoned their founder's cardinal doctrine is, on the other hand, equally inaccurate. A chief concern of the General Conference of 1860 was to keep the "border conferences" in Kentucky, Maryland, West Virginia, and Missouri within the denomination, and hence to contribute—so its leaders hoped—to the campaign to prevent the secession of those states from the national union. Sustaining an appeal from abolitionists, even sanctified ones, would hardly serve this purpose. The motion to dismiss the committee appointed to consider the difficulties in Genesee was, in fact, carried after one of the Buffalo group proclaimed his adherence to states' rights in politics and conference rights in the church, and a delegate from the Baltimore Conference responded with an appeal which set off a wave of speeches in its support! [52]

The Bishops' Address presaging this action was remarkably mild. After reproving those "whose presentation of the doctrine of Christian perfection" had recently varied from the standard Methodist authors "in the terms and

[50] Cf. Conable, *op. cit.*, pp. 650-51, 653-60, *passim*, with Hogue, *op. cit.*, I, 115, 193-207, 248-64, 294-96, 319, 322.
[51] Benjamin T. Roberts, *Holiness Teachings Compiled from the Editorial Writings of the Late Rev. Benjamin T. Roberts* (North Chili, N. Y., 1893), pp. 209, 212, 241-42. Concerning matters referred to earlier in the paragraph, Hogue, *op. cit.*, I, pp. 57-67, cites testimony completely contradicting that quoted in Conable, *op. cit.*, pp. 630-33, 638-39. On the question of emotional excesses, cf. Hogue, *op. cit.*, I, pp. 125-26, 128, 130-34, 169-70, with Conable, *op. cit.*, pp. 637, 641, 662.
[52] Hogue, *op. cit.*, I, 295.

forms of expression used," in much the same vein as the pastoral address of 1852, they continued as follows:

These individuals claim to be strictly Wesleyan in their views of the doctrine, and probably are so substantially. Nor do we impugn their motives. But, in our judgment, in denouncing those in the ministry and laity who do not sympathize with them and adopt their measures . . . they have erred, and in a few instances caused secessions. *It is our opinion that there was no occasion for these special-ties. Our ministers are generally Wesleyan in their faith and preaching touching this subject.*[53]

Disobedience to discipline was the cardinal sin in Methodism, and doubly so when accompanied by encouragement to schism. If Roberts and McCreery were not guilty of these offenses at their trials in 1858, they were by the time the General Conference assembled. Then only the last formal steps remained for the organization of a new denomination. That at least some of their party were by nature unruly, harsh in judgment, and willing to make a public scandal of the sins of others is, moreover, evident from their own testimony.[54]

Many champions of holiness refrained from supporting the "Nazarites" out of unwillingness to identify the cause with such behavior, or with the abolitionism, anti-Masonry, and laymen's rights which they espoused. Jesse Peck, who was present at the Genesee Conference in 1855, framed the first resolution against the alleged organization of *Nazaritism;* he was writing *The Central Idea of Christianity* at the time. William Taylor preached alongside Bishop Simpson at the crucial assembly of 1859.[55] A member of the Oneida Conference who supported Roberts' appeal in 1860 had, in fact, just published a little hand-book in which he condemned lay agitation for increased constitutional powers as vigorously as he supported entire sanctification by faith. Both the Oneida and East Genesee conferences enjoyed a concurrent holiness revival without untoward event; neither, significantly, suffered from a sharp urban-rural cleavage.[56]

[53] *Journal of the General Conference of the Methodist Episcopal Church . . . 1860* (New York, 1860), p. 317. Italics are mine.
[54] See Hogue, *Free Methodist Church,* I, pp. 96-103, *passim,* 159, 161-62; cf. Conable, *op. cit.,* pp. 648-49, 656.
[55] Conable, *op. cit.,* pp. 639, 655, 665. Hogue, *op. cit.,* I, pp. 35, 81-82, indicates the curious opposition to Bishop Hamline.
[56] William E. Reddy, *Inside Views of Methodism . . .* (New York, 1859), pp. 16, 26, 45-51, 59-61; cf. Hogue, *op. cit.,* I, pp. 104, 114, 295, and esp. pp. 115 and 204, citing the recantation made by the Genesee Conference at its centennial in 1910.

The issues which drove the Genesee Conference to division seem thus to have been as much personal and sociological as religious. The rupture could scarcely have occurred had the conflict over holiness not been involved from the beginning with a struggle for place and power in which platforms of moral reform in church and state played a major part. The doctrine of entire sanctification and the crusade to restore "old-fashioned Methodism" were emotional symbols as well as issues vital to the fray.

In western New York, however, and to some degree in other places, the controversy enabled opponents of the second blessing to seize the initiative. A prominent pastor led the attack for several years in the Philadelphia Conference.[57] Though slavery rather than doctrinal standards may have been the decisive factor, it is significant that the General Conference of 1864 made Daniel Curry editor of *The Christian Advocate and Journal* and chose Davis W. Clark to be a bishop in preference to Randolph S. Foster and Jesse Peck.[58] Frances Willard, founder and long-term president of the Women's Christian Temperance Union, later testified that she lost the grace of perfect love from failure to testify to it while serving, during the year 1866, as preceptress of the Genesee Wesleyan Seminary in Lima, New York.

Miss Willard's story is worth telling for its own sake. Both John Dempster and Randolph Foster had been instrumental in her conversion in 1859, while she was a somewhat rebellious student at the Female College in Evanston, Illinois. When Mrs. L. L. Hamline arrived there in 1865, she arranged for the restless, complex girl to help organize the first national association of Methodist women, a temporary group which raised funds to construct Heck Hall at nearby Garrett Seminary. She also gave Frances the writings of Jesse Peck and Phoebe Palmer and encouraged her to read the lives of John Fletcher and Hester Ann Rogers. Dr. and Mrs. Palmer conducted a long revival in the Evanston church the next spring, and the young woman professed sanctification. On her departure for Lima, however, a distinguished minister warned her that the Free Methodists had "done great harm in western New York by their excesses in the doctrine and experience of holiness," and added: "You know I believe thoroughly in and profess it, but just now our church has suffered so much from the

[57] See Wheatley, *Phoebe Palmer*, pp. 307, 450, 452, 551-54, 579; Simpson, *Cyclopedia of Methodism*, p. 446.
[58] Simpson, *Cyclopedia of Methodism*, pp. 272, 516; Curry, *Davis W. Clark*, pp. 173, 184; *The Daily Christian Advocate* (Philadelphia), May 21, 1864.

"Nazarites," as they are called, that I fear if you speak and act as zealously at Lima in this cause as you do here it may make trouble." [59]

This statement, like so many others made during these years, only supports the thesis that "perfect love" was still a central quest of Wesleyan religion. Methodist leaders were not yet ready to allow a direct challenge to what all regarded as a chief distinguishing belief of their denominations.[60] Opponents dared no more than to impugn the methods and terminology of its special pleaders or to argue the precise forms of "worldliness" its subjects must renounce. The departure of the Free Methodist fringe deprived antagonists of some favorite targets and thus may in the long run have strengthened the cause within the church. Continuous discussion certainly provoked a more precise explanation of what it meant to be "sanctified wholly." R. S. Foster, Phoebe Palmer, and Jesse Peck, for example, helped many seekers by clarifying the distinction between "essential human nature" and the "carnal mind," one of which God meant to save and the other to cleanse away. And, notwithstanding a recent student's opinion to the contrary, even quite radical advocates of the second blessing carefully stressed the growth and discipline which must both precede and follow the "instantaneous" reception of perfect love.[61]

Jesse Peck wrote the editor of *The Guide to Holiness* from the West Coast in 1858 that the recent controversies had cleared the air and brought unity of opinion nearer than ever before. "Old definitions, and well-established principles," he declared, were "more than ever satisfactory to the church." The doctrine was prominent in Methodist preaching in California, Peck reported. He had spent many days at the district camp meeting without hearing "in public or in private a single unsound opinion on the subject . . . from preacher or layman." [62] His satisfaction might have been even greater could he have foreseen the revival which after the Civil War was to sweep him into the bishop's chair!

[59] See her testimony in S. Olin Garrison, *Forty Witnesses, Covering the Whole Range of Christian Experience* (New York, 1888), p. 97.

[60] See D. D. Whedon, "Doctrines of Methodism," *Bibliotheca Sacra,* XIX (1862), pp. 269-72; *Harper's Monthly,* XVIII (1859), p. 841; Jacob J. Abbott, "Boardman's Higher Christian Life," *Bibliotheca Sacra,* XVII (1860), p. 519; and Wheatley, *Phoebe Palmer,* p. 323, for contemporary observations not cited earlier.

[61] William Taylor, *Story of My Life,* pp. 73-75; Foster, *Christian Purity* (1869), pp. 63-69; Peck, *Central Idea,* pp. 41-47. On the question of growth in holiness, contrast Peters, *Christian Perfection,* pp. 112, 190, with Wallace, *Entire Holiness,* pp. 91-92, 93-95, and Roberts, *Holiness Teachings,* pp. 209-12.

[62] *The Guide to Holiness,* XXXIV (July-December, 1858), 143-44.

IX

Revivalism and Perfectionism

❧

The foregoing two chapters suggest a new interpretation of the revival of 1858, ushered in as it was by Finney's preaching in Boston and Baptist Henry Clay Fish's call for a return to Pentecostal piety. Fish lamented most the weakness of an unconsecrated church and urged every Christian to strive for "the glorious gift of sanctification." The Rev. George B. Ide joined him in the conviction that the church could never meet her responsibilities to American society until her children "come up to that high measure of evangelical sanctification" which the Scriptures require.[1] The previous year, the Lutheran *Evangelical Quarterly Review* had printed a serious evaluation of the growing interest in Christian perfection which, though rejecting the specifically Wesleyan view, agreed that the times required and the Bible taught that Christians must attain personal holiness.[2]

When the revival broke out, it seemed to its champions a "modern Pentecost" in which the "gift of power" bestowed on believers of every sect was preparing the way for the conversion of the world and the early advent of the kingdom of God on earth. "We need the gift of the Spirit, and we need it now," wrote James W. Alexander at its height; "we need it to break the power of sin in professing Christians and to nail their lusts to the cross."[3] The phenomenal success of William E. Boardman's volume, *The Higher Christian Life*, published at the height of the awakening, can only be explained in terms of the universal awareness of this want. No wonder that Dr. and Mrs. Palmer found Baptist, Presbyterian, and Congregational pulpits thrown open to them that summer! Apostolic unction

---

[1] Henry C. Fish, *Primitive Piety Revived* . . . (Boston, 1857), pp. 69-70, 86, 87-90, 98-101; cf. *The Christian Review*, XXIV (1859), p. 321; XXV (1860), p. 153.

[2] A. L. Bridgman, "A High Standard of Piety Demanded by the Times," *The Evangelical Quarterly Review*, VII (1855), pp. 364-66, 366-68, 371 ff.

[3] James Waddell Alexander, *The Revival and Its Lessons* . . . (New York, 1858), p. 9. Cf. for an identical conviction Charles Pettit McIlvaine, *Bishop McIlvaine on the Revival of Religion* (Philadelphia, 1858), p. 4; and, generally, Talbott W. Chambers, *The Noon Prayer Meeting of the North Dutch Church, Fulton Street, New York* . . . (New York, 1858), pp. 80, 245, 248, 267. See earlier, pp. 58, 86-88.

was the burden of every prayer. At an all-day union meeting in Baltimore in 1859 prominent pastors of nearly every denomination joined in urging a distinct experience of the baptism of the Holy Spirit subsequent to conversion. The Rev. R. Fuller, minister at the Seventh Avenue Baptist Church, concluded his remarks with a request to sing Charles Wesley's hymn:

> O for a heart to praise my God,
> A heart from sin set free.[4]

The spiritual tide carried many urban Methodist pastors into the experience which in rural Genesee was at the same moment causing bitter controversy. Alfred Cookman, who was sanctified in 1857 while pastor of Green Street Church, Philadelphia, was the most famous of these. He founded that fall the city's first noonday prayer meeting. Through its influence he became an important leader of the next year's awakening. At his succeeding pastorates in Philadelphia, New York City, Wilmington, and Newark, Cookman invariably organized a weekday meeting for the promotion of holiness, patterned after Mrs. Palmer's, and carried on an intensely "spiritual" program. That such a ministry gained favor with the denomination's laymen is indicated by the invitations he received to become pastor of large congregations in Boston, Chicago, Cincinnati, and Washington on the occasion of his transfer to Newark in 1870.[5]

About 1860 Cookman began spending every summer making the rounds of Methodist camp meetings in the East, preaching with great success on sanctification. The New York *Christian Advocate and Journal* reported his progress regularly. In 1865, for example, its front page carried the story of an evening meeting for clergymen at Shrewsbury camp near Baltimore where, after a "frank and full" exchange of views on holiness, Cookman led three presiding elders and nineteen other ministers into the blessing. The tides of emotion and earnest prayer swept on until dawn. "Whenever and wherever the work of sanctification revived among professing Christians," the newspaper quoted him as saying, "the work of God revived in the conversion of sinners." [6]

   [4] Richard Wheatley, *Life and Letters of Phoebe Palmer* (New York, 1876), pp. 334-35; Y.M.C.A., Baltimore, *Proceedings of the All-Day Prayer Meeting . . . September 27, 1859* (Baltimore, 1859), pp. 6, 10-11, 17, 19, 23.
   [5] Henry B. Ridgaway, *The Life of the Rev. Alfred Cookman . . .* (New York, 1874), pp. 115, 193-98, 229, 235-36, 239, 258, 281, 292-93, 311, 345, 402-5.
   [6] Quoted from *The Christian Advocate and Journal* in Ridgaway, *op. cit.*, pp. 305-6; see generally pp. 300-8.

As the Civil War drew to a close, many other New York City and Philadelphia pastors joined Cookman in thanksgiving that the Methodist Centenary year, 1866, would find "the spotless banner of Christian purity" floating triumphantly over American Wesleyanism. John Swannell Inskip, was sanctified in 1864 while preaching on the experience in his own pulpit in Newark, a year after his wife had found it at Sing Sing camp meeting. At his next charge, the Green Street Church, New York, Inskip led the city's Methodist preacher's meeting, of which he was chairman, in a weekly discussion of the theme. He was destined soon to become president of the National Camp Meeting Association for the Promotion of Holiness, an organization which for one brief decade made entire sanctification a rallying cry of the denomination through the length and breadth of the land.[7] John C. McClintock, who in 1867 was to become the first president of Drew Theological Seminary, fervently pleaded in a centenary sermon delivered in his own pulpit, St. John's, New York, that the Methodist ministry must hold to

the great central idea of the whole book of God, from the beginning to the end,—*the holiness of the human soul, heart, mind, and will.* It may be called fanaticism but that, dear friends, is our mission. If we keep to that, the next century is ours. Our work is a moral work; that is to say, the work of making men holy. Our preaching is to that, our church agencies are for that, our schools, colleges, universities, and theological seminaries are for that. There is our mission. There is our glory. There is our power, and there shall be our triumph.[8]

That holiness had become the key to Methodist evangelism was evident from the immensely successful tour Dr. and Mrs. Palmer conducted the year after Grant's victory ended the Civil War. They were at Evanston, site of Garrett Biblical Institute, for three weeks, then at McKendree College, Lebanon, Illinois, whence the president, Robert Allyn, reported that scores had "experienced the blessing of perfect love." They visited "cen-

[7] *Ibid.*, p. 302; Phoebe Palmer, *Pioneer Experiences, or the Gift of Power Received by Faith* . . . (New York, 1867), pp. 52-60; *The Christian Advocate and Journal*, May-June, 1867, pp. 141, 149, 157, 181, 189; A. McLean and Joel W. Eaton, eds., *Penuel; or Face to Face with God* (New York, 1869), pp. 6-15; and George Hughes, *Days of Power in the Forest Temple. A Review of the Wonderful Work of God at Fourteen National Camp-Meetings, from 1867 to 1872* (Boston, 1874), pp. 39-60.

[8] Quoted in *Proceedings of Holiness Conferences* . . . *1877* (Philadelphia, ca. 1878), pp. 139-40, from *The Methodist*, Feb. 3, 1866. See the sketch in Matthew Simpson, *Cyclopedia of Methodism* . . . (Philadelphia, 1878), p. 573.

tennial camp meetings" held under the auspices of conference districts at Albion, Palmyra, and Ann Arbor, Michigan; Greenbush, Ontario; Des Plaines, Illinois (the Chicago District camp); Lima, Indiana; and Watertown, New York. Scores of pastors professed the blessing and pledged to return to their home communities and "uphold the banner of holiness." Meanwhile, Anthony Atwood, president of the Philadelphia preachers' meeting, reported in the fall that the gospel of sanctification "never took hold of our ministers and people in this city as now." [9]

A sufficient number of Baptist ministers also experienced the second work of grace during the revival of 1858 to begin a noteworthy "higher life" movement in their denomination. Chief among them was John Q. Adams, pastor of the North Baptist Church, New York. Adams found the blessing at Mrs. Palmer's house, after a woman parishioner had shared with him her copy of Boardman's famous book.[10] Certain of his congregation objected, however, when Adams preached the doctrine; whereupon Adams resigned and on July 1, 1859, after an all-day prayer meeting, organized eighty-one of the poorer members into the Antioch Baptist Church. The new group occupied temporary quarters in a hall of the Metropolitan Academy in lower Manhattan. A council of recognition representing forty of the churches in the New York Baptist Association "extended fellowship" to them the following October, and several pastors joined Adams in preaching holiness. But the opposition of the North church was sufficient to prevent the Antioch people from securing institutional membership in the association. Fifty-two converts were baptized the first year, however—more than in any but two other Baptist congregations in the city—and forty-one members were received by transfer. Despite the great poverty of the congregation and the failure of their first efforts to purchase a vacated downtown church building, the work continued to prosper.[11]

In 1863 Adams began publishing a monthly magazine, *The Christian*, which served to unify and inspire the growing company of Baptist min-

[9] *The Guide to Holiness*, L (July-December, 1866), p. 188. See, on the Palmers's tour, the same, pp. 58-59, 88-91, 122-23, 152-54; LI (January-June, 1867), p. 155; S. Olin Garrison, *Forty Witnesses, Covering the Whole Range of Christian Experience* (New York, 1888), p. 95.

[10] John Quincy Adams, ed., *Experiences of the Higher Christian Life in the Baptist Denomination* . . . (New York, 1870), pp. 17, 21, 134, 135, 142; *Sanctification: A Sermon Preached in the North Baptist Church, New York, June 12, 1859* (New York, 1859), p. 3; and *The Christian, Devoted to the Advancement of Gospel Holiness*, I, (1863), pp. 56-58.

[11] The Antioch Baptist Church. *First Annual Report* . . . *1860*, pp. 3-15; *Third Annual Report* . . . *1862*, pp. 3-4, 14.

isters who had experienced sanctification. Their chief stumbling block had been sectarian prejudice, which in some cases had restrained them from preaching the doctrine even when they enjoyed the blessing. "The devil said 'Methodism,'" as one of them put it, "but the Lord said gospel truth." [12] Adams himself led the way in rejecting sectarianism, despite the fact that he had earlier become well known for his authorship of a book entitled *Baptists, the Only Thorough Religious Reformers*.[13] Mrs. Palmer's influence upon the group was marked. Her idea of "only believing" was the keynote of their testimony, just as in many localities her Tuesday Meeting was a pattern for their evangelism. All of them tended to emphasize experience over creeds and to make practical consecration their chief concern.[14] By 1867 they were sufficiently numerous to sponsor a public service at the anniversary meetings in Chicago of the national Baptist societies. Their books and pamphlets multiplied in number, and every season of revival brought additional clergymen into the circle.[15]

The rising fame of Baptist evangelist A. B. Earle, who was sanctified in 1859, the same year in which he preached eighty consecutive sermons in the Tremont Temple at Boston, greatly helped Adams' movement. When Jacob Knapp came into contact the following winter with Boston Baptists who professed sanctification, he confided that he had himself never been troubled with too much holiness. But Emerson Andrews, another prominent evangelist of the denomination, clearly preached a second work of grace. Earle's subsequent role in union city-wide revivals at Fall River, Chelsea, Springfield, and Haverhill, Massachusetts, Ithaca, New York, and Washington, D. C. is striking proof of the popularity of perfectionism. Boston welcomed Earle back in 1862 for a three-month campaign at Tremont Temple, and again in 1866 for a union meeting where Baptist pastors joined with those from the Park Street and Mount Vernon

[12] The quotation is from Adams, *Experiences*, p. 227; cf. pp. 32, 33, 166, 167, 176. See also the correspondence in *The Christian*, I (1863), pp. 45-46, 92, 120-22.

[13] Cf. *The Christian*, I (1863), pp. 52-54, 160, 192, with John Q. Adams, *Baptists, the Only Thorough Religious Reformers* (New York, 1853, and many later editions), *passim*.

[14] *The Christian*, I (1863), pp. 15, 176; Adams, *Experiences*, pp. 27, 34, 113, 116-17, 131, 134, 137, 143-44, 167-69, 177, 277.

[15] See *The Christian*, V (1867), pp. 148, 277-78, the latter selection being a rebuke to the "practical antinomianism" of "sinning Christians"; VI (1868), p. 51; Antioch Baptist Church. *First Annual Report . . . 1860*, p. 13, and *Seventh Annual Report . . . 1866*, pp. 3-4; and, for examples of general literature, William L. Parsons, *Satan's Devices and the Believer's Victory* (Boston, 1864), and D. F. Newton, *The Sword That Cuts, the Fire That Burns* (New York, 1867).

Congregational churches. In 1866 the ministerial union of San Francisco invited him to California, where, at the behest of Edward N. Kirk and others, he spent the next two years.[16]

Earle's book on holiness, *The Rest of Faith*, like his evangelistic sermons, was thoughtful and free from sectarian cant. He was convinced that Christians of all denominations were gripped by a great hunger for the "fullness of Christ's love." The record of his success in Boston explains why Dr. and Mrs. Palmer found such great interest there in 1864 among clergymen of many persuasions. They accepted an invitation to remain at Tremont Temple for ten days.[17]

Another indication of the popularity of holiness sentiments in this era of revivals is the way in which the perfectionist view of the first work of grace gained ground after 1858. Evangelicals readily agreed with the Unitarian editor who declared that the gospel "undertakes to effect an entire change, a radical reformation in human character" through a "wonderful crisis which takes place in the profoundest depths of our nature."[18] Bishop McIlvaine warned Ohio Episcopal clergymen in 1863 that neither sacraments nor church ordinances nor Sacred Scripture could substitute for an immediate experience of Christ. They must, he said, preach constantly the doctrine that the Holy Spirit comes to the human heart to destroy "the carnal mind" and to make the sinner "a new creature in Christ Jesus." The deliverance from sin is "so complete that to the believer there is no condemnation."[19]

Looking back, then, across the narrative of this and the preceding two chapters, we may conclude that the popularity of Christian perfection, in both its Oberlin and Wesleyan forms, increased steadily in American Prot-

[16] Absalom B. Earle, *Bringing In Sheaves* (Boston, 1869), pp. 269, 270, 280-363, *passim*, 373. See earlier, pp. 74-75. Cf. *The Watchman and Reflector*, March 26 and Apr. 19, 1863; P. C. Headley, *Evangelists in the Church: Philip, A.D., 35, to Moody and Sankey, A.D. 1875* (Boston, 1875), pp. 346-47, 349-59, *passim*; Jacob Knapp, *Autobiography of Elder Jacob Knapp* (New York, 1868), p. 178; Emerson Andrews, *Living Life; or Autobiography of the Rev. Emerson Andrews, Evangelist* (Boston, 1875), pp. 313-318.

[17] Wheatley, *Phoebe Palmer*, p. 409. See, again, Earle, *Bringing In Sheeves*, pp. 363-64; cf. pp. 239-51 for his defense of interdenominational revivals. See also A. B. Earle, *The Rest of Faith* (Boston, 1867); and contrast John C. Stockbridge, *A Memoir of the Life and Correspondence of Rev. Baron Stow, D.D. . . .* (Boston, 1871), p. 311 with Charles K. Whipple, "The Boston Revival, and Its Leader," *The Radical: a Monthly Magazine Devoted to Religion*, I (1865-66), 429-38.

[18] *The Watchman and Reflector*, Jan. 22, 1863. Cf. Austin Phelps, "Conversion, Its Nature," *Bibliotheca Sacra*, XXIII (1866), pp. 53-55 for the spread of the Oberlin view.

[19] Charles Pettit McIlvaine, *The Work of Preaching Christ . . .* (New York, 1863), pp. 14, 26, 44-45, 49-50, 51-54.

estantism between 1840 and 1870. Although one branch of the Oberlin gospel tree bore holiness from the first bloom of grace and the other insisted on blossoming twice, the fruit of both was the sanctification of heart and conduct. In the Methodist fold the greatest intellectual leaders joined with several of the most highly regarded bishops to breathe new life into the ancient aim "to reform the nation and spread scriptural holiness over these lands." Phoebe Palmer and her husband exerted an immense influence over the Wesleyan clergy through the New York Tuesday Meeting, *The Guide to Holiness*, and their ardent evangelism at camp meetings all over the country. Despite the fact that after 1848 serious controversy broke out in the denomination over the public testimonies upon which these advocates of the second blessing insisted and the new "altar phraseology" which Mrs. Palmer created, few men dared publicly to challenge the doctrine itself. The principal result of the debate, as likewise of the Free Methodist secession in 1859, was to establish the centrality of "perfect love" in the church's teachings. The stream of popular holiness literature flowed thereafter without abatement, and the bishops gave hearty encouragement to the organized effort to bring Methodist preachers into the experience.

Elsewhere, particularly in the cities, perfectionism also prospered, borne forward on revival tides. Thomas C. Upham, professor of philosophy at Bowdoin College, joined Wesleyanism to mysticism in a dozen thoughtful books which bridged the chasm between Christian piety and transcendentalism. Mrs. Palmer had secured Upham's sanctification in 1839. During the revival of 1858 Presbyterian William E. Boardman initiated the "Higher Life" movement, with the express aim of making the doctrine interdenominational. From 1859 to 1874, when Dwight L. Moody's fame eclipsed them, Boardman and A. B. Earle—a Baptist likewise chiefly known for his advocacy of the second blessing—were easily the two most respected evangelists in America. Presbyterians, Congregationalists, and Baptists who could not accept their radical idea of two works of grace meanwhile turned quite naturally toward the emphasis growing at Oberlin on a perfect life through the initial experience of conversion.

What were the causes of this remarkable fruitage of perfectionist fervor in mid-nineteenth-century America?

Most obvious is the fact that the movement embodied in somewhat radical fashion the religious ideals and customs stemming from the new revivalism. Evangelism spawned Arminianism, and Arminianism of both the Wesleyan and Oberlin varieties bore perfectionism.[20] Holiness was so generally identified with interchurch fellowship that a call issued by the Evangelical Alliance for a national week of prayer in January, 1863, equated the increase of one with the growth of the other.[21] Parishioners who led their pastors into the higher life demonstrated time and again the new spiritual eminence of laymen. Most important, the ethical earnestness native to revivalism attained fullest expression in the doctrine of entire consecration to God's will, an idea which was the pith and marrow of the holiness crusade. At the high tide of revivalism, perfectionism was the crest of the wave.

That a romantic and transcendentalist generation joined readily in the mystic quest for union with God and "perfect love" should, moreover, not surprise us. Thomas C. Upham must have been already steeped in the literature of Catholic sainthood when he met Phoebe Palmer, for his first treatise on holiness, *Principles of the Interior or Hidden Life*, employed quotations from twelve great mystics.[22] George Peck, who asserted that no work in English stated and applied the doctrine of sanctification better than this volume, was amazed to find that the Unitarian *Religious Miscellany*, *The Arminian Quarterly*, and *The New Englander* approved its main position—the last differing only on the point of instantaneous attainment.[23]

The kinship of the belief in the Holy Spirit's "abiding presence" to Ralph Waldo Emerson's idea of communion with the oversoul was apparent to such widely different witnesses as Stephen Olin, Phoebe Palmer, Gilbert Haven, Andrew Preston Peabody, and Emerson himself. Peabody, who succeeded Frederic D. Huntington at Harvard, explained this rela-

---

[20] See earlier, pp. 80-94, *passim* and the quotation from Samuel S. Schmucker, p. 58.

[21] *The American Missionary*, XII (1863), p. 7. Cf. Daniel P. Noyes, "The Church and the Churches," *Bibliotheca Sacra*, XX (1863), pp. 350-51, 355; Charles Adams, "Wesley the Catholic," *The Methodist Quarterly Review*, XXXII (1850), pp. 177, 191; W. Scott, "Remarks on I Corinthians XIII, 9-13," the same, pp. 377, 380-82, 384; and *The Christian*, I (1863), p. 160, praising the "spirit of true Christian union" in a Free Methodist camp meeting in Broome County, N. Y.

[22] Benjamin Breckinridge Warfield, *Perfectionism*, (New York, 1931), II, 371-73; cf. pp. 371-410, *passim*. For an example of popular interest, see "The Youth and Early Manhood of Fénélon," *Zion's Herald*, Oct. 25 and Nov. 8, 1854.

[23] George O. Peck, "Dr. Upham's Works," *The Methodist Quarterly Review*, XXVIII (1846); see 252-57 for a biting satire on transcendentalism. Note the mystical interests of the period of the great revival in "Notes on the Mystics," *The Christian Review*, XXV (1860), pp. 557-76; *The Watchman and Reflector*, July 2, 1857, containing a report of a Newton Seminary graduate's essay on "Union with Christ by the Agency of the Holy Spirit"; and Henry C. Fish, *Primitive Piety*, pp. 138-40.

tionship in a Pentecost Sunday sermon at Appleton Chapel in the early seventies.[24] In 1864 a Baptist minister's little volume, *The Celestial Dawn; or Connection of Earth and Heaven*, wove together golden strands from Wesley, Upham, Finney, Wordsworth, and the Catholic mystics to form a magic carpet of evangelical transcendentalism. "Pure truth," he declared, "is an inbreathing of God; . . . holy love is the life of God and celestial beings. So far as we are admissive of these, earth and heaven become one in our experience."[25]

Indeed the whole stream of nineteenth-century popular romanticism was a fitting context for the optimism which ruled in Phoebe Palmer's parlors as Americans sought "immediate sanctification by faith." A similar mood lay back of New Harmony, the Oneida Community, and the Washingtonian movement, as well as Brook Farm. The merging of the romantic spirit with the boundless hopefulness of the postwar years in no wise lessened the receptiveness of multitudes awakened by a generation of revivals to the confident promise, "If we walk in the light as He is in the light, we have fellowship one with another, and the blood of Jesus Christ God's son cleanseth us from all sin."[26]

Two sociological facts bear on this point: the growth of city life and the enlarged role of women in religious affairs. Perfectionism in America seems to have been typical not of frontier but of urban communities. There the social discipline of the church was more consistent. The migration of both native and foreign-born agricultural populations to the cities produced a host of personal frustrations. Individuals once securely integrated within a simpler society felt themselves "lost" in the crowds, if not the sin, of the city. To be "found" in a revival was a thrilling emotional experience. Those converts whose religious training and psychological orientation permitted it turned readily to a subjective, individualistic quest for personal holiness, for "union with Christ." From the Arkansas frontier a Methodist local preacher wrote *The Guide to Holiness* in 1856:

[24] Andrew Preston Peabody, *Christian Belief and Life* (Boston, 1875), pp. 232-39; Gilbert Haven, "Wesley and Modern Philosophy," *The Methodist Quarterly Review*, LXI (1879), pp. 9, 16; John McClintock, "Stephen Olin," *The Methodist Quarterly Review*, XXXVI (1854), pp. 17-18. Cf. on the same point, Henry Steele Commager, *Theodore Parker* (Boston, 1936), p. 267; Stow Persons, *Free Religion, an American Faith* (New Haven, 1947), p. 21.

[25] W. F. Evans, *The Celestial Dawn; or Connection of Earth and Heaven* (Boston, 1864), p. vi, and *passim*; cf. identical sentiments in Peabody, *Belief and Life*, pp. 160-68, and *The Guide to Holiness*, XXXIV (July-December, 1858), pp. 122-23.

[26] I John 1:7. See Ralph Henry Gabriel, "Evangelical Religion and Popular Romanticism in Early Nineteenth Century America," *Church History*, XIX (1950), p. 41.

Not a single minister of God within this state (and I am generally acquainted with the ministry of the different denominations) has as yet attained this grace, though several of my Methodist brethren preach it. . . . How I would rejoice "to sit in heavenly places in Christ Jesus" with all those who have enjoyed, and do enjoy this blessing in Boston and New York.[27]

The theory that mystical and perfectionist religion thrives when feminine influence is dominant may find some support in the fact that women like Mrs. Palmer and Mrs. Upham led their husbands into the experience.[28] Many others, including Mrs. William E. Boardman, the second Mrs. Finney, Mrs. Leonidas Hamline, Mrs. Edmund S. Janes, Mrs. John Inskip, and Mrs. Alfred Cookman assumed prominent roles concurrently with the sanctification of their several spouses. Such women conducted week-day holiness meetings, wrote articles and sentimental poetry for *The Guide*, devoured the biographies of early Methodist female saints, and spent summers at camp meetings supervising children's work and leading their more timid sisters into the emancipating blessing.[29]

Such a generalization bears some scrutiny, however, for Phoebe Palmer heartily opposed the mystic tendencies of both Thomas C. Upham and Frederic Dan Huntington. She warned Upham that his emphasis on intuitive experience to the neglect of scriptural formulas was leading some to think they had reached a state of union with God which Paul himself did not attain in this life. Nor, she continued, did Upham's doctrine of "the death of the will" fit the New Testament picture of Christ, whose will in her opinion was "not *dead*, but in subjection to the will of His Father," and whose humanity was proof that "natural propensities . . . are not sinful, only as they have become debased by the Fall." The function of God's sanctifying grace, she said, is to turn human drives into holy channels. About the same time she wrote Huntington that, while admiring his un-

[27] *The Guide to Holiness*, XXX (1856), p. 158. Cf. Thomas Guthrie, *The City: Its Sins and Its Sorrows* . . . (Glasgow, 1862), pp. 8-9; and "The Perils and Advantages of a Christian Life in the City," *The Independent*, Dec. 16, 1858.
[28] Herbert Moller, "Sex Composition and Correlated Culture Patterns of Colonial America," *The William and Mary Quarterly*, II (1949), p. 146.
[29] Any issue of *The Guide to Holiness* will verify this point: see L (July-December, 1866), in which half of the signed articles are by women; XXXII (July-December, 1857), 45-47, 131; and the interesting extract from Jesse T. Peck, *The True Woman, or Life and Happiness at Home and Abroad* (New York, 1856), quoted in the same, p. 129. Cf. George Coles, *Heroines of Methodism* . . . (New York, 1857), pp. 4, 135-36, 203-4 and *passim*; and Abel Stevens, *The Women of Methodism: Its Three Foundresses* . . . (New York, 1866), pp. 3-4, 15. Twenty of the twenty-five testimonies of lay persons in Adams, *Higher Life in the Baptist Denomination*, were from women, as were most of those in John Eyre, *Full Sanctification Realized* . . . (London, 1850).

reserved consecration, she feared his desire for some inner "sign or wonder" of mystic revelation. Sanctification was not an experience of constant ecstasy but a "state of continuous trust." That trust was, in her view, a rational act based upon the awareness of our complete personal consecration to God's will and full confidence in the promises of his Word.[80]

All of which suggests a third and quite utilitarian impulse of the holiness revival, the hunger for an experience which would "make Christianity work." Finney, the reformer, Mrs. Palmer, the pioneer of many benevolent and missionary enterprises and William E. Boardman, organizer and executive head of The United States Christian Commission, did not seem mystic dreamers to their generation. They rather exhibited the consecration to Christian service which their preaching declared to be in will the prerequisite and in life the fruit of entire sanctification. The movement they led was one of the great efforts by which the plain men of the century tried to put their religious ideals to work.

Thus James Caughey wrote of *Christianity in Earnest*, Boardman of "gospel efficiency," and Phoebe Palmer of *Faith and Its Effects*—her trust in God must get results.[81] Perfectionists of all varieties rang the changes on Henry Clay Fish's theme that the Spirit's baptism was the secret of pulpit power and the fountain of that energy which alone could accomplish the evangelization of the world.[82] They met on common ground with the Unitarian editor who declared in 1857 that the "perilous experiment of liberty" in America, accompanied as it was by the passing away of "old creeds and usages," could only succeed if the ministry were baptized with the Holy Spirit and each disciple clothed anew with the "tongues of fire."[83] During the war the American Tract Society published an Ameri-

[80] Quoted in Wheatley, *Phoebe Palmer*, pp. 401-2, 518, 520, 575-76; pp. 510-77, *passim*, contain numerous letters touching on the same theme. See especially pp. 540-41, 542-44.

[81] William Edwin Boardman, *He that Overcometh, or a Conquering Gospel* (Boston, 1869), pp. 207-303, *passim*. Caughey's phrase persisted in the name of B. T. Roberts's periodical, *The Earnest Christian and Golden Rule, Devoted to the Promotion of Experimental and Practical Piety* (Buffalo; Rochester, N. Y., v. 1-58, 1860-89) and another published in Canada, *Earnest Christianity* (Toronto, v. 1-4, 1873-76). Cf. G. W. Huntley, "Holiness Essential to Usefulness," *The Christian*, II (1864), pp. 8-10.

[82] Henry C. Fish, "Power in the Pulpit," *The Christian Review*, XXVII (1862), pp. 141-42 was cited in a previous chapter. Cf. B. W. Gorham, "Personal Holiness and Ministerial Efficiency," *The Guide to Holiness*, XXXI (January-June, 1857), pp. 5-7, 153-54; Adams, *Higher Life in the Baptist Denomination*, p. 119; and, for a later non-perfectionist statement, Nehemiah Adams, *The Power and Office of the Holy Spirit* . . . (Boston, 1866), *passim*.

[83] Quoted in *The Watchman and Reflector*, Feb. 19, 1857. Cf. George Ellis, *Regeneration and Sanctification* . . . (Charlestown, Mass., 1842), pp. 11, 21, 26.

can edition of Hannah More's *Practical Piety*, a famous handbook of the English evangelical awakening, which maintained that every genuine religious experience—especially Christian holiness—must express itself ethically. "All the doctrines of the Gospel," she wrote, "are practical principles." [84]

Enthusiasm for Christian perfection was evangelical Protestantism's answer to the moral strivings of the age.[85] The Unitarian revolt had earlier shown that Americans would be less interested in dogma than in ethics. But the challenge of its leaders to some of the ancient principles of the Christian faith and their preoccupation with intellectual concerns cut them off from the masses. This was especially true of the two most interested in a radical reformation of society—Emerson and Parker. Out of the heart of revival Christianity came by mid-century a platform more widely acceptable and as realistically concerned with alleviating social evil. It called for the miraculous baptism of believers in the Holy Ghost and the consecration of their lives and possessions to the building of the kingdom of God. Horace Bushnell, always an intriguing figure to historians because he stood midway between both camps, appears in this light not so much a pioneer as a symbol of his times. Men such as he and Frederic Dan Huntington united for a sophisticated audience the principles of Christian liberalism and evangelical faith which were fused among the masses by the fires of the perfectionist awakening.[86]

Immersion in the events of the period, however, ought not to blind us to one other important determinant of the impulse to holiness, the persistence in history of a great ideal. The favorable response of Methodist officials to Finney and Phoebe Palmer would have been impossible had not their founder been the foremost advocate of Christian perfection in modern times. Every book on the subject cited in the foregoing pages refers to Wesley; most of them quote him at great length. The Epworth reformer, in turn, drew inspiration from the Moravians, Luther, Augustine, and,

[84] Hannah More, *Practical Piety; or the Influence of the Religion of the Heart on the Conduct of Life* (New York, 1863), pp. 31, 35, 162-68; cf. *The Christian Review*, XXIV (1859), p. 157. For a modern Episcopal expression of the same theme see Samuel M. Shoemaker, Jr., *Religion That Works. Sermons of Practical Christian Life* (New York, 1938), pp. 119 ff.

[85] Contrast Howard R. Murphy, "The Ethical Revolt Against Christian Orthodoxy in Early Victorian England," *The American Historical Review*, LX (1955), pp. 800-17.

[86] See Bushnell's *Sermons for the New Life* (7th ed., New York, 1869), pp. 106-26, 265-81, *passim*.

above all, the New Testament—the book sacred to nineteenth-century Christians as the very bread of life.

One can, after all, hardly write of Boardman and Bangs and ignore Jesus, whose most famous sermon applied the theme, "Blessed are the pure in heart," with the admonition, "Be ye therefore perfect, even as your Father which is in heaven is perfect." Or disregard Paul, whose many prayers for the perfection of the saints are typified in his exhortation to the Thessalonians, "And the very God of peace sanctify you wholly; and I pray God your whole spirit and soul and body be preserved blameless unto the coming of our Lord Jesus Christ." Thomas Upham's quest of union with God and A. B. Earle's testimony to "the rest of faith" were but a latter-day echo of Augustine's confession, "Thou madest us for Thyself, and our heart is restless, until it repose in Thee." [87]

[87] *The Confessions of St. Augustine* (tr. Edward B. Pusey; New York, 1951), p. 1. Cf. R. Newton Flew, *Idea of Perfection*, for a connected narrative covering all of Christian history until Wesley. The Scripture quotations are from Matt. 5:8, 48 and I Thess. 5:23.

X

The Evangelical Origins
of Social Christianity

The rapid growth of concern with purely social issues such as poverty, workingmen's rights, the liquor traffic, slum housing, and racial bitterness is the chief feature distinguishing American religion after 1865 from that of the first half of the nineteenth century. Such matters in some cases supplanted entirely the earlier pre-occupation with salvation from personal sin and the life hereafter. Seminaries reorganized their programs to stress sociology. Institutional churches and social settlement work became prominent in the cities. Crusades for the rights of oppressed groups of all sorts absorbed the energies of hundreds of clergymen.

The vanguard of the movement went far beyond the earlier Christian emphasis on almsgiving to a search for the causes of human suffering and a campaign to reconstruct social and economic relations upon a Christian pattern. At its height evangelicals like William Booth and Charles M. Sheldon stood as stanchly for reform as their more liberal brethren. Outstanding among the latter were Washington Gladden—Congregationalist pastor in Columbus, Ohio, and labor's fast friend—and Walter Rauschenbush, professor at the Baptist seminary in Rochester. Gladden's hymn, "O Master, Let Me Walk With Thee," hauntingly expresses the spiritual content of his many appeals in behalf of workingmen's rights. The same note of reverence echoes in Rauschenbush's *Prayers of the Social Awakening* and in his little book on *The Social Principles of Jesus*.

The best-known recent works on the beginnings of social Christianity have leaned toward either an intellectual or a sociological interpretation and placed chief emphasis upon the events which followed the Civil War. Pressure from urban maladjustments and industrial strife, the challenge of Darwinian philosophy and the new psychology, and the influence of the optimistic and communitarian spirit of the age seemed to Charles Howard Hopkins, Aaron I. Abell, Henry F. May, and James Dombrowski the chief factors which turned Christian minds toward social reconstruc-

148

tion.[1] That humanitarian impulses flowed earlier from hearts warmed at Finney's revival fires has not been forgotten, of course.[2] But for the past half-century church historians have assumed that revivals and perfectionism declined in public favor after about 1842, the year in which Elder Jacob Knapp was banished from Boston and the Oberlin preachers suffered widespread attacks for their "fanaticism." Thus scholars have eliminated these two forces from consideration as causes of the movement which seemed to emerge later on.

The discovery that the doctrine of sanctification and the methods of mass evangelism played an increasingly important role in the program of the churches *after* 1842 compels a revaluation of their impact on every facet of the contemporary religious scene. Here, then, is offered an evangelical explanation of the origins of the social gospel. The thesis of the remaining chapters of this book is that, whatever may have been the role of other factors, the quest for perfection joined with compassion for poor and needy sinners and a rebirth of millennial expectation to make popular Protestantism a mighty social force long before the slavery conflict erupted into war.

In many ways, of course, the evangelists' preoccupation with personal religious experience could nurture an exclusively spiritual faith. Their chief concern was to prepare men for another world, their most earnest prayer for a miraculous "outpouring of the Holy Spirit" which would break the shackles of human sin. Opposition to social evil was often only an occasional skirmish in their war on personal wickedness.[3] Charles G. Finney, for example, inspired many an abolitionist. But he never thought himself primarily a reformer. He composed his *Lectures on Revivals* in 1834 partly to help Joshua Leavitt, editor of *The New York Evangelist*,

[1] Aaron I. Abell, *The Urban Impact on American Protestantism, 1865-1900* (Harvard Historical Studies, LIV, Cambridge, 1943), pp. 3-26; Henry F. May, *Protestant Churches and Industrial America* (New York, 1949); Charles Howard Hopkins, *The Rise of the Social Gospel in American Protestantism, 1865-1913* (New Haven, 1940); James Dombrowski, *The Early Days of Christian Socialism in America* (New York, 1936), preface, pp. 1-13, and *passim*. The two named last pay very scant attention to Baptist and Methodist sources. Dombrowski did not consider any Methodist seminaries in his chapter on the significance of such institutions, pp. 60-73. Hopkins' *History of the Y.M.C.A. in North America* (New York, 1951) does, however, give due credit to revivalism.

[2] Gilbert H. Barnes, *The Antislavery Impulse, 1830-1844* (New York, 1933); Alice Felt Tyler, *Freedom's Ferment: Phases of American Social History to 1860* (Minneapolis, 1944), pp. 489-97; and Benjamin Platt Thomas, *Theodore Dwight Weld, Crusader for Freedom* (New Brunswick, N. J., 1950), all stress this fact.

[3] See, for example, Lewis G. Vander Velde, "Notes on the Diary of George Duffield," *The Mississippi Valley Historical Review*, XXXV (1937-38), p. 61.

REVIVALISM AND SOCIAL REFORM

rescue that paper from the near ruin which Leavitt's strong stand against slavery had brought upon it. Two decades later Elder Jacob Knapp blamed only himself when a Louisville congregation halted one of his campaigns upon learning that Knapp was about to break his self-imposed silence on slavery. Though always an abolitionist, he believed his first work was to save souls not free slaves. "I let all debatable subjects alone," James Caughey wrote from England in 1857; "have nothing to do with re-formers as reformers, but as *soul-savers* I know all good men." A sincere revivalist had little choice when the alternative was to drive penitents from the place of prayer.[4]

The violence of the slavery controversy only made the problem more difficult. True enough, a Baptist minister wrote, the aim of the Christian faith was "to revolutionize the world and bring all powers under its own sway." But had not Christ himself set an example of love and longsuffering toward the authors of oppression?[5]

When right-wing Calvinists and Episcopalians accepted revival measures, they became the chief spokesmen for such spiritual conservatism. The editor of Boston's *Puritan Recorder* attempted in 1854 to show that past American awakenings had prospered in proportion to their "holiness," by which he meant the extent to which they "drew a wide line between politics and religion, between the interests of this world and of another."[6] The Episcopal *Church Journal* attributed the success of lay leadership in the revival of 1858 to the public reaction against "Kansas and antislavery preachers" who had neglected spiritual tasks. That only their church's share of the awakening had begun under clerical auspices seemed to these editors proof that the people preferred a politically conservative ministry.[7] Similarly, the pastoral address which Charles P. McIlvaine prepared for circulation on behalf of the board of Episcopal bishops in 1862 condemned Southerners for rebellion but not slavery and warned Northern Chris-tians of the dangers which periods of public excitement bring to the

---

[4] James Caughey, Sheffield, November, 1857, to Slade Robinson, Toronto, quoted in *The Guide to Holiness*, XXXIII (February, 1858), p. 50; Charles G. Finney, *Memoirs* (New York, 1876), pp. 328-30; Jacob Knapp, *Autobiography* (New York, 1868), pp. 172-73.

[5] Eli Noyes, *Lectures on the Truth of the Bible* (Boston, 1853), pp. 263-72, *passim*. Cf. John McClintock's praise for Fletcher Harper's conservatism in *The Methodist Quarterly Review*, XXXVII (1855), p. 145, with the latter's statement on p. 15 of this volume.

[6] *The Puritan Recorder*, Feb. 23, 1854. Cf. "Political Preaching," Feb. 5, 1857.

[7] Anon., *The Revival System and the Paraclete. A Series of Articles from the Church Journal* (New York, 1858), pp. 60-62.

life of the spirit. "Let not love of country make your love to God and your gracious Saviour less fervent," the address ran. "Immense as is the present earthly interest, it is only earthly." [8]

But liberalism on social issues, not reaction, was the dominant note which evangelical preachers sounded before 1860. The most influential of them, from Albert Barnes and Samuel S. Schmucker to Edward Norris Kirk and Matthew Simpson, defined carefully the relationship between personal salvation and community improvement and never tired of glowing descriptions of the social and economic millennium which they believed revival Christianity would bring into existence. Even the doctrine of human depravity seemed to such men a demonstration of the solidarity of the race and the brotherhood of man, a crushing rebuke to "all contempt of even the vilest" of Adam's sons.[9] That they thought individual regeneration a chief means of social reform does not set them apart from their postwar successors. As late as 1910, according to the foremost student of the subject, the central feature of Christian social method in America remained the dedication of person and resources to the will of God. Thus, Lyman Abbott and Josiah Strong would have agreed with the editor of the Baptist *Watchman and Reflector* who insisted in the year 1857 that legislation alone could not "reach down to the root of our social evils." For this, he wrote, "moral and Christian power must be invoked. . . . The great panacea is the gospel of Christ." [10]

These later reformers might also have shared the same editor's enthusiasm for Frederic Dan Huntington's declaration before a Unitarian gathering planning a denominational tract society, that "the world's salvation consists in a spiritual redemption . . . and *not* in a mere natural development of the human powers according to natural laws." The books Unitarians circulated, Huntington said,

[8] Charles Pettit McIlvaine *Pastoral Letter of the Bishops of the Protestant Episcopal Church . . . Delivered before the General Convention . . . N. Y., Friday October 17, 1862* (New York, 1862), pp. 11-12; William Wilson Manross, *A History of the American Episcopal Church* (2nd ed., New York, 1950), pp. 290-92. Cf. McIlvaine's *The Work of Preaching Christ . . .* (New York, 1863), pp. 9, 14-15, 19, 24; and Samuel I. Prime, *Five Years of Prayer, with the Answers* (New York, 1864), pp. 31-32, 34-36.

[9] *The Watchman and Reflector*, Nov. 12, 1857; Stephen Olin, *Works* (New York, 1860), II, pp. 347-53. Cf., for example, Gilbert Haven, *National Sermons: Sermons, Speeches and Letters on Slavery and Its War . . .* (Boston, 1869), pp. 136-37, 345, with Walter Rauschenbusch's use of the same theme, in *Theology of the Social Gospel* (New York, 1917), pp. 57-58.

[10] *The Watchman and Reflector*, Nov. 12, 1857; Hopkins, *Social Gospel*, pp. 75-76, 138-39, 142-43, 148.

must affirm the radical and essential distinction between morality and piety, insisting on the latter as the vital root of the former. They must recognize the offices of the Holy Spirit, the Comforter, in regenerating the soul, sanctifying it, flooding it with grace, and raising it to glory. And finally, they must fearlessly and unqualifiedly apply the principles and spirit of the Lord Jesus, not only to the ordinary labor and familiar relations of man's life in the world, but to all popular combinations of sin, organized iniquities, and public crimes, like intemperance, slavery, and war. . . .[11]

In fact, if evangelicals insisted upon moral solutions to social questions, they never forgot that personal sin often had communal roots. Albert Barnes pointed in 1842 to the "evils of alliance, of compact, of confederation" characteristic of urban life, to "sins of common pursuit, where one man keeps another in countenance, or one man leads on the many to transgression." Sin is never solitary, he declared, nor can it be banished piecemeal from society.

One sin is interlocked with others and is sustained by others. . . . The only power in the universe which can meet and overcome such combined evil is the power of the Spirit of God. There are evils of alliance and confederation in every city which can never be met but by a general revival of religion.[12]

Fifteen years later The Watchman's editor, a leader in the crusade for just such a nation-wide awakening, reproved those who were taking refuge from the gloomy social outlook in purely spiritual contemplation. True, he acknowledged, the slave power was gaining ground every day. The American Republic, instead of being superseded by the kingdom of Christ "as the star of dawn is swallowed up in the perfect day," might have to be overturned in judgment before Christians could enjoy millennial peace. But, declared this earnest Baptist, the triumph of the gospel calls for its victory over all evil, not a mere deliverance of individual Christians from harm.

It is something more than a gathering together of those who shall be saved in a future state, leaving the world to destruction; it contemplates the organiza-

<hr>

[11] Quoted in The Watchman and Reflector, March 23, 1854.
[12] Albert Barnes, "Revivals of Religion in Cities and Large Towns," The American National Preacher, XV (1841), pp. 12-13, 15. A similar statement appears in Olin, Works, II, 85, and Edward Norris Kirk, The Church Essential to the Republic . . . (New York, 1848), pp. 5, 14.

tion and supremacy of goodness in human society—the doing of God's will *on earth*—the coming of His Kingdom hither, as well as our going hence to it. . . . True, when his work in this respect is accomplished, we are taught that there will be new heavens and a new earth, in which all external circumstances shall be conformed to the spiritual glory of that consummation. . . . Meanwhile, it is ours, not only to fit ourselves and others for a better world, but to labor to make this world better.[13]

The growth of slavery could only be halted, the writer continued, when Christians comprehended the infinite value which Christ had attached to every human creature through his incarnation, sufferings, and atoning death. Men must "learn to regard slavery as not merely the denial of rights conferred in original creation, but as an outrage on the nature which the Son of God was pleased to make the temple of His divinity." For this reason, he believed that the growth of the "pure spirit" of Christianity would be more effective against the extension of the institution than a hundred legislative prohibitions. The latter were indispensable, even as they were "altogether rightful." But if the church of Christ were "more suffused with His spirit," their necessity would be greatly diminished. "Oppression and violence could not with their darkness affront *that* light," he cried; "faith and love and purity would prevail, because vivified and directed by One who has all power, as He is to have all dominion."[14]

It is no wonder that when the intermittent and local awakenings characteristic of the years after 1842 gave way in 1858 to a Pentecost of seemingly miraculous proportions, revivalists were convinced that the conquest of social and political evil was near at hand. For long afterward they were apt to ascribe humanitarian progress to the force of the gospel.[15] As late as 1880 a Freewill Baptist minister predicted confidently that the faith which had "swept slavery from the earth, elevated women from a state of bondage," and "weakened the grasp of despots" would ultimately triumph over every ill. "War will eventually cease," he cried. "The strong

[13] *The Watchman and Reflector*, March 26, 1857. See earlier, pp. 48-49.
[14] *The Watchman and Reflector*, March 26, 1857. Cf. "Need of a Deeper Piety," the same, Jan. 15, 1863.
[15] Jesse T. Peck, *The History of the Great Republic, Considered from a Christian Standpoint* (New York, 1868), pp. 560, 562; "The Power," *The American Missionary (Magazine)*, VIII (1864), p. 34.

will foster the weak, capital befriend labor . . . and the spirit of mutual helpfulness pervade all the ranks of society." [16]

What was needed to accomplish these ends was more and purer piety. Hence the importance of the fervor for Christian perfection which spread through the churches after 1835. All of the socially potent doctrines of revivalism reached white heat in the Oberlin and Wesleyan experience of sanctification—ethical seriousness, the call to full personal consecration, the belief in God's immanence, in his readiness to transform the present world through the outpoured Holy Ghost, and the exaltation of Christian love. [17]

William Arthur most clearly expounded for nineteenth-century Methodists the social implications of their belief in deliverance from all sin and in entire consecration. In his book *The Tongue of Fire*, which appeared in a half-dozen editions in England and America after 1854, Arthur warned that the two most dangerous perversions of the gospel were to look upon it as "a salvation for the soul after it leaves the body, but no salvation from sin while there," and as "a means of forming a holy community in the world to come, but never in this."

Nothing short of the general renewal of society ought to satisfy any soldier of Christ. . . . Much as Satan glories in his power over an individual, how much greater must be his glorying over a nation embodying, in its laws and usages, disobedience to God, wrong to man, and contamination to morals? To destroy all national holds of evil; to root sin out of institutions; to hold up to view the gospel ideal of a righteous nation . . . is one of the first duties of those whose position or mode of thought gives them any influence in general questions. In so doing they are at once glorifying the Redeemer, by displaying the benignity of his influence over human society, and removing hindrances to individual conversions, some of which act by direct incentive to vice, others by upholding a state of things the acknowledged basis of which is, "Forget God."

Satan might be content to let Christianity turn over the subsoil, if he is in perpetuity to sow the surface with thorns and briers; but the gospel is come to renew the face of the earth. [18]

Other Methodist perfectionists struck a similar note. The editor of

[16] *Doctrine and Life. Sermons by Free Baptist Ministers* (Dover, N. H., 1880), p. 34.
[17] See earlier, pp. 141-42, 145-46.
[18] William Arthur, *The Tongue of Fire* . . . (New York, 1880), pp. 145-46. On Arthur's general prominence, see T. Bowman Stephenson, *William Arthur, A Brief Biography* (John Tedford, ed., *The Library of Methodist Biography*, New York, n.d.), p. 111; and Matthew Simpson, ed., *Cyclopedia of Methodism* . . . (Philadelphia, 1878), p. 55.

Zion's Herald declared in 1854 that spirituality must be expressed in irreproachable morality and unceasing efforts to reform society, lest the "adversaries of Christ" be permitted to appear more interested in the welfare of mankind than the friends of the gospel. Every Christian should seek to overthrow slavery, intemperance, political corruption, and all other public vices. A few weeks later the same journal argued that only "entire self-devotion to Christ" could produce the systematic benevolence which was the hope of the poor. The way to avoid the sin of covetousness was "to subject our property, with ourselves, to the dominion of Christ." *The Guide to Holiness* printed in 1856 Finney's letter advising ministers "to inquire affectionately and particularly" into the political beliefs of their parishioners, "whether they are cleaving to a party without regard to principles," as well as "in what manner they demean themselves toward those who are in their employment." [19]

Elsewhere, a professor at Ohio Wesleyan University echoed Wesley's dictum that the increase of personal wealth was the most subtle foe to a life of personal consecration. The sanctified Christian is "a living sacrifice"; he must relieve the poor, visit the sick and imprisoned, and instruct the ignorant in the ways of the Lord. [20] Somewhat later, the president of another Methodist college wrote in *The Guide to Holiness* against the "kind of passive, quiescent, sentimental offering, which some souls seem to make of themselves to God." The consecration which the gospel contemplates, he insisted, is one of service to others. "That faith and consecration, if such there be, which do not lead to service and sacrifice, are of no value. . . . The power of the Gospel is proved by the service rendered to man in the name of Christ."

The idea of full personal consecration had made great headway since the days when Lyman Beecher undercut Charles G. Finney's pleas to a Boston audience to devote their property and talents to Christ with the

[19] *The Guide to Holiness*, XXIX (January-June, 1856), p. 35; *Zion's Herald*, Nov. 29, and Dec. 13, 1854. The same sentiment appeared earlier in "Holiness—Its Effects," *Zion's Herald*, March 10, 1852. See also "Property—Its Abuses and True Uses," the same, Dec. 20, 1854; "Is Systematic Benevolence a Duty," the same, Dec. 27, 1854; and Stephen Olin's sermon of 1848, "The Gospel Basis of Charity," *Works*, II, 86-89.

[20] Frederick Merrick, "Consecration to God," in Davis W. Clark, ed., *The Methodist Episcopal Pulpit; a Collection of Original Sermons from Living Ministers of the M. E. Church* (New York, 1850), pp. 134-36. Cf. the same appeal, but based on intense otherworldiness, in Richard Treffry's perennially popular *Treatise on Christian Perfection* (Boston, 1888, and many earlier editions), pp. 213-14.

REVIVALISM AND SOCIAL REFORM

assurance that they need have no fear since the Lord would give it all back! [21]

The concept of divine immanence was another revival theme which the holiness movement expressed in radical terms. In the preaching of the evangelists, God was not only transcendent, set over against his creatures. He was near at hand. They thought themselves not so much voices crying in the wilderness as heralds and footmen for Him who had come to baptize with the Holy Ghost and fire and make sinners into saints. Christ's judgments were taking place now. He was threshing men and institutions on the floor of his righteousness, winnowing the wheat from the chaff. [22]

Because of such convictions Finney became the first to elaborate clearly the doctrine that the Christian covenant was supreme in human affairs, a "higher law" than the Constitution. A generation of his co-workers engraved the concept on the minds of praying men while William H. Seward was fashioning it into a political creed. [23] Similarly, it was a revivalist editor who most fearlessly denounced the sins of the wealthy after the financial crash of 1857. Speculators who could pay "decent attention to the externals of religion on the Sabbath," he cried, while ignoring the sufferings of the poor and enslaved and laying an "embargo of almost famine prices upon bread," were guilty of "deep-seated, practical infidelity." God was "rising out of his place to hear the cry of the 'poor and needy' and visit rebuke on their oppressors." [24]

[21] Finney, *Memoirs*, pp. 315-16. A. C. George, "Consecration Must Be Perpetual and Active," *The Guide to Holiness*, LI (January-June, 1867), pp. 171-73; cf. Richard Wheatley, *The Life and Letters of Phoebe Palmer* (New York, 1876), pp. 569-70. See also, "Not Your Own," *The Christian*, II (1864), pp. 194-95, for the utterly serious light in which holiness Baptists held the doctrine of stewardship.

[22] John R. Bodo, *The Protestant Clergy and Public Issues, 1812-1848* (Princeton, N. J., 1954), documents fully the social significance of Calvinist theocratic concepts in the period, but without reference to the manner in which revival pleas impressed them upon the popular mind.

[23] Charles C. Cole, *The Social Ideas of the Northern Evangelists, 1826-1860* (New York, 1854), pp. 208-10, cites Finney's address of 1839 before the Ohio Anti-Slavery Society. Cf. Gilbert Haven, "The Higher Law," *National Sermons*, pp. 5-7, 11-13; William Hosmer, *The Higher Law in Its Relation to Civil Government, with Particular Reference to Slavery and the Fugitive Slave Law* (Auburn, N. Y., 1852), *passim*; and Robert D. Clark, *Life of Matthew Simpson* (New York, 1956), pp. 158-60.

[24] *The Watchman and Reflector*, Oct. 8, 1857. See also Jesse T. Peck, "The Burning, Fiery Furnace," *The Guide to Holiness*, XXXIII (January-June, 1858), pp. 1-3; Henry C. Fish, *Primitive Piety Revived* . . . (Boston, 1855), pp. 44-45, 55-62, *passim*; Olin, *Works*, II, pp. 85-88; and wartime repetitions of the theme in *The Watchman and Reflector*, editorials for Jan. 15, and Apr. 9, 1863.

One form of Calvinist quietism might leave the Almighty to accomplish such judgments alone. But the perfectionists joined a thoroughgoing attack on sin and a radical doctrine of God's immanence with Arminian views of human responsibility, free will, and 'universal election. True enough, wrote William Arthur, only divine power could renew fallen men in that holiness the Creator had intended. Statesmen and philanthropists were too prone to neglect this fact. But, he insisted, evangelical Christians on their part had insufficiently studied the relationship of personal regeneration to social need and too often rejected organized efforts at reform. "Fearful social evils," he warned,

may coëxist with a state of society wherein many are holy, and all have a large amount of Christian light. Base usages fostering intemperance, alienation of class from class in feeling and interest, systematic frauds in commerce, neglect of workmen by masters, neglect of children by their parents, whole classes living by sin, usages checking marriage and encouraging licentiousness, human dwellings which make the idea of home odious, and the existence of modesty impossible, are but specimens of the evils which may be left age after age, cursing a people among whom Christianity is the recognized standard of society.[25]

To be indifferent to these things, Arthur continued, was as unfaithful to Christian morals as "hoping to remedy them without spreading practical holiness among individuals" was contrary to gospel truth. Some premillennialists and Calvinists, he said, might be willing to believe that the Christian dispensation was "a kind of interlude between the Lord's lifetime upon earth and a future earthly reign," in which the gospel was preached "for the conversion of a few and the condemnation of the many." But Arthur believed that the nineteenth-century revival of holiness proved that Christ was here now, in the person of the Holy Spirit, accomplishing the regeneration of the earth which must precede his personal reign. What every Christian needed to speed the fulfillment of this plan was the baptism of fire and of the Holy Ghost.[26]

As late as 1883 Daniel Steele, leader of a coterie of Boston University professors promoting sanctification, wrote a preface for Catherine Booth's *Aggressive Christianity* which praised her for believing that the gospel aims both to destroy sin in the individual soul "through the power of the Holy Spirit wholly sanctifying it by the instantaneous finishing stroke

[25] Arthur, *Tongue of Fire*, pp. 129-30; see pp. 110-129, *passim*.
[26] *Ibid.*, pp. 335, 346-47, 348-50.

given to original sin" and to banish sin from society as well, until the whole world is subdued "to Jesus, its rightful King." Catherine Booth, Steele wrote, was "no gloomy pessimist, wailing the decay of Christianity." Rather, she understood "this glorious consummation" to be "within the reach of the present generation of believers," if only they would allow the Holy Spirit a complete, a sanctifying control.[27]

The revival idea that love to God and man was the chief fruit of Christian experience had equally significant consequences in social theory. Here, too, the propagandists of perfection occupied the highest ground. Finney, Boardman, and Phoebe Palmer were convincing preachers of charity precisely because they believed themselves forever indebted to God's saving compassion and sanctified in the fullness of his love.

A major burden of Mrs. Palmer's preaching and writing was to warn converts against selfishly seeking "ecstatic enjoyment." Holiness made one a servant—at times a suffering servant—of his fellow men. "Sympathy with Jesus in the great work which brought him from heaven to earth" and the achievement of "entire unselfishness" were to her the true marks of sanctification. She was thus fully in accord with Wesley's doctrine that the second work of grace replaced the carnal mind with a dominant "holy temper" of perfect love.[28] Whether such a transformation actually took place is less important to historical analysis than the fact that thousands believed it had and testified publicly to the fact, placing themselves under a double compulsion to live as if it were true.

Methodist social teachings were saturated with this notion. The essence of the Christian revelation seemed to two New England pastors to be "the mighty outbreaking of an infinite heart" rather than merely "an effulgence of the infinite mind." Christ's true followers, one of them wrote, must partake of his "purest sympathy for human suffering" and devote their money and time to relieving the poor.[29] The editor of *Zion's Herald* maintained that "true Christian charity," born of love for the Lord, comprehended "both the complex nature of men and the true philosophy of

---

[27] Catherine Booth, *Aggressive Christianity: Practical Sermons* (Boston, 1883), pp. 11-12. Cf. William Booth, *In Darkest England and the Way Out* (New York, 1890), preface.

[28] Wheatley, *Phoebe Palmer*, pp. 529-31, 546. See earlier, p. 144. Cf. Thomas C. Upham, *Life and Religious Opinions and Experience of Madame de la Mothe Guyon . . .* (New York, 1874), I, vi.

[29] L. P. Brockett, "The Relation of Christianity to Humanitarian Effort," *The Methodist Quarterly Review*, XL (1858), pp. 455-57; Charles Adams, "Charity to the Poor," in Clark, *Methodist Episcopal Pulpit*, pp. 292-94, 297-98. Contrast Hopkins, *Social Gospel*, p. 318.

social regeneration." It ministered alike to temporal and spiritual needs.[30] According to William Arthur, the chief aim of Christianity was "to unite all men in loving brotherhood." The "family feeling" which glowed in the church after Pentecost and still lived in Methodist testimony and class meetings was to become the divine order of society.[31] Such an emotion enabled even a loyal Methodist like Nathan Bangs to transcend denominational prejudice, and caused another to believe, in the year of the great revival, that though slavery was not yet destroyed, sympathy for "the whole human brotherhood" would increase till the millennial triumph, when "health, holiness, and happiness" would pervade the earth.[32]

A precisely similar mood carried Frederic Dan Huntington through the period of his evangelical conversion to the time when, as Episcopal bishop of western New York, he was to spearhead the social crusade in that denomination. Huntington served until his death as the first president of the Church Association in the Interests of Labor, wrote numerous tracts supporting Christian socialism, championed the rights of the Onondaga Indians, and, with his son, the Rev. James Huntington, opened at Syracuse in 1877 a "shelter" for unwed mothers.[33] "God binds men together," he wrote in 1862, "and trains them up through the mutual affections, sacrifices, and services of corporate institutions: first the Family, secondly the State, thirdly the Church." The philosophy of "sheer individualism" is unchristian, Huntington continued. It violates the purest and most unselfish aspirations of humanity. "Christ comes, not to make righteous individuals, but to build a righteous kingdom, whereof each individual is a member, so that no one can say to another, I have no need of thee." [34]

Edward Beecher long before had pointed to the power of such sentiments, in a flaming appeal for social reconstruction published in 1835. The kingdom of Christ was first of all spiritual, he declared, and could "make no real progress except by an increase in holiness." This alone could

[30] *Zion's Herald*, Dec. 13, 1854. But contrast Jesse T. Crane, "The Moral Value of a Material World," *The Methodist Quarterly Review*, XL (1858), p. 234.

[31] Arthur, *Tongue of Fire*, pp. 117, 138-41; contrast generally the whole passage, "Fellowship and Brotherhood," pp. 137-44, with the traditional churchly view in Philip Schaff, *America* . . . (New York, 1855), p. 123.

[32] L. P. Brockett, *loc. cit.*, pp. 470-71; Abel Stevens, *Life and Times of Nathan Bangs, D.D.* (New York, 1863), p. 363.

[33] See Arria S. Huntington, *Memoir and Letters of Frederic Dan Huntington* . . . (Boston, 1906), pp. 324-28, 353, 355-56; and Huntington's sermon on "The Social Conscience," *Christian Believing and Living* (New York, 1859), p. 438.

[34] Arria Huntington, *Huntington*, p. 251. Cf. the prospectus of his journal, *The Church Monthly*, I (1861), p. 1.

produce the personal consecration, the "moral sensibility to the evils of sin," and the brotherly love among denominations necessary to the regeneration of the world.[35] "There is a state of mind," Beecher cried, "which if first produced will secure all else . . . by the spontaneous impulse of ardent and overflowing love." It is "that SUPREME DEVOTEDNESS TO GOD" which makes it "essential to our happiness" to do all we can for him. The times demanded "Holy Emotion, full and ardent to the highest degree."[36] Harriet Beecher Stowe was to demonstrate the truth of this contention twenty years later in a way her brother scarcely could have foreseen, when she fired antislavery sentiments with the story of Topsy and Little Eva, Simon Legree and Uncle Tom. Scores of reformers, from John B. Gough of temperance fame to William Jennings Bryan, operated on the same plan.[37]

Beecher's statement illustrates the emotional fanaticism which, as Oliver W. Elsbree pointed out twenty years ago, Samuel Hopkins's doctrine of "disinterested benevolence" inspired among American Calvinists, thrusting them into social crusades which coolly rational men might approve but scarcely join. Hopkins, who was in early life a close associate of Jonathan Edwards and pastor from 1770-1803 of the Congregational church at Newport, Rhode Island, exerted an immense influence over the younger clergy, largely through his complete dedication to the things of the Spirit. He taught that the truly consecrated Christian must so fully love the Lord as to be willing if need be to be damned for his glory.[38]

The kinship between "Hopkinsianism" and the Methodist doctrine of perfect love was evident throughout the nineteenth century. Wellman J. Warner, a student of R. H. Tawney, expounded in 1930 the impact of Wesleyan perfectionism on early English industrial society, in a volume which American writers rarely cite. The experience of sanctification,

[35] Edward Beecher, "The Nature, Importance, and Means of Eminent Holiness Throughout the Church," *The American National Preacher*, X (1835), pp. 195, 197, 198, 201; cf. pp. 209, 212.

[36] *Ibid.*, pp. 203, 219.

[37] See earlier, pp. 88, 105; Ralph H. Gabriel, "Evangelical Religion and Popular Romanticism in Early Nineteenth-Century America," *Church History*, XIX (1950), pp. 42-45; and Richard Hofstadter's essay on Bryan, "The Democrat as Revivalist," in his *The American Political Tradition* (New York, 1948).

[38] Oliver Wendell Elsbree, "Samuel Hopkins and the Doctrine of Benevolence," *The New England Quarterly*, VIII (1935), pp. 535, 548-49. Elsbree libels the Methodists, as Hopkins, *Social Gospel*, a volume which seems preoccupied with the transformation of conservative Calvinism, neglects them: see pp. 25, 36, 43-48, 86 ff., 99, 102, 113, 238, 289-92. Cf. John M. Mecklin, *The Story of American Dissent* (New York, 1934), pp. 20-21.

Warner said, socialized the individual disposition and released in men the mystic power to make benevolent motives work.[39]

Thus did the mid-century preachers furrow the ground from which the social gospel sprang. Evangelists facing urban challenges early proclaimed the unity and interdependence of the race. Edward Beecher, E. N. Kirk, Albert Barnes, George B. Cheever, and a host of lesser men saw with surprising clarity the social implications of their prized ideals of righteous living, brotherly love, and the immanence of God through the outpoured Holy Spirit. They moved rapidly toward a systematic elaboration of Christian humanitarian doctrine. Perfectionists like Finney and William Arthur, who added to these ideals a passion for full personal consecration and freedom from all sin, actually led the way. By the time of the Civil War the conviction had become commonplace that society must be reconstructed through the power of a sanctifying gospel and all the evils of cruelty, slavery, poverty, and greed be done away. The enlargement of millennial hopes, as we shall see later on, illustrates and in part explains the churchman's new sense of social responsibility.

Only their evangelical trust in divine grace to supplement human efforts and their retention of the historic "heavenly hope" of the faith set these pioneers apart from the Christian social reformers of a later age. The doctrine of divine immanence set forth in the "Andover Theology" in 1880 was, in fact, no more than a tepid restatement of liberal revivalist thinking on the subject during the preceding forty years. The volume entitled *Progressive Orthodoxy*, which announced the Andover platform, stressed the regenerating, perfecting power of God in the soul in the same way as had William Arthur and Asa Mahan. The opinion that the aim of the gospel was to produce in individuals an "actual and manifest likeness to Christ," which would, by its spread, renovate the whole of society, was by then new only to those who persisted in their devotion to Orthodox Calvinism. Thomas C. Upham, the philosopher of mystic perfectionism, had stated it formally in 1852.[40] Only the more or less

[39] Wellman Joel Warner, *The Wesleyan Movement in the Industrial Revolution* (London, 1930), pp. 65-66; see also pp. 61-72, 281-82. Contrast Hunter Dickinson Farish, *The Circuit Rider Dismounts; a Social History of Southern Methodism, 1865-1900* (Richmond, Va., 1938), pp. 71-72; and Sidney E. Mead's review of Wade Crawford Barclay, *Early American Methodism, 1769-1844*, Vol. II, *To Reform the Nation* (*History of American Methodism*, Part I, New York, 1949), in *The William and Mary Quarterly*, 3rd ser., VII (1951), pp. 596-98.

[40] See Thomas C. Upham, *A Treatise on Divine Union . . .* (Boston, 1852), pp. 267-68; *Progressive Orthodoxy: a Contribution to the Christian Interpretation of Christian Doctrines,*

conscious relation of the idea to Charles Darwin's theory of evolution was novel, something scarcely possible for men who wrote before 1865.

If God seemed near in nineteenth-century America, it was not because an elite circle of theologians read Darwin's book on *The Descent of Man*. It was rather due to the fact that in countless revivals the "tongue of fire" had descended on the disciples, freeing them from the bondage of sin and selfishness, and dedicating them to the task of making over the world. Nor was the Christian contribution to the nation's heritage of hope simply belief in the rational perfectibility of men who had not "committed" original sin.[41] Another optimism was abroad in the land, one tied more closely to the religious traditions of the people. It promised a baptism of the Holy Ghost which would purify men's hearts by faith and bring them into fellowship with Christ's self-denying love. In 1870 John Humphrey Noyes, the most radical "perfectionist" of them all, predicted that "the next phase of National history will be that of Revivalism and Socialism, harmonized and working together for the Kingdom of Heaven."[42]

---

by the Editors of "The Andover Review" (Boston, 1886), pp. 126-27; Sidney E. Mead, *Nathaniel W. Taylor, 1786-1858, A Connecticut Liberal* (Chicago, 1942), pp. viii-ix, 211-33; and Hopkins, *Social Gospel*, pp. 61-66, 115.

[41] See Boyd C. Shafer, "The American Heritage of Hope, 1865-1940," *The Mississippi Valley Historical Review*, XXXVII (1950-51), pp. 440-41.

[42] Quoted from John Humphrey Noyes, *The History of American Socialisms* (Philadelphia, 1870), p. 28, in Alice Felt Tyler, *Freedom's Ferment* . . . p. 186.

XI

The Churches Help the Poor

〜

The acid test of social theories is their exemplification in practice. Even in this "land of plenty" poverty became a persistent reality after 1837. It stemmed in part from the new immigration and the uncertainties of employment in an infant industrial economy. But the Calvinist ethic of frugality and industry, which held individuals morally accountable for their destitution, was the prevailing tradition in America. Almsgiving was frequently regarded as an undue interference with divine justice. What, then, did the churches actually do to help the underprivileged in the twenty years after 1840? The answer to this question will serve to measure the sincerity of the new social concern.

In a charity sermon which he preached in Boston during the revival of 1842, evangelist Edward Norris Kirk warned that the rise of urban poverty in America posed a new challenge to religion. "Our whole system of education, our modes of life, our very standards of personal piety," declared the newly called pastor of Mt. Vernon Congregational Church, "need great renovation." Instead of shielding their children from the knowledge of suffering, parents must teach them "that the removal of human wretchedness, and the elevation of degraded man is the business of life." He denounced those who opposed charity on the grounds that it frustrated God's punishment of vice and indolence, noting Albert Barnes's argument that medical care and the preaching of the gospel were open to the same objection. Nor would indiscriminate almsgiving do. "When men love their neighbors as themselves, the causes of poverty will be sought out, and the remedy applied as far as possible." [1] It was too soon for men like Kirk to recognize much more than personal factors like "improvidence, intemperance, and discouragement" among those causes. But he was courageous enough to assert that by catering to the upper classes, the churches contributed to Sabbath drunkenness, and that in any case, none had the right to allow children to suffer for their parents' sins. [2]

[1] Edward Norris Kirk, A Plea for the Poor . . . (Boston, 1843), pp. 20, 23, 26, 40.
[2] Ibid., pp. 28-36.

Such evangelical concern for the plight of the masses increased steadily. Thirteen years later the editors of *The Independent* scornfully dismissed a move for a Congregational liturgy on the grounds that city churches had already neglected too much "the immense class of working poor" to favor "the rich and comfortable." The usual "Sabbath feasts of taste and music," where "sweet moods of pensive thought" soothed the minds of those who spent the week in a "pleasant, trivial round of parlor-parties" were, the editors declared, unworthy of men who claimed to follow Christ's "stern life of continued self-forgetfulness." [3]

A year before the same journal had regretted the spasmodic nature of most poor relief, especially its failure to deal with the economic factors in urban destitution. Cities attracted impoverished migrants while at the same time giving businessmen the opportunity to amass fortunes quickly. Sharp contrasts became a plague. The "numerous and multiplying institutions of benevolence and reform" were, the editors believed, praiseworthy improvements over the private charity upon which village and farming communities still relied. But until "the great question of wages" was solved, the chasm between rich and poor would open wider every day. For the time being, however, they dared only to advocate "low rents, commodious, cleanly, healthy buildings, upon the most approved plan of lodging-houses," and the Maine prohibition law "in its most stringent application." [4]

The movement of churches to the uptown areas, where "worship was conditioned on a good pew rent," alarmed those who shared this concern. [5] That competition in impressive edifices toppled even Baptist and Methodist prejudices against pew rents helped to dramatize the issue. The General Conference of the latter church voted in 1852 to sanction the practice, already prevalent in Boston, after prominent New Yorkers spoke in its support. Though the pastoral address of the conference deplored the growing love of riches and advised that Wesley's followers should avoid costly buildings, their metropolitan congregations, as one wag commented, went so far over to "pewsyism" as to leave the free-church field to the Episcopalians and the Broadway Tabernacle. [6]

[3] "A Gospel to the Rich," *The Independent*, May 24, 1855.
[4] "How to Help the Poor," the same, May 25, 1854; "Poverty in Cities," the same, Dec. 28, 1854. See the answer to the earlier article, "'Cures' for Social Diseases," June 8, 1854.
[5] "A Gospel to the Rich," *loc. cit.*; "The Broadway Tabernacle—Downtown Churches," the same, July 19, 1855.
[6] *Zion's Herald*, June 16, 1852 reports both the debates and the pastoral address. See

THE CHURCHES HELP THE POOR

During the Civil War Hiram Mattison and several other dissident clergymen who had been fighting for lay representation in the annual and general conferences organized The Independent Methodist Church. Its major objects were declared to be

to carry the Gospel to the poor; to unite different denominations for home mission purposes; to establish union churches in waste places where no single sect could succeed; to meet in halls and cheap places for worship, so as to avoid unnecessary expense; and to come back as far as possible to the faith and zeal and simplicity of the Puritans and the early Methodists. .

The Boston unit was described as "Congregational in government, Baptist as respects immersion, and Methodist in doctrine and modes of worship." [7]

Stephen Colwell, a Pennsylvania ironmaster and Old School Presbyterian layman, aroused interest in other aspects of the problem through the controversial volume, *New Themes for the Protestant Clergy*, which he published anonymously in 1851. In appearance this strange book was a vigorous attack on Protestant neglect of the poor, particularly in Philadelphia. Its less obvious purpose was to refute the principles of organized benevolence and make way for Colwell's own many-sided social program. The latter included tariffs and other legislation to protect workmen's wages (he did not mention manufacturers' profits), and the union of all Protestant sects, so as to enable them to Christianize the school system, restrain the power of Catholicism, and subject American politics to the rule of religion. [8]

Samuel Allibone, an Episcopal laymen prominent in the Philadelphia Sunday School Union, who was later to achieve modest fame as a literary

also George Prentice, *The Life of Gilbert Haven, Bishop of the Methodist Episcopal Church* (New York, 1883), pp. 149, 272; James Waddell Alexander, *Forty Years' Familiar Letters* . . . (New York, 1860), II, pp. 282, 283; *The Watchman and Reflector*, Dec. 7, 1854; and Stephen Olin, *The Works of Stephen Olin, D.D., L.L.D.* (New York, 1860), I, pp. 85-87. See earlier, pp. 65-66.

[7] *The Independent*, Sept. 10, 1863; *The American Missionary* (*Magazine*), VI (1862), p. 35.

[8] Stephen Colwell, *New Themes for the Protestant Clergy: Creeds Without Charity, Theology Without Humanity, and Protestantism Without Chrisianity* . . . (Philadelphia, 1851), pp. 161-62, 242, 263-64, 272-75; Stephen Colwell, *The Position of Christianity in the United States* . . . (Philadelphia, 1854), pp. 78-81, 89, 98, 100-13, *passim*.

Broadus Mitchell wrote the *D.A.B.* sketch. Colwell's other works which bear on the argument raised in *New Themes* include: *Some Aid to a Clear Perception of Our Actual Dependence upon Home Production* . . . (Johnathan B. Wise, *pseud.*, Philadelphia, 1849); *Politics for American Citizens* . . . (Philadelphia, 1852); and *The Claims of Labor, and Their Precedence to the Claims of Free Trade* (Philadelphia, 1861).

bibliographer, retorted in a long review that Colwell had willfully ignored the great amount of charitable work the Philadelphia churches performed. He had, moreover, spared the Catholic clergy, disregarded the relation of intemperance to pauperism, and indulged in such general bitterness as to cause some booksellers to reject the volume, thinking it written by an infidel. If its author attended church, Allibone wrote, he was probably not aware that many of the people with whom he sat had spent part of the week searching out the needy in their homes, bringing them spiritual and material aid.[9]

It was the first clash in what became the familiar battle between those who labored with the roots of social ills and those who dealt with symptoms. Allibone's naïveté in social economics was no worse, however, than Colwell's romantic trust in capitalism and Christian virtue. Aside from legislation to protect workers from unfair competition, the author of *New Themes* would leave all charity to private initiative. "The work of the real disciples of Christ," he wrote, "must be performed by them individually, and not by the church." The love for men which ought to "glow in the bosom of individual Christians" could "never dwell in a corporation or ecclesiastical organization." [10] In a later book he declared that the world was rejecting the "sectarian churches" and coming rather to rely upon "the invisible workings of sanctified human affections . . . being exerted in every practicable direction for both the earthly and heavenly interests" of men. The pastor of the largest Old School congregation in New York City wrote to a friend at Princeton that Colwell seemed to favor a plan which should "dissolve all churches, charities, and associations, and solve the great social problem by this formula, 'Let every man be perfectly good.'"[11]

An argument between Old School Presbyterians is, however, scarcely a reliable index to the social thought of American Protestants. Reactionary Calvinists might still rant that the "increase of a spurious charity" in organizations which ignored "the doctrine, form of government, worship,

[9] Samuel A. Allibone, *A Review, by a Layman, of a Work Entitled, "New Themes for the Protestant Clergy . . ."* (Philadelphia, 1852), p. 66, and generally, pp. 17-22, 30-37, 56-58, 73, 81-96. Cf. Colwell, *New Themes*, pp. 173, 187-88, and especially 183-85, where he scores the Catholic social philosophy but praises the church's concern for the poor. Victor H. Paltsits wrote the sketch of Allibone in the *D.A.B.*

[10] Colwell, *New Themes*, pp. 161-62, 242, 272-73; Allibone, *Review*, pp. 31, 52. Aaron I. Abell, *The Urban Impact on American Protestantism, 1865-1900* (Harvard Historical Studies, LIV, Cambridge, 1943), pp. 4-5, relies uncritically on Colwell.

[11] Colwell, *Position of Christianity*, pp. 134-35; Alexander, *Familiar Letters*, II, 166; cf. p. 275.

and discipline which the Bible teaches" was "ineffectual for the elevation and purification of mankind." But few would listen to them.[12]

The experience of evangelicals in co-operative benevolent and missionary enterprises was rapidly awakening a new sense of responsibility for those whom a soulless industrial system had thrown upon the refuse heap of the city's slums. The American Sunday School Union, for example, gave increasing attention to unchurched urban children. William E. Boardman was called from the Michigan frontier in 1855 to direct the "Students Mission Service," which gave hundreds of future ministers an unforgettable contact with impoverishment. By 1859 the New York City chapter of the Union reported that 40 per cent of the 65,000 who attended its schools were from families which did not attend church.[13]

Local units of the Home Missionary and Tract societies performed similar roles, moving rapidly from simple evangelism to the establishment of mission churches and Sunday schools, job placement, resettlement of destitute children and youths, and the distribution of clothing, food, and money to the poor.[14] Samuel Allibone described how 5,000 volunteers, representing most of the 160 church-sponsored and 40 other charitable societies in Philadelphia, had divided the city into sections for systematic visitation and relief of every indigent home.[15] Better organization and more intelligent planning might come after the war, but they would never kindle greater zeal.

In a similar manner, the first twenty-five years of temperance agitation awakened Christian sensitivity to social need. It also spread the thesis that society was responsible for some poor men's sins. "So long as religion stands by," wrote Thomas Guthrie, "silent and unprotesting against the temptations with which men, greedy of gain, and Governments, greedy of revenue, surround the wretched victims of this basest vice . . . it appears to me utter mockery for her to go with the word of God in her hand, teaching them

[12] Alexander Blaikie, *The Philosophy of Sectarianism* . . . (2nd ed., Boston, 1855), pp. v-vi; cf. pp. 240-41, 297.

[13] Mary M. Boardman (Mrs. W. E.), *Life and Labours of the Rev. W. E. Boardman* (New York, 1887), pp. 99-101; anon., *The American Christian Record* . . . (New York, 1860), p. 358. The latter volume, pp. 298-309, 337-39, 401 and *passim*, contains statistical summaries of the work of various benevolent societies.

[14] See *The Puritan Recorder*, Feb. 2 and 23, 1854, for reports of the Boston City Missionary Society and the Albany City Tract Society; *The Watchman and Reflector*, March 16, 1854, Feb. 12, 1857, Apr. 29, 1858, and Feb. 26, 1863, for samples of similar reports on other organizations, the last referring to the Portsmouth, New Hampshire, city mission; and William Taylor, *Story of My Life* . . . (New York, 1896), pp. 232-33.

[15] Allibone, *Review*, pp. 60-66.

to say, 'Lead us not into temptation.'"[16] Though the temperance movement stemmed from the Puritan zeal of evangelists like Edward Beecher,
Edward N. Kirk, Emerson Andrews, Finney, Barnes, and the Methodists,
its aim was to reform society, not simply to regulate private behavior.[17] Its
supporters were convinced that drunkenness was the prime cause of
pauperism. They seem to have fixed the conviction in many minds that to
banish one was to destroy the other. Even *The Atlantic Monthly* managed
a hurrah in one of its early issues for ministers who carried on the fight
against "drunkenness and want, ignorance, idleness," and "lust."[18]

That intemperance seemed to go hand in hand with Roman Catholic
immigration served only to heighten evangelical solicitude. In sharp contrast to those who allowed hatred of the hierarchy or fear for their own
economic security to destroy compassion for the unfortunate, the revivalists
believed the churches' task was to save Catholics, not scorn them. In order
to meet the challenge, Robert Baird and others organized in the 1830's The
Foreign Evangelical Society, the American Protestant Society, and, later,
the Christian Alliance. These all merged in 1849 to form The American
and Foreign Christian Union, with Baird as publicist and chief agent.
Many thoughtful men considered such efforts an integral part of the plan
for the redemption of the race.[19]

Finally, the example of Christian welfare work in the Old World
confirmed the dawning awareness of obligation to the poor. Religious
newspapers reviewed English books and pointed to European examples
in their efforts to quicken humanitarian impulses. In a famous volume
describing the vices of city life, Thomas Guthrie, the Scottish pioneer of

[16] Thomas Guthrie, *The City: Its Sins and Its Sorrows* . . . (Glasgow, 1862), p. 60.
Many other editions of this work appeared in England and America between 1857 and
1873.

[17] See Horace Bushnell, *Work and Play, or Literary Varieties* (New York, 1864), pp.
99-100; Philip Schaff, *America.* . . . (New York, 1855), pp. 45-46; and Charles C. Cole,
The Social Ideas of the Northern Evangelists, 1826-1860 (New York, 1954), pp. 116-24.
For the revivalists who took an early lead in the crusade, see David O. Mears, *Life of
Edward Norris Kirk* (Boston, 1877), pp. 75-90; Henry Martyn Baird, *Life of the Rev.
Robert Baird, D.D.* (New York, 1866), pp. 105-43, on the temperance mission in Europe,
and pp. 341 ff.; Emerson Andrews, *Living Life or Autobiography* . . . (Boston, 1875), p. 69;
George Prentice, *Wilbur Fisk* (Boston, 1890), pp. 180-94.

[18] Allibone, *Review*, pp. 81-96; *The Atlantic Monthly*, I (1858), p. 864.

[19] See James W. Alexander, *The Revival and Its Lessons* . . . (New York, 1858), pp.
176, 177-82; *The Watchman and Reflector*, Sept. 3, 1857; the articles cited earlier in *The
Independent*, May 25, June 8, and Dec. 28, 1854; H. M. Baird, *Baird*, pp. 99, 253. Cf. Ray
Allen Billington, *The Protestant Crusade, 1800-1860. A Study of the Origins of American
Nativism* (New York, 1938), pp. 322 ff.

"ragged schools," helped to popularize a threefold program of education, prohibition, and Protestant union for systematic evangelism and benevolence. The plan was neatly tailored to fit American conditions. His scheme of dividing cities into areas assigned to each congregation, copied from a successful long-term experiment in Hamburg, Germany, was exactly the same as that in operation in Philadelphia in 1851.[20] As we have seen, the plan spread to all major cities during and after the great revival, driving thousands of middle-class churchmen into the alleys and cellars which the poor called home. Once there, they could not rest content with a purely personal and "spiritual" ministry.[21]

Phoebe Palmer's pioneer work in social welfare projects illustrates the part which urban evangelization played in the origins of the Christian social movement. She enrolled as a tract distributor in New York's slums in the early 1840's and retained a regular assignment until long after she had become Methodism's most prominent perfectionist leader. At the same time she began taking part in prison ministry at the Tombs. Then followed a successful agitation in the Ladies Home Missionary Society of the Methodist Episcopal Church for the establishment of Hedding Church, a mission to the poor. In 1854 Dr. and Mrs. Palmer withdrew from the Allen Street congregation to join another Methodist mission church.

Very early in these activities Mrs. Palmer began making generous personal gifts to meet material needs she found in the slums. She expressed disdain for "the querulous spirit which is ever denouncing the rich, merely because they are so," but warned that great possessions were a curse to those who did not hold them "as social responsibilities, for which an account of stewardship must be rendered." By 1847 she was corresponding secretary of The New York Female Assistance Society for the Relief and Religious Instruction of the Sick Poor, an office which she held for eleven years. At the same time she supported at least one orphanage and other charities.[22]

---

[20] Guthrie, The City, pp. 85, 87, 107-8 and, in general, 33-63. Cf. "Sin and Sorrow in the Cities," The Watchman and Reflector, Dec. 3, 1857; The Independent, Sept. 25, 1851, for an essay on English "open-air preaching"; and Alexander, Familiar Letters, II, pp. 275, 282.

[21] See again, earlier, pp. 65-66. Cf. Alexander, The Revival, p. 11, and Henry M. Dexter, The Spread of the Gospel in the City Among the Poor . . . (Boston, 1866), pp. 8-10, for later promotion of the plan.

[22] Richard Wheatley, The Life and Letters of Phoebe Palmer (New York, 1876), pp. 205-10, 214-27, 189-91, 600-01. On Wheatley's interest in social work, see Matthew Simpson, Cyclopedia of Methodism . . . (Philadelphia, 1878), p. 936.

Phoebe Palmer's crowning achievement, however, was the founding in 1850 of the Five Points Mission, to which can be traced the beginnings of Protestant institutional work in the slums. The Ladies Home Missionary Society had already established seven other missions to the poor when Mrs. Palmer persuaded its advisory committee of Methodist men to buy and demolish the "Old Brewery," located in the city's most squalid neighborhood, and build accommodations for an early type of settlement house. Among those prominent in the men's group were Bishop Edmund S. Janes, Dr. Palmer, W. B. Skidmore, Leonard Kirby, and Daniel Drew. The new structure contained a chapel, parsonage, schoolrooms, baths, and twenty apartments designed to be furnished without charge to families who would otherwise support themselves and obey the rules of the mission. The New York Conference appointed as minister in charge the Rev. Lewis Morris Pease. The project caught the public imagination immediately, especially after five Broadway hotels provided Thanksgiving dinners for five hundred persons that fall.[23]

Long before the mission quarters were completed, however, Pease realized that something more than sermons would be required to reclaim derelict women and their children. They needed jobs, food, clothing, and the kind of home where, in the absence of husbands and fathers, they could be gradually restored to a self-respecting life. The "family apartments" were plainly going to be of little help. Although the officers of the ladies' missionary society at first believed that their constitution prohibited them from supporting his plan, the pastor, acting on his own initiative, persuaded a shirt manufacturer to let out piece work and turned the rented hall which was a gospel center at night into a garment shop by day.

When Pease and his wife proposed to move their home into the Five Points, however, the women turned thumbs down. He resigned and rented two dwellings, conveniently emptied when a friendly judge arranged a police raid. There he opened The Five Points House of Industry. By 1854 his organization was supporting five hundred people.[24]

Both institutions continued thereafter side by side. The Methodist

[23] *The Independent*, Dec. 19, 1850; Henry Cammann and H. N. Camp, *The Charities of New York, Brooklyn and Staten Island* (New York, 1868), pp. 349-60.
[24] See Cammann and Camp, *op. cit.*, pp. 303-14; and "The Five Points House of Industry," *The American Church Monthly*, III (1858), pp. 216-22, for general accounts, the latter quite scornful of the religious predilections of the Ladies Home Missionary Society.

women soon decided that day schools, placement of indigent children in the country, and the distribution of food and clothing were within their province. Numerous pamphlets and short-lived periodicals publicized the settlements. Religious journals of all persuasions praised them highly.[25] Low Church Episcopalians seem by 1856 to have provided most of Pease's support. His new six-story building, completed that year, housed shops, schoolrooms, living quarters, and a chapel. The Five Points became a regular stop for visitors interested in the wonders of New York piety.[26]

Similar ventures multiplied rapidly elsewhere, particularly among Methodist women whose spiritual emancipation was achieved in weekday meetings for the promotion of holiness. Some of the group surrounding Mrs. Palmer helped to organize in 1858 The Ladies Christian Association of the City of New York, later called The Ladies Christian Union. It pioneered in the endeavors which the Y.W.C.A. was later to carry on, early supplementing prayer meetings and Bible classes with a boarding-house at 67 Amity place and a "young women's home" on Fourteenth Street. Others served on the governing boards of a rescue home for young delinquents, "half prison and half school," an asylum for the deaf, and another which in 1854 sheltered 500 Negro orphans.[27] When Chicago Methodist women organized to support a rescue venture modeled after the Five Points, *The Northwestern Christian Advocate* prophesied that the cause of city missions was "destined to actuate the heart of the church with a power little dreamed of." [28]

The missions to immigrants and sailors which had long engaged the attention of the most fervently pious Methodists now gained new support

[25] *Zion's Herald*, Dec. 27, 1854; *The Puritan Recorder*, Feb. 23, 1854; *The Methodist Quarterly Review*, XXXVI (1854), p. 315; *The Independent*, March 29, 1855. See also *The Old Brewery, and the New Mission House at the Five Points. By the Ladies of the Mission* (New York, 1854); and, anon., *American Christian Record*, pp. 380, 401, the latter providing statistics for both organizations in 1859.

[26] "The Five Points House of Industry," *loc. cit.*, pp. 220-22; anon., *America As I Found It* (London, 1852), pp. 66-68; Amelia Murray, *Letters from The United States, Cuba, and Canada* (New York, 1856), p. 157.

[27] James Dixon, *Personal Narrative of a Tour Through a Part of The United States and Canada* . . . (New York, 1849), p. 45; anon., *America As I Found It*, pp. 64-66; J. H. Grand Pièrre, *A Parisian Pastor's Glance at America* (Boston, 1854), p. 83.

Cammann and Camp, *Charities*, pp. 34, 264, 349-60, 503-4, 509, show that Mrs. C. R. Duel, Mrs. W. B. Skidmore, Mrs. S. A. Lankford, and Mrs. J. A. Wright, all of them Mrs. Palmer's associates, were prominent in the activities of The New York State Women's Hospital, The Colored Orphans Asylum, and The Ladies Christian Association. For the prominence of women on the governing boards and visiting committees of many of such charities, see pp. 33, 81, 214, 223, 256, 264, 282, 287, 329, and *passim*.

[28] *The Christian Advocate and Journal*, Jan. 18, 1855; Cf. *Zion's Herald*, Nov. 24, 1852.

and extended their social ministry. Baptist "seamen's bethels" also appeared in New York, Boston, and other cities.[29] Stephen H. Tyng, the most prominent Episcopal clergyman in the nation and leader of the church's evangelical wing, was the guiding spirit in The American Female Guardian Society and Home for the Friendless, after he became pastor in 1845 of St. George's Church, New York. By 1868 this organization maintained six industrial schools; numerous "visitation committees" sought out candidates for its care.[30] In Boston, Unitarians established the Temporary Home for the Destitute, which specialized in resettling children, and St. Stephen's Episcopal Church conducted an intensely evangelistic mission to the poor which in 1860 spent nearly $6,000 for "temporal aid." [31]

By the time of the revival of 1858, in fact, scores of wealthy city congregations of all communions operated chapels for the underprivileged as a regular part of their work, one in New York having established five.[32] No fewer than seventy-six missions were functioning in the national metropolis at the close of the Civil War, twenty-two of them under the city's Mission and Tract society, fourteen attached to Presbyterian churches, eight to Episcopal, seven to Methodist, and others variously sponsored. Even the Universalist congregation maintained one, located at Third Avenue near Fifty-Second Street.[33]

Though Frederic Dan Huntington's dream of a great Episcopal free church in Boston's Back Bay district was never realized, the Rector's Aid Society in his parish conducted a permanent mission to the poor, estab-

---

[29] See earlier, p. 39; *The Watchman and Reflector*, Jan. 1854, Apr. 23 and Oct. 8. 1857, and Feb. 4, 1858; *The Puritan Recorder*, Feb. 12, 1857, reporting a revival at the "Cherry Street Chapel," New York.

[30] Cammann and Camp, *op. cit.*, pp. 290 ff. Cf. Tyng's *D.A.B.* sketch, by E. Clowes Chorley; and Stephen H. Tyng, *Lectures on the Law and the Gospel* (New York, 1848), pp. 235-36, 239, 242, 287-88, for his nearly perfectionist evangelicalism.

[31] *The Christian Register*, Feb. 6, 1858, p. 1; St. Stephen's Chapel. *Report of the Mission to the Poor* (No. 18, Boston, 1861), pp. 11-15, and *passim*; and an earlier *Report* (No. 10, Boston, 1853).

[32] Isabella (Bird) Bishop, *The Aspects of Religion in The United States* . . . (London, 1859), pp. 175-76; Alexander, *Familiar Letters*, II, pp. 277, 282; Samuel Irenaeus Prime, *The Power of Prayer* . . . (New York, 1859), pp. 220-52, *passim*, 258, 262, 263; William C. Conant, *Narratives of Remarkable Conversions and Revival Incidents* . . . (New York, 1858), pp. 364, 366, 376. Conant was editor of the Five Points Magazine, *The Message.* See earlier, p. 69.

[33] These figures are compiled from the tables in New York City Mission and Tract Society, *Walks About New York. Facts and Figures Gathered from Various Sources* (New York, 1865), pp. 19-29.

lished the nonsectarian Chapel of the Good Shepherd in 1866 and, later on, built Huntington House.[34] One of the parishioners, Dr. Charles Cullis, like Dr. Walter Palmer a "homeopathic physician," organized in 1861, with his pastor's encouragement, a Home for Consumptives. The institution soon became famous as a "faith work" because of its methods of healing and of raising funds. Relying entirely on gifts from the public, in the manner and under the inspiration of George Mueller in England, Cullis built eleven cottages on a tract of land at Grove Hall, near Boston. In the city, meanwhile, he maintained the Beacon Hill Church, the Lewis Mission, Faith Training College, and the Cottage Street Church. The good doctor publicized his projects through the Willard Tract Depository, a printing firm which early specialized in holiness books by Hannah Whitall Smith and William E. Boardman. In 1873 Boardman himself prepared the fullest account of Cullis' many ventures.[35]

A chief result of such activities was to marry spiritual to social service. Organizations which still specialized in soul winning now carefully defined the import of that work for the improvement of society. The annual report of the New York City Tract Society for 1859, for example, claimed that an apprenticeship in tract visitation had trained and inspired the men who later founded some of Manhattan's largest charitable endeavors. Samuel R. Halliday, who began his career in this way, served in turn as city missionary in Providence, Rhode Island, head of The Five Points House of Industry, and, finally, as parish assistant to Henry Ward Beecher. The Methodist clergyman who first proposed streamlining and combining the one hundred odd welfare societies in New York thus expressed a commonplace idea when he remarked that concern for "the temporal as well as the spiritual interests of the masses" must underlie their work. "The church of Christ," wrote Bishop Simpson,

[34] Arria S. Huntington, *Memoir and Letters of Frederic Dan Huntington* . . . (New York, 1906), pp. 240-42; Frederic D. Huntington, "Moral Principles of Church Building," *The Church Monthly*, II (July-December, 1861), p. 4; William R. Huntington, "The Mission Sunday School," the same, III (January-June, 1862), pp. 38-41; Mary L. Bissell, "Work for Laywomen," the same, pp. 102-4, concerning district visitation; and Samuel H. Hilliard, "Lay Mission-Work," the same, pp. 137-41.

[35] See William E. Boardman, *Faith Work Under Dr. Cullis, in Boston* (Boston, 1873); Arria Huntington, *Huntington*, p. 241; *The Christian*, V (1867), pp. 281-83, indicating support from holiness Baptists; and Cullis's testimony to sanctification in S. Olin Garrison, ed., *Forty Witnesses, Covering the Whole Range of Christian Experience* (New York, 1888), pp. 220-22. Henry R. Viets wrote the article in the *D.A.B.*

must grope her way into the alleys and courts and purlieus of the city, and up the broken staircase, and into the bare room, and beside the loathsome sufferer. . . . For she was organized, commissioned, and equipped for the moral renovation of the world.[86]

True, men like Horace Bushnell and Francis Wayland held out for what President Herbert Hoover was later to call "rugged individualism." The stern old Calvinist recipe for poverty occasionally cropped up even in *The Independent's* columns.[87] But even the most orthodox of Old School men did not escape the tide of human sympathy. One of them declared in *The Princeton Review* that relieving impoverishment was one of the three historic purposes of the church, along with preaching the gospel and maintaining order and purity among the faithful. The ordination of deacons in the primitive Christian community was intended, he said, to give "dignity and sacredness" to the cause of the poor, so as to "win their hearts to him who is able and willing to supply all their spiritual wants." The American churches were risking an alienation of the lowest class as serious as that in Europe, this writer warned, unless they abandoned pew rents, gave up sophisticated sermons, restored the diaconate to its central place in church order, and provided it the means to supply the temporal needs of the unfortunate.

From 1858 onwards, in fact, revivalists issued repeated warnings against the danger that the love of money would benumb social concern. In an address before Yale alumni in 1861 James M. Sturtevant, president of Illinois College, scorned wealthy merchants who had "thought it out of taste . . . to be troubled about politics" while they let slavery fester in the land. George Barrell Cheever mocked the "worship of the Golden Calves of America," and Gilbert Haven, foremost Methodist abolitionist, warned

[86] Quoted in New York City Mission and Tract Society, *Walks About New York*, p. 120. See also, the same, *Annual Report . . . 1859*, pp. 14-15, 17; Samuel R. Halliday, *Winning Souls: Sketches and Incidents During Forty Years of Pastoral Work* (New York, 1873), p. i; and C. C. Goss, *Charities of New York City* (New York, ca. 1870), pp. 1, 20, 21 ff. Cf. the social emphasis in holiness Baptist circles in The Antioch Baptist Church, *Third Annual Report* (New York, 1862), pp. 7-9, and *Seventh Annual Report* (New York, 1866), pp. 6-8, and *The Christian*, I (1863), pp. 31-32, 47-48, and II (1864), p. 120.
[87] Contrast *The Independent*, March 15 and 22, 1855, and the review of the resettlement program at the Five Points in the following issue, March 29, with quotations made earlier, p. 164. Cf. Cole, *Northern Evangelists*, pp. 169-70, 175-83, perhaps over-emphasizing Bushnell and Wayland; and James W. Alexander, John Todd and others, *The Man of Business, Considered in His Various Relations* (New York, 1857), pp. 3-5, 23, 30-31, 36-37, teaching divine ordination of social and economic inequality, and a wage level determined by the law of supply and demand.

his fellow clergymen that usury was as hard to preach against as slavery. "Some rich brother, who has waxed fat on these ill-gotten gains," he said, "will denounce you as an intermeddler, while his conduct uncensured, and himself undisciplined, keeps scores from the church." [88]

In such a climate of opinion the Y.M.C.A. could not but thrive. Evangelical compassion flowing from the heart of American church life thrust it forward, first into rescue missions and then into the general welfare work which large city congregations had already adopted. The "Y" institutionalized the aims which Edward N. Kirk had proposed in 1850 for the Mount Vernon Association of Young Men, from which the parent unit in Boston developed. These were to help young men grow "in the love of God, in the faith of Christ, in brotherly love" and "in zeal for human welfare." [89]

Perfectionist and revivalist sentiment even more completely dominated the United States Christian Commission's social work. William E. Boardman, the executive secretary, explained that only by reaching soldiers personally through deeds of healing and charity could the agents of the Commission win the chance to tell them "of Jesus, his love, his sacrifice, his readiness to pardon, his perfect righteousness—all, all the sinner's own by simple faith." He believed that Christ had raised up in these last days a new apostleship, composed of "men full of faith and the Holy Ghost," who loved humanity enough to "leave their houses and go without fee or reward to bear the great tidings of a Saviour to the lost." John Wesley's preachers, Boardman declared, had carried the gospel to the British armies a hundred years before Florence Nightingale had gone to heal their bodies; now, for the first time, the two were combined.[40]

Small wonder that Methodist officials like Alfred Cookman and Bishops Edmund S. Janes and Matthew Simpson gave so much valuable aid to the Commission's program, or that pious women organized Ladies' Christian Commission units to raise its funds. The nineteenth-century

---

[88] "Relation of the Church to the Poor," *The Princeton Review*, XXXIV (1862), 612-13, 618, 623, 626, 631; Julian M. Sturtevant, *The Lessons of Our National Conflict* . . . (New Haven, 1861), p. 10; Gilbert Haven, *National Sermons* . . . (Boston, 1869), p. 387; see earlier p. 156.

[89] David O. Mears, *Life of Edward Norris Kirk D.D.* (Boston, 1877), p. 219, and pp. 79, 216-27, *passim; Zion's Herald*, Jan. 21 and March 31, 1852; Charles Howard Hopkins, *History of the Y.M.C.A.* . . . (New York, 1951), pp. 26-27, 45-47; "The United States Christian Commission," *The Evangelical Quarterly Review*, XVI (1865), pp. 264, 266-68; *Christ in the Army: a Selection of Sketches of the Work of The U. S. Christian Commission* (Philadelphia, 1865), pp. 17-18.

[40] *Christ in the Army*, pp. 24-25, 27.

quest for holiness was turned into avenues of service, instead of the byways of mystic contemplation. "Entirely consecrated to service, and then filled with God," cried Cookman in his sermon on sanctification before the national anniversary service of the Y.M.C.A. in 1869. "A co-worker with omnipotence. I challenge the world to supply a more sublime ideal of character, of experience, of life." [41]

It is incorrect, of course, to suppose that liberal Christians and rational men who rejected religious sentiments were in all cases less interested in the plight of the poor. As in the antislavery agitation, Unitarians and Universalists frequently exercised leadership and usually expounded humanitarian theories in advance of their time.[42] Evangelicals themselves testified that "infidel" reformers had sometimes shamed the churches into action, though they insisted that the idea of charity was intrinsically Christian. As one English visitor complained, the fact that revivalists often made total abstinence from liquor "the very rock of salvation" alienated the two groups as much as did the liberal scorn of otherworldly notions. But the preponderance of wealth and numbers was on the side of the evangelicals. The power which earliest opposed the organized evils of urban society and stretched out hands of mercy to help the poor was sanctified compassion. Glowing hopes for the establishment of the kingdom of Christ on earth lighted its way. "Infidelity makes a great outcry about its philanthropy," growled the conservative New York Observer in 1855, "but religion does the work.[43]

Thus declined the ancient distinctions between piety and moralism, spiritual and social service. The prayer of all disciples, "Thy kingdom come, Thy will be done in earth, as it is in heaven" took on new significance as the soul-winning impulse drove Christians into systematic efforts to relieve the miseries of the urban poor. Home mission, Sunday-school, tract, and temperance agents early felt the weight of organized evil in the

[41] Quoted in Henry B. Ridgaway, The Life of the Rev. Alfred Cookman . . . (New York, 1874), pp. 370-71. Cf. William Warren Sweet, The Methodist Episcopal Church and the Civil War (Cincinnati, [1912]), pp. 149, 162, 163-65; Christ in the Army, pp. 40-46; Hopkins, Y.M.C.A., pp. 89-94, 96-98. See earlier; pp. 76-77.

[42] See, for example, E. H. Chapin, Moral Aspects of City Life (New York, 1853), and the same author's Humanity in the City (New York, 1855), reviewed in The Independent, Jan. 26, 1854, and March 1, 1855; and L. P. Brockett and Mary C. Vaughan, Woman's Work in the Civil War . . . (Rochester, N. Y., 1867), on the Sanitary Commission.

[43] The New York Observer, May, 1855, quoted in Anson Phelps Stokes, Church and State in the United States (New York, 1950), II, pp. 190-91. See, again, "The Five Points House of Industry," loc. cit., pp. 210-12; and anon., America As I Found It, p. 71.

festering slums. The flight of the churches from destitute neighborhoods alarmed them while Old World pioneers in Christian social service presented inspiring examples. The rolling tide of Catholic immigration which impelled some men toward nativism challenged earnest believers to gospel work. Individual churches soon joined the interdenominational societies in distributing food and clothing, finding employment, resettling children, and providing medical aid for the lowest classes. The revival of 1858 was in many respects the harvest reaped from this gospel seed. It convinced churchmen everywhere that the story of the Good Samaritan was a parable for their times.

Institutional work meanwhile began, we have also seen, with Phoebe Palmer's Five Points Mission and its offspring, The Five Points House of Industry. Though rudimentary settlement houses such as these remained a rarity, hundreds of city missions existed by 1860, most of them offering temporal ministries far greater than the bowl of stew and occasional night's lodging characteristic in such establishments today. The wartime social services of the United States Christian Commission and the Y.M.-C.A. stemmed directly from these roots and were grounded on the same compassion for "lost" men. A large corps of perfectionists flocked to their banners. By the year of Appomattox evangelicals of all persuasions—even Princeton professors—were attacking the abuses of wealth and acknowledging that relief of the impoverished and oppressed was a primary task of the Christian church.

"A charge to keep I have," sang the assembled Methodist preachers in the great hymn which became their battle song, "a God to glorify, a never-dying soul to save, and fit it for the sky." But the second stanza turned all its solemn weight on the side of social compassion:

> To serve the present age,
>   My calling to fulfill;
> O may it all my powers engage
>   To do my Master's will!

XII

Christian Liberty and Human Bondage.
The Paradox of Slavery

☙

The American Civil War has held perennial fascination for students of our national history. No president has been the subject of more biographies than Abraham Lincoln, no social institution has provoked more fervid study than slavery. The military campaigns whose bloody events are conjured up with the words "Chancellorsville," "Gettysburg," and "Lookout Mountain" have not lost their power to sadden or inspire.

In myth and symbol as well as in fact, the epic story speaks to our deepest emotions. Its overtones of paradox and paranoia are reminiscent of Greek tragedy. Brothers strive, greed beds with altruism. Victors, save for Lincoln, seem shameful in triumph, and vanquished heroes cast their lengthening spell year by year on the popular mind. Whatever may be one's technical criticism of Carl Sandburg's life of the war president, even the most hardbitten historian senses how fitting it is that a poet should speak to break the silence of Appomattox.

That these powerful emotions should have generated sound historical curiosity as well as mystic awe, and so promoted our real knowledge of events, was to be expected. A vast array of monographs and biographies are slowly making it possible for us to know a great deal about the causes and nature of the war for the Union and the persons and forces cast in leading roles upon its stage.

At first, in the 1880's, most historians treated the war as an inevitable clash between the moral force of righteousness and the sin of slavery. In this view the abolitionist agitators were the heroes, seers of destiny who were able to bend history to their purposes because they were in harmony with Eternal Right. Among these, the Boston party of radical Unitarians, led by William Lloyd Garrison, Wendell Phillips, and Theodore Parker, received the lion's share of credit, even though it was recognized that persons from other sections and from evangelical backgrounds, like James G. Birney, Harriet Beecher Stowe, and Theodore Dwight Weld, played a part. After all, most good historical writing was still being done around Boston—and by Unitarians at that.

A generation later Edward Channing and Charles A. Beard penetrated beneath what they thought was the veneer of moral argument to uncover other bases for the sectional strife. Channing asserted that the emergence in the North and South of two distinct ways of life, involving differences in economic organization, social patterns, and religious and political ideals, made the war inevitable. To Beard, on the other hand, the real "irrepressible conflict" was between two groups of rising capitalists—the great planters and the new industrialists. Each sought to seize control of the national government as a means of securing a major share of the country's wealth. Both points of view fit well the temper of twentieth-century thought. They inspired so many brilliant studies of facets of the war's origin that scholars lost interest in the role of the abolitionists.

When, therefore, in the early 1930's, Gilbert H. Barnes and Dwight L. Dumond published volumes which emphasized the role of evangelical zealots like Finney's convert Weld, the Quaker sisters Sarah and Angeline Grimké, and the Presbyterian brothers Arthur and Lewis Tappan, over that of Garrison's party, many historians showed only faint interest. These labors were soon to win greater recognition. For by 1940, James G. Randall in the North and Avery Craven, a Southerner by birth, were mounting an impressive attack upon the whole idea that the war was unavoidable. They declared, rather, that it was the work of a "blundering generation" which was driven along by a motley crew of religious fanatics, slave-driving speculators, fire-eating orators and publicists, and politicians who clothed their ambitions in pious garb. The abolitionists became important again, simply because they were numbered among the screwballs.[1]

Until very recently, however, none of these interpretations has inspired or seemed to require a thoroughgoing analysis of the work and preaching of the main body of "moderate" antislavery Christians in the North.[2] The first generation of historians accepted uncritically the strange libel of Garrison and Birney that their parties alone were the true friends

[1] Howard K. Beale, "What Historians Have Said About the Causes of the Civil War" in *Theory and Practice in Historical Study: a Report of the Committee on Historiography* (Social Science Research Council, Bulletin, No. 54), pp. 55-102, reviews all but the most recent literature.

[2] Charles C. Cole, *The Social Ideas of the Northern Evangelists, 1826-1860* (New York, 1854), pp. 192-220, contains a fine chapter on slavery.

of the slave and the churches the bulwark of his oppressors. The libel became a legend in the Beard-Channing era, despite the fact that it had lost its significance for historical interpretation. Intellectuals of the early part of this century found great delight in pillorying religion. Now, as amended by Professors Barnes and Dumond, the story serves well the thesis that war is something manufactured by madmen.

Many thoughtful contemporaries took a different view. European visitors carefully explained to their countrymen why American Christians opposed to slavery would have nothing to do with abolitionist parties. By striking at the Bible and the Constitution, as Georges Fisch expressed it, the radicals had placed themselves "outside the great religious current that was carrying the nation on." Isabella Bishop told of attending a Garrisonian convention in Boston in 1858 at which Wendell Phillips denounced both George Washington and Jesus Christ as traitors to humanity, the one for giving us the Constitution, the other, the New Testament. Among the twenty-three similar speeches she heard there were two in which Parker Pilsbury and a bloomered advocate of woman's rights declared themselves "bold enough to deny the creation of credulity and priestcraft named the Deity." In the view of such travelers, the decisive body of Northern antislavery sentiment lay in the hearts of the moderate Christians. Though cautious in their utterances and sometimes maddeningly conservative in their actions, they at last threw their weight into the balance against human bondage.[3]

The din of controversy both retarded this event and obscured it from public view. We may first ask ourselves, therefore, what lay back of the noisy struggle among those who professed one common object, freedom for the slave?

Abolitionism's House Divided

As is now well known, religious radicals of both Unitarian and evangelical persuasions co-operated to kindle the first blaze of antislavery feeling which swept over the nation. Charles G. Finney probably won as many converts to the cause as William Lloyd Garrison, even though he shunned the role of a political agitator for that of a winner of souls. Among these were Weld, Arthur Tappan, first president of the American

[3] Georges Fisch, *Nine Months in the United States During the Crisis* (London 1863), pp. 120-24; Isabella (Bird) Bishop, *The Aspects of Religion in the United States* . . . (London, 1859), pp. 81-92. Cf. A. É. de Gasparin, *The Uprising of a Great People* . . . (tr. Mary L. Booth; 4th ed., New York, 1861), pp. 90-91.

Antislavery Society, and Joshua Leavitt, editor first of *The Evangelist* and then of *The Emancipator*. Revivalists like Edward Norris Kirk, Nathaniel S. S. Beman, and Jacob Knapp, together with hundreds of Methodist and New School pastors, lent spiritual support to the movement.

Recognition of the prominence of such men should not, however, obscure their debt to Garrison's *Liberator*, a fact which they freely acknowledged. Orange Scott, a thoroughly orthodox and evangelistic Methodist presiding elder, actually won over a majority of the New England Conference to abolitionism in 1835 by sending them a three-month subscription to the magazine. Garrison, Scott noted, thoroughly exploded the dream of re-colonizing the Negroes in Africa, previously an important stumbling block. Thereafter, Unitarians spoke frequently against slavery in evangelical pulpits.[4]

There was nothing mysterious about this alliance. An uncompromising stand against slavery *as a sin* fitted alike the pattern of Methodist per-fectionism, New School revivalism, and the intensely ethical concerns of radical Quaker and Unitarian religion. Andrew Jackson's presidency wit-nessed an immense enlargement of the average man's interest in politics. For the deeply pious, for those awakened in the revivals of 1828-36, such participation required a moral platform. The abolition of slavery was the one most ready to hand. It was, moreover, easily identifiable with their religious traditions. Wesley had called the traffic in human beings the "sum of all villainies." Samuel Hopkins had fearlessly denounced those in his congregation at Newport who profited from it. The spiritual heirs of these two men were the holiness and revival preachers of the nineteenth century.

By 1845, however, the unity of the movement had been completely shattered. Garrison had ousted the evangelicals from the American Anti-Slavery Society. The Methodist bishops had driven the most radical agitators from their fold, but could not prevent the wedge of controversy from splitting the denomination, North and South. Old School theologians had joined with proslavery Southerners to force the revivalistic synods

[4] Lucius C. Matlack, *The Life of Rev. Orange Scott* . . . (New York, 1847), pp. 33-34; Matthew Simpson, ed., *Cyclopedia of Methodism* . . . (Philadelphia, 1878), p. 191.

Cf., on the role of evangelicals generally and their relations with Garrison, Eugene P. Southall, "Arthur Tappan and the Antislavery Movement," *Journal of Negro History*, XV (1930), pp. 187, 191, 196; Gilbert H. Barnes, *The Antislavery Impulse, 1830-1844* (New York, 1933); and Gilbert H. Barnes and Dwight L. Dumond, eds., *Letters of Theodore Dwight Weld, Angeline Grimké Weld and Sarah Grimké, 1822-1844* (New York, 1934).

out of the Presbyterian church and to develop a biblical and theological defense of the South's peculiar institution. Meanwhile Congregationalists and New School Presbyterians both suffered from the charges of fanaticism raised against Finney's Oberlin College when the perfectionist revival broke out there. The former group, struggling hard in New England to ward off Garrison's bitter attacks upon the church, the Bible, and the ancient creeds, could scarcely avoid the conclusion that religious and social radicalism contained elements of real danger to the faith.

Trouble between the evangelicals and the radical Unitarians began in 1836 and 1837, when the sisters Grimké toured New England as agents of the antislavery society. By their example, if nothing more, they gave encouragement to the infant movement for woman's rights, about which proponents of abolition were by no means united. Garrison, with characteristic rashness, determined to force the society to accept women on a basis of equality with men. He was by this time moving rapidly toward a program of "universal reform" somewhat similar to the complete reconstruction of society for which Edward Beecher had called two years before. Only in Garrison's case, Christianity was not to be an instrument but an object of attack. He would soon champion not only freedom for the slave and the legal equality of the sexes, but the destruction as well of the "sinful" governments of church and state which had permitted these evils to exist so long.[5]

When, therefore, the evangelicals protested this propaganda on behalf of woman's rights, *The Liberator* burst into flaming attacks upon the clergy and the churches. In a Fourth-of-July oration at Providence in 1837, the embattled editor announced

that our doom as a nation is sealed; that the day of our probation has ended, and we are not saved. . . . *The downfall of the republic seems inevitable.* . . . The corruptions of the Church, so-called, are obviously more deep and incurable than those of the state, and, therefore, the Church, in spite of every precaution, is first to be dashed to pieces. . . . The political dismemberment of our union is ultimately to follow.[6]

Three months later Garrison printed a letter from James Boyle, a "per-

[5] Samuel J. May, *Some Recollections of Our Antislavery Conflict* (Boston, 1869), pp. 233-37, 239-40 is pro-Garrison. Cf. *Appeal of Clerical Abolitionists on Anti-Slavery Measures* (Boston, 1838), and Massachusetts Abolition Society, *The True History of the Late Division in the Anti-Slavery Societies . . .* (Boston, 1841), pp. 1-12.
[6] Quoted from *The Liberator*, VII (1837), p. 123, in Massachusetts Abolition Society, *Second Annual Report . . . 1841* (Boston, 1841), p. 11.

fectionist" of Newark, Ohio, who announced grandly, "My hope for the Millennium begins where Dr. Beecher's expires, viz., AT THE OVERTHROW OF THIS NATION. . . . God, by His Spirit, has moved me to nominate Jesus Christ for the Presidency, not only of the United States, but of the World." [7]

Here, so the Methodist, Baptist, and Congregational preachers in the antislavery society believed, was transcendentalist utopianism gone completely daft. They first urged Garrison, as proprietor of *The Liberator*, to dissociate the magazine from its official connection with the society. They succeeded only in enraging him. When they proposed a second journal, cheaper in price and slanted to a more popular audience, he denounced them publicly as traitors to the cause of the slave, wicked plotters who wished by ousting him to destroy a movement they could no longer control. They replied in private remonstrance and, finally, in public print that Garrison was the real renegade. For he had determined to drive from the antislavery ranks all but the few who would adopt his platform of universal reform. [8]

Throughout 1838 Garrison waged as furious a campaign against the church and the ministry as against the slave traffic. His control of the official publication, together with the rather loose organization under which the society functioned, enabled him to oust his opponents at the annual meeting in 1839. The next year, with similar tactics, he seized control of the national convention in New York. Weld, Birney, and Arthur Tappan—who had been both New York state and national president from the beginning—shepherded the evangelicals into the American and Foreign Antislavery Society. Boston divines had already set in motion the separate Massachusetts unit.

But the tumult and strife did irreparable harm to the cause, especially in New England. The Massachusetts Abolition Society, never in a very healthy condition, shouted itself hoarse in a vain attempt to drown out the lion of *The Liberator*. In the churches the counsels of conservative men prevailed—of saintly leaders whose goals were mystic and other-worldly and of editors and ecclesiastical officials anxious for the peace and prosperity of their flocks. The Christian witness against the century's most glaring evil died away. Deeply discouraged, Weld, Birney and

[7] *Ibid.*, p. 12.
[8] *Ibid.*, pp. 13-16, 29-32. Cf. May, *Recollections*, pp. 241-45; and *Appeal of Clerical Abolitionists*.

scores of evangelicals began, like Garrison, to denounce the sins of the Levites as much as the Simon Legrees. Birney declared in 1850 that the churches had been for a decade "in the rear of society." "With the exception of small denominations, which I greatly honor for their conduct in this particular," he wrote, "the church cannot disappoint me much in its anti-slavery measures, because I look for so little—hardly anything, indeed, from it." [9]

The tense battle which was being fought out during the same year in the Methodist conferences in New England and upper New York, testing whether the bishops could restrain the moral sentiment of their church, illustrates this crisis of Christian antislavery. In 1835 Bishop Elijah Hedding transferred Orange Scott from the Springfield to the Providence district. The next year he removed him from the presiding eldership altogether, in retaliation, so Scott alleged, for the latter's skillful leadership of the antislavery delegation at the General Conference in Cincinnati. Scott accepted appointment as pastor in Lowell, Massachusetts. There he set out with his colleague, Joel Parker, "to secure the outpouring of the Holy Spirit among the people" and so "to bring all over to the cause of Christ, and the bleeding slave." They were so successful that within a year the city became a swarming ground for Methodist abolitionists. [10]

Scott thereupon requested inactive status in the conference to become a full-time agent of the American Antislavery Society. His particular speciality was to arrange lectures at the seat of Methodist conferences, much to the disgust of Bishop Hedding. The latter imported Wilbur Fisk, Nathan Bangs, and other prominent New York City clergymen to present competing addresses against abolitionism, allowing them the use of the conference floor. Perversely, as even Methodist preachers are wont to act under such circumstances, the crowds followed Scott. When Hedding himself preferred charges against the reformer in 1838, the conference by a resounding vote found him not guilty. Before long, three hundred pastors in Eastern districts professed loyalty to the cause, and *Zion's Herald*,

[9] James G. Birney to The Christian Antislavery Society, Apr. 2, 1850, quoted in Dwight L. Dumond, ed., *Letters of James Gillespie Birney, 1831-1857* (New York, 1938), II, 1134; cf. James G. Birney, *The American Churches, the Bulwarks of American Slavery* (2nd ed., Newburyport, Mass., 1842). See generally, Mass. Abolition Society, *Second Annual Report*, pp. 33-54; Alice F. Tyler, *Freedom's Ferment . . .* (Minneapolis, 1944), pp. 490-97; and David O. Mears, *Life of Edward Norris Kirk, DD.* (Boston, 1877), pp. 247-48.
[10] Matlack, *Orange Scott*, pp. 33-35, 38, gives Scott's own account.

the Boston Methodist weekly, had become its champion. Meanwhile, Scott had been equally successful in evangelizing western New York.[11]

By 1840, however, public reaction from Garrison's strange course enabled the bishops to bring a moderate party to power and thus to press Scott and his followers toward insubordination to Methodist discipline. The new editor of *Zion's Herald* announced that its columns would be open to all expressions of opinion which were free from "personal wrangling." But he pledged himself to the principle that the church could be "evangelically antislavery" and still allow masters the privileges of membership. Despairing of further success, Scott, LaRoy Sunderland, and Luther Lee in 1843 led several thousand New York laymen and their pastors into the Wesleyan Methodist Church, renouncing episcopacy as heartily as compromise with slaveholders. In the long run this action weakened abolition in the mother church by identifying it with schism. The New Englanders, however, by threatening to join the Wesleyans, were able to force the North-South division at the General Conference the following year.[12]

Similar but even more serious troubles beset the antislavery party in the Presbyterian Church. If the conclusions which C. Bruce Staiger presented in *The Mississippi Valley Historical Review* seven years ago are correct, the expulsion of the New School from the General Assembly in 1837 resulted from a covert "deal" between conservative Scotch-Irish churchmen who opposed the revivalists' doctrinal heresies and Southerners who feared their antislavery principles. The latter had been until 1836 apathetic toward the theological issues which Finney, Albert Barnes, Lyman Beecher, and George Duffield had raised when they espoused free will and natural ability. Near the close of the General Assembly that year, however, delegates from the conservative New York, New Jersey, and Philadelphia presbyteries made known their willingness to abandon the church's historic stand against slavery if Southerners would help them oust the rapidly growing "Puritan" party. That zeal for orthodoxy should have swept slave-state synods the following year is scant surprise. The "Exscinding Act" of 1837 rid the church by a single stroke of both abolitionism and Arminianism, so Staiger concluded, and under

[11] *Ibid.,* pp. 39-40, 122-25, 130-39; Abel Stevens, *Life and Times of Nathan Bangs, D.D.* (New York, 1863), pp. 313-23.
[12] Stevens, *Nathan Bangs,* pp. 318-23; Charles Baumer Swaney, *Episcopal Methodism and Slavery; with Sidelights on Ecclesiastical Politics* (Boston, 1926), pp. 117-37; Whitney Rogers Cross, *The Burned-Over District . . .* (Ithaca, N. Y., 1950), pp. 263-67.

circumstances which left Princeton theologians free to explain piously that it was all done to preserve the faith of the fathers. Scarcely two years had passed before news of the perfectionist awakening at Oberlin gave dramatic point to the Old School charge that revivalism, fanaticism, and reform went hand in hand.[13]

Meanwhile, Princeton professors joined Southern preachers in working out a maddeningly ingenious defense of slavery which, disseminated through the columns of *The New York Observer*, cut further ground from beneath its evangelical opponents. God had chosen some to be masters and some to be servants, the argument ran, in much the same way as certain men were elected to be saved and others to be damned. The Scriptures revealed this divine sanction of slavery—the Old Testament by precept and example and the New Testament by its silence. The apostles had not thought the church "a moral institute of universal good" but a channel of personal salvation, a doorway to everlasting life.[14]

Such reasoning was calculated to cut the heart out of revivalist and perfectionist incitement to reform, appealing as it did to ancient creed, sacred book, and mystic aspiration. It was the antithesis to the moral optimism which, through revival experience and millennial vision, had penetrated great segments of the Northern church. On the strength of it Princeton deserted the theocratic and humanitarian tradition which had flourished there until the 1830's and turned rapidly back toward ultra-Calvinism.[15] As late as 1862 the pastor of the largest Old School church in New York City warned preachers of the gospel to stick to the old-time religion. "Christ and Him crucified," he said, was their only proper subject. The public appetite for sermons on "literary and ethical questions, questions of social and moral reform," and "other matters of a curious and

[13] C. Bruce Staiger, "Abolitionism and the Presbyterian Schism of 1837-1838," *The Mississippi Valley Historical Review*, XXVI (1949-50), pp. 395, 399-400, 404-6, 408-9, covers only events leading up to the division; cf. E. H. Gillett, *History of the Presbyterian Church . . .* (Philadelphia, 1864), II, pp. 547-52. See earlier, pp. 26-28.

[14] James H. Thornwell, *Report on the Subject of Slavery. Presented to the Synod of South Carolina . . .* (Columbia, S. C., 1852), is summarized in William S. Jenkins, *Proslavery Thought in the Old South* (Chapel Hill, N. C., 1935), pp. 207-9; cf., in the latter, pp. 215-16.

[15] Fisch, *Nine Months*, pp. 45-47; J. H. Grand Pièrre, *A Parisian Pastor's Glance at America* (Boston, 1854), pp. 128, 129. Cf. Gillett, *Presbyterian Church*, II, p. 554. Jenkins, *Proslavery Thought*, pp. 207-18, and, generally, pp. 200-241, and Adelaide Avery Lyons, "Religious Defense of Slavery in the North," Trinity College Historical Society, *Historical Papers*, series XIII (Durham, N. C., 1919), review a mass of material without much reference to the fact that most of it was Old School in origin.

novel character" would serve only to corrupt the sacred calling of the pulpit.[16]

Never did venerable religious doctrine fit so well the interests of the classes who now came to hear it preached. In the Ohio Valley, where free farmers were bound to the slave states by numerous ties of kinship and commerce, as well as among the mercantile classes of New York, Philadelphia, St. Louis, and Chicago, the principles of Old School Presbyterianism came to seem the apex of religion. The denomination increased its membership from 126,000 to 292,000 in twenty years. When, in the middle fifties, antislavery members of its Midwestern synods became sufficiently numerous to found a seminary which they hoped would be a counterweight to Princeton, Nathan L. Rice—then editor of *The St. Louis Presbyterian*—canvassed the presbyteries against it. With Cyrus McCormick's timely financial help Rice seized the institution in the name of the General Assembly.[17] In the South, meanwhile, the mood of orthodoxy became an obsession. "We have got to hating everything with the prefix of free," cried one black-belt editor; "free farms, free labor, free society, free will, free thinking, free children, and free schools—all belonging to the same brand of damnable isms."[18]

Thus from the day that Garrison seized control of the American Antislavery Society, the evangelicals, as one of them put it, were "between the upper and the nether millstones of a *pro-slavery* Christianity, and an *anti-Christian* abolitionism."[19] The one party associated freedom with infidelity and championed revolution against church and state. The other identified both Holy Writ and ancient creed with oppression. Had not morality been larger in human hearts than movements to support it and liberty a braver force than those who sang of it at Fourth-of-July celebrations, the slave might yet have languished in his bonds.

[16] Nathan L. Rice, *The Pulpit: Its Relation to Our National Crisis* . . . (New York, 1862), pp. 10-11, 22; Jenkins, *Proslavery Thought*, pp. 200-7, 218-24. See also, Alexander McCaine, *Slavery Defended from Scripture, Against the Attacks of the Abolitionists, in a Speech Delivered Before the General Conference of the Methodist Protestant Church* . . . (Baltimore, 1842).

[17] Thomas E. Thomas, *Correspondence* . . . *Mainly Relating to the Anti-Slavery Conflict in Ohio, Especially in the Presbyterian Church* (Dayton, Ohio, 1909), pp. 92-99. Cf. Gillett, *Presbyterian Church*, II, pp. 549, 568-69. On McCormick Seminary, see Thomas Cary Johnson, *The Life and Letters of Benjamin Morgan Palmer* (Richmond, 1906), p. 192 and *passim*; and William E. Dodd, "The Fight for the Northwest," *The American Historical Review*, XVI (1910-11), pp. 781-82.

[18] Quoted in Abel Stevens, "Slavery—The Times," *The Methodist Quarterly Review*, XXXIX (1857), p. 273.

[19] Anon., "The Vital Forces of the Age," *The Christian Review*, XXVI (1861), p. 566.

The Inner Dilemmas of Evangelical Antislavery

Within the heart of spiritual Protestantism itself, however, lay the contradictory ideals, and in its internal organization the opposing interests which are principally to blame for its weakness in the slavery fight. These dilemmas must be stated and illustrated here before we can appreciate fully the achievement of those revivalists and perfectionists who transcended them. Two involved political questions and another two their ecclesiastical equivalents. A final one raised a purely religious issue. They are as follows:

(a) Whether churchmen might any more than politicians jeopardize the unity of the nation in pursuit of freedom for the slave. (b) At what point the solidarity of national religious and benevolent societies became less important than a clear witness against human bondage. (c) Whether the proper role of the churches in a democratic society was to regulate individual conduct or to impose Christian principles upon social and legal institutions. (d) Whether in disciplining individual conduct the central or the local governing bodies of the sects should act, and by what procedures. And, (e), whether Christians might do violence for loving ends.

Count Agénor de Gasparin concluded in 1861 that proslavery compromises had flourished in America chiefly among those who were "desirous, above every thing, of avoiding both the dismemberment of the United States, and that of the churches." Disunion in either case jeopardized what to the nineteenth century were religious values. Most evangelical clergymen believed that the nation's chief mission was to cradle a faith which should conquer the world. Its unity seemed to them as priceless a treasure as the churchly bonds through which they hoped that Americans themselves might be fully Christianized. Thus, when speaking of slavery in 1848, a Baptist propagandist for home missions cried, "When shall this stumbling-block in the way of the world's evangelization be removed?" But in the next breath he declared, "If this nation shall make shipwreck on the rocks of disunion, . . . who, *who* will be held responsible but American Christians, holding, as they do, the balance of moral and political power?" God had placed in their charge not only the civil and spiritual destinies of this country, he said, but "the master work of evangelizing Foreign Nations" as well.[20]

---

[20] Gasparin, *Uprising*, p. 75; James L. Batchelder, *The United States, the West, and the State of Ohio, as Missionary Fields* (Cincinnati, 1848), pp. 20, 22, 30-31. Cf. Jesse T. Peck, *The History of the Great Republic, Considered from a Christian Standpoint*

Prominent statesmen helped to spread this notion. Henry Clay wrote of the division of the Methodist Episcopal Church: "Scarcely any public occurrence has happened for a long time that gave me so much real concern and pain." Such a separation would not necessarily produce a dissolution of the political union, Clay said, but the example would be fraught with great danger. John C. Calhoun underscored the point from another angle in the debates over the compromise of 1850.[21]

Whether such a danger actually existed is less important here than the fact that many churchmen who were sincerely opposed to slavery believed it did. According to Abel Stevens, this was true of the Methodist bishops and their chief spokesman—Nathan Bangs—during the years prior to the rupture of 1844. Bangs warned New England audiences that their denomination was "the chief religious and, in a sense, the chief social tie between the Northern and Southern states." As late as 1857 Stevens, who had succeeded Bangs as defender of the moderate position in the church, ridiculed the "abstractionists" who thought good men should render a verdict on social issues independently of results. Consequences, he insisted, are the first criterion by which duty is established. Christian reformers, prone to weigh issues on a moral scale alone, ought to support compensated emancipation, since it was the only program likely to bring economic as well as moral force to bear against the evil. Typical, also, was the antislavery Baptist editor who berated Theodore Parker for smashing "with a huge battering ram against all the bulwarks of society," when he neither accepted the responsibility nor displayed the genius to rebuild what he so eagerly destroyed.[22]

Looking backward in 1863, Gilbert Haven—perhaps the most respected Methodist abolitionist—explained in conciliatory tones the significance of this danger of disunion. The abolitionists, he admitted, though sound on the rights of man, had been unmindful of the necessity of the union to attain and preserve those rights. While one party cried, "Union at any cost. Down with the abolitionists who are destroying it," the other with equal fervor answered, "The Rights of every man at any cost. Down with the Union, if it stands in the way of liberty." The shock of arms, Haven

(New York, 1868), p. 570; and "Slavery and the War," *The Watchman and Reflector*, Jan. 1, 1863, for comments in agreement with the one quoted from Gasparin.
[21] Clay is quoted in James M. Buckley, *Constitutional and Parliamentary History of the Methodist Episcopal Church* (New York, 1912), p. 475.
[22] Stevens, *Nathan Bangs*, p. 316; Stevens, "Slavery—The Times," *loc. cit.*, pp. 260. 445, 448, 454; *The Watchman and Reflector*, March 16, 1854, p. 2.

observed, had united these two factions. The one now saw that union meant universal liberty; and the other, that "abolitionism meant union, and only under its banner could the nation be preserved." Equal rights were seen to mean every man's rights. Democracy was identical with abolitionism.[23]

A parallel fear for the unity of national religious organizations lay athwart any antislavery path which the churches or benevolent societies might choose. Here, certainly, the danger was real, not imaginary. Nor did it exist simply because proslavery sentiments flourished among members residing in the South. The religious attack declared slavery a sin and proposed to disfellowship all whom it had contaminated. Such a platform could not fail to alienate thousands who regarded themselves or others as sincerely opposed to the institution but caught by circumstances in the temporary obligation to maintain it.

For this reason, only sects confined to the northernmost portions of free territory—Congregationalists, Unitarians, Universalists, and smaller groups like the Freewill Baptists and Wesleyan Methodists—could take a stand without offending major sections of their membership. Since the larger of these had no effective instruments of central government, their numerous local pronouncements on slavery gained scant notice and the diverse opinions which they did shelter provoked no constitutional crisis. Methodists, Lutherans, Episcopalians, and New School Presbyterians labored under opposite conditions, as did the interdenominational societies like the Evangelical Alliance, the Y.M.C.A., and the American Tract Society.

Though the Baptists were national in scope, they escaped much turmoil both before and after the establishment of sectional missionary boards by their stout insistence upon congregational order. "One of the brethren" of the Philadelphia Association protested in 1857 a Boston editor's inference that their group had not denounced slavery. Indeed they had, he insisted, and quoted resolutions of 1789 and 1805 to prove it! But, he added, "The churches of the body select their own ways to seek the removal of an evil, the existence of which, it is believed, they unanimously deplore."[24]

The Methodists, by contrast, had developed the most tightly knit or-

[23] Gilbert Haven, *National Sermons: Sermons, Speeches and Letters on Slavery and Its War* . . . (Boston, 1869), p. 383.
[24] *The Watchman and Reflector*, Oct. 29, 1857, p. 1. On the Congregationalists, see Mass. Abolition Society, *Second Annual Report*, pp. 43-46.

ganization in the country. They were accustomed to speaking with a united voice. But the fear of schism bridled the tongue of the General Conference at every stage of the controversy. When, despite all the bishops could do, the church divided in 1844, feverish backstage compromises saved for the North the "border" conferences in Maryland, Kentucky, and Missouri. From that time the cornerstone of the Northern bishops' policy was to keep them in.[25]

Their prescription was silence. Supporters of this course argued that the church could be antislavery without saying so. "What am I in virtue of being a Methodist?" asked Charles Adams of the editor of *Zion's Herald* in 1852. "I reply that I am an extirpationist. . . . I am the cleanest-sweeping—the most pertinacious—net dragging—all-devouring abolitionist under heaven." The General Conference was no more obligated to issue another statement against slavery, Adams said, than against "theft, adultery, bigamy, murder, or any . . . of the other vices and crimes unseparated and inseparable from the horrible slavery of this country." He concluded that those who criticized the church at this point were giving it an underserved reputation for conniving with the evil, exactly as Orange Scott's Wesleyan Methodists had done ten years before.[26]

A preacher from rural New England fired back that the people had every right to expect a statement on slavery from the General Conference, if nothing more than to disallow the charge of compromise. The tragedy was, he said, that the membership of that assembly was more conservative in temper than the church as a whole. Safe, moderate men always stood the best chance of election as delegates, men who loved more than their duty "the honor of a seat in so dignified a body—rich breakfasts, sumptuous dinners, exhilarating teas, good smokes in summer-houses or shady bowers, downy beds, [and] seeing the lions and elephants." Pitted against these weaklings, he noted, were veteran delegates from the border conferences, bent on silencing public argument at any cost.[27]

Despite such mutterings the policy of silence prevailed. The pastoral ad-

[25] George Prentice, *Wilbur Fisk* (Boston, 1890), pp. 218-19; Stevens, *Nathan Bangs*, pp. 317-20; Swaney, *Episcopal Methodism and Slavery*, pp. 174-88, 219-31; Robert D. Clark, *Life of Matthew Simpson* (New York, 1956), pp. 212-14.

[26] *Zion's Herald*, Sept. 15, 1852, p. 2; Sept. 22, 1852, p. 2; cf. issues for July 28, 1852, p. 1, and Aug. 11, 1852, p. 2.

[27] *Zion's Herald*, Oct. 6, 1852, p. 2; cf. the letter from a Plainfield, Vt., reader, Oct. 13, 1852, p. 4.

dress issued by the General Conference in 1856 insisted that the debates that year "brought out fully the fact, that none of the members . . . entertained pro-slavery sentiments" and that "little or no mercenary slave-holding" existed in the church. "The effect of such action upon the interests of the border conferences," the address continued, "probably alone prevented a constitutional majority from voting to recommend a change of our General Rules on the subject." A year later Abel Stevens wrote that these Southern districts were "the very battle-field of the question" and the only ones in which the church had "direct access to the slave." To break with them would not help the Negro. The schism of 1844 had proved that such a course would only insulate his masters from contact with the Northern conscience. Stevens urged instead that the home mission program be expanded to provide additional conferences to sustain antislavery Methodists in the South.[28]

The reminder is appropriate, however, that Abel Stevens, like most of the bishops, key editors, and missionary, publishing, and Sabbath-school executives of the denomination, lived in New York City where "safe" opinions stemmed from more than ecclesiastical concerns. The cotton trade siphoned off much of the South's wealth to Park Avenue millionaires. For them, peace was more profitable than principle. Methodist ministers, to be sure, had few such persons in their congregations. But the atmosphere of the national metropolis was friendly to the voice of moderation. Even in 1860 the delegation which represented the city at the General Conference was content to see the resolution lost which forbade mercenary slave-holding, so long as that body denounced the institution itself as immoral.[29]

New England Methodists and those from upstate New York took a dim view of "border-conference politics." A Providence, Rhode Island, minister wrote in 1857, on his return from a tour of Kentucky and Maryland, that societies which the missionary board supported as "vanguards of liberty" were, in fact, filled with proslavery members who denied to all comers that theirs was an antislavery church. Even clergymen had houses full of slaves—the titles often being held by their fathers-in-law! To one cynical observer the difference between the Northern and Southern Methodists

---

[28] Abel Stevens, "American Slavery—Its Progress and Prospects," *The Methodist Review*, XXXIX (1857), pp. 461-63. See earlier, p. 131.

[29] Daniel Curry, *Life-Story of Davis Wasgatt Clark, D.D., Bishop of the Methodist Episcopal Church* (New York, 1874), pp. 167-74. Cf. generally Philip S. Foner, *Business and Slavery* (Chapel Hill, N. C., 1941), pp. 168, 318-21.

was not one of principle but of degree—retail *versus* wholesale. Southern editors, naturally, missed no chance to advertise this view.[80]

The interdenominational benevolent societies were in similar straits. In 1846 Stephen Olin wrote his friend Abel Stevens from London, where he was attending the initial meeting of the Evangelical Alliance, that if he knew his own heart, he "would go as far as anybody to counterwork the detestable system" of slavery. He would "gladly sacrifice the Evangelical Alliance, and a thousand alliances, for its removal." But, Olin added, "I am frank to say that I do not see how this great object can be forwarded at all by attempting to complicate our plans for Christian union with it." When the conference yielded to such sentiments, a representative of the American and Foreign Antislavery Society cried in anguish that this was the same course which had muzzled the voice of reform in America: Churchmen chose brotherly love toward one another in preference to charity for the Negro.[81]

A similar compromise prevailed when the Y.M.C.A. launched first a national then an international organization in 1854 and 1855. Abel Stevens, spokesman for the American delegation at Paris in 1855, persuaded that assembly to adopt a constitution forbidding pronouncements on the subject. His plea was that such a course would help to convince the antislavery associations in America that they must abandon hope for free discussion here![82]

With like motives the Executive Committee of the American Tract Society for years excluded all mention of slavery in its publications, in a hypocritically literal interpretation of the rule that its tracts must be "calculated to receive the approbation of all evangelical Christians." In the early 'fifties several Congregational Associations joined with *The Independent* in a friendly but unsuccessful effort to get this policy reversed. In 1856 the Directors appointed an investigating committee, composed of a dozen distinguished churchmen. George H. Stuart, Mark Hopkins, Francis

[80] See letters to the editor in *Zion's Herald*, Jan. 21, 1852, p. 4, and March 3, 1852, p. 2; George Prentice, *The Life of Gilbert Haven* . . . (New York, 1883), pp. 231-33, 238-39; Charles K. Whipple, *The Methodist Church and Slavery* (New York, 1859), pp. 13-15, 19, 20-21.

[81] Stephen Olin, London, 1846, to Abel Stevens, in Julia M. Olin, ed., *The Life and Letters of Stephen Olin* (New York, 1853), II, 318-19; American and Foreign Anti-Slavery Society, *Remonstrance Against the Course Pursued by the Evangelical Alliance on the Subject of American Slavery* (New York, 1847), pp. 1-9.

[82] Charles Howard Hopkins, *History of the Y.M.C.A.* . . . (New York, 1951), pp. 60, 64, 77, 80.

Wayland, Albert Barnes, and S. S. Schmucker were in the group. Their unanimous recommendation, decided upon in only one meeting, was that the society had every right and duty to publish against the *evils* of slavery, as distinct from the institution itself, or the mode of its abolition, or the question of communion with slaveholders. But the publishing committee professed themselves unable to find a manuscript which even on this point would meet the approval of all Christians! The stalemate continued until 1858, when a large number of the directors withdrew. Several new societies were formed, and the Massachusetts unit began publishing antislavery materials on its own.[33]

James Russell Lowell's article in *The Atlantic Monthly*, describing and deploring these events, brought all the issues into focus. If the founders of the Tract Society, he wrote, could have foreseen that their successors

would hold their peace about the body of Cuffee dancing to the music of the cart whip, provided only they could save the soul of Sambo alive by presenting him a pamphlet, which he could not read, on the depravity of the double-shuffle, . . . they would have shrunk in horror.

Lowell went on to decry in bitter terms a Christianity which was shocked "at a dance or a Sunday-drive, while it was blandly silent about the separation of families, . . . the selling [of] Christian girls for Christian harems" and all the "thousand horrors" of that iniquitous institution. And he laid his finger on one especially tender spot. The benevolent societies of the nation, like many of the denominations, maintained their headquarters in New York City, where the cotton trade was king. There most easily prevailed the counsels of the Christian capitalists, whose growing wealth had numbed their youthful passions for reform.[34]

A third major dilemma of evangelical abolitionism sprang from the argument that the only political role proper to the churches in a democratic state was the regulation of private conduct. They must not seek by organized action to impose Christian principles upon laws and institutions. Interestingly, at this point the clergymen who withdrew from the Massachusetts Antislavery Society had parted company with Garrison. "The

[33] *The Independent*, Jan. 28, 1858, p. 4; cf. editorials in the issues for Sept. 20 and Nov. 22, 1855.
[34] James Russell Lowell, "The American Tract Society," *The Atlantic Monthly*, II (1857-58), pp. 246-51. Cf. Joshua Leavitt, N. Y., January 23 and April 10, 1855, to James G. Birney, quoted in Dumond, ed., *Letters of J. G. Birney*, II, 1168-69, 1171-73, revealing the domestication of a reformer.

duty of acting politically was the cornerstone of our society," they insisted, and the editor of *The Liberator*, by making war on government and parties, had renounced it. They resolved to carry on the public campaign to eliminate the institution from the nation and to support as well measures which would exclude slaveholders from the church.[35]

Within the denominations, however, most debates raged around the issue of disciplining members. American ecclesiastics took seriously the separated condition of state and church and, as we have seen, heartily supported the "voluntary system." They were wary of partisan alignments. Wilbur Fisk warned that Methodism had been evangelically powerful because she had remained politically neutral. Albert Barnes insisted for twenty years that if the churches would eliminate slaveholders from their own number, the evil would disappear from society as well. And he wished to exhaust every alternative of propaganda and appeal calculated to awaken their consciences before forcibly excluding them.[36]

By contrast, many Methodists who professed loathing for the national plague argued that to disfellowship masters would succeed only in removing from the influence of the gospel the very men who needed it most. Moreover, as John McClintock, editor of *The Methodist Review*, pointed out in 1854, to purify the church alone would not sanctify the nation. The great work to be done, he wrote, was to regenerate the sentiment of the community; "not to curse and malign individual slaveholders, but to break up the false public morality in which the system finds its main support."[37] The danger in such advice was that moral conviction in the pulpit should yield to the self-interest which was allowed to flourish in the pew. The ancient evangelical practice was to fence sinners out. The terrible irony of the action of the General Conference of the Methodist Episcopal Church, South, which in 1857 expunged from the discipline the rule forbidding the buying and selling of human beings, but maintained in all their vigor those affecting dress, dancing, card-playing, and attendance at the theater, was not lost upon the radical abolitionists.[38]

Whenever the churches dared attempt to regulate the relation of their

[35] Mass. Abolition Society, *Second Annual Report*, p. 47.
[36] Prentice, *Wilbur Fisk*, pp. 211-12; Albert Barnes, *The Church and Slavery* (2nd. ed., Philadelphia, 1857), pp. 150-51, 164-65.
[37] John McClintock, "Stephen Olin," *The Methodist Quarterly Review*, XXXVI (1854), pp. 31-33.
[38] Charles K. Whipple, *The Methodist Church and Slavery* (New York, 1859), pp. 11-12.

members to slavery, however, convincing protests arose, even in the most episcopally governed bodies, that the separate divisions—dioceses, synods, presbyteries, annual conferences, and associations—ought more properly to handle the question. Many denominations had developed, either by chance or design, a framework of polity similar to that of the nation. Religious "states rights" grew up naturally in the shadow of the political concept which bore that name.

And whether general or local governing units pondered action, innumerable alternative procedures offered themselves—each with its separate set of problems. Were just ministers, or all communicants, or simply bishops, to be forbidden to hold slaves? (Constitutionally, Methodism was an organization of clergymen, above the congregational level.) Was any distinction to be made between mercenary and paternalistic slaveholding? If not excluding them, should the church discipline masters for unchristian conduct of their responsibilities, and, if so, how? Might enslaved church members testify in such cases, when in the civil courts it was forbidden? Were those who supported abolitionist parties or served on the Underground Railroad, thus contributing to the subversion of the laws of the land, to be condoned, or punished?

The fate of a Troy, New York, Methodist Episcopal Conference resolution, which in 1854 proposed the exclusion of all slaveholders, is instructive. Unquestionably antislavery conferences like the Oneida, East Maine, and Erie joined those in border territory in rejecting it on the grounds that one might accept or retain ownership of a Negro as a charitable act. An Iowa Conference committee four years later objected to a similar memorial on the plea that it would prevent good Methodists from buying slaves in order to free them! [39]

The tangled story of New School Presbyterian action and inaction illustrates all these problems of procedure. The fact that certain presbyteries in East Tennessee, Kentucky, Virginia, and South Carolina adhered to the denomination on doctrinal grounds, at the time of the division from the Old School, complicated matters. Although the General Assembly courageously refused year after year to choke off discussion, it voted as early as 1839 to refer all memorials back to the synods and presbyteries "to take such order thereon as in their judgment will be the most judicious and adapted to remove the evil." Four years later, three days of argument re-

[39] *Zion's Herald*, Nov. 22, 1854, p. 186; *Minutes of the Iowa Conference of the Methodist Episcopal Church* . . . (1858), pp. 14-16.

sulted in a stalemate, aptly summed up in the resolution adopted at its end:

> Whereas, there is in this Assembly great diversity of opinion as to the proper and best mode of action on the subject of slavery; and whereas, in such circumstances, any expression of sentiment would carry with it but little weight, as it would be passed by a small majority and must operate to produce alienation and division, ... Resolved, that the Assembly do not think it for the edification of the church, for their body to take any action on the subject.[40]

In 1845 the Assembly declared, by a vote of ninety-two to twenty-nine, that although "the system of slavery, as it exists in the United States, . . . is intrinsically an unrighteous and oppressive system," the delegates would not attempt "to determine the degree of moral turpitude on the part of individuals involved in it." Rather, they exhorted their "beloved brethren" to "remove it from them as speedily as possible, by all appropriate means" and at the same time to avoid "all divisive and schismatical measures tending to destroy the unity and disturb the peace of the church." [41]

Debates in the succeeding meetings of the group reflected the reawakening of the Northern conscience in the years 1848-54. They turned on the question whether the Assembly should vote to encourage and, later, to require presbyteries to bar masters from communion. A committee was appointed in 1855 to determine whether the national body might constitutionally take such action. When a majority reported the next year that it had the right, prolonged discussion broke out, and decision was deferred. The following year the Presbytery of Lexington, Kentucky, served notice that many of its ministers and members owned Negroes "from principle." Here was proof, if any were needed, of the failure of the policy of inaction to keep the church united. The practical result was that only presbyteries in antislavery territory took a stand, leaving the institution elsewhere unrebuked and very much alive.

The General Assembly voted to condemn the Lexington unit and asked it to modify its stand. Southern delegates protested that this was an "indirect" exscinding act as odious as that which in 1837 had driven the New School synods from the parent church. During the next year twenty-one

---

[40] Quoted in Barnes, *Church and Slavery*, pp. 72-73, 75, from the *Minutes of the General Assembly of the Presbyterian Church*, (1839), p. 22; (1843), pp. 18-19. Cf. Gillett, *Presbyterian Church*, II, 549-50.

[41] Quoted in Barnes, *op. cit.*, pp. 76-78.

border presbyteries withdrew to form the United Synod of the Presbyterian Church, carrying with them fifteen thousand members. They refused to join even the Old School communion, regarding its principles insufficiently clear in defense of slaveholding! [42]

Through all these churchly debates over political and ecclesiastical measures, finally, ran the thread of an essentially religious paradox—whether Christians might do violence in pursuit of charitable ends. The dilemma was as old as the faith itself, Jesus having been, in a sense, crucified upon the arms of it. In Gethsemane he had bidden Peter to sheathe his sword. How then could his disciples march off to holy war, singing "John Brown's body lies amold'ring in the grave"?

Even in William Lloyd Garrison the ideal of Christian love operated to deter as well as to inspire antislavery action. Partly under the influence of the antinomian perfectionist, John Humphrey Noyes, Garrison decided in 1837 that Christians must renounce all allegiance to violent and coercive governments. Only thus could they bear the cross of Christ and be crucified unto the world. To this end Garrison announced in December of that year his readiness to lead a new and radical peace crusade, one which would show that the Quakers had erred only in not going far enough. The outcome was the organization in 1838 of The New England Non-Resistance Society, in which Bronson Alcott, Sarah Grimké, and Abby Kelley, as well as the editor of *The Liberator*, played leading roles.[43] Thus, in the name of charity, did Garrison dissociate himself from responsible policy during the very year in which the irresponsible rancor of his journalism reached high pitch. While disdaining the muck of politics, the transcendentalist agitators thereafter threw mud by the wheelbarrow at all who did not occupy their "lofty ground." Christian love had indeed found a strange apostle.

At the opposite extreme stood those who, as one editor complained, displayed a full measure of the graces of forbearance toward slaveholders. *The New York Observer*, he noted, "deprecates any unkind words, or harsh judgment, or rigid church discipline, and aims to win the offenders to a right course by the majestic power of Christian love." Because of this "sentiment of confraternity," one of the moderate Methodists confessed later, "we preached carefully, or not at all, the great common rights of manhood and the fearful crimes of slavery . . . until we had actually

---

[42] *Ibid.*, pp. 84-107, *passim;* Gillett, *Presbyterian Church*, II, 555-58.
[43] Tyler, *Freedom's Ferment*, pp. 411-14.

manufactured an entire department of law and logic and gospel and etiquette to accommodate it." [44]

During the war Southern clergymen did not hesitate to show what use they could make of the doctrine of love. In an "Address to Christians Throughout the World" they asked how measures of violence could "coerce a people to brotherly kindness, unity, and devotion to each other." They denounced as "worthy of universal reprobation" Lincoln's proclamation that the slaves in rebellious areas of the South were free. It was, they said, "in no proper sense an act of mercy to the slave, but of malice toward the master." This, and the bloody carnage, persuaded others besides Albert Barnes that year that peace should be concluded on terms acceptable to the South. [45]

Thus for two decades Garrison cried "war" but refused to fight, and the proslavery clergy answered "peace" when there was no peace. Caught in the middle, evangelicals dared not forsake either the slave or the Golden Rule. Nor could they simply rest in the hope Wilbur Fisk proffered, in opposition to the Methodist abolitionists of New England, that love would destroy evil unattended. The spirit of the gospel, Fisk opined, thrust the nation irresistibly toward freedom. But men like George Barrell Cheever knew that, however much the law of love stood in contradiction to human bondage, that law would not prevail until men bore a cross for it. [46]

The time had come, wrote the editors of Boston's Baptist newspaper in 1857, for Northern Christians to realize that charity and forbearance were not winning, but simply emboldening the slaveholders. "It seems to us quite idle to talk longer of the existence of sound views among the great body of Southern Christians," they wrote. Conservative men in the North were "deceiving themselves, and inflicting fatal injury on the cause of righteousness, by such a pretence." Southern churchmen were, in fact, now asking that slavery be conceded "to be no sin, nor an evil, but a blessing to both races. It must be confessed to be consonant with Christianity, and a providential institution for the conversion of Pagan Africa." No longer could sincere believers allow Christ's decree to be broken and

[44] The Watchman and Reflector, July 16, 1857, p. 2; Peck, Great Republic, p. 570.
[45] Quoted in Peter G. Mode, Sourcebook and Bibliographical Guide for American Church History (Menasha, Wisc., 1921), pp. 611-13; The Watchman and Reflector, Feb. 12, 1863.
[46] Prentice, Wilbur Fisk, pp. 207-8, 211-12; George Barrell Cheever, God Against Slavery, and the Freedom and Duty of the Pulpit to Rebuke It, As a Sin Against God (New York, 1857), pp. 94-95, 100, 101. Cf. Matlack, Orange Scott, pp. 256, 261, for Scott's thoughts on I Corinthians 13.

fail, in the name of that precept, to rebuke its traducers. They must now rise up to declare with united voice

that slavery tramples on the great law, "Thou shalt love thy neighbor as thyself"; that it is inconsistent with the spirit of the gospel of Christ; and those who support it and seek to perpetuate a system of oppression forfeit their title to the name Christian.[47]

Thereafter the "terrible logic of events," as the New York *Christian Advocate and Journal* put it, rapidly hammered the ploughshare of love into a sword. That paper, so long a foe of radicalism, was by 1861 calling for immediate emancipation of the Negroes. In Boston Edward N. Kirk's Thanksgiving sermon the same year glorified war as fervently as Horace Greeley ever did. Basing his remarks upon the Psalm which begins, "I will sing of mercy and judgment," Kirk declared that there could be no compassion for the slave without vengeance for his master. "Blessed be the war," cried this erstwhile champion of the peace crusade; for it had given the lie to Quaker quietism and destroyed the myth that the God of the New Testament was not the sovereign of the Old.[48]

No peace without war. No love without hate. Julia Ward Howe's paradoxical Christ, who came in the beauty of the lilies to trample out the grapes of wrath, was a mirror of the age.

Nathan Bangs died a month after the Battle of Shiloh, convinced that God had at last "taken the problem into His own almighty hand." He was working out its solution, Bangs believed, "with such retribution, on Church and State, North and South, as should astonish all the civilized world, and rebuke alike the truculence and cowardice of men." By their compromises, wrote another, the churches had only brought judgment upon themselves. "The divine purpose had transferred to war the honor of freeing the oppressed."[49]

Abraham Lincoln said it more eloquently in his immortal second inaugural address. Only so, in the conviction that sovereign Deity had seized the helm of events to punish in bloody conflict the sins of both sections and all parties, could Christians fight to free the slaves—with malice toward

[47] *The Watchman and Reflector*, Oct. 1, 1857, p. 2.
[48] *The American Missionary*, V (1861), p. 268, quoted and commented upon the *Christian Advocate's* statement. See also Mears, *Kirk*, pp. 283, 291.
[49] Stevens, *Nathan Bangs*, p. 322. Cf. Julian M. Sturtevant, *The Lessons of Our National Conflict. Address to the Alumni of Yale College* . . . (New Haven, 1861), pp. 18-20; *The Watchman and Reflector*, Jan. 1, 1863, p. 1.

none, with charity for all. The judgments of the Lord were true and right-eous altogether. His was the scourge of war which should requite the bondsman's toil.

Here is, perhaps, the place to note how similar was Lincoln's enigmatic stand on slavery to that of the churchmen. Like them, he had experienced a full range of inward tension on the subject, seeking all the while Webster's promised land of "liberty and union." When, however, Federal bayonets were drawn in Boston to enforce the Fugitive Slave Act and Kansas bled from the repeal of the Missouri Compromise, he, like they, saw more paradox than promise in the famous orator's phrase. The union, shield of liberty, now seemed on the verge of becoming an instrument of tyranny.

Lincoln's first recourse—and it seemed to antislavery clergymen a re-sponsible one, however much based, as we now know, on a misunderstand-ing of geography—was to unite with the Republican party on a platform forbidding the further extension of slavery in the Western territories. They thought thus to set the institution in the way of ultimate extinction. When, however, the Dred Scott Decision placed the supreme law of the land in array against this program—or so, at least, Lincoln said it did—the issue was fatefully joined. He wrote his "House Divided" speech the next spring, while churchmen sought the Baptism with the Holy Ghost.[50]

Whether the deepening of moral conviction in the year 1858 was as important a cause of the conflict as the estrangement of Stephen A. Douglas from the Southern Democrats, to the latter of which events Lincoln contributed perhaps more than the former, is a question others must answer. In any case, the prairie politician won nomination and election to the presidency two years later. War came then, as much because the South's leaders could not believe in Lincoln's essential conservatism as that they would not endure his moral opposition to slavery. Here, too, the parallel is obvious between what happened among the statesmen and what occurred between the two camps of clergymen—North and South.

Both before and during the war, therefore, the citizens who by ethical conviction were best able to share Lincoln's ends and by painful experi-ence most qualified to understand his conservative means were the evan-gelical ministers in the North. Many of them considered themselves his

[50] Albert J. Beveridge, *Abraham Lincoln, 1809-1858* (Boston, 1928), II, 30-32, 151-52, 218-22, 238-39, 244-54, 358-61, 500-13, makes these points clear.

friends and advisors, none more so than Bishop Matthew Simpson, who gave the address at the president's burial in Springfield.[51]

Not only in America were they the mainstay of Republicanism. A swarm of preachers from the revivalist camp shared with Minister Charles Francis Adams the task of explaining to the British people how a war carried on ostensibly to save the union was in fact destined to give the deathblow to slavery. Most of them wrote and spoke without any collaboration with the administration in Washington. Others, like J. M. Sturtevant, president of Illinois College, and George B. Cheever, went with Lincoln's or the party's blessing. The list of those who were in England early in the war included some of the most respected evangelicals of America—Charles G. Finney, Henry Ward Beecher, William Taylor, William Arthur (an Englishman popular in this country), Dr. and Mrs. Walter C. Palmer, and Bishop Charles P. McIlvaine. Among the English liberals and nonconformists, especially, their testimony helped to neutralize the arguments which were pulling the Queen's government perilously close to alliance with the South.[52]

The conflicts which dogged the path of Christians who sought freedom for the slave, then, began in the late 1830's with the disruption of the American Antislavery Society, the suppression of radical abolitionists in the Methodist conferences, and the expulsion of the New School synods from the Presbyterian Church, U.S.A. The fabrication under Princeton auspices of proslavery arguments which appealed to ancient evangelical prejudices occurred at about the same time. A decade of indecision followed, during which churchmen seemed disarmed by the political, ecclesiastical, and religious issues which the slavery crisis raised.

In retrospect, the confusion which these dilemmas produced in the various denominations seems to have been neither more nor less than that in American society as a whole. Vested interests combined with pious dreams and ties of brotherly sentiment to make the unity of both church and nation a thing more precious than freedom for the Negro. The conservative

[51] William Warren Sweet, *The Methodist Episcopal Church and the Civil War* (Cincinnati, 1912), pp. 155-57, 159; Clark, *Matthew Simpson*, pp. 240-46.

[52] See William Arthur's introduction to Fisch, *Nine Months*, dated Dec. 6, 1862, pp. x, xii; William Taylor, *Cause and Probable Results of the Civil War in America* (London, 1862); Charles H. Rammelkamp, "The Reverberations of the Slavery Conflict in a Pioneer College," *The Mississippi Valley Historical Review*, XIV (1927-28), pp. 459-60; William Wilson Manross, *A History of the American Episcopal Church* (2nd ed., New York, 1950), p. 294; George I. Rockwood, *Cheever, Lincoln and the Causes of the Civil War* (Worcester, Mass., 1936), pp. 30-31.

temper which preferred to let well enough alone rather than cope with thorny problems became as strong in ecclesiastical assemblies as in the halls of Congress. Everywhere men of good will—whether saints or skeptics—rejected all thought of armed conflict even while adopting measures which, in the name of human brotherhood, drove the country toward a brother's war. Slavery, and the poison of racial prejudice which it created, was to be the nation's rock of offense. Its woe was not to be restricted to those from whom the offense came. The fathers had sinned, and the children's teeth were set on edge.

XIII

The Spiritual Warfare
Against Slavery

۞

By and large, churchmen in tune with the new revivalism could most easily cut through the dilemmas which held other Christians back from the campaign to free the Negroes. Their moral fervor, the habit of reducing complex matters to simple terms, and their restless enthusiasm had tempered the blade of reform during President Jackson's era. The thesis of this chapter is that after the silent 'forties, during which evangelical abolition faltered and revivals waned, a new generation of soul winners united with veterans like Charles G. Finney and Albert Barnes to summon the churches to their duty. From 1850 onward, the reverberations of this moral strife opened widening fissures in the solidarity of the nation. The antislavery leaders believed that the conflict of conscience would result in the peaceful emancipation of the Negro. Instead, it piled up the combustibles of civil war.

To be sure, the impact of political events, not the preacher's cry, awakened mid-century America to the menace of the "slave power." The debates over the Wilmot Proviso, the Compromise of 1850, the Kansas-Nebraska Act, and the Dred Scott Decision rang each in turn, to use Thomas Jefferson's phrase, a firebell in the night. But in the vanguard of those who answered the alarm were the evangelists, whose compassion for men and hatred of sin struck once more an answering chord in the nation's heart.

Chiefly significant is the fact that revival Christianity had since 1830 adjusted itself to urban conditions. It was more thoughtful in temper, more chastened by bitter experience with schismatics and fanatics, more firmly entrenched in positions of ecclesiastical and educational leadership than before. These gains enabled the evangelistic clergymen to exert an influence upon city dwellers, who now occupied the pivotal position in the antislavery fight. Horace Greeley, William Lloyd Garrison, and the preachers who represented the American and Foreign Antislavery Society had kept alive the sentiment for freedom in rural and small-town districts along the northern edge of the free states. Balanced against the inhabitants of this zone were the farmers and townspeople of the lower Middle West, who idolized Stephen A. Douglas, champion of compromise. Moral conviction was most needed to overcome the weight of economic interest in the cities, and so tip the scales for liberty. The crucial battle for men's minds was fought in Boston, New York, and Philadelphia; in Buffalo, Pittsburgh, and Chicago. Here revivalists played a leading role.[1]

By 1852 a score of religious newspapers had become the harbingers of a renewed campaign against the national curse. In Boston the Methodist *Zion's Herald,* muted for ten years, rang out the antislavery theme clearly again after Daniel Wise had replaced Abel Stevens as its editor. "We are for peace, purity, liberty and temperance," Wise declared in his maiden utterance. "Toward slavery, especially, we cannot show aught but undisguised abhorrence. Our only business with it, shall be to seek its 'extirpation' by all judicious and prudent means; especially from the Church of Christ." The only criterion by which he proposed to screen abolitionist articles was whether or not they would promote the spread of scriptural holiness! Within a few weeks his editorial on "The Christian as a Citizen" declared that "political action is moral action" because the Lord expects our *every* act to be holy; to withdraw from politics is to encourage the growth of evil in the world.[2]

By its side in Boston appeared *The Congregationalist,* equally committed to the cause, and the Baptist *Watchman and Reflector,* more cautious, more spiritually minded, but on that very account immensely effective when its well-written editorials appealed to moral sentiment against the South's cherished institution. *The Christian Register,* organ of all but Theodore Parker's wing of Unitarians, was no more advanced in its views than any of these.[3]

Methodists in upper New York State looked to *The Northern Christian Advocate.* Prior to 1856 William Hosmer, a leader of the radical holiness party whose battles with the episcopacy were eventually to produce the Free Methodist Church, was its editor. Hosmer dedicated his volume, *The Higher Law,* published in 1852, to William H. Seward. He declared slavery to be in conflict with God's laws of love, of improvement, of

[1] See earlier, pp. 59-60, 72-73.
[2] *Zion's Herald,* July 7, 1852, p. 2, and Aug. 11, 1852, p. 2. Cf. "Civilization and Slavery," the same, Aug. 18, 1852, p. 4.
[3] Frank L. Mott, *A History of American Magazines, 1850-1865* (Cambridge, Mass., 1938), pp. 67-68, and *passim,* discusses many of these.

purity, and of equality. "Holiness or moral purity is one of the most essential principles of the gospel," Hosmer wrote, "but slavery is a violation of that right." As for equality, Christianity was in his eyes a system of "spiritual agrarianism" which put prince and peasant, master and servant on a common plane. Men had no right to make a constitution which sanctioned human bondage. If they did, the believer's duty was to defy it.

The fact that a law is constitutional amounts to nothing, unless it is also pure; it must harmonize with the law of God, or be set at naught by all upright men. Wicked laws not only may be broken, but absolutely must be broken; there is no other way to escape the wrath of God. . . . When the fundamental law of the land is proved to be a conspiracy against human rights, law ceases to be law, and becomes a wanton outrage on society.[4]

The collection of Hosmer's editorials which appeared the next year under the title, Slavery and the Church, illustrates even more clearly how perfectionism combined with millennial aspiration to turn Methodists toward reform. The mission of the church, he wrote, is "to establish the kingdom of God on earth by the banishment of unrighteousness, and the introduction of universal holiness." The exclusion of slaveholders from fellowship was prerequisite to this end. Failing this, he declared, "we should only have, on a large scale, what now occurs in lesser degree, wherever slavery is tolerated in the church—a religion without holiness—gospel progress without gospel morals." Christianity would become a curse, "sanctioning and perpetuating vices which it was designed to remove." The Scripture would be "made to serve the purpose of chains and manacles" and the church converted into a slave pen. No, he cried, the gospel is "a system of holiness." It cannot be allied to evil. The work of conversion is, and must be, an indiscriminate war against sin, "all sin—sin of every kind and degree."[5]

The same conference which in 1852 placed Hosmer and Wise in charge of their papers elected the notorious compromiser Thomas E. Bond to edit the New York Christian Advocate and Journal. Bond's supporters claimed he was the one person best qualified to quell the disturbance

[4] William Hosmer, The Higher Law in Its Relation to Civil Government, with Particular Reference to Slavery and the Fugitive Slave Law (Auburn, N. Y., 1852), pp. 175-76, 178; see also pp. 100-03. Zion's Herald, May 26, 1852, p. 3, and Sept. 13, 1854, p. 146, applauded Hosmer's paper heartily; cf. Abel Stevens, Life and Times of Nathan Bangs D.D. (New York, 1863), p. 322 for a less favorable description.

[5] William Hosmer, Slavery and the Church (Auburn, N. Y., 1853), pp. 129-30, 155-57, 164.

over laymen's rights. The antislavery party believed, however, that their real purpose was to retain Methodism's largest weekly in the service of the bishops' tender solicitude for the border conferences. The stage was set for an editorial war but not, as in 1844, a division of the denomination.

"Were the out and out antislavery portion of the church to withdraw," one of the Genesee preachers wrote in *Zion's Herald*, "there would be no M.E. church left. *Majorities* never secede." Whole conferences were committed, he declared, "old men, strong men, young men together; and no thought of secession enters their mind. . . . Slavery, not we, not the North, will leave the church." Daniel Wise counseled the New England conferences that if Dr. Bond should attack them as he had the New York State abolitionists, they should receive it in dignified silence. "Only let us adhere to our great work of spreading scriptural holiness throughout these lands," he said, "and leave unprofitable controversies alone; thus God will bless the labors of our hands, and crown all our spiritual principles with success." [6]

Though the radical party failed to force their program through the General Conference during the next eight years, their spokesmen became the conscience of Methodism. John McClintock reviewed Hosmer's work very favorably in the denominational quarterly, though he insisted that thousands unwillingly connected with the institution were innocent of personal guilt. Even Dr. Bond had to defend himself against the charge that he was an abolitionist because he agreed that slaveholding "for gain" was a sin. [7] In 1857 Edward Thomson, president of Ohio Wesleyan University, denounced as a subterfuge the argument that Christians in the South should retain their slaves in obedience to state laws forbidding manumission. The truth is, he said:

that Christian doctrine is liable to be perverted and Christian practice lowered by the Church. . . . He is not an innovator, but a restorer of the Gospel, who applies it to the sins of the times. The soft and slippered Christianity which disturbs no one, is not the Christainity of Christ, who brought upon himself persecutions and revilings wherever he went, or of Paul, who turned the world upside down. [8]

---

[6] *Zion's Herald*, Oct. 20 and Dec. 22, 1852; cf. Nov. 12, 1852, p. 4.

[7] *The Methodist Quarterly Review*, XXV (1853), pp. 143-45; LXIV (1882), pp. 392-93; *The Christian Advocate and Journal*, Jan. 18, 1855, p. 10. Cf., in the latter publication, the editorials for Jan. 11, 1855, p. 6, Feb. 1, 1855, p. 18, and the article by J. L. Crane in the issue for Jan. 3, 1856, p. 1.

[8] Edward Thomson, "Slavery," *The Methodist Quarterly Review*, XXXIX (1857), pp. 533, 539-40.

REVIVALISM AND SOCIAL REFORM

In New York City, nevertheless, antislavery leadership in the religious press belonged not to the Methodist and Baptist newspapers but to *The Independent,* founded by influential Congregationalist pastors in December, 1848. Joseph Thompson, R. S. Storrs, Henry Ward Beecher, and George B. Cheever dedicated their paper to fighting the extension of slavery in the territories and promoting various other moral reforms through political action. They reflected most accurately the ideas of revival Christians who stood midway between cautious evangelists like Albert Barnes and George Duffield on one hand and the radical perfectionists of Oberlin and New York State on the other. Moreover, they represented a denomination whose strength outside the national metropolis lay in antislavery territory—New England, the Mohawk Valley, and northern Ohio. They could, therefore, proceed without much restraint other than their own good judgment required. Joshua Leavitt, who had gained fame as abolitionist head of *The Evangelist* in the 1830's and later of *The Emancipator,* served as managing editor.[9]

By contrast, the New School pastors and their paper, *The Evangelist,* the only other important antislavery weekly in New York, were preoccupied with the internal problems of their sect. Whatever they said affected the fortunes of revival Presbyterianism in the border areas southward. The city itself was their chief battleground with the Old School. *The Observer* was published there and Princeton Seminary lay nearby.

At first *The Independent* limited itself to the freesoil platform, secure in the belief that an institution which did "hourly violence to the moral sense of those who maintain it" was destined to pass away, if it could only be hemmed in. The debates over the Compromise of 1850, however, cast doubt on this comforting idea. An editorial published in the fall of that year expressed the opinion that the masses of the people in the North had "become more deeply imbued with hatred of the slave system than ever before." Though the editors did not propose to interfere with it as it existed in the South otherwise than by moral means—"argument, persuasion, and Christian appeal"—they now demanded that it should "cease forever in the District of Columbia" and that fugitives from its bondage should be "as free as the wind when they entered the North."[10]

Douglas's Kansas-Nebraska Bill destroyed the free-soil platform as a

[9] *The Independent,* Jan. 4, 1849, p. 1, and Dec. 19, 1850, p. 2.
[10] Cf., the same, the editorial for Oct. 10, 1850, p. 2, with that of Jan. 3, 1850, 2; see also the supplement for the issue of March 21, 1850.

practical policy but made it all the more appealing as a rallying point for popular resentment against the growing power of the slave states in Washington. During the debates over this measure *The Independent* printed in full the speeches of Senators William H. Seward, Charles Sumner, and Salmon P. Chase. After the bill had passed, the editors declared ominously that even should it be repealed, a peaceable solution of the question had become impossible.

Do what we will, we can not now get rid of slavery without *suffering*. . . . The Fugitive-Slave Law and the Nebraska bill have assumed the conservation of slavery by the national arm. And a Christian nation that in this age has voluntarily given itself to the crime of oppression must suffer the judgments of heaven. . . . Slavery will go down. . . . But the law of divine retribution is now arrayed against us, and will work itself out.[11]

Six months later an editorial with the title "Where Are We Drifting?" declared that the country was "marching as straight upon disunion as ever people did, and blindfolded." For the sake of peace and union the South had been given an advantage which, once secured, they would "use to goad the North to inevitable rupture." Those who advised acquiescence now counseled "disunion and belligerency hereafter."[12]

At this point George Barrell Cheever emerged to prominence on the paper's editorial board. More even than Beecher, Cheever by his flaming essays on the higher law scattered the fog of pious compromise which between periods of excitement settled inexorably upon New York.[13] Cheever had become pastor in 1845 of the Church of the Puritans, organized to provide an arena for the exercise of his talents as an agitator. He had campaigned steadily against all forms of "evil," including especially Unitarianism, Catholicism, intemperance, Sabbath desecration, slavery, and the worship of wealth.[14]

In a dozen books and pamphlets whose titles rang with tones of prophetic

[11] The same, June 8, 1854. See also issues that year for May 18, p. 156, May 25, p. 164, and June 15, pp. 186-87.
[12] The same, Jan. 18, 1855, p. 1.
[13] See, for examples, Cheever's editorials, "The Sure Aggressive Tyranny of Slave Legislation," the same, March 8, 1855, p. 73, and "The Sphere of Conscience as the Judge and Interpreter of Law," the same, May 31, 1855, p. 169.
[14] George I. Rockwood, *Cheever, Lincoln and Causes of the Civil War* (Worcester, Mass., 1936), pp. 40-55, and *passim*, greatly emphasizes Cheever's role. Cf. Earl Morse Wilbur, *A History of Unitarianism in Transylvania, England, and America* (Cambridge, 1952), II, 453.

denunciation Cheever set forth the doctrine that slavery was both a personal and a national sin, and that ministers of the Gospel were God's chosen instruments for destroying it. In a democracy, he declared, the people and the government become enmeshed together in guilt for wicked laws. Private conscience, the only guarantee of public integrity, may be prostrated to "support the nation's sin." Unless the people determine upon "resistance in behalf of God, they go to ruin together." Clergymen must awaken in every Christian the will to renounce and disobey evil statutes. "Only by being faithful to God," he said, "can a people keep their freedom." [15]

Here was a preacher whose vituperative skill equalled Garrison's and whose zeal for the application of ethical principles to social problems was as great as Theodore Parker's. Yet as much as any revivalist he loved the souls of men, revered the Bible as final authority and maintained unwavering allegiance to evangelical doctrine. The idea of the higher law, which the transcendentalists supported by a philosophy nobody understood and the politicians by combinations of interest which few could trust, Cheever established upon the prophecies of Isaiah and Jeremiah. He spoke to the many, they to the initiated few. And an aura of divine sanction rested upon every word he uttered. [16]

Cheever's preaching drew blood, a fact plain from the howls of disapproval which rose weekly from *The New York Observer* and James Gordon Bennett's *New York World.* These two papers circulated more widely in the South than any other religious or secular journals. They served notice upon the partisans of bondage that the churchly indecision of the 'forties had come to an end. Abolition was no longer the hobby of fanatics but the moral objective of the greatest preachers in the free states. When the Rev. Frederick A. Ross accepted Cheever's challenge and declared the "sin theory" the "only honest ground for opposition to slavery" and the doctrine that it was ordained by God as a positive good its only worthy defense, the conflict of conscience was set in battle array. [17]

---

[15] George Barrell Cheever, *God Against Slavery: and the Freedom and Duty of the Pulpit to Rebuke It, as a Sin Against God* (New York, 1857), pp. 24-25. Cf. generally, by the same author, *Fire and Hammer of God's Word Against the Sin of Slavery* (New York, 1858); *Commission from God Against the Sin of Slavery* (Boston, 1858); and *The Guilt of Slavery and the Crime of Slaveholding, Demonstrated from the Hebrew and Greek Scriptures* (Boston, 1860). The *D.A.B.* sketch of Cheever's career is by Frederick T. Persons.

[16] Cheever, *God Against Slavery*, pp. 46-47; Rockwood, *Cheever, Lincoln*, pp. 44, 52; see earlier, pp. 53, 65, 88, 199.

[17] Rockwood, *op. cit.*, pp. 14, 19, 73-76, 79-81, and *passim*, elaborates this point;

Revivalists of all persuasions contributed to the goal for which such anti-slavery editors were striving in the cities of the North. In Newark, Henry Clay Fish cried out in the name both of national liberty and human brotherhood against the slave power. "We are linked together, bone of the same bone, and flesh of the same flesh—the members of one common family," he declared. Francis Wayland told the "Nebraska meeting" in Providence that he valued the union as much as any man. He "would cheerfully sacrifice to it everything but truth and justice and liberty." But, he added, "To form a union for the sake of perpetuating oppression is to make myself an oppressor. . . . The Union itself becomes to me an accursed thing, if I must first steep it in the tears and blood of those for whom Chirst died."[18]

The only major exceptions were the Methodist perfectionists surrounding Phoebe Palmer. Her fast friends, Bishops Edmund Janes and Leonidas Hamline, were the architects of the policy of silence which later became the regret of Northern Methodism. George and Jesse Peck, Nathan Bangs, Alfred Cookman, and a host of her other admirers supported it fully. Although Henry V. Degen, editor of *The Guide to Holiness*, pointed to the moral issues at stake in the election of 1856 and asked his readers to pray for the success of God's man, he identified neither the man nor the issues. "We have naturally but little relish for politics," Degen explained, "and if we had, we are not disposed to leave our appropriate mission, and enter the political arena. But the times are ominous, and if ever we needed divine intervention, we need it now." [19]

As titular head of the holiness revival Mrs. Palmer's position was a difficult one. The schisms of 1843 and 1844 had laid both abolitionism and perfectionism under continuing suspicion of disloyalty. The decade after 1850 produced a welter of conflict over methods and terminology which seriously endangered her movement. The Free Methodist agitation in western New York did not help matters. Her friendship with the church's leaders was, therefore, absolutely vital.

Frederick A. Ross, *Slavery Ordained of God* (Philadelphia, 1859), contains speeches made before the New School General Assembly in 1853 and 1856.

[18] *The Watchman and Reflector*, March 30, 1854, pp. 49-50; Henry C. Fish, *Freedom or Despotism. The Voice of Our Brother's Blood* . . . (Newark, 1856), p. 12. Cf., in the latter work, pp. 16-17, and David O. Mears, *Life of Edward Norris Kirk D.D.* (Boston, 1877), pp. 247-48.

[19] *The Guide to Holiness*, XXX (July-December, 1856), p. 127; Richard Wheatley, . . . *Phoebe Palmer* (New York, 1876), pp. 218, 315, 552, 599-601. See also earlier p. 123, and Jesse T. Peck, *The History of the Great Republic* . . . (New York, 1868), pp. 573-74.

In such circumstances the otherworldly and spiritual aspects of Phoebe Palmer's quest for perfect love readily won out over the impulse to anti-slavery reform. Although early to take part in the relief of the widowed, orphaned, and imprisoned or in any other task which required the exercise of compassion, her New York and Philadelphia coterie were laggards in whatever demanded stern attacks on persons and institutions. Nor did they champion women's rights, either, despite the spiritual equality with men which their leader and others in the group achieved. Denouncing social and political injustice remained for them a prerogative of divinity. Thus when Mrs. Palmer received news in England of the Emancipation Proclamation, she wrote an American friend that for many years she had anticipated "days of sadness, when the righteous Judge would chasten us" for "the cruel wrongs of the slave." But, like so many "spiritual" Christians, she had left the issue in the hands of Providence, never doubting "that the God of battles would give us victory."[20]

Quite the opposite happened when perfectionist experience combined, as in Finney, with a hearty tradition of social responsibility and a personal preoccupation with reform. The results in that case were politically explosive, as indeed they were in the late 1840's when, as we have seen, Mrs. Palmer's doctrines reached Methodist abolitionists in New England and upper New York. There the Wesleyan Methodists had cultivated holiness and humanitarianism together from the beginning. "We are organized," Orange Scott wrote in 1845, on "principles that require us to stand out prominently before the world as a class of religious and moral reformers." He urged his followers to seek and find the second blessing. "Deep experience in the things of God" was "essential to the peace and usefulness of all Christians," but especially "to any class of Christian Reformers."[21]

The subtitle of the hymnbook *Miriam's Timbrel*, which the young Wesleyan denomination published, illustrates this combination of social and spiritual ideals so rare in the twentieth century. It announced *Sacred Songs, Suited to Revival Occasions; and Also for Antislavery, Peace, Temperance, and Reform Meetings.* In it appeared such gems as this one, sung to the tune of "America":

> Ye who in bondage pine,
> Shut out from light divine,
> Bereft of hope;

[20] Phoebe Palmer, *Four Years in the Old World* . . . (New York, 1864), p. 647.
[21] Matlack, *Orange Scott*, pp. 245, 248, 251, quotes Scott's editorials; cf. pp. 252-61.

Whose limbs are worn with chains
Whose tears bedew our plains
Whose blood our glory stains
  In gloom who grope.

Shout! for the hour draws nigh,
That gives you liberty!
  And from the dust,
So long your vile embrace,
Uprising take your place
Among earth's noblest race
  By right the first!

Another substituted a dialogue between slaves and reformers for the responses in the familiar hymn, "Watchman, Tell Us of the Night." Called "The Bondsman's Hope," it began,

Freemen! tell us of the night,
What its signs of promise are!
Bondmen! lo! yon spreading light—
Freedom's glorious, beaming star!

A hymn of judgment entitled "Where is thy brother?" asked,

What mean ye that ye bruise and bind
My people, saith the Lord,
And starve your craving brother's mind
That asks to hear my word? [22]

The social radicalism of John Humphrey Noyes and William Lloyd Garrison sprang from an acceptance of the spirit though not the form of such Christian perfectionism. For hundreds of more orthodox clergymen, creed and charity found mystic union in religious experience, whether or not they called it "holiness."

Aside from Mrs. Palmer's group, in fact, the appeal to otherworldliness was more characteristic of liturgical and antirevival Christians than their opposites. We have already noted the Old School's campaign against "political preaching." *The Christian Review*, a Baptist quarterly which among the periodicals of that denomination gave least and last place to

[22] *Miriam's Timbrel* . . . (2nd. ed., Mansfield, Ohio, 1853), pp. 92-93, 97-98, 129-30.

revivalism, maintained silence on slavery until the war broke out. The Lutheran synods, in which the tide of pietistic fervor had begun to subside before the awakening of the national conscience reached its full extent, avoided controversy by appealing to the confessional nature of their church. Samuel S. Schmucker, the revival leader of the General Synod, and the perfectionist Franckean Synod in New York State were exceptions, as illustrated in the title of Schmucker's sermon, *The Christian Pulpit, the Rightful Guardian of Morals in Political, No Less Than in Private Life.*[23] Charles P. McIlvaine and the Low Church Protestant Episcopal bishops, though in principle opposed to slavery, endured with becoming dignity the silence which High Church and Southern prelates imposed upon them until war came. Then, with equally becoming charity, they ignored all social issues save the sin of rebellion and so exalted the spiritual and heavenly ends of the faith that a tranquil reunion with the Southern churches was possible soon after the peace of 1865. The attitude of the Roman Catholic hierarchy was, incidentally, about the same.[24]

Revival clergymen sounded a different note. As the crisis deepened, their convictions hardened. "There is a spirit abroad in the land," wrote Philadelphia's most famous citizen, Albert Barnes, in 1856, and "a voice uttered everywhere against slavery so loud and clear that it will ultimately be regarded." A year later the Baptist newspaper which was leading the return to revivalism in that denomination called for a review of every phase of the church's relation to the system. "Everything like indecision on this great question should be shunned," its editors declared; "lukewarmness is intolerable." What they proposed seemed naïve to men of Parker's stripe, but not to those who understood the dynamics of evangelical moral sentiment. "It is a time for prayer," they said, "for faithful dealing with ourselves, for a more earnest consecration to Christ, and the cultivation of a warmer benevolence for the souls he came to save."[25]

[23] "The National Crisis," *The Christian Review,* XXVI (1861), pp. 491-95, 507-8; Charles William Heathcote, *The Lutheran Church and the Civil War* (New York, 1919), pp. 54-65; Robert Fortenbaugh, "American Lutheran Synods and Slavery, 1830-1860," *The Journal of Religion,* XIII (1933), pp. 72, 74, 91. Schmucker's sermon was published at Gettysburg, Pa., in 1846. See earlier, pp. 55-60.

[24] William W. Manross, *A History of the American Episcopal Church* (2nd. ed., rev., New York, 1950), pp. 290-92; see pp. 150-51.
On the Catholic attitude see Madeleine Hooke Rice, *American Catholic Opinion in the Slavery Controversy* (New York, 1944), pp. 155-57, 275-96; and Anson Phelps Stokes, *Church and State in the United States* (New York, 1950), II, pp. 185-89.

[25] *The Watchman and Reflector,* March 26, 1857, p. 2; Albert Barnes, *The Church and Slavery* (2nd. ed., Philadelphia, 1857), p. 151.

The appearance of Charles G. Finney and Elder Jacob Knapp at union revivals in the largest churches of Boston, New York, Baltimore, Buffalo, and Cincinnati in 1857 and 1858 indicated the direction such heart searching was to take. That men like Cheever, Edward N. Kirk, Wayland, Beecher, and Barnes took a prominent part in the nationwide awakening which followed is sufficient evidence that its leaders sought no escape from social responsibility. Horace Greeley believed rather that a rebirth of conscience was under way which should finally destroy slavery. Two clear-eyed Frenchmen who visited the country on the eve of the war agreed. Georges Fisch pointed to the fact that a half million men "had passed through all the anguish of repentance, and . . . had learned, through a living, personal contact with Jesus Christ, what charity really is." Count Agénor de Gasparin concluded that the revival of 1858 had been a profound agitation of national conviction which had paved the way to the election of Lincoln. "The great moral force which is struggling with American slavery," he wrote, "is the Gospel." [26]

In retrospect, the peculiar power of these Christian knights of antislavery seems to have stemmed from the spirit of compassion toward sinning and suffering men which cropped out in their most heated denunciations of the "cherished institution." Herein lay the difference between Garrison and Finney in the 'thirties, and between Parker and Cheever in the 'fifties. The revivalists were the heirs of a tradition which judged sin even as it bore its cross. They might stigmatize all the vices of which slaveholders were guilty, but they had to love them still. They could not, therefore, either advocate secession of the North from the union, as Garrison did, nor send an army of John Browns to wreak vengeance upon the children of Belial. As the editor of an antislavery missionary magazine put it, "God will secure the deliverance of the oppressed. Our work is to promote it by the pure Gospel of Christ, with its faithful application to all sin, and emphatically, to the great enormities of slavery." [27] In this way they bound themselves and a widening circle in the nation to that union and liberty which Webster and Clay sought,

[26] See editorials in *The New York Tribune*, March 1, and 6, 1858; Agénor É. de Gasparin, *The Uprising of a Great People* . . . (tr. Mary L. Booth; 4th ed., New York, 1861), pp. 83, 86-87; Georges Fisch, *Nine Months in the United States* . . . (London, 1863), p. 151, and generally pp. 147-66; and earlier, pp. 86-88.

[27] *The American Missionary* (Magazine), III, 6 (June, 1859), p. 131; II (November, 1859), p. 251. Cf. Cheever, *God Against Slavery*, pp. 94-95; and *The Watchman and Reflector*, March 30, 1854, quoting with approval an identical statement in *The Independent*.

REVIVALISM AND SOCIAL REFORM

while at the same time heaping faggots on the fire of division which those stalwart compromisers so greatly feared.

Other forces, immense, complex, unpredictable, were also at work, thrusting the nation toward Armageddon. But no avenue of propaganda could have been devised more effectively to harden Northern antipathy toward slavery than the pulpits and the pens of such men. Nor could any have so deeply enflamed Southern pride. When in the great revival year Lincoln wedded politics to religion with the warning that a house divided against itself could not stand, the South did not forget.

Two by-products of the spiritual attack upon slavery deserve particular emphasis: the rehabilitation of the Bible as an instrument of reform, and the contribution which the revivalists made to the idea of an American theocracy.

The use of the Holy Scriptures in defense of slavery deeply alarmed evangelicals. In 1845 a writer in Yale's *New Englander* challenged those who did so to

meet the infidel on the question of the *internal evidence* of the divinity and truth of the Bible, *if you can. Prove* that any book, which authorizes and commands this "Complicated villainy," as John Wesley called it, is from the God of love, *if you can.*

Albert Barnes charged that "all attempts to show that the Bible sanctioned human bondage" contributed "to just that extent, to sustain and diffuse infidelity in the world. This I maturely and firmly believe." [28]

Cheever, Barnes, and Joseph P. Thompson, representing the Congregationalist-New School tradition, and Charles Elliott, president of Iowa Wesleyan College and a close friend of Bishop Hamline, each published volumes designed to show that the Bible was an antislavery book. Cheever acknowledged that he wrote *The Guilt of Slavery and the Crime of Slaveholding; Demonstrated from the Hebrew and Greek Scriptures* out of "the conviction of the impossibility of a divine revelation sanctioning so

[28] See "Slavery and the Bible," *The New Englander*, XV (1857), pp. 129-30, quoting a review published in that journal twelve years before; and Barnes, *Church and Slavery*, pp. 10-11. Cf. John Dempster's review of William Goodell, *American Slave Code in Theory and Practice . . .* (New York, 1858), in *The Methodist Quarterly Review*, XL (1858), pp. 362-82; Peck, *The Great Republic*, pp. 573-74; and, especially, William W. Patton, *Slavery and Infidelity: or Slavery in the Church Insures Infidelity in the World* (Cincinnati, 1857). Patton's work, which elaborated Barnes's point at great length, received a lengthy notice in *The New Englander*, XV (1857), pp. 129-34.

diabolical a cruelty and crime." As usual, his enthusiasm outran his logic and exegetical skill. Hebrew servitude, he said, was honorable and voluntary. In contrast to the Egyptian system, it consisted of "paid and rewarded labor"; the Jews were a society of free men. A second treatise which Cheever published in 1857 enlarged upon the same point, but added the thought that such patriarchal slavery as did exist in Israel was contrary to the divine intention and brought with it a curse.[29]

Thompson wrote a companion volume called *The New Testament on Slavery*. He reasoned that the institution existed in the apostolic age only as a creature of Roman law. Nowhere did Paul acknowledge its rightfulness in the sight of God. Rather, by placing the relationship of masters and servants "under the higher law of Christian love and equality," the apostles "decreed the virtual abolition of slavery, and did in time abolish it wherever Christianity gained the ascendancy in society or in the state." Those who argued that the command to obey one's master sanctioned holding men as chattels might as easily prove that Christ's exhortation to turn the other cheek gave divine approval to assault and battery.[30]

Charles Elliott, a leader of the moderate party of Iowa Methodists, took the same position. Paul's teachings on the sovereignty of God, the equality of the races, the brotherhood of man, and universal redemption, together with his injunctions to shun sin and do good to all men, assaulted the foundation upon which Roman slavery stood. Moreover, Elliott pointed out, obedience to the apostles' principles of justice, equity, kindness, and holiness would require masters to grant freedom to their servants as far as it was in their power.[31]

An important by-product of such arguments was the spread of a rational and historical approach to the interpretation of Scripture, long before German critical scholarship became a seminary fashion. Joseph P. Thompson explained that the New Testament epistles were

---

[29] Cheever, *Guilt of Slavery*, pp. iv, ix-xx; *God Against Slavery*, pp. 9-15, and *passim*. The substance of the former volume first appeared as a series of articles in *Bibliotheca Sacra* in 1855 and 1856. Cf. Albert Barnes, *An Inquiry into the Scriptural Views of Slavery* (Philadelphia, 1846).

[30] Joseph P. Thompson, *Teachings of the New Testament on Slavery* (New York, 1856) is quoted here from the review in *The New Englander*, XV (1857), pp. 110, 113.

[31] Charles Elliott, *The Bible and Slavery* . . . (Cincinnati, 1857), pp. 336-54; the quotation is from pp. 351-52. Charles Adams, also a "moderate," found Elliott much too conservative for his taste, in *The Methodist Quarterly Review*, XXXIX (1857), pp. 634-44. Cf. Aaron W. Haines, *The Makers of Iowa Methodism* . . . (Cincinnati, 1900), p. 180.

not tracts published to act upon society at large; nor were they collected and generally circulated, as now, in a book; but they were manuscript letters, which were sent to little companies composed generally of poor and uninfluential persons. . . . These considerations . . . fully account for the omission in the epistles of many topics relating to society at large.

The outbreak of war forced a contributor to even so conservative a journal as the Baptist *Christian Review* to acknowledge the distinction between biblical revelation "as an objective fact," and as a truth disclosed "to man's spiritual apprehension, to the grasp of his intellectual conceptions." The first is a perfected work, the writer stated, while the second is "ever advancing . . . yet never passing beyond" the written Word. Significantly, the chief factor which he thought responsible for the increase of antislavery interpretation of the Bible was "the majesty and power of God's onward-marching providence." [32]

In 1860 a French visitor who was close to the antislavery evangelicals noted that they had at last realized that "a revelation, to be divine, does not cease to be progressive." If God deemed it proper "to give to his people, so long as they needed it, a legislation adopted to their social condition," such decrees might also have been "divinely abrogated afterward." Moreover, he continued, the Gospels do not contain "a moral code, promulgated article by article" but rather a Golden Rule, in which lay the germ of "a series of commandments, of transformations, of progression, which we have not nearly exhausted." The Christian sense of right is relentless, he said, and those American pastors who preached the law of love struck shackles from the slave's back more certainly than those who proposed to take the sword to free him. [33]

Such a view of progressive revelation was only a few steps short of that which Horace Bushnell had expressed nearly twenty years earlier. "If there is, by God's appointment, and is always to be, a progress in law," Bushnell wrote, nothing more is wanted for the final condemnation of an institution than to demonstrate that its day is now past. "If it can be shown that Christianity itself expects, and deliberately prepares, just this kind of advancement in the social capability of mankind, slavery is

---

[32] See again *The New Englander*, XV (1857), p. 113; and "Does the Bible Sanction Slavery?" *The Christian Review*, XXVII (1862), pp. 584-85.
[33] Gasparin, *Uprising*, pp. 93-94, 99-100. Cf. Fisch, *Nine Months*, pp. 130-31.

THE SPIRITUAL WARFARE AGAINST SLAVERY

then just as truly ruled out by the Scriptures, as if it were specifically con-demned." [34]

Thus by making the law of love the key to the Scriptures and subject-ing them to a Christian version of the doctrine of progress, Northern evangelicals escaped the strait jacket of literalism in which proslavery preachers were fatefully binding the conscience of the South.[35] In suc-ceeding years, the Grand Army of the Republic sang "Glory, Hallelujah, His truth is marching on," while Dixieland became the "Bible Belt," heart of fundamentalist America. Many of its citizens have believed ever since that the good book was a shield against social innovation.

Meanwhile, revival religion's war on slavery sustained the theocratic ideal that God must rule American society, during the very decades when Orthodox Calvinists were forsaking it.[36] To be sure, politics never became the principal business of the evangelistic pulpit, except possibly in the case of Cheever. But the nineteenth-century soul winners were at war with all sin. The persistence across many years of a political crisis whose central issue was a moral one inevitably linked their declarations with public issues. When this happened, the sense of divine judgment which preachers of hell-fire and damnation could conjure up made them more effective propagandists of the higher law than any other class of citizens. That they on occasion applied the concept to divorce, the trade in alcohol, vice and its protection, corrupt politics, secret societies, Sab-bath desecration, and the love of money in all its forms—whether from cotton or commerce—did not lessen their impact on the popular mind. After 1850 no Princeton graduate remotely approximated the influence which men from Andover, Yale, Oberlin, Connecticut Wesleyan, and Union Theological Seminary exerted on behalf of the doctrine of God's sovereignty over American laws and institutions.[37]

[34] Horace Bushnell, Work and Play; or Literary Varieties (New York, 1864), pp. v-vi. Cf. the essay, "The Growth of Law," the same, pp. 78-123, and Charles C. Cole, Jr., "Horace Bushnell and the Slavery Question," The New England Quarterly, XXIII (1950), pp. 19-30.

[35] William Sumner Jenkins, Pro-Slavery Thought in the Old South (Chapel Hill, N. C., 1935), pp. 218-24, suggests this point. Cf. Elliott, Bible and Slavery, pp. 283-84, and Hosmer, Higher Law, p. 175, the latter stressing the law of holiness rather than that of love. See also pp. 199-201.

[36] John R. Bodo, The Protestant Clergy and Public Issues, 1812-1848 (Princeton, N. J., 1954), recounts fully the earlier Calvinist contributions.

[37] Barnes, Church and Slavery, pp. 159-60; "Higher Law and Divorces," The Inde-pendent, July 5, 1855, p. 212; the same, Aug. 31, 1854, p. 276. The American Missionary (Magazine), IV, 7 (July, 1860), 149, and 8 (August, 1860), p. 181, condemned tobacco and slavery together.

The preaching of Gilbert Haven, the best-known Methodist abolitionist and, after 1872, a much-loved bishop in that denomination, will best serve to illustrate this fact. It demonstrates also the persistence into the nineteenth century of John Wesley's fervor for reform. Haven's youthful training in a Malden, Massachusetts, home stamped devotion to holiness and abolition deep upon his character. While at Connecticut Wesleyan University, where Wilbur Fisk was president, he taught a Sunday-school class of young women at the Negro church in Middletown. He wrote his mother that this was proof of his fidelity and warned her with tongue in cheek that she must prepare to receive with great affection a dusky daughter-in-law.[38]

The young minister's sermon on "The Higher Law," delivered during the debate over the Compromise of 1850, struck the notes of devotion and denunciation which characterized most of his later preaching. "In Christ, not in the Constitution, must we put our trust," Haven declared. "On his law should we meditate, not on that which nails him, scourged and bleeding, to that fatal cross." The next year, in his first pastorate at Northampton, Massachusetts, he expressed similar views in the community Fast Day sermon, "to the great joy of the Abolitionists," he wrote a friend, "and the great rage of the Websterian portion of the audience." Meanwhile, he read Jonathan Edwards' sermon on the religious affections, and books by Asa Mahan and T. C. Upham on entire sanctification. He was to seek the latter blessing intermittently until after the war.[39]

Three years later Haven announced to a Wilbraham, Massachusetts, congregation the views on race which set him apart from the general run of reformers. Caste feeling based on color was, he said, the cornerstone of American slavery. Yet "the Bible constantly proclaims the absolute oneness of the race of man, in Adam, Noah, and Christ." Christians who set out to destroy the institution must welcome the Negro to their homes and tables, and accept the biblical sanction of inter-racial marriage.[40]

Haven spent the following years in Methodist pastorates near Boston, speaking often at antislavery meetings. He fled from the sorrow of his wife's death to accept a chaplaincy with the Eighth Massachusetts Regiment when war broke out. In Maryland, Christian connivance with the

[38] George Prentice, *The Life of Gilbert Haven* . . . (New York, 1883), pp. 42-43, 59, 70-73, 94.
[39] *Ibid.*, pp. 292, 107, 137; Gilbert Haven, *National Sermons* . . . (Boston, 1869), pp. 109-10.
[40] Haven, *op. cit.*, pp. 137, 142-45, 146-48.

evil disgusted him. "Thank God, the kingdom of heaven is at hand," he wrote to his friends at home. "The march of events in the political, the religious, the social world, all show that He is soon to appear who will unloose these heavy burdens and let the oppressed go free, and break every yoke."[41]

Back in Boston in the spring of 1863, Haven addressed the preachers of the New England Conference on the means by which they must seek to establish this Kingdom. His sermon closely paralleled the ideas which William Arthur had publicized six years before. Haven denounced those who urged ministers to shun politics and preach only "Christ crucified," while wicked men go on "establishing the state on injustice and framing iniquity by a law." Such counselors, he warned, were as dangerous as those who asked for silence on the sins of the theater, fiction reading, and usury! God had appointed the minister to "watch over souls" as one who must give an account. His duty, therefore, was to seek to make everything contribute to their salvation.

Will a wicked system of government imperil the spiritual welfare of its subjects? He must resist it unto the death. Will social vices tend to their corruption? They must be attacked and overthrown. . . . Would not a holy society, a correct system of government, a pure and lofty literature . . . tend to the salvation of more souls than corrupted morals, despotic government, and debasing literature? Christ crucified, preached to a community under the pressure of all manner of inward and outward lust, will be proclaimed almost as vainly as in Pandemonium itself. He is most successfully lifted up when all the surroundings approximate to the divinity of this central truth. . . . Christ crucified is the grand banner of the church. . . . But to come and hug that flag-staff with apparent fondness, while the enemy is plowing the outer lines with his diabolic artillery, is not affection—it is cowardice.[42]

The remainder of this sermon reiterated Haven's views on racial equality, but in a setting of millennial hope. Divisions on account of language and color, he said, were a consequence of the Fall. As the world approached its ultimate redemption, mankind must recover its unity of race and tongue and become a brotherhood of one family of God's children. "America is the center of the history of the world today," he wrote; "to save this land to universal liberty and universal brotherhood, supported by universal law

---

[41] Quoted in Prentice, *Gilbert Haven*, p. 230; cf. pp. 219, 227-35.
[42] Haven, *National Sermons*, pp. 340-42; cf. pp. 337-38. On the question of riches, see, the same, p. 387; Prentice, *Gilbert Haven*, p. 242; and earlier, pp. 156-57, 174-75.

and sanctified by universal piety, is to save all lands."[43] Though it required "all our sons, all our treasure, all our generation" to destroy the enemies within and without, America would triumph. Then other nations would behold "the image of the transfigured Christ shining in our uplifted face," he exulted. "European caste and tyranny, tottering everywhere to its downfall," would speedily disappear. America would govern the earth, "not in the boastful spirit of national pride, but in the humble spirit of Christian love." Only then should we be a member of "an equal, universal, happy family, the family of Christ." To such a goal, Haven concluded, the Methodist preachers must pledge themselves, purging out "all the old leaven of malice and wickedness" that they might become "a new lump, sanctified and set apart for the Master's use."[44]

Haven's preaching, like William Hosmer's editorials, expressed the views of hundreds in whom revival fervor fused perfectionist ethics and millennial aspiration into a rationale for social reform. The war itself hastened this process. J. M. Sturtevant told Yale alumni that the prophetic "reign of peace on earth" was "not to be ushered in by leaving crime unpunished, and unoffending virtue unprotected, and giving up this present world to men of violence and blood, to tyrannize over it to their heart's content." Rather, he said, Christians must effect "such changes in the social, political, and moral condition of the world . . . as shall render a long reign of justice possible." Four years later even the conservative Lutheran quarterly displayed renewed interest in theocratic doctrines.[45]

Here, then, was a new kind of theocratic ideal, one which rested not so much on faith in God's ancient decrees as in his immediate involvement with the march of human events. God had come—through the providences of history as well as the outpouring of the Holy Ghost—to dispense both mercy and judgment and cleanse America of its sin. The evangelists saw both majesty and mystery in his strange ways with men. The vision enabled them to break out of the bars of conservatism and other-

[43] Haven, *National Sermons*, pp. 349-50, 356, 358; cf., pp. 439-72, his Fast Day sermon for the next year called "The World War: Aristocracy and Democracy." See also, "The Church and the Negro," pp. 361-72, delivered before the Church Anti-Slavery Society at Tremont Temple, June 10, 1863.

[44] *Ibid.*, p. 359.

[45] Julian M. Sturtevant, *The Lessons of Our National Conflict* . . . (New Haven, 1861), p. 54; Robert D. Clark, *Life of Matthew Simpson* (New York, 1956), pp. 219 ff.; Henry Ziegler, "Politics in the Pulpit," *The Evangelical Quarterly Review*, XVI (1865), pp. 245-58; F. W. Conrad, "The Ministers of the Gospel, the Moral Watchmen of the Nations," the same, pp. 366-92.

worldiness, of brotherly love and economic interest which so long had kept the American church from exerting its full strength in the slavery fight.

In summary, the revivalists seem to have carried the brunt of the religious attack upon the Negro's bondage. Especially after 1850, editors of denominational newspapers like Daniel Wise of Boston's *Zion's Herald*, and George B. Cheever of *The Independent*, helped bring about an awakening of conscience in the cities—then the focal points in the battle for men's minds. Albert Barnes, Gilbert Haven, Charles G. Finney, and scores of lesser men ably seconded them, though Phoebe Palmer's immediate circle of Methodist perfectionists stood aloof from the controversy. The Awakening of 1858 appeared to contemporaries to deepen the national soul-searching and so pave the way to the election of Lincoln and the coming of the war. One important by-product of the long debate was that the evangelists adopted a liberal view of scriptural interpretation, freeing the Bible from complicity with oppression. Another was the reinforcement of their conviction that Christ must be king of the nation's affairs, economic and political, as well as religious.

That President Lincoln often employed language similar to that of Haven and Cheever is perhaps not so much proof that the preachers influenced him as that both church and state were undergoing a profound crisis of conscience and conduct. Every moral, religious, and political ideal of a free people was imperiled, whether by peace or by war. The anguish of Antietam's field made this fact clear. Out of the fullness of national suffering came, for one brief moment, wholeness of understanding about the nature and meaning of the American way. As brothers fought to death, brotherhood sprang to life. Even the ponderous rhetoric of the revivalists could not hide its beauty nor dim its promise for a later day.

Sadly, however, the demagoguery of the reconstruction era, in which many churchmen shared, revealed the tragic shallowness of the dedication which the conflict had summoned forth. What C. Vann Woodward has called the "reunion and reaction" of the 'seventies portended the return of the nation, like many a Methodist convert, to the slough of privilege and prejudice.

At the war's end a contributor to the promising young magazine, *The Nation*, wrote hopefully of "The One Humanity," in tones reminiscent of Gilbert Haven. God had placed before the country this question of race, he said. It was destined to be the stone of stumbling which should make or break "our Israel." The aim of a Christian state, "its lofty ideal, its divine mission," was "to help all the weak, to lift up all the fallen, to raise to the highest culture of which he is capable every son of Adam. . . ."[46]

After eighty years we stagger still at the promise. No wonder that historians appeared who denounced as idiocy a war which had settled so little.

[46] *The Nation*, I (Oct. 26, 1865), pp. 520-21. Contrast the racial prejudice expressed in such antirevival writings as Philip Schaff, *America . . .* (New York, 1855), pp. viii-ix, 51, with the following: T. V. Moore, "Unity of the Human Race," *The Methodist Quarterly Review*, XXXIII (1851), p. 348; *The Watchman and Reflector*, Oct. 29, 1857, p. 2; "Backman on the Unity of the Human Race," *The Evangelical Quarterly Review*, VII (1855), pp. 400-12; *The American Missionary* (*Magazine*), VI (1862), p. 106; Gasparin, *Uprising*, pp. 103-4, 205-7; and the opinions of Gilbert Haven described above.

XIV

The Gospel of the Kingdom

⊘∼⊙

Much of the preceding discussion indicates that revivalism and perfectionism became socially volatile only when combined with the doctrine of Christ's imminent conquest of the earth. Edward Beecher's declaration of 1835, referred to earlier, is a case in point. The churches of America were "aroused as never before," he wrote in 1835, to the belief that "a glorious advent of the kingdom of God" was near at hand. No longer did the conversion of the world seem the "distant vision of inspired prophets." Christians were coming to see that their task was

not merely to preach the gospel to every creature, but to reorganize human society in accordance with the law of God. To abolish all corruptions in religion and all abuses in the social system and, so far as it has been erected on false principles, to take it down and erect it anew.[1]

The attacks upon the evils of slavery, intemperance, pauperism, ignorance, and vice were, Beecher felt, portents of an "agitation of the whole community" destined to continue "till the heavens and the earth have been broken at the advent of God; till the last remnant of rebellion has passed away from the earth, and the human race shall repose in peace beneath the authority of Him whose right it is to reign." Characteristically, he spelled out in capital letters the concern which, though most important of all, he thought was being neglected; namely, "the immediate production of an elevated state of personal holiness throughout the universal church—such a standard as God requires, and the present exigencies of the world demand."[2]

---

[1] Edward Beecher, "The Nature, Importance, and Means of Eminent Holiness Throughout the Church," *The American National Preacher*, X (1835), pp. 193-94. Robert Ellis Thompson, *A History of the Presbyterian Churches in the United States* (Philip Schaff and others, eds., *The American Church History Series*, VI, New York, 1895), pp. 129-31, long ago suggested, rather vaguely, the relationship of perfectionism and millennialism to the genesis of the social movement. Cf. John R. Bodo, *The Protestant Clergy and Public Issues, 1812-1848* (Princeton, N. J., 1954), pp. 251-52, and C. C. Cole, *The Social Ideas of the Northern Evangelists, 1826-1860* (New York, 1954), pp. 232-33.

[2] Beecher, *loc. cit.* See earlier, pp. 159-60.

This theme was a keynote of both revival and reform propaganda for the next three decades. Samuel S. Schmucker appealed in 1839 for organic union of all Protestant bodies and the training of 25,000 missionaries in co-operative seminaries, on the ground that "the Son of God appears to be coming in his glory, conquering and to conquer the kingdoms of the earth." [3] Charles Adams, a member of the New England Methodist conference, cited the progress of Bible and tract societies and the commitment of all major denominations to the missionary cause as proof that the "outspreading and triumph of the kingdom of God" was ushering in an era of "righteousness, peace, and happiness." Witnesses on all sides agreed with him that those who shared this hope were the pioneers and chief support of both home and foreign missions.[4] By the late 1850's prominent Baptist and Methodist journals preached church union as strongly as Schmucker had, appealing to the same millennial motivation and praying for the success of a similar evangelistic crusade.[5]

"A grand feature of our times is that *all* is *Progress*," exulted the editors of *The Independent* in 1851. Christianity and culture seemed to be marching together "onward and upward" toward the "grand consummation of prophecy in a civilized, an enlightened, and a sanctified world" and the establishment of "that spiritual kingdom which God has ordained shall triumph and endure." Their only worry was that "mere physical, social, and political development," the growth of "wealth and knowledge and liberty," should fill the horizon of human hopes. "Nay; what is the chaff to the wheat? Let it be a future of Holiness." [6] Three years later Philip

[3] Samuel Simon Schmucker, *Fraternal Appeal to the American Churches, with a Plan for Catholic Union, on Apostolic Principles* (2nd. ed., New York, 1839), pp. 139-40. Cf. "Even so, Come, Lord Jesus," *The Christian Union and Religious Memorial*, I (1848), p. 29; and James L. Batchelder, *The United States, the West, and the State of Ohio, as Missionary Fields* (Cincinnati, 1848), p. 84.

[4] Charles Adams, *Evangelism in the Middle of the Nineteenth Century* . . . (Boston, 1851), pp. 17, 27-29, 31. Cf. the review of a prize-winning essay by John A. Jameson, *Responsibility of American Merchants for the Conversion of the World to Christ*, in *The Independent*, Apr. 5, 1855; "History of Opinions Respecting the Millennium," *The American Theological Review*, I (1859), p. 655; and Oliver W. Elsbree, "The Rise of the Missionary Spirit in New England, 1790-1815," *The New England Quarterly*, I (1928), p. 318.

[5] "That They All May Be One," *The Watchman and Reflector*, Apr. 16, 1857; "Oneness of the Faith and of the Knowledge of the Son of God," the same, Sept. 24, 1857; "Divine and Human Methods to Establish Unity in the Christian Church," the same, Oct. 1, 1857; William Nast, "The Berlin Conference of 1857," *The Methodist Quarterly Review*, XL (1858), p. 428.

[6] "The Coming Age," *The Independent*, Jan. 16, 1851.

Schaff told a Berlin audience that the growing hold of Protestantism upon the American people made Christ's triumph sure. Their missions, he said, both to the uncivilized and "the nominal Christians of the Old World," and their colonization of Christianized slaves in Africa were hastening the day when the whole earth would be filled with his glory and "all nations walk in the light of eternal truth and love." [7]

The revival of 1858 greatly quickened all such hopes. It seemed, as one put it, "the careful preparation for some overwhelming manifestation" in which the "Spirit's fire" would descend over all the land. "The strong towers of sin shall fall, the glory of the Lord shall be displayed, and the millenial [sic] glory shall dawn upon the earth." Bishop McIlvaine soberly admonished his Episcopal brethren to believe that in these last days "a work of the Spirit of God" would be done which would be to Pentecost what the harvest is to the first fruits of the garden.[8] "Who does not see," asked a Dutch Reformed pastor in Philadelphia,

that, with the termination of injustice and oppression, of cruelty and deceit; with the establishment of righteousness in every statute book, and in every provision of human legislation and human jurisprudence; with art and science sanctified by the truth of God, and holiness to the Lord graven upon the walls of our high places, and the whole earth drinking in the rain of righteousness, . . . this world would be renovated by the power of holiness. . . . Oh! this is the reign of Jesus.[9]

The awakening convinced one traveler from Britain that "the transformation of society into the kingdom of Christ" was to be the great work of the American churches. In the growth of the new nation, Isabella Bird Bishop believed she could

trace the unhasting yet unresting progress of a kingdom ordained ere time began, to be completed when time shall be no more . . . when earth's monarchies shall be overthrown, and earth's republics shall bow before the sway of a

[7] Philip Schaff, *America* . . . (New York, 1855), pp. 260, 265; cf. pp. xvi-xvii.
[8] Y.M.C.A. Baltimore, *Proceedings of the All-Day Prayer Meeeting . . . September 27, 1859* (Baltimore, 1859), pp. 10-11; Charles Pettit McIlvaine, *Bishop McIlvaine on the Revival of Religion* (Philadelphia, 1858), p. 19. Note, however, that the volume, *The New York Pulpit in the Revival of 1858—A Memorial Volume of Sermons* (New York, 1858), contains no specific emphasis upon millennial aspiration.
[9] Joseph F. Berg, *The Second Advent of Jesus Christ, Not Premillennial* (Philadelphia, 1859), pp. 125-26; see also, p. 157.

despotic sceptre, and the crown of universal empire shall be placed upon the head of our Lord Jesus Christ.[10]

That William Miller's bizarre crusade to convince the nation that Christ would return in 1843 had not discredited millennialism is obvious. Nor should his movement be considered a sectarian protest against the abandonment of the doctrine by the churches, as a recent sympathetic study concludes. Rather, Miller appeared at the point when revival fires were bringing hopes for the Second Advent to feverish intensity.[11] The attitudes which evangelists like Jacob Knapp, Phoebe Palmer, and the Oberlin and Methodist preachers expressed toward Miller indicate that he gained adherents by advocating a sensational variant of the views they all preached. Prominent revivalists remained charitable to him even after the Lord's failure to appear at the appointed hour provoked general public derision and occasioned the strange legends about white-robed saints waiting in hilltop assemblies for the summons from above.[12]

As in the case of perfectionism, preoccupation with the erratic behavior of strange sects has obscured the wider scene. Actually the chief effect of the reaction from Millerism was to speed the adoption of a fervent postmillennialism, attuned to the prevailing optimism of the age. Preachers of all persuasions turned to the belief that their mission was to prepare the world for Christ's coming by reducing it to the lordship of his gospel.[13]

[10] *The Aspects of Religion in the United States* . . . (London, 1859), pp. 188-89.

[11] Contrast Ira Brown, "Watchers for the Second Coming: the Millenarian Tradition in America," *The Mississippi Valley Historical Review*, XXXIX (1952-53), p. 452, and Dixon Ryan Fox, *Ideas in Motion* (New York, 1935), pp. 110-20, with "The Coming of Christ," *The Methodist Quarterly Review*, XXIV (1842), pp. 352-78; George Duffield, *Millenarianism Defended* . . . (New York, 1843); and Robert S. Fletcher, *A History of Oberlin College, from Its Foundation Through the Civil War* (Oberlin, 1943), I, pp. 222-23.

[12] See Jacob Knapp, *Autobiography* . . . (New York, 1868), pp. 144-45; Phoebe Palmer to William Miller, Oct. 24, 1844, in Richard Wheatley, *Phoebe Palmer* . . . (New York, 1876), pp. 512-13; the same, pp. 513, 514; Albert C. Johnson, *Advent Christian History* . . . (Boston, 1918), pp. 112-14, 207, 214, suggesting the close association of holiness adventists with Methodism and their use of the camp meeting method; and, especially, J. Litch, "The Rise and Progress of Adventism," *The Advent Shield and Review*, I (1844-45), pp. 60-73, 90-91.

[13] Cf. Ralph H. Gabriel, *The Course of American Democratic Thought; an Intellectual History Since 1815* (New York, 1940), pp. 34-37. For early examples of the reaction towards postmillennialism, see "The Millenium [sic] of Revelation xx," *The Methodist Quarterly Review*, XXV (1843), pp. 83-110; "Millennial Traditions," the same, pp. 421-46; Adams, *Evangelism*, p. 17; David Brown, *Christ's Second Coming. Will It Be Pre-Millennial?* (New York, 1851), a Baptist volume; and Thomas Wickes, *An Exposition of the Apocalypse* (New York, 1851), by a Congregational pastor in Marietta, Ohio.

When, therefore, in 1844 Joshua Himes argued in *The Advent Shield and Review* that the pope was antichrist and the conversion of the world impossible until the Second Advent, he only made it less likely that the average minister, however conservative a Calvinist, would agree with him.[14] Old School Presbyterians, conservative Lutherans, and certain Princeton-educated Episcopalians were, in fact, highly embarrassed at being forced to choose between a view now widely tagged with the epithet, "chiliast," and one which lent itself to the support of theological and social liberalism. Not until the dark days preceding the Civil War, when a serious writer in *The American Theological Review* described Miller as simply "unwise enough to fix upon a time," did premillennialism again secure open espousal in respectable quarters.[15]

Two other factors, meanwhile, contributed to the surge of postmillennialism. The clergy's growing sense of social responsibility encouraged the identification of America's destiny with the Christian's hope. And their tendency toward practical Arminianism elicited from even Scottish and Puritan preachers a new reliance upon human measures to hasten the dawning day.

The key question was whether those efforts should include social as well as spiritual action. One conservative writer, for example, agreed in 1859 that most American Protestants believed that "at some period, yet future, the influence of the Great Deceiver" would be restrained and the Spirit of God "remarkably poured out," bringing wars, injustice, oppression, and cruelty to an end. But like many other Old School Presbyterians, he was not willing to encourage "reformers" to work toward this goal, nor to identify the progress of liberal democratic culture with the triumph of Christianity.[16] *The Independent*, on the other hand, organ of revivalist and reforming Congregationalism in New York City, joined fervent hopes with equally fervent pleas for individuals to accept their responsibility to help usher in the Kingdom.[17]

Similarly, in a valedictory describing the relation between revivals and

[14] *The Advent Shield and Review*, I (1844-45), pp. 89, 252, 264.
[15] "History of Opinions Respecting the Millennium," *loc. cit.*, pp. 654-55.
[16] *Ibid.* Cf. Lewis Cheeseman, *Differences Between Old and New School Presbyterians* . . . (Rochester, N. Y., 1848), pp. 166-67; Berg, *The Second Advent*, pp. 38, 116-19, 125-26, 164; and Daniel P. Noyes, "The Church and the Churches," *Bibliotheca Sacra*, XX (1863), p. 364. Anon., *The Revival System and the Paraclete. A Series of Articles from the Church Journal* (New York, 1858), pp. 35-36, illustrates Episcopal premillennialism.
[17] "The Christian's Errand," *The Independent*, July 26, 1855; "Individual Responsibility," Aug. 23, 1855.

progress written in 1859, the aging Albert Barnes declared himself "hopeful in regard to truth, to religion, to liberty, to the advancement of the race." The increase of the comforts of life and the progress of science (even geology) were, he believed, providential agents, along with the "great enterprises of Christian benevolence," in the "recovery and redemption of the race." [18] Edward Beecher also blew once more a trumpet call, as clear as any Walter Rauschenbusch later sounded, for the coronation of Christ as king. Because Jesus said his dominion is not of this world, Beecher wrote in 1865 in *Bibliotheca Sacra,* many had regarded civil government, commerce, the arts and sciences and education as in some sense secular, of necessity worldly and unsanctified. "Yet the very end for which the church was ordained," Beecher declared, is to make each of these institutions "a harmonious and consistent part of his kingdom." [19]

Not the vagaries of Adventists but the tragedy of civil war first shook the faith of American evangelicals in the triumph of this kingdom over personal and social evil. Most deeply affected were the Baptists, whose theological journal, *The Christian Review,* affords an index to one reactionary current of thought. In 1857 George B. Taylor's article mirrored the contemporary hopes for what he called a "social millennium." Arguing both from man's historic progress and the doctrine of God's sovereignty, Taylor declared the "cheering promise" of scripture to be that "a period of blessedness far exceeding the wildest dreams of poetic phrenzy" was soon to be humanity's lot. His optimism reached stellar proportions with the inclusion of possible unfallen inhabitants of other planets in the hoped-for future. [20]

After the attack on Fort Sumter, however, the editors confessed it had been mere self-flattery to suppose that America should "escape the devastating wars which have marked the fluctuating fortunes of European Empire," or to think that "in a .pathway of unbroken peace we should sweep forward into the cloudless splendors" of the millennial era. "Our visions," they mourned, "have been suddenly, rudely dispelled." Shortly thereafter two long articles made plain their abandonment of all hopes

[18] Albert Barnes, *Life at Three-Score* . . . (Philadelphia, 1859), p. 73; see also pp. 16-17, 20, 33-35.

[19] Edward Beecher, "The Scriptural Philosophy of Congregationalism and of Councils," *Bibliotheca Sacra,* XXII (1865), pp. 238, 287-88. Cf. the identical sentiment in Beriah Green to James G. Birney, Whitesboro, N. Y., Apr. 6, 1852, quoted in Dwight L. Dumond, ed., *Letters of James Gillespie Birney, 1831-1857* (New York, 1938), II, p. 1143.

[20] George B. Taylor, "Society's Future," *The Christian Review,* XXII (1857), pp. 376-78, 380.

for a golden age on earth. The first was a biblical attack on the pre-millennialist "chiliasm" of the Adventists, differing from the usual only in the intensity of its emotion. Popular prepudice against Millerism was still strong enough to deter them from taking that historic path to pessimism. The second article appealed to both Augustine and the Scriptures to deny that Christ would ever personally rule on earth. He will return, perhaps soon, the author declared, but only to judge the sinners, destroy the world, and gather the elect to their eternal home. The same year two articles in the Lutheran theological journal covered exactly the same ground.[21]

Others of stanchly optimistic backgrounds endured similar heart searchings. James I. T. Coolidge wrote a purely premillennialist essay for Frederic Dan Huntington's new Episcopal journal. *The Congregational Quarterly* avoided the theme altogether from 1860-67. The Baptist *Watchman and Reflector,* hitherto a champion of liberal evangelicalism, saluted the year 1863 with the chastened assurance that "amid all the wars and rumors of wars" God reigned, dividing nations and dissolving states as "only a part of the eternal plan by which he will turn and overturn, until Jesus comes to reign, and the kingdoms of the earth shall be given to the saints of the most high." Meanwhile, Adventist sects flourished again in various sections of New England, feeding on despair.[22]

The trial which broke the faith of some, however, served only to sober and strengthen others. In an essay on the "moral results" of the war, prepared in 1864 to help publicize the United States Christian Commission, the Rev. Robert Patterson explained that, until the conflict, Christians had "never dreamed of the rough combat with the powers of darkness which an earnest effort to convert the world demands." American religion had acquired a "respectable burgess" character, he wrote, "fat, well clad in broad cloth, with gilt Bible, Gothic church and organ," while an "under-

[21] "The National Crisis," the same, XXVI (1861), p. 492; J. T. Smith, "The First Resurrection and the Millennium, in Revelation XX:1-6," the same, XXVII (1862), pp. 445-46, 462; Heman Lincoln, "The Millennium of the Bible," the same, XXVIII (1863), pp. 131-40. Cf. "The New Heavens and The New Earth," *Evangelical Quarterly Review,* XII (1860-61), pp. 242-55, and G. Seyffarth, "Chiliasm, Critically Examined, According to the Statements of the New and Old Testaments, with Reference to the Most Recent Theory of the Millennium," the same, pp. 341-401. Somewhat earlier appeared the first work of the man who was to become the foremost Lutheran expositor of premillennialism: J. A. Seiss, *The Last Times: an Earnest Discussion of Momentous Themes* (Baltimore, 1856).
[22] J. I. T. Coolidge, "Looking for the Advent," *The Church Monthly,* III (January-June, 1862), pp. 2-3; *The Watchman and Reflector,* Jan. 1 and March 5, 1863; Johnson, *Advent Christian History,* pp. 207, 214.

ground class" it did not touch grew steadily larger in the great cities. What the churches needed was the kind of revival sweeping the army, one which would consider the social as well as the spiritual needs of men. Only thus could they prepare America for the "last great struggle between freedom and slavery, truth and error," for which the Lord was mustering the nations of the earth:

> We are entering, fellow-citizens, upon a period foretold by prophets of old . . . , a period of the overthrow of despotism, and the down-fall of anti-Christ. . . .
>
> Arise, then, Christians of America, and gird yourselves for this great undertaking. . . . Let every prayer meeting in the land wrestle with God for a revival, and we shall see such an outpouring of the Spirit as will convert the army, revive the church, and regenerate the nation.[23]

"The new year will . . . be a momentous one," wrote the editor of the antislavery American Missionary Association's monthly in January, 1862, one in which every child of God and "lover of his race" must hold "himself, and all that he has, consecrated unreservedly to the Master's service, to be used, as he sees fit, for the establishment of his Kingdom of peace and righteousness in our land and throughout the earth." [24]

Such a blending of the sense of impending judgment with millennial ardor and social realism was characteristic in wartime revival appeals.[25] An awakened generation learned at Fredericksburg and Antietam a new understanding of "the glory of the coming of the Lord." Julia Ward Howe set it to unforgettable words and music, in her famous "Battle Hymn." Christ the king was the scourge of sin. He was sifting out the hearts of men before his judgment seat. The wine of peace was to flow blood red from the sword of his wrath.

Contrary to the view that the holiness movement represented a flight from temporal realities, most of its leaders held optimistic views of a temporal millennium and of the necessity of social action to achieve it. Thomas C. Upham and Bishop Leonidas L. Hamline rejoiced in 1846, as

---

[23] *Christ in the Army: a Selection of Sketches of the Work of The U. S. Christian Commission* (Philadelphia, 1865), pp. 135, 139-41.

[24] *The American Missionary (Magazine)*, VI (1862), p. 10. Cf. the similar sentiment with which E. H. Gillett closed his *History of the Presbyterian Church in the United States of America* (Philadelphia, 1864), II, 571, 573.

[25] See, for examples, Levi Sternberg, "Revivals," *The Evangelical Quarterly Review*, XV (1864), pp. 286-87; John E. Todd, *Revivals of Religion . . .* (Boston, 1866), p. 4.

had Professor John Morgan of Oberlin the year before, that the rapid spread of the experience of sanctification marked the beginning of the last dispensation, in which the gospel would conquer the world. "Behold here the dominion of the Holy Ghost, the triumph of the Millenium [sic], the reign of holy love!" [26] William Hosmer, leading writer in the Genesee Methodist Conference holiness revival, declared in 1852 that the business of ministers was "to proclaim the Higher Law, and the Higher Law as paramount to all other laws." They were "heralds of the kingdom of God, and when that kingdom is condemned, they must appear in its defense, or Christ is betrayed in the house of his friends." [27] Leading Methodist journals meanwhile rejected the premillennialist denial of the possibility of the world's conversion and called for "a higher, holier standard of piety" to hasten it.[28] In a camp-meeting sermon preached about the time of the second battle at Bull Run, George Peck declared that the coming reign of Jesus required every minister to testify against wickedness wherever found, including "the vices of trade, the vices of the professions, and the vices of politics." [29]

At the close of the war Jesse Peck published a lengthy religious interpretation of the history of the United States. Its basic assumptions were that God was the actual soverign of all nations, that his purpose "to advance the human race beyond all its precedents in intelligence, goodness, and power" formed the American republic, and that the Christian religion was the "life—force and organizing power" by which he was building a community of holy men and holy institutions made perfect through his sanctifying will.[30] Bishop Matthew Simpson and John C. McClintock, both of whom were moving closer to the "second blessing" leaders, preached Methodist Centenary sermons in 1866 which were filled with millennial

---

[26] Upham, *Life . . . of Madame de la Mothe Guyon* . . . (New York, 1874), II, p. 56. Cf. Leonidas L. Hamline, *The Works of Rev. Leonidas L. Hamline, D.D.* (F. G. Hibbard, ed., New York, 1871), II, 356-59, 445-52; and John Morgan, "The Gift of the Holy Ghost," *The Oberlin Quarterly Review*, I (1845), pp. 115-16.

[27] William Hosmer, *The Higher Law* . . . (Auburn, N. Y., 1852), p. v.

[28] "The Great Want of the Times," *Zion's Herald*, Nov. 15, 1854; "The World's Conversion a Practicable Idea," the same, Nov. 22, 1854; James Nichols, "Tendency of Current Events in the Moral and Material World," *The Methodist Quarterly Review*, XXXIV (1852), pp. 82-85; "The Signs of the Times," the same, XXXV (1853), pp. 440, 443-44; William Nast, "The Berlin Conference of 1857," the same, XL (1858), p. 428.

[29] George O. Peck, "The Signs of the Times," in *Our Country: Its Trial and Its Triumph* . . . (New York, 1865), pp. 36, 38.

[30] *The History of the Great Republic* . . . (New York, 1868), pp. viii, 513, 704-8.

expectation. "Another hundred years," cried Simpson in a dramatic climax, and

the earth shall stand in beauty and glory; a hundred years and the banner of the cross shall shine triumphant over every mountain top and every valley, and the islands of the sea shall give their treasures to Immanuel; a hundred years and they will be singing in heaven and throughout the earth: "Hallelujah! The Lord God omnipotent reigneth."

Let Methodists make this year, he exhorted, one of heart searching, "a year of pure consecration," and of "wide catholic feeling" for all Christians. Let them show their movement to be not only "the power of God in the salvation of sinners," but "the love of God for all Christians and for all classes—the power of Christ in human form." [31]

Outside Methodist ranks, the same spirit prevailed. Though Baptists who promoted sanctification were affected by their denomination's swing toward pessimism, some of them dared during the war to identify perfect love with pacifism while others carried the idea of consecration of property into the most radical millennial idealism.[32] When the Union victory freed William E. Boardman from the Christian Commission, he set to work as a fulltime evangelist, preaching a conquering, overcoming gospel—one which would master sin in society even as it destroyed it in individuals. "No other question," he wrote in 1869, "looms up before the thoughtful Christian mind in the immediate future with such grandeur as this of the conversion of the industrial, commercial, political, educational, and social interests of the world to Christ." [33]

Boardman's program, to be sure, was as naïve as his aims were high. It called for Christians to go into business and industry with faith and prayer, to "push the competition upon the principles of truth and righteousness," and thus drive to the wall "the servants of the devil and all their corrupt and selfish practices." This, he cried, "would be the beginning of the end for the millennial triumph." The significant point is, however,

---

[31] Quoted from *Pittsburgh Christian Advocate*, Apr. 21, 1866, in Wallace Guy Smeltzer, *Methodism on the Headwaters of the Ohio* . . . (Nashville, 1951), pp. 234-35; McClintock's sermon is quoted earlier, p. 137. Cf. an identical sentiment in Henry B. Ridgaway, *The Life of Rev. Alfred Cookman* . . . (New York, 1874), pp. 354-59.

[32] See James Morrison, "The Coming of Christ," *The Christian*, I (1863), pp. 164-65; Cf. "H.P.B.," Brooklyn, N. Y., Sept. 16, 1863, to John Q. Adams, the same, pp. 171-72; "Shall Christians Fight," the same, II (1864), pp. 61-64.

[33] William Edwin Boardman, *He That Overcometh* . . . (Boston, 1869), p. 232.

that, like the other holiness preachers, Boardman refused to consign secular relations to Satan. Though for him the kingdom of Christ was spiritual, he believed that it must rule the temporal world, not shun it. Happily, its embattled hosts seemed in his eyes destined to enjoy the worldly spoils of their heavenly conquest.[84]

In the postwar period the evangelical ideology of the millennium merged without a break into what came to be called the social gospel. The triumph of Yankee arms restored the faith of even Princeton conservatives that Christianity and civilization were marching forward toward perfection.[85] Gilbert Haven, who had been Methodism's most notable abolitionist, predicted that the grace of Christ would "renew the land in holiness and love," halt the sale of alcoholic beverages, end the "luxurious absorption by a few families of the people's wealth," spread universal education, and establish economic security for all. Later, in a Thanksgiving sermon celebrating, ironically enough, the election of Ulysses S. Grant to the presidency, Haven urged Methodists to make their lives an offering by which to speed the achievement of social equality, racial intermarriage, woman's suffrage, temperance reform, and other beauties of the millennium.

Let Christ abolish sin from your souls, of whatever sort, by His indwelling grace. Let your heart become His peaceful realm, with its every passion, thought, and purpose subject to His sway. Labor by every word and deed to make all other hearts equally perfect. Strive to bring the laws of society into subjection to His control. Root up the gnarled tusks of prejudice. Toil cheerfully, hopefully, faithfully, to bring in the Grand Sabbatic Year, the Jubilee of Heaven.[86]

Six years later an article in Yale's *New Englander* restated the case for postmillennialism in evolutionary terms, referring not to Darwin, however, but to Christ's parable of the mustard seed. The Rev. George T. Ladd argued that premillennialism contradicts the facts of human progress and "degrades the Gospel as a present and prospective power." He believed that it tends to let down the tone of the Christian life and to discourage ministers from feeling that they are working "for the Ages" and "for the race."

[84] *Ibid.*, pp. 208-9, 233; the "gospel of success" is underlined on pp. 231-32, 234.
[85] L. P. Hickok, "Humanity Progressing to Perfection," *The American Presbyterian and Theological Review*, n s., VI (1868), pp. 532, 550. Cf. the first article on the subject for many years in *The Congregational Quarterly*: J. Torrey Smith, "The Second Advent of Our Lord," VII (1867), pp. 195-214, reviewing favorably Brown, *Christ's Second Coming*, which had just been reissued in a Glasgow edition.
[86] Gilbert Haven, *National Sermons* . . . (Boston, 1869), pp. 387, 601-2, 629-30.

Christ's teaching, Ladd said, is far grander. It promises the evolution of the Kingdom, not through "a godless and aimless development," but by means of an "expanding of forces and powers already planted by God within the world as seeds." Under the "constant rule and presence of Christ" and the "constant working of the Holy Spirit," these were ultimately to accomplish "the conversion and sanctifying of the world." [37]

A public meeting of the Christian Labor Union, held in Boston in May, 1875, put the matter more bluntly. The "God of the Bible," its resolution ran, had set forth in that book a twofold plan of redemption—one part "to cure men in their innate tendency to evil" and the other "to establish in the earth that divine order and conduct of human society which Jesus Christ called the Kingdom of God." [38]

The most significant millenarian doctrines of the mid-nineteenth century were not those of William Miller, but those which grew out of evangelical Protestantism's crusade to Christianize the land. Revivalistic Calvinists like Edward and Henry Ward Beecher and Albert Barnes, Oberlin perfectionists, and Methodists great and small were ardent postmillennialists, bent like John the Baptist on preparing a kingdom for the King. Social reforms of all sorts fit into their scheme. The chief result of the Millerite excitement seems to have been to hasten the acceptance of this doctrine among Baptists and Presbyterians previously attached to the premillennial view. That clergymen identified the popular belief in America's mission with the Christian hope and drifted steadily toward Arminianism, with its emphasis upon free will and human ability, strengthened the trend.

True, Old School Calvinists who feared antislavery agitation spawned on the eve of the sectional conflict an antimillennial variant of the beliefs which Miller's demise had discredited. The carnage of war shrouded certain Baptist and Lutheran groups in such pessimism as to encourage its growth. By and large, however, the peace of 1865 found leaders of the revivalistic sects consecrated to the task of building a Christian commonwealth in America. The trial by arms had served only to imbue them with a new sense of the reality of divine judgment and the stubbornness of the evils which they faced.

[37] George T. Ladd, "What Is the True Doctrine of Christ's Second Coming," *The New Englander*, XXXIII (1874), pp. 369, 377-79, 381-83.
[38] Quoted from *Equity*, June, 1875, pp. 17-18, in Aaron I. Abell, *The Urban Impact on American Protestantism, 1865-1900*, (Harvard Historical Studies, LIV, Cambridge, 1943) p. 24, Cf. Charles H. Hopkins, *The Rise of the Social Gospel in American Protestantism, 1865-1913* (New Haven, 1940), pp. 42-49, and Edward H. Rogers, *National Life in the Spirit World* (Chelsea, Mass., 1891), pp. 2, 9-11, 64.

Not Darwinian philosophy or the new sociology but the nearness men felt to God in the mid-century awakenings catalyzed the Kingdom ideology whose elements Edward Beecher had weighed out in 1835. In these "last days" God had poured out his Spirit on all flesh. Sons and daughters prophesied. Old men dreamed dreams and young men saw visions. And they all worked in a fury of passion lest the "great and terrible day. of His wrath" should overtake them unprepared.

CRITICAL ESSAY
ON THE SOURCES OF INFORMATION

❧

Modern Scholarly Works

Two volumes have recently appeared which converge on the subject of this research from different angles. Charles C. Cole, Jr., *The Social Ideas of the Northern Evangelists, 1826-1860* (New York, 1954) covers adequately the opinions of a rather diverse group of individual leaders, but not their relations to the movements in church life which they represent. John R. Bodo, *The Protestant Clergy and Public Issues, 1812-1848* (Princeton, N. J., 1954) is misnamed, since it considers only those educated ministers of New England and the Middle Atlantic states who supported the idea of an American theocracy. Both volumes shed light on the interrelation of church and society during the period.

Other studies of established reputation are Aaron Ignatius Abell, *The Urban Impact on American Protestantism, 1865-1900* (*Harvard Historical Studies*, LIV, Cambridge, 1943), which attributes the socialization of religious institutions to the new urban environment; and Alice Felt Tyler, *Freedom's Ferment; Phases of American Social History to 1860* (Minneapolis, 1944), which explains spiritual and social factors in the movements for humanitarian reform. Whitney Rogers Cross, *The Burned-over District; the Social and Intellectual History of Enthusiastic Religion in Western New York, 1800-1850* (Ithaca, N. Y., 1950) is an admirable regional study, marred only by unawareness of the extent of "enthusiasm" in seaboard cities. Charles Howard Hopkins, *History of the Y.M.C.A. in North America* (New York, 1951) meticulously commemorates an institution in which interdenominational revivalism was dominant.

The quest for holiness is illumined in Robert S. Fletcher, *A History of Oberlin College; from Its Foundation Through the Civil War* (Oberlin, Ohio, 1943), originally a Harvard dissertation, and John Leland Peters, *Christian Perfection and American Methodism* (New York and Nashville, 1956), begun at Yale. Neither these two works, however, nor the much older collection of essays by the dour Princetonian, Benjamin B. Warfield, *Perfectionism* (New York, 1931), uncover the social dynamics of the movement. For background the beginner cannot do better than to consult Harold Lindstrom, *Wesley and Sanctification, a Study in the Doctrine of Salvation* (Stockholm, 1946) and, on social issues, Wellman Joel Warner,

CRITICAL ESSAY ON THE SOURCES OF INFORMATION

The Wesleyan Movement in the Industrial Revolution (London, 1930), the latter by a student of R. H. Tawney.

Gilbert H. Barnes, *The Antislavery Impulse, 1830-1844* (N. Y., 1933), and Dwight L. Dumond, *Antislavery Origins of the Civil War in the United States* (Ann Arbor, Mich., 1939), explore in great detail earlier phases of the evangelical attack on slavery. Benjamin Platt Thomas, *Theodore Weld, Crusader for Freedom* (New Brunswick, N. J., 1950), and the volumes of the James G. Birney and Weld-Grimké correspondence which Dumond and Barnes edited, fill out the story. Cole's chapter in *The Northern Evangelists* and George I. Rockwood, *Cheever, Lincoln and the Causes of the Civil War* (Worcester, Mass., 1936), provide stimulating insights into the later agitation. The proslavery argument is analyzed, though without much reference to the inner life of the churches, in William Sumner Jenkins, *Pro-Slavery Thought in the Old South* (Chapel Hill, N. C., 1935), and, more sketchily, in Adelaide Avery Lyons, "Religious Defense of Slavery in the North" (Trinity College Historical Society, *Historical Papers*, ser. 13, Durham, N. C., 1919).

The best treatment of a particular denomination is Thomas E. Drake, *Quakers and Slavery in America* (New Haven, Conn., 1950). Lewis G. Vander Velde, *The Presbyterian Churches and the Federal Union, 1861-1869* (*Harvard Historical Studies*, XXXIII, Cambridge, 1932), is superficial on doctrine, while Charles W. Heathcote, *The Lutheran Church and the Civil War* (New York, 1919), is based on incomplete research. Neither William Warren Sweet's filial *The Methodist Episcopal Church and the Civil War* (Cincinnati, 1912) nor Charles Baumer Swaney's rather cynical *Episcopal Methodism and Slavery; with Sidelights on Ecclesiastical Politics* (Boston, 1926) display much understanding of the relation of Wesleyan religion to reform. Outstanding articles are C. Bruce Staiger, "Abolitionism and the Presbyterian Schism of 1837-1838," *The Mississippi Valley Historical Review*, XXVI (1949-50), 391-414; Robert Fortenbaugh, "American Lutheran Synods and Slavery, 1830-1860," *The Journal of Religion*, XIII (1933), 72-92.

Most denominational histories written during the past fifty years underplay or omit altogether the story of revivalist and perfectionist strivings. Exceptions are those treating smaller sects, such as Wilson T. Hogue's rather unscholarly *History of the Free Methodist Church of North America* (Chicago, 1915) and Raymond W. Albright's fine *History of the Evangelical Church* (Harrisburg, Pa., 1942). Wade Crawford Barclay, *To Reform the Nation* (vol. II of *Early American Methodism, 1769-1844*, New York, 1949), part of a projected multi-volume work on our chief Protestant denomination, bids fair to reverse the trend for the larger groups. Barclay pays due attention to holiness piety and relates it to the social scene. William Wilson Manross, *A History of the American Episcopal Church* (2nd. ed., rev., New York, 1950), slights the Low Church evangelicals. Oscar N. Olson, *The Augustana Lutheran Church in America: Pioneer Period, 1846-1860* (Rock Island, Ill., 1950), disowns revivalism.

General Contemporary Materials

European travelers made stimulating observations about every facet of American church life, following the lead of Alexis de Tocqueville, *Democracy in America* (tr. Henry Reeve; rev. ed. New York, 1900). Most useful for the later period are two volumes by Isabella (Bird) Bishop, *The Aspects of Religion in the United States of America* (London, 1859), covering especially the revival of 1858 and the sectional crisis, and *The Englishwoman in America* (London, 1856). Three French evangelical pastors recorded impressions particularly valuable for denominations in the Calvinist tradition: J. H. Grand Pièrre, *A Parisian Pastor's Glance at America* (Boston, 1854), Agénor Étienne de Gasparin, *The Uprising of a Great People. The United States in 1861* (tr. Mary L. Booth; New York, 1861), and Georges Fisch, *Nine Months in the United States During the Crisis* (London, 1863). James Dixon, *Personal Narrative of a Tour Through a Part of the United States and Canada, with Notices of Methodism in America* (New York, 1849), is a panorama of Methodism.

Even more enlightening are the efforts Americans made to explain our religious institutions to churchmen in the Old World. Robert Baird's three volumes, *View of Religion in America* (New York, 1844), *The Progress and Prospects of Christianity in the United States* . . . (London, 1851), and *State and Prospects of Religion in America* (London, 1855), reflect the efforts of a New School preacher to allay European prejudices against revivals and the voluntary system of church membership and support. Baird was one of the chief architects of the Evangelical Alliance. Alexander Blaikie, *The Philosophy of Sectarianism; or, a Classified View of the Christian Sects in the United States* . . . (Boston, 1854), takes the opposite view, as does Philip Schaff, *America. A Sketch of the Political, Social, and Religious Character of the United States of North America* (New York, 1855). Schaff's work is a partisan deprecation of the pietist and revivalist practices which had invaded Lutheran and German Reformed churches.

Handbooks explaining the nature and work of all the different denominations were popular then, as now. They yield valuable statistics and lists of publications and educational institutions. Most useful are *The American Christian Record* . . . (New York, 1860), and two reflecting a Methodist point of view—Charles Adams, *Evangelism in the Middle of the Nineteenth Century* . . . (Boston, 1851), and Charles C. Goss, *Statistical History of the First Century of American Methodism* . . . (New York, 1866). Joseph Belcher, *The Religious Denominations in the United States, their History, Doctrine, Government, and Statistics* (Philadelphia, 1856), is a Baptist pastor's careful summary which usually gives the sources of its statistics.

All of the foregoing contain information on revivals of religion and the relation of the sects to state and society. On the latter point, however, Stephen Colwell, *The Position of Christianity in the United States* (Philadelphia, 1854), is uniquely important. Albert Barnes, *The Gospel Necessary to Our Country* (Washington, 1852), and works by two Methodists, William Henry Milburn, *The Rifle, Axe, and Saddle-Bags* . . . (New York, 1856), and Jesse T. Peck, *The History of the Great Republic, Considered from the Christian Stand-Point* (New York, 1868), contain more propaganda than analysis.

General accounts of religious awakenings in the period appear in P. C. Headley, *Evangelists in the Church. Philip, A. D., 35, to Moody and Sankey, A. D., 1875*

(Boston, 1875), biographical essays based on contemporary sources now rarely available; and Heman Humphrey, *Revival Sketches and Manual* (New York, 1859). A. P. Marvin, "Three Eras of Revivals in the United States," *Bibliotheca Sacra*, XVI (1859), 279-301, covers mostly earlier periods. Martin Moore, *Boston Revival, 1842 . . .* (Boston, 1842) is superficial. For the awakening of 1858, however, abundant materials may be found in William C. Conant, *Narratives of Remarkable Conversions and Revival Incidents . . .* (New York, 1858), an uncritical summary of newspaper reports printed at the height of the excitement; Talbot W. Chambers, *The Noon Prayer Meeting of the North Dutch Church, Fulton Street, New York . . .* (New York, 1858), an indispensable inside account of the awakening's origin; and Samuel I. Prime, *The Power of Prayer, as Illustrated in the Wonderful Displays of Divine Grace in the Fulton Street and Other Meetings . . .* (New York, 1859), which charts its course both in and outside New York City.

Religious enthusiasm in wartime found many chroniclers. Samuel I. Prime, *Five Years of Prayer, With the Answers* (New York, 1864), covers the home front, while *Christ in the Army: a Selection of Sketches of the Work of the U. S. Christian Commission* (Philadelphia, 1865), and J. William Jones, *Christ in the Camp; or, Religion in Lee's Army* (Richmond, 1887), recount the events in the armed forces.

Contemporary Descriptions of Particular Denominations

Abel Stevens, *History of the Methodist Episcopal Church in the United States* (New York, 1864-1867) and E. H. Gillett, *History of the Presbyterian Church in the United States of America* (Philadelphia, 1864) are in many ways still the best accounts of those two denominations, though Stevens is skimpy on the years covered by this study while Gillett is complete. Two of the volumes in *The American Church History Series*, edited by Philip Schaff and others toward the end of the century, deserve special mention both for their scholarly merit and for the fact that they were written from distant memory of the events of the prewar period. These are Henry Eyster Jacobs, *A History of the Evangelical Lutheran Church in the United States* (New York, 1893) and Albert Henry Newman, *A History of the Baptist Churches in the United States* (New York, 1894). Charles C. Tiffany, *A History of the Protestant Episcopal Church in the United States of America* (New York, 1895), in the same series, is more generous toward the Low Church party than the volume by W. W. Manross mentioned above.

Invaluable mines of information also are Samuel S. Schmucker, *The American Lutheran Church . . .* (5th ed., Philadelphia, 1852), which defends the revivalist position dominant in the General Synod; Elisha Bates, *The Doctrines of Friends . . .* (Philadelphia, 1868), the platform of the evangelical party; George Ellis, *Half-Century of the Unitarian Controversy* (Boston, 1857), explaining the beliefs of the moderate majority which opposed Theodore Parker; Lewis Cheeseman, *Differences Between Old and New School Presbyterians* (Rochester, N. Y., 1848), which reflects the accommodation of the Old School to revival measures in the "burned-over" district; and Matthew Simpson, ed., *Cyclopedia of Methodism . . .* (Philadelphia, 1878). Of the dozens of Methodist conference histories, F. W. Conable, *History of* the *Genesee Annual Conference* . . . (New York, 1876), is important for its bitterly prejudiced account of Free Methodist origins.

Among the useful periodical articles are Francis Springer, "Lutheranism in the United States," *The Evangelical Quarterly Review*, XI (1859-60), 96-110, and anon., "The Present Position of the Lutheran Church," on pp. 12-43 of the same volume. The former supported the "New Lutheran," the latter, the confessional position. Henry Cowles, "Ohio Congregationalism," *The Congregational Quarterly*, V (1863-64), 136-43, portrays Oberlin's early withdrawal from the Plan of Union. William Hurlin, "The Freewill Baptists; Their History and Doctrines," *The Christian Review*, XXVII (1862), 556-84, is an excellent short summary. Andover's quarterly journal, *Bibliotheca Sacra*, printed during the war a series of articles on theology. George Duffield, "Doctrines of the New School Presbyterian Church," XX (1863), 606-15, is more conservative than the pattern prevailing in his denomination; while Daniel D. Whedon, "The Doctrines of Methodism," XIX (1862), 241-73, is more liberal.

Church Periodicals

The learned theological reviews, usually published quarterly, are the most accessible but the least useful of the religious serials. However, when studied with due reference to the biographical and historical material available elsewhere, they reveal the adjustment of the most conservative thought of the churches to changing times. The chief limitation is that most of their contents were long book reviews. *The Methodist Quarterly Review* (XXIII-XLVIII, New York, 1841-66) was surprisingly friendly to the holiness advocates. The *Lutheran Evangelical Quarterly Review* (VII-XVI, Gettysburg, Penn., 1856-65) refereed the truce between the revivalist and confessional parties. *The Christian Review* (XX-XXVII, Boston, 1855-56, New York, 1857-62), the Baptist organ, maintained the antirevival, Calvinist tradition.

Congregationalist and Presbyterian journals must be classified along doctrinal lines. Liberal and friendly to humanitarian endeavors, if not always to revivalism, were Andover's *Bibliotheca Sacra* (I-XXII, Andover, Mass. 1844-64) and Yale's *The New Englander* (I-XXI, New Haven, Conn., 1843-63). *The Congregational Quarterly* (I-VII, Boston, 1859-65) and *The Oberlin Quarterly Review* (I-IV, Oberlin, Ohio, 1845-49) defended both evangelism and reform. The latter championed perfectionism and the former encouraged the growth of sectarian sentiment in the denomination. On the other hand, *The Boston Review: Devoted to Theology and Literature* (I-VI, Boston, 1861-66) and *The American Theological Review* (I-VI, New York, 1859-64) depicted the conservative reaction against "new measures" and social reconstruction, a position which *The Princeton Review* (XIII-XXIV, Princeton, N. J., 1841-62) had maintained for two decades.

Monthly magazines came one step nearer the march of events. Though useful for their book reviews, they mainly contained signed articles on religious and social questions. *The American National Preacher* (X-XV, Philadelphia, 1836-41) was a highly significant outlet for New School opinion during the years of controversy. *The Christian Union and Religious Memorial* . . . (I-III, New York, 1848-50),

CRITICAL ESSAY ON THE SOURCES OF INFORMATION

edited by Robert Baird, worked for interdenominational alliance; and *The American Missionary (Magazine)* (IV-IX, New York, 1858-63) promoted the work of the antislavery American Missionary Association. All of these were ostensibly interdenominational and promoted revivals and humanitarian reform. *Harper's New Monthly Magazine* (VII-XX, New York, 1853-60), though not ecclesiastically sponsored, reflected a conservative Methodist viewpoint on social issues.

More limited in appeal were those monthlies representing one movement. Frederic Dan Huntington's *The Monthly Religious Magazine* (IX-XXVI, Boston, 1853-61) is a neglected source of information about moderate Unitarianism. After Huntington entered the Low Church Episcopal ministry, he edited *The Church Monthly* (I-III, Boston, 1861-63). *The Guide to Holiness* (I-L, Boston, 1839-63) was the voice of the Methodist "second blessing" advocates; *The Christian; Devoted to the Advancement of Gospel Holiness* (I-VI, New York, 1863-68) furthered the higher-life doctrine among Baptists. *The Advent Shield and Review* (I, Boston, 1844-45), an ephemeral Millerite publication, contains invaluable first-hand accounts of Adventist origins.

The denominational weekly newspapers are, however, the best source for religious opinion on social and political matters and accounts of revivals and humanitarian projects. Among the more than one hundred such publications, I have chosen to work through the following representative ones. *The Christian Advocate and Journal* (New York, 1850-60), the principal Methodist weekly, was often silent on social issues, as contrasted with most others of the denomination, especially *Zion's Herald* (Boston, 1850-61). *The New York Evangelist* (New York, 1848-54), organ of New School Presbyterians, was likewise more conservative than the Congregationalist *Independent* (New York, 1848-59), edited by Henry Ward Beecher, Joseph P. Thompson, and George B. Cheever. The Old School *New York Observer* supported Princeton and proslavery compromise. In Boston *The Watchman and Reflector* (1853-63) reflected Baptist revivalism and social concern, as *The Congregationalist* (Boston, 1851-61) did for a sister denomination. *The Puritan Recorder* (Boston, 1851-61), welcomed revivals but not reform and endeavored to keep alive among Congregationalists the older Calvinism.

Biographical and Devotional Literature

Most nineteenth-century volumes of "lives and letters" carried lengthy quotations from diaries and correspondence. The shorter and more literary biographies which came into vogue after the Civil War were rarely annotated and are consequently of less value to the historian. Those of most general usefulness are Charles G. Finney, *Memoirs* (New York, 1876), a remarkably objective chronicle based upon his journals and other writings; Henry Martyn Baird, *Life of the Rev. Robert Baird, D.D.* (New York, 1866), a scholarly tribute to the causes of temperance reform and ecumenicity; David O. Mears, *Life of Edward Norris Kirk* (Boston, 1877), which quotes inaccessible documents at length; Arria S. Huntington, *Memoir and Letters of Frederic Dan Huntington . . .* (Boston, 1906), an accurate introduction to evangelical Unitarianism; and Richard Wheatley, *The Life and Letters of Mrs.*

243

Phoebe Palmer (New York, 1876), a lengthy index to the wide impact of perfectionism.

Among indispensable biographies of holiness leaders are five written about Methodists: Abel Stevens, *Life and Times of Nathan Bangs, D.D.* (New York, 1863), both comprehensive and partial; F. G. Hibbard, *Biography of Rev. Leonidas L. Hamline* . . . (Cincinnati, 1880), to be compared with Dr. Walter C. Palmer's life of the same man, published in New York in 1880; Henry B. Ridgaway, *Life of Alfred Cookman* . . . (New York, 1874), the most thorough and objective of the group; George Hughes, *The Beloved Physician, Walter C. Palmer* . . . (New York, 1884), which is studded with material from the manuscripts of the illustrious Phoebe's husband; and Lucius C. Matlack, *The Life of Rev. Orange Scott* . . . (New York, 1847), important for its record of Wesleyan Methodist abolitionism. Mary M. Boardman (Mrs. William E.), *Life and Labours of Rev. W. E. Boardman* (New York, 1887) traces the "higher-life" movement outside the Methodist fold in England and America, while Absalom B. Earle's autobiography, *Bringing in Sheaves* (Boston, 1868) discloses the perfectionism of the Baptist movement's most famous wartime soul winner.

Samples of other evangelists' stories are Emerson Andrews, *Living Life* . . . (Boston, 1872), and Jacob Knapp, *Autobiography* . . . (New York, 1868), which depict the triumph of revivalism in the Baptist denomination; Helen Dunn Gates, *Life and Labors of Rev. Ransom Dunn* . . . (Boston, 1901), about an urban Freewill Baptist pastor; Samuel B. Halliday, *Winning Souls* . . . (New York, 1873), the reminiscences of a Congregationalist evangelist and city missionary; William Taylor's ponderous *Story of My Life* . . . (New York, 1896), no less partisan from the fact that it is based on manuscripts written at the time of the events it describes; and P. C. Headley, ed., *The Harvest Work of the Holy Spirit* . . . (6th ed., Boston, 1862), containing newspaper accounts of the beginning of Congregationalist E. P. Hammond's career.

The mountain of sermonic material defies description but demands selective study. The chief pitfall is that although title pages often carry no reference to the author's denominational allegiance, the great university libraries contain more sermons by Unitarians than by those who preached to the masses. Useful collections for the student of popular religion are Boston Congregational Council, *Addresses to Church Members by the Congregational Pastors of Boston* . . . (Boston, 1866), trumpeting for "new measures"; James Waddell Alexander, *The Revival and Its Lessons* . . . (N. Y., 1858), containing seventeen "sermons for the people," by a reluctant revivalist from the Old School; anon., *The New York Pulpit in the Revival of 1858—A Memorial Volume of Sermons* (N. Y., 1858); Davis W. Clark, comp., *Methodist Episcopal Pulpit: a Collection of Original Sermons* (George Peck, ed., New York, 1850); Stephen H. Tyng, *Lectures on The Law and The Gospel* (New York, 1848), illustrating Low Church Episcopal evangelism; and Frederic Dan Huntington, *Christian Believing and Living* (Boston, 1859), proclaiming the famous Harvard preacher's conversion to Trinitarianism. Charles G. Finney's volumes, *Lectures on Revivals* . . . (New York, 1835), *Sermons on Important Subjects* (3rd ed., New York, 1836), and *Lectures to Professing Christians*

(New York, 1837), display the aspirations out of which the perfectionist revival was born. Collected writings of nearly every prominent clergyman, including the Methodists, eventually appeared in print. Bishop Leonidas L. Hamline's *Works* (F. G. Hibbard, ed., New York, 1871) are important to us because of their expression of Methodist perfectionism.

Revivalist and Perfectionist Propaganda

Scattered through the foregoing parts of this essay are references to many volumes which furthered the spread of revival measures in churches hitherto reluctant to receive them. Others devoted particularly to this end were Henry Clay Fish, *Primitive Piety Revived . . .* (Boston, 1855), which heralded the awakening of 1858 among Baptists and Congregationalists; Robert Aikman, *The Relations of the Ministry to Revivals of Religion . . .* (New York, 1863), an Old School declaration; Frederic Dan Huntington, *Permanent Realities of Religion and the Present Religious Interest* (Boston, 1858), which summoned Harvard to penitence; and Charles P. McIlvaine, *Bishop McIlvaine on the Revival of Religion . . .* (Philadelphia, 1858), a Low Church bishop's tract.

In the theological journals, too, men of conservative backgrounds chorused the message which, in Finney's lectures and Albert Barnes's essay, "Revivals of Religion in Cities and Large Towns," *The American National Preacher*, XV (1841), 1-24, had once come from voices crying in the wilderness. Henry M. Dexter, "Congregationalism Specially Adapted to Promote Revivals of Religion," *The Congregational Quarterly*, III (1861), 52-58, Levi Sternberg, "Revivals," *The Evangelical Quarterly Review*, XV (1864), 273-92, and Henry Clay Fish, "Power in the Pulpit," *The Christian Review*, XXVII (1862), 118-42, spoke for three powerful denominations. Typical of the arch-Calvinist, the liturgical, and the humanist opposition were, anon., "Spurious Revivals," *The American Theological Review*, I (1859), 82-87; A. M. Ziegler, "Treatment of the Awakened," *The Evangelical Quarterly Review*, IX (1857-58), 237-56; and Charles K. Whipple, "The Boston Revival, and Its Leader," *The Radical*, I (1866), 429-38, an attack on A. B. Earle.

Perfectionism, likewise, won its way slowly into the columns of the learned quarterlies. The Oberlin view was expounded in John Morgan, "The Gift of the Holy Ghost," *The Oberlin Quarterly Review*, I (1845), 90-116; disowned in James H. Fairchild, "The Doctrine of Sanctification at Oberlin," *The Congregational Quarterly*, XVIII (1876); and scorned in J. C. Lord, "Finney's Sermons on Sanctification and Mahan on Christian Perfection," *The Princeton Review*, XIII (1841), 231-49. *The Methodist Quarterly Review* was the exception. George Peck, "Dr. Upham's Works," XXVIII (1846), 248-65, extended a Wesleyan welcome to the mystic philosopher of holiness. Jesse T. Peck, "Philosophy of Christian Perfection," XXX (1848), 293-323, and Wesley Kenney, "The Central Idea of Christianity," XXXIX (1857), 84-104, describing Peck's volume, illustrate that journal's friendliness. *The Guide to Holiness* became the vehicle for most such writing in the denomination, however, as best indicated in Nathan Bangs's series, "Christian Perfection," XIX (January-June, 1851), 37-41, 49-55, 74-79, 121-129; and XX (July-December, 1851), 29-31, 49-55, 73-75, 86-90, 109-12, 121-23. A. L.

Bridgman, "A High Standard of Piety Demanded by the Times," *The Evangelical Quarterly Review*, VII (1855), 364-76, expresses interest but not approval; Jacob J. Abbott, "Boardman's Higher Christian Life," *Bibliotheca Sacra*, XVII (1860), 508-34, is antagonistic.

Scores of books and pamphlets swelled the stream of popular perfectionist propaganda. James Caughey, Phoebe Palmer, and Thomas C. Upham must have together published at least forty of them, as the footnotes on pp. 105-6 and 117-19 suggest. I will list here only twenty-two titles which seem essential to an understanding of the movement. Most of these appeared in numerous editions.

Charles G. Finney, *Views of Sanctification* (Oberlin, Ohio, 1840), containing essays which appeared earlier in *The Oberlin Evangelist*, and Asa Mahan, *Scripture Doctrine of Christian Perfection* . . . (Boston, 1840), expound the earlier Oberlin doctrine. George O. Peck, *The Scripture Doctrine of Christian Perfection Stated and Defended* (New York, 1842), is a kindly and semi-official Methodist rejoinder, consisting of lectures delivered in several New York City churches. George Hughes, *Fragrant Memories of the Tuesday Meeting and Guide to Holiness* . . . (New York, 1886), is a sentimental but detailed account of the course of Mrs. Palmer's group. Phoebe Palmer, *The Way of Holiness* . . . (New York, 1851), is her most influential tract. D. S. King, ed., *The Riches of Grace* . . . (Boston, 1847) is a collection of unsigned testimonies given at the Tuesday Meeting, the first of a long cycle of such books.

Important among later Methodist contributions to holiness literature are Nathan Bangs, *Letters on the Necessity, Nature, and Fruits of Sanctification* (New York, 1851); Randolph S. Foster, *Nature and Blessedness of Christian Purity* (New York, 1851; rev. ed., entitled *Christian Purity; or, the Heritage of Faith*, New York, 1869); and Jesse T. Peck, *The Central Idea of Christianity* (Boston, 1856), all clearly "second blessing." William Arthur, *The Tongue of Fire; or, the True Power of Christianity* (New York, 1856, and many other editions, the first printed in London) applied the doctrine to social problems. Phoebe Palmer, *Pioneer Experiences: or The Gift of Power Received by Faith* . . . (New York, 1867), contained eighty signed testimonies. James Caughey, *Helps to a Life of Holiness* . . . (5th ed., Boston, 1852) illustrated the popular evangelism. Merritt Caldwell, *The Philosophy of Christian Perfection* . . . (Philadelphia, 1849), the first "psychological" study, provoked a minor controversy, while Tobias Spicer, *The Way from Sin to Sanctification, Holiness and Heaven* (4th ed., New York, 1857) criticized Mrs. Palmer's terminology.

Meanwhile, Thomas C. Upham cultivated interest among the mystic-minded outside the Methodist fold with volumes such as *Principles of the Interior, or Hidden Life* . . . (2nd, ed., New York, 1845) and *A Treatise on Divine Union* . . . (Boston, 1851). Even more important was William E. Boardman's *The Higher Christian Life* (Boston, 1858), which related the doctrine to the practical quests of Revivalistic Calvinism and became one of the half dozen most influential religious books of the era. Boradman's *He That Overcometh: or, a Conquering Gospel* (Boston, 1869) was a more starry-eyed "application." John Quincy Adams, ed., *Experiences of the Higher Christian Life in the Baptist Denomination* . . . (New

York, 1870), illustrates another phase. John H. Wallace, *Entire Holiness* . . . (Auburn, N. Y., 1853), demonstrates the solid Wesleyan orthodoxy of the Genesee Conference agitators, while Benjamin T. Roberts, *Holiness Teachings* . . . (North Chili, N. Y., 1893), shows the effects of sectarianization of the doctrine among the Free Methodists.

The Record of Evangelical Reform

Edward Beecher, "The Nature, Importance, and Means of Eminent Holiness Throughout the Church," *The American National Preacher*, X (1835), 193-224, best distills the ideas which, scattered through Finney's lectures and the literature of temperance and abolition, were responsible for the birth of social Christianity. The same author summarized his doctrine of the kingdom, foreshadowing George D. Herron and Walter Rauschenbusch, in "The Scriptural Philosophy of Congregationalism and of Councils," *Bibliotheca Sacra*, XXII (1865), 356-83. Edward N. Kirk, *A Plea for the Poor* . . . (Boston, 1843), is a more prosaic illustration of the impulse revivals gave to social service. Stephen Colwell, *New Themes for the Protestant Clergy* . . . (Philadelphia, 1851), is a much over-rated attack on the churches, prejudiced by the author's strange program of reform. It must be compared with Samuel A. Allibone, *A Review, by a Layman, of a Work Entitled, "New Themes for the Protestant Clergy* . . ." (Philadelphia, 1852), an occasionally naïve but factually rich rejoinder. Thomas Guthrie, *The City, Its Sins and Its Sorrows* . . . (New York, 1873, and many earlier editions) awakened compassion for the poor in both England and America. L. P. Brockett, "The Relation of Christianity to Humanitarian Effort," *The Methodist Quarterly Review*, XL (1858), 452-70, and, anon., "The Relation of the Church to the Poor," *The Princeton Review* XXXIX (1862), 601-35, illustrate the growth of the new sense of responsibility in other quarters.

Records of early efforts at social service may be found in anon., "The Five Points House of Industry," *The American Church Monthly*, III (1858), 209-22, 289-97, 350-60, and New York City Tract Society, *Annual Report[s]* . . . *with the . . . Annual Report[s] of the Female Branch* (New York, 1838-63), as well as in the biographies and interdenominational handbooks described above. The religious weeklies printed frequent summaries and reports of such work. Henry Cammann and H. N. Camp, *The Charities of New York, Brooklyn and Staten Island* (New York, 1868), is an invaluable catalogue, which includes historical statements, statistics, and lists of officers. The New York City Mission and Tract Society, *Walks About New York. Facts and Figures Gathered from Various Sources* (New York, 1865), is best on city missions. Lemuel Moss, *Annals of the United States Christian Commission* (Philadelphia, 1868), and L. P. Brockett, *Woman's Work in the Civil War* . . . (New York, 1867) stress the social aspects of wartime evangelism.

Matlack's *Orange Scott* and the Massachusetts Abolition Society, *Second Annual Report* . . . (Boston, 1841), shed light on the earlier phases of evangelical antislavery in New England and western New York. Albert Barnes, *The Church and Slavery* (2nd ed., Philadelphia, 1857), defends the New School Presbyterian Church's course, while Abel Stevens, "Slavery—The Times," *The Methodist Quarterly Review*, XXXIX (1857), 260-80, and "American Slavery—Its Progress and Prospects," the same, 437-63, seek to exonerate Methodism. Significant volumes by the three most influential abolitionists from the revivalist camp are George Barrell Cheever, *God Against Slavery; and the Freedom and Duty of the Pulpit to Rebuke It* . . . (New York, 1857), platform of New York City Congregationalists; William Hosmer, *The Higher Law* . . . (Auburn, N. Y., 1852), by a Methodist editor from the Genesee country; and Gilbert Haven, *National Sermons: Speeches and Letters on Slavery and Its War* (Boston, 1869), important for its millennial and racial views.

The attack on the scriptural defense of the institution began with Albert Barnes, *An Inquiry into the Scriptural Views of Slavery* (Philadelphia, 1846), which set the trend toward rational interpretation of the Bible. George B. Cheever, *The Guilt of Slavery and the Crime of Slaveholding, Demonstrated from the Hebrew and Greek Scriptures* (Boston, 1860), was as impetuous as Methodist Charles Elliott's volume, *The Bible and Slavery* . . . (Cincinnati, 1857), was restrained. The article, "Slavery and the Bible," *The New Englander*, XV (1857), 102-34, reviews several such works.

The literature of millennialism is immense, but almost unfailingly rich in social ideas. On the eve of the Civil War numerous works signaled the conversion of hitherto conservative groups to optimistic postmillennialism. Joseph F. Berg, *The Second Advent of Jesus Christ, Not Premillennial* (Philadelphia, 1859), is a Dutch Reformed view. David Brown, *On the Second Advent. Will It Be Pre-Millennial?* (New York, 1851), and George B. Taylor, "Society's Future," *The Christian Review*, XXII (1857), 356-79, are Baptist contributions. L. P. Hickok, "Humanity Progressing to Perfection," *The American Presbyterian and Theological Review*, n. s. VI (1868), 532-50; and George T. Ladd, "What is the True Doctrine of Christ's Second Coming?" *The New Englander*, XXIII (1874), 356-83, indicate the postwar thrust of Christian hope. Phoebe Palmer, *Promise of the Father; or a Neglected Specialty of the Last Days* . . . (Boston, 1859), announced a sort of Pentecostal feminist crusade.

INDEX

Church membership: requirements for,
18; statistics of, 17, 20-21
Civil War: causes of, 178-80, 189-90, 199-
203, 204, 215-16; religious results of,
231-34, 236; revivals in the, 76-78
Clark, Davis W., 128-29, 133
Clarke, James Freeman, 46
Class structure and religion, 24, 80, 164,
231-32
Colwell, Stephen, 34, 40-41, 165-66
Congregational Church, 17, 21, 28, 43,
53, 96; revivalism in the, 50-53, 73, 75-
76; and slavery, 190, 208-10, 216-17
Congregationalist, The, 51, 89, 205
Connecticut Wesleyan University, 60
Cookman, Alfred, 74, 136-37, 175-76, 211
Coolidge, James I. T., 99-100, 231
Cowles, Henry, 53, 104, 110
Cullis, Charles C., 173
Cumberland Presbyterian Church, 20, 27-
28, 88

Darwinism, 162, 235-36
Depressions, economic, and religion, 63-
65
Dexter, Henry Martyn, 75
Disciples of Christ, 21, 29, 59, 88
Divine agency, doctrine of, 55, 61, 71,
80, 90-91, 109, 112, 114, 117, 151-52,
200-201
Divine immanence, doctrine of: and the
Holy Spirit, 61, 97-99, 102, 142-43,
145, 156-58, 161-62, 176, 218; and
judgment of social evil, 156, 209-10,
219-21, 232
Douglas, Stephen A., 205
Drew Theological Seminary, 121, 137
Duffield, George, 26, 53, 108-9, 208
Dutch Reformed Church, 19, 63

Earle, A. B., 74, 75, 139-40
East-West religious differences, 22-23, 25-
26, 27, 48, 62, 75
Education, higher, and religion, 36, 85.
See also Revivalism in colleges
Edwards, Jonathan, 87, 90, 220
Ellis, George E., 95, 100
Emerson, Ralph Waldo, 9, 31, 92, 98,
102, 142, 210
Emotionalism, religious, 24, 46, 60, 93,
99, 130, 158
Ethical seriousness, 80, 85-88, 98-100, 223
European travelers' views, 18-19, 37-38,
41-42, 215, 227-28

Evangelical Alliance, 19, 42-43, 45, 59,
83, 142, 193
Evangelical Arminianism, 33
Evangelical Association, 31

Feminism. *See* Women's rights
Finney, Charles G., 9, 28, 45, 52, 60,
66, 73, 81, 82, 86, 89, 92-93, 97, 102,
103-13, 135, 149, 155-56, 180, 204,
212, 215
Fish, Henry C., 49, 81, 86, 135, 145, 211
Fisk, Wilbur, 91, 121, 184, 195, 199
Five Points Mission, 172-73
Foster, Randolph S., 121, 123, 133, 134
Free will. *See* Arminianism *and* Natural
ability
Free Methodist Church, 129-34, 141, 205,
211-12
Freewill Baptists, 20, 26, 47, 89, 90
Friends, Society of, 20, 31, 59, 88

Garrett Seminary, 121, 133, 137
Garrison, William Lloyd, 178-84, 194-95,
198, 204, 213, 215
German Methodists, 31
German Reformed Church, 21, 92
Gettysburg Seminary, 55-56
Greeley, Horace, 63, 87, 204, 215
Grimké, Sarah and Angeline, 179, 182,
198
Guide to Holiness, The, 116, 120, 124,
134, 143-44, 155, 211
Gurney, John J., 31, 59

Hamline, Leonidas L., 119-20, 123, 125-
26, 133, 211, 232
Hammond, Edward P., 50, 73-74
Harper, Fletcher, 15-16
Harvard University, 70, 95-101
Haven, Gilbert, 35-36, 142, 189-90, 220-
22, 235
Hedding, Elijah, 119, 184
Hicks, Elias, 31, 59
Higher law, doctrine of the, 156, 205-6,
209-10, 220-22, 233
Hopkins, Mark, 50, 88, 93, 193
Hopkins, Samuel, and the doctrine of dis-
interested benevolence, 9, 160, 181
Hosmer, William, 129, 205-6, 222, 233
Humanitarian concern, 36, 45-46, 148,
152-53, 176-77; Arminianism and, 92,
229; perfectionism and, 154-61, 211-12;
revivalism and, 60-61, 71, 77-79, 86-88,
149-51, 161, 173-74, 231-32. *See also*
Poor

REVIVALISM AND SOCIAL REFORM

Poor: evangelization of the, 65-66, 69, 101; relief of the, 163-76

Pragmatism in religion, 48, 61-62, 92-93, 96, 145-46

Premillennialism, 228-29, 230-31, 233, 235

Presbyterianism, division of 1837, 26-28, 185-86

Presbyterianism, New School: 21, 22, 26-28; and perfectionism, 108-9; and revivals, 53-54; and slavery, 185-86, 196-98, 208, 216-17

Presbyterianism, Old School: 19, 21, 22, 26-28, 40, 229; and revivals, 54-55; and slavery, 186-87, 198, 208, 213

Princeton University, 55, 108, 185-86, 208, 219, 235

Protestant Episcopal Church, 21, 28, 29-30, 101, 214, 231

Public schools, religion in, 41

Puritan Recorder, The, 51, 90

Randall, Benjamin, 26

Rauschenbusch, Walter, 148, 230

Regeneration, doctrine of, 98-100, 109-11, 113, 140

Republican party, 201-2, 208-9

Revivalism, 7-8, 32; in city churches, 8-10, 48, 53-54, 59-60, 62, 65-66, 72-73, 204 ff.; in colleges, 48, 50, 51, 53, 54, 56, 60, 73, 137-38; decrease of emotionalism in, 46, 60, 69-70; and the educated clergy, 48, 50, 60; and liberal theology, 46, 60-61; and practical church work, 48, 61-62; and professional evangelists, 46, 47-48, 49, 72-74, 118; and union city-wide campaigns, 72-73. See also Slavery

Revivalism in the denominations: Baptist, 23-25, 47-49, 59, 66-68, 74; Congregational, 50-53, 66-67, 75-76, 139-40; Episcopal, 30, 69-70; Freewill Baptist, 26, 47; Lutheran, 30-31, 55-59, 74; Methodist, 23-25, 46-47, 66, 74-75; New School Presbyterian, 26-28, 53-54; Old School Presbyterian, 54-55, 66, 69, 74; Unitarians and Universalists in the revival of 1858, 70-71, 75, 99-100

Revivalistic Calvinism, 32

Roberts, Benjamin T., 130-32

Roman Catholic Church, 40-41, 214

Rural-urban differences, 9, 22-24, 47-48, 56, 59, 62, 67-68, 78, 115, 122, 124, 129-33, 136-37, 141, 143-44, 152, 164, 191-92

Sabbath observance, 37, 209

Sacramental theory, 30

Schaff, Philip, 18, 26, 28, 30-31, 35, 55, 84, 226-27

Schmucker, Samuel S., 42, 55-56, 58, 81, 214, 226

Scott, Orange, 183, 184-85, 212

Sectarian rivalry, 19, 34, 42-43, 57-58, 61. See also Interdenominational harmony

Secularism, 16

Separation of church and state. See Voluntary system

Simpson, Matthew, 120, 130, 173-74, 175, 202, 233

Slavery, 2, 23, 27, 42-43, 47, 64, 78, 185-86, 180-83; Baptists and, 190; Congregationalists and, 190, 193-94; and denominational unity, 190-92; Methodists and, 184-85, 190-93, 195-96; perfectionism and, 205-6, 211-13, 220-22; Presbyterians and, 26-27, 185-87, 196-98; religious defense of, 181-82, 199-200, 210; revivalism and antislavery, 87-88, 129-31, 149-50, 152-53, 180, 200-202, 204-24, 225

Small sects, 8, 18-19, 38, 79

Southern churches, 17, 22-23, 26-27, 77-78, 199, 219

Southern Baptist Convention, 23. See also Baptists

Spiritualism, 29

Sprecher, Samuel, 55

Stevens, Abel, 42, 121, 189, 192-93, 205

Stowe, Harriet B., 82, 87, 160, 179

Stuart, George H., 76, 193

Sturtevant, James M., 85, 174, 202, 222

Sunday schools, 65-66. See also American Sunday School Union

Tappan, Arthur, 179

Taylor, Nathaniel W., 28, 50, 89, 91

Taylor, William, 74, 118-19, 132

Temperance reform, 37, 133-34, 164, 166, 167-68, 176, 225

Theocracy, doctrine of, 7, 216, 219-23, 224-37

Thompson, Joseph P., 216, 217-18

Thomson, Edward, 207

Tocqueville, Alexis de, 35, 89

Toleration, religious, 34, 35-36, 221-22

Traditionalism, 32, 58, 85, 213-14

Transcendentalism, 8, 87, 96, 97-98, 102, 105, 113, 141-43, 183, 210

Trinity, doctrine of the, 99-100

INDEX

Tyng, Dudley A., 69, 82
Tyng, Stephen H., 29, 30, 69, 172

Union Theological Seminary, 49, 53, 92
Unitarianism, 21, 31-32, 41, 86-87, 95-102, 147, 176, 181, 190
United Brethren in Christ, 20, 31
United States Christian Commission, 76-78, 145, 175-76, 231, 234
Universalist Church, 21, 29, 190
University of Rochester, 48, 49
Upham, Thomas C., 105-6, 124, 141-44, 161, 220, 232

Voluntary system, 18, 19, 34-35, 59-60, 195

Walther, C. F. W., 57
Watchman and Reflector, The, 48, 67, 152-53, 205, 231
Wayland, Francis, 48, 81, 82, 174, 194, 211, 215
Wealth, Christian view of, 87, 155-57, 164, 174-75, 209

Wesley, John, 9, 25, 83, 103, 114-16, 196, 181
Wesleyan Methodist Church, 25, 116, 184-85, 190, 211-12
West, evangelization of the, 39-40, 54, 74
Whedon, Daniel, 91-92
Willard, Frances, 133-34
Williams College, 50
Wise, Daniel, 117, 126, 205, 207, 223
Witness of the Spirit, doctrine of the, 51, 125-27
Wittenberg College, 55, 60
Women's rights, 82, 124, 133, 144-45, 169-71, 182, 212

Yale University, 50, 51
Young Men's Christian Association, 39, 51, 52, 63, 65, 76, 175-76, 193

Zion's Herald, 117-18, 126, 155, 184-85, 191, 205, 207, 223

CPSIA information can be obtained
at www.ICGtesting.com
Printed in the USA
BVHW042118031119
562799BV00008B/29/P